# CALDERÓN DE LA BARCA: SIX PLAYS

## Translated and with introductions by Edwin Honig

## IASTA PRESS

Institute for Advanced Studies in the Theatre Arts - New York

*In memory of a Spanish grandmother*

**Esther Mulliver Honig**
**(1869-1943)**

# Calderón de la Barca: Six Plays

## Contents

# Acknowledgments

The publication of **Calderón de la Barca: Six Plays** would have been impossible without the assistance of a number of organizations and individuals to whom I am expressly indebted.

After the original Hill and Wang publication of **Calderón: Four Plays** in the early sixties, I was invited to see my translation of **The Phantom Lady** impressively performed in Washington, D.C., by an ambitious theatre arts organization, the Institute for Advanced Studies in the Theatre Arts (IASTA). Many years later, while searching for a publisher who would reprint the four plays along with two others—a 1970 translation of **Life is A Dream** and a new translation of **The Crown of Absalom**—I learned that IASTA was still alive and now producing films and books on classical theatre subjects. IASTA immediately approved my request to publish the six plays. I am now doubly grateful to IASTA's president, Dr. John D. Mitchell, who initiated The Phantom Lady in 1965; and to IASTA's present staff as well, for making this project one of their own.

Particular mention must surely be made of IASTA's talented Director of Development, Francine Douwes Whitney, who not only worked hard on securing the grants to publish the book, but also typeset and designed it. Thanks are in order to Alida Morgan, who diligently computer-scanned the various texts and proofread and corrected them all up to the final version.

The publication of **Six Plays** was supported by a generous grant from the Program for Cultural Cooperation of the Spanish Ministry of Culture, and instrumentalized by its Program Coordinator, Holly Zimmerman at the University of Minnesota. Further aid came in the form of a private award to Brown University's Creative Writing Department; and thanks are due to Gale Nelson for facilitating this process.

Finally I wish to thank the theatres and schools that have used my versions of the **Four Plays** since 1961. Without their tacit and spoken enthusiasm for the works of Calderón, **Six Plays** would not have seemed the necessary and worthwhile undertaking that it has been.

E. Honig
Providence, RI, 1993

## Introduction

In the crude engraving prefacing a late seventeenth-century edition of Calderón's collected works, the distracted look of an elderly melancholiac stares out at the reader. The portrait seems an unintentional caricature of an earlier one done by Juan de Alfaro Gómez, showing a younger disdainful head emerging from the dark cape and tunic of a Knight of Santiago. Disdain softened by resignation dominates still another portrait revealing a clerical gentleman, in severe habit and flowing cape, holding a copy of his plays opened to the title page of **Bien vengas, mal, si vienes solo (Welcome, Evil, If You Come Alone)**. And still the haunted, indrawn stare prevails. For a man who lived eighty-one years (1600-1681), and more than fifty in close touch with Court society, the record is sketchy, the relevant facts of his existence singularly bare. As if to emphasize that all this is due to the playwright's characteristic reserve, unmarred by legend or exploit, the commentators have coined a phrase, "the biography of silence."

Pedro Calderón de la Barca was born in Madrid on January 17, 1600, the third child and second son of María Henao y Riaño and Don Diego, the Secretary of the Council of the Treasury, a significant minor post at Court. The family followed the King to Valladolid and back to Madrid before Calderón's matriculation at the Imperial College of the Jesuits in 1608. The college curriculum at the time would have included readings in the Latin of Cicero, Virgil, Seneca, Catullus, and Propertius, and enough Greek to read St. John Chrysostom. His mother, who wanted her son to become a priest, died suddenly in 1610. Four years later, Calderón enrolled at the University of Alcalá to study logic and rhetoric; that same year his father was remarried. But in 1615 his father died, leaving a will which acknowledges the paternity of an illegitimate son, Francisco, thereafter accepted by the Calderón household as a relative and servant; as for Pedro, "I charge and beseech [him], under no circumstances to quit his studies, but rather to continue and finish them."

From 1616 to 1620, the young Calderón divided his time between Madrid and the two university cities of Alcalá and Salamanca, where he had embarked on a course in canon law; but there is no record of his having completed the course, as is sometimes maintained. His earliest known verses date from this period, and in 1620, he entered a poetry competition held in Madrid in honor of the beatification of San Isidro. Lope de Vega, one of the judges on this occasion, bestowed some general words of praise on Calderón's efforts. During this time there was a litigation between the Calderón brothers and their stepmother, which was settled satisfactorily upon her remarriage in 1618. There is, in addition, a record of a suit against them for having killed a relative of the Duke of Frias, of a huge fine being levied, and subsequently of an exonerating settlement effected out of court.

Calderón's literary career began in earnest in the early 1620s with the winning of several poetry prizes. His first play, **Amor, honor y poder (Love, Honor and Power)** was performed at Court in June 1623; another, **La selva confusa (The Tangled Forest)**, in July; and a play about the Maccabees in

September of the same year. There is no record of his whereabouts in the next two years, though he is believed to have been soldiering in Italy and Flanders, this mainly because of the vivid geographical details which turn up in his play **El sitio de Breda** (**The Siege of Breda**), the same subject as Velásquez's celebrated painting, **The Lances**.

Of the fifteen plays he wrote by 1630, at least two were destined to become world famous: **La dama duende** (**The Phantom Lady**) and **El príncipe constante** (**The Constant Prince**). In the latter play Calderón undertook to satirize the florid Gongoristic style of the Court preacher, Hortensio Félix y Arteaga. The playwright was motivated by the preacher's attack upon him following the second and last of the cape-and-sword escapades in which Calderón is purported to have engaged. Seeking revenge on the actor Pedro de Villegas, who had wounded his brother in a duel, Calderón pursued him into a nunnery where he is said to have molested the nuns. One of the nuns was Lope de Vega's daughter Marcela, and her father complained about the incident to the Duke of Sessa. Calderón was put under house arrest for a few days. The incident spurred the young playwright's growing popularity and brought him into greater favor at Court. By 1637 he had written forty-one more plays, among them almost all the great secular dramas by which he is best known.

When Lope de Vega died in 1635, Calderón succeeded him as director of all theatrical functions at Court. Two years later he was made a Knight of Santiago after a magnificent *zarzuela* which he had superintended at the opening of the new palace of the Buen Retiro. "This was a musical play," as Gerald Brenan reports in **The Literature of the Spanish People**, "on the theme of Ulysses and Circe, which was later printed as **El mayor encanto amor** (**Love, The Great Enchanter**). No play had ever been given under such splendid circumstances. A floating stage was built on the large *estanque*, or oblong pond, and lit with three thousand lanterns. Cosme Lotti, an Italian stage machinist, designed the décor, which included a shipwreck, a triumphal watercar pulled by dolphins, and the destruction of Circe's palace to the accompaniment of artillery and fireworks. The king and his suite watched from gondolas."

By 1637 two volumes of his plays had been brought out under the nominal editorship of José Calderón, his brother.

If Calderón's star was fixed in the 1630s, the following decade saw it overcast by national and personal misfortunes. In 1640 Portugal successfully revolted against the Spanish crown, and in the same year Calderón went off with the army to put down a rebellion in Catalonia occasioned by outrages against the peasantry committed by Spanish soldiers stationed there. The disillusioning experience is strikingly borne out in his play **El alcalde de Zalamea** (**The Mayor of Zalamea**). The closing of the public and Court theatres, his own ill health after the military campaign, and his withdrawal from military service caused him to become a member of the Duke of Alba's household, where he stayed for four years (1646-1650). Within a relatively short period both his brothers were killed and his mistress died, leaving him a son. His resignation from his post at Court (1650) was immediately followed by his entrance into the priesthood. By 1653 he had written thirty-three more plays—a few, as before, in collaboration—and twenty-one *autos,* the allegorical dramas to which he was to devote the remainder of his life. He was given a chaplaincy in Toledo until prevailed on by the king to return to his former post at Court in 1663, where he remained until his death. (It was also at Court that he wrote and directed his mythological plays.)

The third (1664), fourth (1672), and fifth (1677) volumes of his collected plays were edited by friends, but in the latter year Calderón himself also collected and published his *autos* and wrote a preface to them. In 1680 he answered a request to provide a list of his plays, which he determined as 110 secular dramas and 70 of the rest. In 1669 a French diplomat reported that he had spoken with Calderón and gathered from the conversation the playwright had almost no general knowledge and despite his hoary locks, knew least of all about the rules of drama. On the other hand, there is a contemporary report that on the day of his death, May 25, 1681, Calderón was writing a new *auto,* so that "he died, as they say of the swan, singing."

Of the plays in this volume, the first four originally appeared as **Calderón: Four Plays,** (Hill and Wang, New York, 1961). Subsequently, Hill and Wang issued **Life is a Dream** in 1970. Now **The Crown of Absalom,** a recent translation of **Los cabellos de Absalón** (literally, **Absalom's Hair**), joins the others to form **Six Plays** under the IASTA Press imprint. In this connection, my book, **Calderón and the Seizures of Honor** (Harvard University Press, Cambridge, 1972), elaborates on the discussion of honor in the Introduction to **Four Plays,** and later in the Introduction to **Life Is a Dream.** Condensed versions of all these now appear here in the separate introductions to each play, except for the one to **The Crown of Absalom,** which is altogether new.

It may be appropriate to indicate how the additional two titles create a new configuration of the views on honor previously represented.

We get a fairly strict paradigmatic view in **Secret Vengeance for Secret Insult** and **Devotion to the Cross;** it is as though Calderón were giving us basic texts on the subject without regard to any social implications of the honor quandary. In **The Mayor of Zalamea,** however, a largely open, more exploratory view of the problem brings up the sexual and class determinants of social justice. Then, more obliquely in **The Phantom Lady,** a romantic comedy, Calderón skirts the insult-vengeance trap to dwell briefly but strikingly on the underlying implications in a domestic situation, of the awakening incest drive. Again in **Life Is a Dream,** which, if classifiable, may be termed an elaborate morality, the Segismundo-Rosaura relationship is resolved (rather unconvincingly) in a compromise, but not without repeated portents of a deep sexual arousal being sounded in Segismundo's attraction to Rosaura and hers to him. (A more explicit incestuous involvement is similarly present between Julia and Eusebio in **Devotion to the Cross.**) The honor code does not permit them to consummate their feelings for one another in marriage. In any event, we are given to see how Segismundo's moral victory in the end is lessened considerably thereby, and also how King David's survival is drastically reduced in **The Crown of Absalom.** In these instances, we seem to be headed off by the technical demands of the form: tragedy, comedy and a hybrid tragicomedy/morality. A more paradigmatic view is enforced by the first, a more humane one offered by comedy and morality, and something in-between the two in tragicomedy. What grows evident from these examples, however, is that in each play honor becomes a prime metaphor for the way people may act and according to the strictest compact of an unwritten social law.

Through the metaphor of honor as a social conditioner of behavior in society, Calderón is enabled to show the actual and highly variable means according to which the conventions of marriage, soldiery, the intermingling of social classes, the bonds of friendship and love both grow and come apart. In this way we recognize what the life of an individual may become in his and her own terms, and in terms of the world which continually modifies their behavior. Consequently, a wider perspective for judging Calderón's primary thematic appeal is offered by **Six Plays** than appeared in the earlier 1961 volume. And such recognition may provide a happier note to end on at present.

## A Note on the Translation

Because rhyme in Spanish is so natural as to be almost inescapable, assonantal patterns are substituted in order to avoid it, particularly in the *romance*, or Spanish ballad, where the octosyllabic line is standard, and in dramatic verse, where it is dominant. In translating Golden Age drama into English, where rhyme is uncommon or simply accidental, the usual solution is to reduce everything to blank verse, or to a prose that sounds like blank verse. But what is thus normalized in principle is lost in effect to the metronomic rhythms, and the tell-tale diction and inversions of the seventeenth century, which forever fixed dramatic blank verse in English. To avoid that pitfall, I use a syllabic line patterned on the octosyllabic *romance*, but different from its model (which sometimes omits and sometimes adds a syllable) in permitting a regular six-to-nine syllable limitation and variation. The basic syllabic quantity allows for a fairly regular beat to emerge in a variety of trimeter, tetrameter, and pentameter lines—familiar to the English ear, yet just strange enough to suggest the Spanish norm. A few exceptions occur, as in the first act of **Secret Vengeance for Secret Insult**, where the formal diction is made to fit into the original's Spanish verse forms, and in the sonnets encountered in this play as well.

The aim is to reflect the essential poetry in Calderón's language and to stick to its prose sense. If these versions of his plays are dramatically effective to readers discouraged by the insipidities of verbal compromise, archaisms, and double-headed anachronisms, then I'll have come close to delivering the substance, and perhaps some of the raw flavor, of the thing in the original.

# SECRET VENGEANCE FOR SECRET INSULT

## (A SECRETO AGRAVIO, SECRETA VENGANZA)

## Secret Vengeance for Secret Insult

In **Secret Vengeance for Secret Insult** the classical honor situation occurs in its barest form. Don Lope de Almeida, the Portuguese king's military commander, has married by proxy a Castilian lady, Doña Leonor. The King releases him from military duty so that Don Lope, according to his own request, may consummate his marriage. Leonor was formerly betrothed to a Spanish nobleman, Don Luis, whom she believes was killed in the wars. As Lope is on his way to join Leonor, he is met by Don Juan, an exiled friend, now secretly returned from Goa where his rash murder of the governor's son over a question of honor has forced him to live in disgrace. Lope takes him into his protection as he joins Leonor, who has meanwhile also made a discovery: Don Luis is alive and has revealed himself to her, disguised as a traveling merchant, intent on regaining her love. In this involvement Sirena, her maid, acts as Leonor's confidante and go-between in the same way that Manrique, his valet, and Don Juan serve Don Lope.

Don Lope is an impetuous military man, unused to the niceties of courtship and the blandishments of marriage; he feels uneasy, impatient, and estranged in his new role as husband. He senses that he has neglected a more important military duty for a problematic and lesser civic duty; he is clearly not cut out to be a lover or a husband. His personal quandary is immediately magnified into a raging cause of injured honor when Don Luis, invited to the house by Leonor in order to make him stop courting her, is discovered hiding there. Instead of killing the intruder, Don Lope, forewarned by his friend's cautionary example, dissembles his fears and jealousy and helps Don Luis escape. "Secret insult most requires secret vengeance" is the principle which leads the offended man to a delayed and complicated series of ruses before drowning her lover, and then burning down the house where he has killed his wife. The King approves the deed, which frees Don Lope to join the military campaign. But though he is perversely heroized for committing a double murder, Don Lope is also left exhausted and ready to end his life on the battlefield, "if indeed misfortune ever ends."

Don Lope's vehement protests against the tyrannical laws of honor do not prevent his carrying them out. Jealous or not, he is a military man who understands the goads of harsh necessity, the inhumanity which makes slaughter a social virtue. But a victory on the battlefield is clear-cut, while a triumph based on conscientious scruples is only pyrrhic, leaving repercussions that chill the blood, debilitate the soul, and turn glory into a simulacrum. Don Lope is evidently a victim of his own deeds, an implement of the insult-vengeance complex, with its dehumanized rationale of an outmoded justice. For us, he is as much a victim as is Kafka's officer surrendering to the torture machine he charges himself to maintain in **The Penal Colony**. It is finally the authoritarian justice machine to which humanity is sacrificed.

If these are the dramatic consequences of the vengeance-for-insult theme, how are they prepared in the ethos of the play? The answer is, first, through a pattern of persistent and elaborate polarities. The conflict

3

between love and war, peace and duty, is established at the start, and is never dropped as an instigative force in Don Lope's behavior. His marriage by proxy that will never be consummated opposes the true passion of love between Leonor and Don Luis. Insult will provoke the cause of honor, and vengeance will annihilate the offenders as though they had never existed. The elemental symbols of fire, water, wind, and earth literally and metaphorically influence the course of action. And these, in turn, are allied with the polarities which enlarge the actions and attributes of all the characters: land and sea, silence and speech, certainty and suspicion, Castile and Portugal, sun and cloud, dissimulation and revelation. In this way, Don Lope's personal impasse is given cosmic dimensions, a world larger than the truth or falsity of his emotions, by which to be measured. And in such an environment the moral questions to which his actions give rise are figuratively extended, beyond the literal resolution of his problems, into the universal problems of order, justice, and renunciation.

A second means of preparing the tragic consequences is evident in the strategy of developing Don Lope's flawed personality. A man who has been traumatically shocked out of his self-esteem, not only by marriage and the loss of his soldierly role, but also by the suspicion of sexual incapacity, Don Lope momentarily loses his identity and must do everything he can in order to regain it. And yet what he does must scrupulously fulfill the law of honor, as though his reputation, his status, his bond to society had not in fact been disturbed. So he must dissemble, play the hypocrite, continually rationalize his doubts, meet duplicity with duplicity, become an underground man living in a state of siege, a "cold war" which he would seem to accept as the normal state of affairs. He must, above all, safeguard the suprapersonal machine of honor to which his identity is wedded and on which his life depends. Honor is his surrogate, secrecy his escutcheon. From this situation proceed his legalistic self-incriminations and defenses, until "the moment is ripe", and he becomes the executioner of honor's law.

A third means of preparation involves the supportive roles of Don Juan, the insulted friend who becomes the mirror and guide of Don Lope's strategy, and Manrique, the servant, whose transforming of his master's problems into comic actions emphasizes their dehumanized absurdity. Without Don Juan's providential appearance at the start and the lengthy sense of outrage he conveys as a man who failed to vindicate his honor because his vengeance revealed and redoubled the insult, Don Lope could not have plotted his own mechanically perfect acts of revenge. And if Don Juan's example instructs and propels him, Manrique defines, by exaggerating the basic incongruities, the ironic insubstantiality of his master's plight. Manrique's flirtation with Leonor's maid Sirena, his zany speeches, his boasting and his fabling on the sick psychology of love reveal the duplicities that his master takes seriously, and show them up for being proverbial riddles which are realistically passed off with a wry grin, a vulgar joke. In this way, Manrique is as consistent as Don Lope but, because he risks nothing, he is completely invulnerable, as his master is not. Yet grounded though it is in worldly realism so that it balances or relieves Don Lope's intolerable ideality, the servant's view is nevertheless as pitiless as his master's and, finally, as inhuman. We cannot expect to find comfort in him for being so complementary to Don Lope, just as we cannot expect anything like a resolution of the dualities and polarities which surcharge the play. The point about such a highly schematized conception of life is that the polarities persist in make-believe, for the sake of the action, as much as they continue to exist in real life, where they are rarely so defined.

# SECRET VENGEANCE FOR SECRET INSULT

# (A SECRETO AGRAVIO, SECRETA VENGANZA)

## DRAMATIS PERSONAE

| | |
|---|---|
| DON SEBASTIAN | King of Portugal |
| DON LOPE DE ALMEIDA | A Portuguese gentleman |
| DON JUAN DE SILVA | Don Lope's friend |
| DON LUIS DE BENAVIDES | A Castilian gentleman |
| DON BERNARDINO | Old man |
| DUKE OF BERGANZA | |
| DOÑA LEONOR | Wife of Don Lope |
| SIRENA | Doña Leonor's maid |
| CELIO | Servant to Don Luis |
| MANRIQUE | Servant to Don Lope |
| Boatman | |
| Retinue | |
| Soldiers | |

*The scene is laid in LISBON, in the neighborhood of the Galician Quarter, and in other places.*

## ACT ONE

*Outside the KING'S country house.*

*Enter KING SEBASTIAN, DON LOPE DE ALMEIDA,*
*MANRIQUE, and the King's retinue.*

**Don Lope.** Once more, great Sire, I humbly beg your leave
to add to that consent which once you gave
me, to be married.
Always attentive to your will and word,
in whose grace I thrive, my purpose now
is to acquaint you with my urgent vow,
which is, with your indulgence, to cast away
these arms, as Mars himself yields the victory
to Love when peace begins and must allow
the olive to succeed the laurel bough.
I have served you, and if today I speak
of it my sole intent is but to seek
reward in one word which graciously allows
me to depart at once to greet my spouse.
**King.** God speed you; your wish is granted.
I am glad to see you married,
and if I were not now about
to wage a war in Africa, I would
hope to stand as your best man.
**Don Lope.** May the laurel always crown your brow
as loftily as it does now.
**King.** Don Lope, I value and respect you highly.

*[Exeunt the KING and retinue*

**Manrique.** You are happy.
**Don Lope.**                          Such glory
and such bliss would ill
disguise one's happiness.
But I'd be happier still
if I could only fly
away today.
**Manrique.**      Like the wind.
**Don Lope.** That would not help me much.
The wind's a sluggish element.
But if Love would only lend
me wings I'd be borne away
by passion's fire. He who'd use
the wind must go by way
of wind's unsteady wallowings.
But the course that Love would choose
requires fiery wings.

**Manrique.** Tell me, sir, and relieve
  my doubts: why the hurry
  to depart at once, supposing you've
  a reason for it?
**Don Lope.**       To marry.
**Manrique.** But, sir, don't you see it's wrong,
  and enough to make the world suspect,
  when a man goes rushing headlong
  into matrimony? If the day
  you are to marry, you elect
  to be impatient of the wind,
  what's left to do, reflect,
  the day you are a widower?

       *Enter DON JUAN DE SILVA, in ragged clothes.*

**Don Juan.** *[to himself]* Oh native land, how differently
  I thought of my return
  that unhappy day I went away!
  Who would not rather stay
  with your sweet earth beneath his feet?
  But the man who's been disgraced
  must always find a place
  anywhere but where he's known.
  Now these people here have no reason
  to see in me the wretch
  I take myself to be.
**Don Lope.** Wait a moment. Incredible!
  Can it be or do I dream?
  Don Juan!
**Don Juan.**     Don Lope!
**Don Lope.**               Still doubting
  such good fortune, my arms
  hang wide and limp; let them
  enclose you in a tight embrace.
**Don Juan.** But wait, and give me time
  to justify myself before
  one so worthy and so honorable.
  For I, who come bereft by fate
  and destitute, am ashamed
  to rouse your generous heart.
**Don Lope.** I must condemn your reasoning,
  for if fortune grants mankind
  all the treasures of the earth,
  only Heaven offers one
  a friend like you. Now see
  what good luck Heaven's brought us!
**Don Juan.** Though your words encourage me,
  there's yet a greater misery.
  Consider what my straits must be

if they're far worse than poverty.
If there were any way
to mitigate my grief,
it would begin, Don Lope,
in your attentive audience.
At the famous Conquest
of the Indies, where the tomb
of night and the cradle of the sun
both shared one place of rest,
there, we two were friends—
such close friends, indeed, that
where we fought our two bodies
had one soul, one heart. There
we lusted not for riches
but for honor's sake, and ever
spent our courage probing
with our ships those distant provinces
as yet unknown to science.
Such vessels were entrusted
to the cause of fortune
by Lusitania's noblemen.
Our fleet surpassed in fact
the fleet that Jason only feigned.
The eulogy for that enterprise
and all our nation's valor,
I leave to a much sweeter voice,
the great Luis de Camoens',
who sang the deeds he fought.
Now it happened afterward
that you, Don Lope, were summoned
home upon your father's death,
and I remained behind—
you well know with what acclaim
from friends and others generally,
the sense of which is sharper now
for being wholly lost.
But there's a sort of balm in it
for one who never outraged fortune
and yet lives so utterly
estranged from fortune now.
In Goa there was a lady,
daughter of a man whom wealth
had made greedier for
greater store of enterprise.
Beauty and discretion,
two virtues normally at odds,
were reconciled in her. I wooed
her gallantly enough to be
worthy of her favor.

9

Yet who that's ever won at first
has not at long last lost?
Who that's ever tasted
happiness has not lived
to see it die? Sport, love,
and fortune are, in this, alike.
Don Manuel de Sosa, son of
the governor of that name,
quite publicly in Goa,
became my rival for the love
of Violante, as she was called,
who inspired my unhappiness.
Don Manuel was a man full of
high spirits, civility,
courage, sense, and gallantry.
I do not deny his virtues,
for though I took his life,
I would not take away
his honor. I made light
of his amorous pretensions,
since, as it was, I knew
I was the one she favored,
and perceiving his chagrin
only increased my happiness.
One day the sun arose in all its
glory (if only those rays
had been expunged forever!)
and with that sun rose Violante.
Surrounded by her servants,
she approached the shore where
a throng had rallied to greet
a galley recently arrived
in our harbor. Its arrival
was the occasion both for public
concourse and my own catastrophe.
We were among a group of friends
and soldiers chatting in the crowd
when Violante came by.
She made her way so gracefully
each felt she drew his heart away:
as if her fleet foot were the moving
cause that bore off all imaginings.
One captain cried, "The woman's
beautiful!" to which Don Manuel
replied, "Which reveals her temperament."
And then the other, "She must be cruel."
"It's not on that account I say it,"
Don Manuel replied, "but that
her beauty hides the worst of it."

At this I said, "No one's yet
deserved her love, for there's no one
worthy of it, and if there were,
it would be I." "Liar!" he cried.
I cannot even now proceed:
my voice struck dumb, tongue-tied,
my body frozen, one throbbing heart,
my senses mummified, one livid
pain, all singing out the insult.
Fatal error of mankind!
Vile universal law!
That any provocation,
reasonable or not, should stain
a man's proud honor which he spends
a lifetime in acquiring,
and that the ancient name
of honesty should fall prostrate
before the faintest voice!
Oh God, that honor's diamond
should be turned to ash and cinders
by a single puff of breath!
That its purity, more radiant
than the sun, should be clouded
by the merest passing breeze!
I have strayed from my story;
passion carried me away.
Forgive me, I shall return to it.
He had scarcely said the word,
Don Lope, when my sword flitted
from its scabbard to his heart,
to all appearances as if
the insult were the lightning
and my sword the thunder.
Drenched in his own blood,
he fell dead upon the sand.
Then, to protect myself, I ran
for refuge to a church of
the Holy Order of St. Francis.
Since the father of Don Manuel
was governor, I was forced to hide.
In fear and trembling, I lay three
days inside a tomb, alive.
Who would have thought that I,
so far the opposite to death,
should lie as one he'd buried there?
So three days passed until,
favored by the friendship
of the captain of that galley
in our port, who was bound

for Lisbon, I went aboard
one night, and by that token
saved my life. I was hidden
in that vessel under monster
winds and waves. Such is life's impious
deceit! Either his sufferance
should not cast out the man
who bears his own dishonor,
or else, if he revenge himself
let him be freed of blame.
For it is wrong to let insult
be punished and not let
the punisher be pardoned.
Today I came to Lisbon
in such poverty I dared not
enter it. This is my story,
no longer miserable because
it brings me happily to you.
This hand you take in greeting,
Don Lope, would return
a thousandfold, if one bereft
by fortune were deservant of
the mercy, honor, kindness
which you bestow upon me.

**Don Lope.** Don Juan de Silva, this is
a grievous tale your burdened heart
has taught your tongue to utter.
I have listened carefully,
and in pondering all you say
conclude there is no argument,
however subtly couched,
to controvert your own.
Which of us can live from birth
untouched by the inclemencies
of fortune and his time?
Who is ever free and who exempt
from negative intention,
a double-purposed heart
rousing the baneful hand
and the tongue's malignancy?
Of these no man is free.
He alone is counted fortunate
who, like you, has cleansed the stain
upon his honor and punished
the transgressor. You're honest:
dark shadows will not tarnish
nor obscure your ancient honor.
In our present friendship
may be seen a virtue like that

of those two herbs, both poison,
so equally opposed that while one
consumes with heat, the other
penetrates with cold, but being
once compounded do achieve
a salutary state both positive
and sound. And so now are we:
you unhappy, I more fortunate:
let's share the difference between us,
and temper my well-being
with your unhappiness, my joy
with your sorrow, my good
with your ill fortune, for none
may hope to do away with
the cause of pleasure or of pain.
I was married in Castile,
by proxy, with the most beautiful
of women . . . (though properly
speaking, beauty is the least
of all her attributes),
noblest, richest, most virtuous
and most wise, a woman of whom
the imagination scarcely
can conceive. Her name is
Doña Leonor de Mendoza,
who, with Don Bernardino
my uncle, arrives today
in the Galician Quarter.
I go there to meet her now
with such glad auspices
as you may witness here. A vessel
gaily decked that waits for her
finds the day too slovenly
adroop in its own light sails,
for good fortune when it tarries
may turn ill when it arrives.
Such is all my happiness,
made happier by the gladness which
your coming adds to it, Don Juan.
Do not let your poverty
give cause for shame or sadness.
I am rich. My house, dear friend,
my table, horses, servants,
all my property, my honor
and my life, they all are yours.
Be comforted that fortune
leaves you one true friend,
and that grim adversity
could not vanquish you; nor

have you lost the spirit
of your valor, the soul
that quickens you, or this arm of mine
that always will defend you.
Do not attempt to answer me:
the finer courtesies between
two friends may be left unsaid.
Come with me now to where you
may privately observe
the happiness awaiting me.
Today my wife arrives in Lisbon,
and these three leagues of sea
(which for me are more like fire)
must be traversed before we meet her,
for she undoubtedly is waiting
on the other side.

**Don Juan.**　　　　　　See that your own
nobility is not cast down,
Don Lope, by my ragged state,
since what the world esteems
is fine clothes, not noble breeding.

**Don Lope.** Then that's the world's illusion
which cannot understand that while gold
may clothe the body, only
nobility can clothe the soul.
Come with me. [*aside*] Come, my sighs, inflate
these sails, and steer love's course
through seas inflamed by passion's fire.

　　　　　　　　　　*[Exeunt DON LOPE and DON JUAN*

**Manrique.** I'll scud away and take the lead
in a common bark they call a scull;
then, being skull-skilled, I'll beg
some token of my new mistress
for the good news her husband comes;
since her wedding day brings
any lady a reward,
for that day ends her maidenhood,
if she is still a maid.

　　　　　　　　　　　　　　*[Exit MANRIQUE*

### A field near the Galician Quarter

*Enter DON BERNARDINO, an old man, DOÑA LEONOR, and SIRENA*

**Don Bernardino.** Here on this pleasant hillside strewn with
flowers, where springtime now comes courting,
here you may rest a while, fair Doña
Leonor, until Don Lope,
your husband, comes for you.

14

He shall pardon your sweet sorrow,
though I see no cause to wonder
why you must grieve, for having come
to Portugal, you are now compelled
to bid Castile farewell.
**Doña Leonor.** Venerable Don Bernardino:
my hushed lament is no
sign of ingratitude
for the great honor fate
and fortune have bestowed.
Now as my sweetheart appears,
I feel joy, and yet, as you know,
joy often comes to one with tears.
**Don Bernardino.** Your excellent discretion
certainly acquits you,
but even though it does,
I shall gladly take the blame.
Meanwhile you shall have time
to overcome your melancholy.
Rest here a while from the rigors
of the sun and its consuming beams.
May Heaven always protect you.

*[Exit DON BERNARDINO*

**Doña Leonor.** Sirena, is he gone now?
**Sirena.**                                   Yes.
**Doña Leonor.** Will anyone overhear us?
**Sirena.** I suspect we are alone.
**Doña Leonor.** Then God relieve me of this burden
of my life, my pent-up breast.
If weeping would only end this
ache that rankles in me, the passion
in my soul that shoots anger
into tears and floods my eyes
and fills my mouth with sighs.
Grant me no peace, no ease,
till they consume my burden,
for all my tears and cries
are kindling points of fire.
May they destroy life's passion
in one torrential flame,
now that my journey's at an end
after miles of sea and wind.
Now my voice is flame and air,
and my tears a sobbing fire.
**Sirena.** What are you saying, madam?
Think of the danger to your honor.
**Doña Leonor.** How can you, who know my sorrow
and my helplessness, offer

15

lessons in restraint? How can
you turn from my complaints
and tell me to be silent?

**Sirena.** I shall listen to them, though I think
that your complaints are now in vain.

**Doña Leonor.** Sirena, how can you call them vain?
Does the flower not complain
when the quickened breeze has stabbed it
and the senile sun creeps
downward to its jeweled tomb?
The proud hillside complains when
the wild wind has gouged it.
And then there's Echo, vocal nymph,
lamenting her misfortune, who grieves
once more beyond her final accent.
The lovelorn ivy frets, though knowing
how to love, when it has lost
the hard tree trunk it used to cling to.
So too any bird complains,
however gently, of one who claims
it for the gilded cage,
where it seems to soothe itself in song
which, even though ignored
as song, comes through as sorrow's rage.
The sea complains upon the shore,
hurling all its watery tongues
against the rocks' opposing lips.
Fire frets that's locked and whirled
by thunders warring on the world.
Then how can I desist
from quarreling with my pain,
if flower, hillside, stone,
Echo, ivy, bird and sun,
tree trunk, sea and wind and thunderbolt
each has its just complaint?

**Sirena.** Yes, but of what use is your
continual despair
now Don Luis is dead
and you are married? What
is it you seek?

**Doña Leonor.**     Alas,
Sirena dear, to say
that Don Luis is dead is to say
I too am dead. For even
though compelled by Heaven,
I'd still be as you see me now:
calm, benumbed, bereft of soul
and will—yes, a woman dead,
and not a woman married.

Those things which I once learned and loved,
all of them, alas, may be removed
or lost, but not forgotten.
Can I forget the vows I've taken?
Love deceives, else how can so clear
a truth be scorned? Whoever has been
constant once cannot afterward
forget, if he truly loved,
or have loved at all if he forget.
Remember what I felt when they
told me of his death? I forced
myself to marry someone else,
as if only to avenge myself!
Now once for all I take leave
of sorrow. Love, I've walked
with you to the altar steps; I leave
you here. You dare not follow further
to the altar of my honor.

*Enter MANRIQUE.*

**Manrique.** How lucky for me to be here first,
how venturesome of me,
oh joy of joys, and doubly
joyous me, to be the first
to press his lips upon your feet
which, overladen with these flowers,
now become the summer's harbingers.
And since I'm quick while others plod,
I'm here to kiss and kiss again,
and kiss as often as I can,
without offending my Lord God.
**Doña Leonor.** Who are you?
**Manrique.**                    The least of servants
to Don Lope, my master
(though not his least of babblers),
and he has sent me in advance
with news of his arrival.
**Doña Leonor.** Well spoken. I was negligent.
Here, take this, and tell me
how you serve your master.
**Manrique.** As Jack of all trades and humors.
Doesn't such a title tell you that
I'm the nobleman's own gentleman?
**Doña Leonor.** How are you his gentleman?
**Manrique.** As the mouth is to the smile.
Body servant, and as such preferred
for matters of close confidence;
and thus the bawd of all his servants,
to any foot the floor. On guard,

17

his major-domo; his chamberlain
when I await my master's hand-
me-downs; his dining steward when
I bite into the choicest ham;
his secretary and least friend
in telling his latest secret;
his chief groom consummate
when I'm too bored to walk
and leap upon his horse's back
to exercise it down the street.
When there's anything of such
importance that it's kept from me,
then I spy for him and may become
his teller later, for where there's some
thing to collect, I'll tell anyone.
When pilfering what I require
in the market, I'm his butler,
and keeper of his stores when
I filch from them; his valiant valet
when I have taken to my heels;
the coachman wearing down his wheels
by day, entrusted with his *billets-
doux*; and so I clearly argue
that as I serve so variously
I serve him constantly:
each an office, one by one,
and all whispering of him at once.

> *Enter DON BERNARDINO, DON LUIS, and CELIO, his servant;
> these three remain some distance removed from DOÑA
> LEONOR, SIRENA, and MANRIQUE.*

**Don Luis.** I am a merchant and deal in diamonds.
  All these now precious flashing stones once
  were of the body of the sun, whose burning mine
  refined the crudest grain to bright perfection.
  In traveling to Lisbon from Castile
  I was struck, in this village, by a marvel
  most divine, incarnate in the lady
  you accompany; the rumor is that she
  is married or will very shortly be.
  And since the custom is at weddings to display
  one's treasure, where jewels and finery
  go together, I'll show you these diamonds,
  no less aglow than starlight; see if such stones,
  the wedding, and your desire may not yield us
  some occasion here for roadside commerce.
**Don Bernardino.** What you guess and what you hope for now strike
  home. Your timing's excellent, for you as well
  as me. Since the bride is sad, I shall

divert her melancholy with a jewel.
Wait here while I go to tell her.
**Don Luis.** Before you go, take this diamond, sir,
as one clear token of my truthfulness;

*[Giving it to him.]*

I cannot doubt but that its excellence
and worth, once she has beheld it, will give you
access to her graciousness.
**Don Bernardino.** How strangely pure!
What depths of brilliance in this jewel. Here,

*[Approaching her.]*

Leonor, my child, there is
a diamond merchant passing by
whose priceless wares you must inspect.
Lay aside your melancholy.
I shall buy the jewel
that pleases you the most.
This diamond in particular comes
as witness to the rest, a beacon
whose beauty's piercing light
strains the sun's own purity,
as if it were the sun's own child.
Here, take it.

*[Gives it to her.]*

**Doña Leonor.** *[aside]* My God! What's this I see?
**Don Bernardino.** Tell me . . .
**Doña Leonor.** *[aside]* I cannot believe it.
**Don Bernardino.** . . . If you wish to see him.
**Doña Leonor.** *[aside]* Alas,
the same, there's no mistaking it . . .
—Have him come! Sirena!

*[DON BERNARDINO walks aside.]*

*[aside]* Release me, love, from this torment,
this enchantment, this abyss.
—This sun-dipped diamond here
is the one I gave to Don Luis
as my pledge. It is his.
Am I deceived by my own tears?
No, it is his. But I must know
how and why it reappears.
**Sirena.** Pretend it's nothing. They're coming now.

*Enter DON LUIS.*

**Don Luis.** Fair lady, I am . . .
**Doña Leonor.** *[aside]* My sorrow's cause,
a ghost in flesh and blood.
**Sirena.** *[aside to her]* I see the reason for
your astonishment. But
conceal it, say nothing yet.

**Don Luis.** I am one who comes here hoping
　　to make happy use of a timely
　　circumstance, so long awaited.
　　The value of my jewels
　　is inestimable.
　　And one among the rest
　　I know you must esteem
　　especially, a perfect prize
　　whose honest beauty I suspect
　　you'll sense at once when this,
　　my jewel of steadfastness,
　　lies fixed upon your breast.
　　Here's another: Cupid's diamond,
　　and worth a treasury
　　which I've designed in jewels
　　closely matched, and therefore have
　　dedicated it to love.
　　My purpose was to answer those
　　accusing love of fickleness
　　with some work made perfect
　　through my constancy alone.
　　The heart I bear contains
　　no counterfeit, no false stone.
　　Further, among my precious rings
　　is one aglow with memories. Once
　　an emerald I had was stolen
　　from me on the highway, mainly,
　　I suppose, for its wondrous hue.
　　It was meant to match this sapphire,
　　but they took the emerald only,
　　leaving this blue stone you see.
　　It was then I shouted in despair,
　　"How deeply vengeful you must be
　　to carry off my hope
　　and leave me to my jealousy!"
　　If it please your loveliness,
　　I have more delights in store
　　that will disclose my memories,
　　my heart, my love, my constancy.
**Don Bernardino.** This merchant is most ingenious.
　　How handsomely his speech awakes
　　one's curiosity to gaze
　　upon his glowing jewels.
**Doña Leonor.** Although the jewels you extol
　　are all you say they are,
　　the occasion you have chosen
　　to display them is inappropriate.
　　I would have delighted in
　　such an exhibition

had it been offered earlier.
But as it is, you come too late.
What would they say of me,
a newly married woman,
if, while awaiting the coming
of my noble husband,
I should offer, not regret,
but fullest sympathy,
to that display you call your heart,
your love, your constancy?
Do not show them, for surely
you'd be ill advised to let
such memories, so long
concealed, now be disesteemed.
And take your diamond too,
although I know I lose thereby
the lovely, faithful light
engendered by the sun itself.
Do not blame me for evasiveness,
but blame yourself for coming
out of time and out of place.

*[A noise offstage.]*

**Manrique.** [*looking back*] Here comes Don Lope, my master.
**Don Luis.** [*aside*] What unhappiness is this
  whose edge can cut so fine?
  Does any sorrow equal mine?
**Doña Leonor.** [*aside*] What spite!
**Don Luis.** [*aside*]                    What cruelty!
**Don Bernardino.** We shall go forth to greet him.

*[Exit DON BERNARDINO*

**Manrique.** Silence, everyone, and listen to
  the first stupidity:
  the swain, whom his lady pleases,
  when he comes to see her, straight away
  gambles with stupidities:
  what he says and what he does
  reveal the gambling cheat.

*[Exit MANRIQUE*

**Don Luis.** How can you answer me this way,
  shameless, fickle, and disloyal
  woman, so pliable and vain,
  and so like a woman, how
  do you propose to justify
  your vagrant memory
  and your broken pledge?
**Doña Leonor.** There's a reason for my broken pledge:
  I believed you dead; I mourned for you,
  though my heart could not forget you.

21

And if I had not yet been married,
now that I see you are alive,
you would soon discover I'm a woman
neither fickle nor disloyal.
But I've been wed by proxy.

**Don Luis.** *By proxy*, yes; that puts it well.
By proxy you've destroyed my fate.
By proxy you've deserted me.
By proxy you've flung my heart away,
and by your proxy I am dead.
This says what you really meant
and not merely what you said.
You've accepted me as dead
is what it comes to; all by proxy.

**Doña Leonor.** I can't, I cannot, oh misery,
answer you. I am in the presence
of my enemy, not my husband.
Yet since you doubt my loyalty,
the words I must address to him
shall speak to you as well.

[*DON LUIS withdraws to one side.*]

*Enter DON LOPE, BERNARDINO, MANRIQUE.*

**Don Lope.**
When praise of your rare loveliness was told,
And rumor everywhere reported it,
I loved you on my faith and, thus accepted,
Leonor was idolized in my heart's hold.
When with astonished heart I now behold
The live Leonor, whose holy image it
Adored, heart blames weak fancy that begot
The copy of the life it had extolled.
For only you may body forth your beauty.
How fortunate I'd be if I were worthy
Of your love, and more, if so you deemed me.
Can I offend you or forget you, truly?
I who loved before I met you, surely,
Now I've seen you, loving is no duty.

**Doña Leonor.**
I signed my troth before I saw you; so
I've lived and died in you alone, because
The object of my love was but your ghost,
Which, being yours, it seemed enough to know.
How happy I would be if I could love you
As in that copy fancy often wrought!
So life might now redeem the common debt
We owed when I humbly signed my troth.
I may be pardoned if my love falls short,
When faltering I come to meet your gaze,

Returning less for what's been dearly bought.
Not I, but you deserve your heart's dispraise,
For though I honor you as spouse, I cannot
Love you as you appeared in former days.

**Don Lope.** Now, my lord and uncle, give me
    your affectionate embrace.
**Don Bernardino.** These arms are the eternal bonds of
    my love and friendship for you.
    But come, do not delay:
    let us at once make ready
    to sail away.
**Don Lope.**      The sea today
    salutes another Venus.
**Manrique.** And as our lover and his lady
    depart in married bliss,
    I could hope (but do forgive me,
    O noble audience),
    our story might end with this.

                  *[Exeunt DON LOPE, DOÑA LEONOR, DON*
                  *BERNARDINO, MANRIQUE and SIRENA*

**Celio.** Sir, now you've been so clearly
    disabused, come to your senses,
    mend your injuries and
    be done with this at last.
    For surely there's no other way;
    you've no alternative.
**Don Luis.** Yes, there is one, Celio.
**Celio.** What can that be?
**Don Luis.**           That's to die,
    the last recourse. It's easy
    to die now I've seen her married,
    now Leonor has scorned my love
    and mocked my hope. What's left
    to kill me when only jealousy
    keeps me alive? Yet she attempted
    to console me, as if to hint
    there's still some hope. When she addressed
    her husband she was in fact
    asking my forgiveness for
    her fickle and forgetful heart.
**Celio.**               What
    do you mean—asking your forgiveness?
    This is the sheerest madness.
**Don Luis.** I'll repeat her very words.
    Notice how they spoke to me.

"I signed my troth before I saw you; so
I've lived and died in you alone, because
The object of my love was but your ghost,
Which, being yours, it seemed enough to know.

How happy I would be if I could love you
As in that copy fancy often wrought!
So life might now redeem the common debt
We owed when I humbly signed my troth.

I may be pardoned if my love falls short,
When faltering I come to meet your gaze,
Returning less for what's been dearly bought.

Not I, but you deserve your heart's dispraise,
For though I honor you as spouse, I cannot
Love you as you appeared in former days."

Well, if this is her apology
for suffering a change of heart,
let my witless hope become
a dagger dipped in poison. For if
I'm to die of sorrow, by Heaven,
I shall do it pleasantly,
and not die for jealousy
but for love. Come, let me boldly
follow up my fate until the end,
and blast all honor, for I must
have Leonor, at any price,
though I pay for her with my life.

## ACT TWO

### A room in DON LOPE'S house in Lisbon

*Enter SIRENA and MANRIQUE.*

**Manrique.** Sirena, dearest heart:
    you play the very Siren,
    which gives me quite a start,
    when you bewitch me simply
    to deceive me; at least pity me
    for suffering your disdain.
    Servants, like their masters, may
    experience the pain
    of unrequited love.
    A little token would be enough.
**Sirena.** What is it I can give you?
**Manrique.** Oh, a great deal, but now
    I want no greater treasure
    than that green fillet which you wear
    so snugly round the waist,

24

like any girl who waits
to be untied behind or
like a kitchen wench about
to be divested of her nice
new fleecy woolen girdle.

**Sirena.** You want my ribbon?

**Manrique.**                              Yes.

**Sirena.** What strange times we live in when
a gallant can be satisfied
with a ribbon.

**Manrique.**          That's it,
and if you hand it over I will
squander all my metaphors today
on a hundred thousand sonnets,
just to sing your praise.

**Sirena.**                              I can't resist
the thought of being so well sonneted.
Here, take it now and go.
I see my mistress coming.

                                        *[Exit MANRIQUE*

*Enter DOÑA LEONOR.*

**Doña Leonor.** I have decided what to do.
I must be absolutely firm,
Sirena, for my life and honor
belong to me no longer
but to my husband, Don Lope.
Go tell Don Luis that as
he's noble, and prizes
his own honor which obliges him,
as a Spaniard and a soldier,
to be courteous, that a lady
(do not say Leonor,
for to any nobleman
simply *lady* should suffice),
that this lady begs him
to banish from his mind
any thought of love for her.
And tell him especially
to consider while he
lingers on a certain street
that the gallantries of Castile
are frowned upon in Portugal.
And tell him that my tears
implore him to go back to Castile
resolved to free me from the fate
of being an unhappy wife.
For Heaven knows, if he does not go
away, he forfeits both our lives.

**Sirena.** I shall tell him all you say,
  if I can only find him.
**Doña Leonor.** When is he not lingering
  somewhere along this street?
  But do not speak with him outside.
  If you meet, go to the inn instead.
**Sirena.** Madam, you are very daring.

*[Exit SIRENA*

*Enter DON LOPE, DON JUAN, and MANRIQUE.*

**Don Lope.** [*aside*] Bright honor, how much must
  still be done on your account.
**Manrique.** They say the King's departure
  for the wars is now imminent.
**Don Lope.** There is no courtier or gentleman
  in all of Lisbon who will not
  think himself most worthy of
  the finest panegyric
  when he comes to die.
**Manrique.**            It's true,
  though I think otherwise.
  For when I come to die
  I want no panegyric,
  nor tragedy nor interlude,
  to be remembered by.
**Don Lope.** Then you're not thinking of
  going off to war in Africa?
**Manrique.** Possibly I'll go, but if so,
  only to have something more
  to brag about, but surely
  not to kill my fellow man
  and vainly break the law of God
  by which I live and bind myself.
  In Africa there's no difference
  I can see in being either
  Moor or Christian. Scripture
  says *Thou shalt not kill*; I'll
  abide by that since I lack the wit
  to interpret God's commandments.
**Don Lope.** Leonor, my dear!
**Doña Leonor.**            Dear husband!
  The time that's passed since last
  I saw you! My love complains
  of every moment it has lost.
**Don Lope.** Spoken like the very lady
  of Castile you are! Do
  put aside the flattery
  and fine phrases. Note that
  we Portuguese prefer

the feeling to its explanation,
for the lover by his very words
devalues all he feels.
If your love is blind, my love
must be mute.
**Manrique.**        Mine the devil's taken.
**Don Lope.** Tell me why it is, Manrique,
that when I'm melancholy
you're always so bright and cheerful?
**Manrique.** First tell me which among
the opposing passions is the better,
happiness or sorrow?
**Don Lope.** Happiness, of course.
**Manrique.**                    Then there you are:
Would you have me put aside
the better for the worse?
You who choose the worse in feeling sad
would do better to be happy.
It would, at any rate,
be more desirable for me
to go from happiness to sorrow
while you do the opposite.

*[Exit MANRIQUE*

**Doña Leonor.** Are you so sad, my lord?
It must be that my heart owes
you so little or else knows
itself even less, for it feels
nothing of your unhappiness.
**Don Lope.** The sum of heritage and duty,
long and worthily sustained,
and binding me by laws
both human and divine,
now stirs my blood, cries out
shrilly to my conscience
to awake from this slothful peace
and this forgetfulness
where my proprietary
laurels lie in dusty sleep.
Renowned Sebastian, our King,
who like the phoenix is the heir
of centuries, goes off today
to war in Africa, leaving
no gentleman behind
in Portugal; for none
will lie abed while fame
cries out abroad. I wish, of course,
to join the King, yet since
I am but newly wed, I cannot

27

offer him my services
until, my dear Leonor,
your own lips grant me leave.
I now must seek that favor of you,
in granting which you honor me
and place me in your debt.
**Doña Leonor.** You have been most thoughtful,
in following necessity,
to smooth the way with speeches
that inspire and encourage me.
Should you absent yourself, my lord,
through any counsel I may give you,
such an action in effect
would be the same as if
I had sentenced myself to death.
Go without my bidding, and your will
shall not refuse what life itself
bestows on you. And further,
since you see how highly I respect
your gallant inclination, you may
guess if I desire my present guide
to be your courage and not my love.
Join King Sebastian, may Heaven
bless his life; the blood of noblemen
is a monarch's patrimony.
Let no one say that woman's
cowardice deprives her husband
of his valor when reason
urges her to strengthen it.
This my heart advises,
though it be the heart that loves you.
However much the stranger
it may sound in saying so,
its sentiment is yours alone.

*[Exit DOÑA LEONOR*

**Don Lope.** Have you ever seen such courage
in your life?
**Don Juan.**      It deserves
to be inscribed and praised
by the pens and tongues of fame.
**Don Lope.** And what would you advise me?
**Don Juan.** Don Lope, I would answer
differently.
**Don Lope.** Tell me how.
**Don Juan.**              A man
who has already laid aside
the bays of Mars and on his head
now wears the laurels of sweet peace,

what need has he to cleanse
his shields again of all the rust
and grime in which they lie?
I might myself be justified
in serving, were it not that, hidden
and in disgrace, I am as good
as dead. Nor can I volunteer:
the King would frown upon a criminal.
If this excuses me,
he'd surely be excused
whose past soldiery sufficiently
acquitted him. Do not go,
my friend; believe me, though
you are dissuaded by a man
and encouraged by a woman.

*[Exit DON JUAN*

**Don Lope.** Heaven help me! Who can prudently
assess his own condition
while someone at the moment
is attempting to advise him?
Who would split himself in two
to find relief in another self?
But that's not it. Rather,
who deliberately would split
his consciousness in two
so that one half may be free
to vent his angry cries,
of which the other half
would continue ignorant?
This way his conscience would never
feel the burden of his voice.
In one breath I might thus become
my own accuser and defender,
yet neither hear nor see
any sign of the proceedings.
Now cowardice, now foolhardiness
have shamed me equally.
How is it one speaks or thinks at all!
For honor has a thousand eyes
to ferret out a fault,
a thousand ears to drink it in,
and only one poor tongue
to articulate its grievances.
What if honor had no eyes or ears
but a thousand tongues instead?
It then would not, as now it must,
being so narrowly regarded,
burst the chest like some exploding mine.
So far so good: I must then

articulate my grievances.
But where shall I begin?
In times of war and peace
my life was always honorable.
Ever loath to mewl complaint
is it any wonder I never
learned its object or necessity?
No one can prepare for what
he does not fear. Do I dare
permit my tongue to say, "If . . . ?"
Stay, be dumb, and utter neither
word nor syllable of my disgrace.
If *you* offend me I can punish you
and sentence you to life or death,
for being insult's victim
and offender both in one,
I may suffer insult
as well as punish it.
Do not say I'm jealous . . .
But there, I've said the word,
and cannot stuff it back
into my heart where it has raged.
How can my heart have brought it forth
for lisping on the lip
and not totally consumed my breath—
the facile exhalation
uttering that hateful word
so different from all others?
The effect of other words is felt
proceeding from the lip inward,
toward the heart, while this word flies
straight out from heart to lip.
What asp or serpent ever died
of its own venom bite?
My God, but I am subject
to the very deed when my own
anguish is the venom
I produce to kill myself.
I am jealous, I have said so.
Now, Heaven help me, but who is
that Castilian gentleman
who hangs about my doors,
my railings, and my threshold,
installed there like a living statue?
In the street, the doorway,
and the church, waiting, turning
like some sunflower to my honor
and forever drinking up its light.
God help me, but what can

Leonor have had in mind,
granting me leave to go so lightly;
no, granting it with such
a happy air, and yet, by
the very words she reasoned with,
obliging me to go away
when I may not have planned to go?
Finally, what can Don Juan
have meant by saying one might go
while declaring I should stay?
Would it not have been more reasonable
for my friend to show his reticence,
and my wife, her feelings of concern?
Would it not have been better had they
taken opposite positions:
Don Juan to urge me on,
and Leonor detain me?
Yes, that would have been better,
far better. But since this is
my burden, let me consider
how I may unburden it.
Surely honor can't be twisted
to condemn a man unjustly
by such subtle arguments as these.
Might it not be that Leonor,
so high-minded, resolute
and wise, should answer as she did
because she feared my reputation
would be harmed if I stayed behind?
It may well be that such indeed
is what she meant and felt
in answering as she did.
Might it not be true that Don Juan
really wanted me to stay,
and offered the argument
of my exemption, while only
seeming to cast doubt on Leonor?
Yes, that may be so. And might it not
also be the case that the lurking
gallant is involved elsewhere?
To press that case further:
when he waits and watches,
when he seems to woo some lady,
does he in any way insult me
or offend against my honor?
Being what she is, Leonor's
reputation is sound;
being what I am, my rectitude
is indisputable; nobody can

obliterate these facts.
And yet, alas, it may be said
of the ever-clear, unsullied sun
that the cloud which does not eclipse it
seeks, at any rate, to do so,
and even though it be unstained,
it's dimmed and so, at last, obscured.
Honor, are there further subtleties
to learn, still unpropounded?
More torments and more burdens,
more sorrows and suspicions,
more fears to hound me with,
more insults to drown me in,
more jealousies to confront me with?
There cannot be, and unless
you've greater means at your disposal
to destroy me, I now know how
I must proceed, with silence,
skill, and cunning, forewarned,
and on my guard, solicitous,
even obsequious, until occasion
give me strength to choose between
my life and death: and meanwhile
come what may, let Heaven be my guide!

*[Exit DON LOPE*

### A street at the door of DON LOPE'S house.

*Enter SIRENA, in a cloak; MANRIQUE, behind her.*

**Sirena.** [*aside*] Whatever I do, I cannot
escape Manrique, and get inside
the house; he has followed me all day.
What shall I do?
**Manrique.**          Girl in a veil,
hurling your glances about
and gliding so stealthily by, what
skill in the art of battle
your movements convey; your figure
exciting despite the gray goat's-
hair cloth you wear, like a boat
sailing by with the wind in its
poop, your slippers embroidered,
your heavy cloak listing apace:
speak now or unveil your face,
else you'll have me believe it's pimpled
and ugly, as they say of the fools
who go muffled and stealthily by,
though the way you dance past in your mules,

I'd say would give them the lie.
**Sirena.** You've nothing more to add?
**Manrique.**                    Nothing.
**Sirena.** And to how many girls have you
   spoken this way?
**Manrique.**          I was
   terribly bashful before.
   On my word of honor, I spoke
   to only five girls all day.
   Now I'm immensely reformed.
**Sirena.** Heaven be praised for a man
   so honest and true! I have
   no more than nine lovers myself.
**Manrique.** I believe you, and since you
   believe me, I must at least
   show you these tokens of love.

                                 *[Takes them out.]*

   First, a lady's bun: this sinful
   bun of hair once-upon-a-time
   played its little role, and by way
   of curler and switch was martyrized
   and shriven. This string of pearls
   is false; they are really lice's eggs,
   which I admire, for when looked at
   from afar they seem to be
   a black panache dotted by a stream
   of snow-white flies. This slender stick
   is actually a whalebone discharged
   by a corset; it was my misfortune
   to receive it in a cudgeling.
   The stick is rich in virtues,
   correcting any breast and
   the roundest hump, for there's
   no figure but plays one false
   by virtue of some whalebone.
   This little slipper you now
   gaze upon in my hand,
   was once a house, I'll have you know,
   where two midgets dwelt but never
   met each other. This is a glove
   which was once a nightingale
   that undoubtedly was mum-dumb
   for a very long time.
   Here, sniff it: it oozes goat grease.
   This ribbon once belonged
   to a high and mighty lady;
   but I disdain it.
**Sirena.**          Why so?
**Manrique.** Because I know she loves me.

Isn't that reason enough?

**Sirena.** Yes.

**Manrique.** The lady I love must be a liar.
    She must deceive and mock me,
    make me jealous continually,
    abuse me, leave me and, in brief,
    must beg to marry me,
    which is the thing I feel
    most strongly about, for though
    this is women's custom anyway,
    I'd only take it as my right
    to make that pleasant which
    must afterwards become
    a very grave affliction.

**Sirena.** And is your lady beautiful?

**Manrique.** No, but she's filthy.

**Sirena.** Then surely
    she's a lady of high quality.

**Manrique.** One eye weeps boiled honey,
    and the other olive oil.

**Sirena.** Is she understanding or prudent?

**Manrique.** As for understanding herself,
    I take it she's prudent, as for
    others understanding her,
    quite the contrary; which means
    she's prudently misunderstood
    or understandably imprudent.

**Sirena.** To show you I'm sincere and shall
    await your loving pleasure,
    I'll accept that ribbon from you.

**Manrique.** Granted, most willingly.

**Sirena.** Alas, alas!

**Manrique.** What's wrong?

**Sirena.** My husband's coming now.
    Begone, quickly; my husband's
    the very devil. Disappear
    around the corner, quickly,
    and meanwhile, sir, when he's passed by,
    I'll await you inside this house.

**Manrique.** What a fine refuge you've discovered;
    I live here myself, and shall return
    in excellent good time.

*[Exit MANRIQUE*

### *A room in DON LOPE'S house*

*Enter SIRENA.*

**Sirena.** I slipped into the house
  without being recognized.
  I've tricked him beautifully,
  but he's tricked me even more
  by shaming and insulting me.
  And saying I was ugly!
  But that wouldn't trouble me,
  even if it were true,
  nor his saying I was stupid
  and dirty; but to say that
  one of my eyes weeps olive oil
  and the other boiled honey!
  No, by God, no! And even
  if my eyes did weep only one
  of those things, it wasn't right
  of him to say so; the idea
  of such a beggar, such an utter knave,
  telling me of my eyes weeps
  olive oil and the other, honey!

*Enter DOÑA LEONOR.*

**Doña Leonor.** Sirena.
**Sirena.**            My lady.
**Doña Leonor.** How anxiously I've waited for you!
  You spoke to him?
**Sirena.**            Yes, he sends
  his answer by this letter
  and promises if he may once
  speak privately with you,
  to go away forever.
**Doña Leonor.** Now I've greater reason for concern.
  Why did you take his letter?
**Sirena.** To bring it to you.
**Doña Leonor.** [*aside*]        Alas,
  how easily cruel hope steals
  into my heart.
**Sirena.**            Why, what does it
  matter if you read the letter?
**Doña Leonor.** Do you really think me capable
  of doing such a thing? Sirena,
  only your opinion keeps me now
  from tearing it to shreds.
  [*aside*] Oh, understand me better,
  little fool—entreat me further.

I am dying to read it.

**Sirena.** How can you blame the mere paper
he has written on, my lady,
and vent your anger by
destroying it?

**Doña Leonor.**    Well then,
I'll accept the letter now,
but only to destroy it.

**Sirena.** Yes, but do read it first.

**Doña Leonor.** [*aside*] That's it, entreat me further.
—How tiresome you are!
Well, to please you, I'll break the seal
and read it, but only for your sake.

**Sirena.** Yes, I see; now open it.

**Doña Leonor.** Well, this is what it says.

[*She opens it and reads.*]

"If I could but obey you, Leonor,
That is, forget you and protect my life,
I'd gladly do so; it would be enough
To know that I could never love you more.
You send me warning of untimely death
If I persist in loving you. Please God
To slay me then, leaving unresolved
My life's endeavor with my passing breath.
Do you pretend you can forget? Can I
Answer the scorn of such forgetfulness
And yet not feel my lips go numb, and die?
I'll have you love me, if you'd bind me thus,
And then forget you when I've kissed your smile!
Joy sooner slips the mind than an offense."

**Sirena.** Does the letter make you cry?
It only speaks of things gone by.

**Doña Leonor.** I weep because it brings to mind
old memories I thought had died.

**Sirena.** A real love is not soon forgotten.

**Doña Leonor.** I was told the man had died
who now springs back alive,
as though an old wound had freshly
broken out again with blood.
His persistence now only
discredits me; if he does not
go away, I shall soon be dead
or ruined, though death would be a fate
far easier to contemplate.

**Sirena.** But you can make him go away.

**Doña Leonor.** How?

**Sirena.**                By seeing him; as he says,

36

see him once, and he'll leave Lisbon.
**Doña Leonor.** How can I manage it, Sirena?
If he'd agree to that, I'd venture
the impossible. How would he
come here?
**Sirena.** Listen closely.
The safest time is now, at twilight,
while it is not too early
to receive a male visitor
nor too late to fear the neighbors
will notice that he's here.
My master, as you know,
never comes home so early.
As for Don Luis, I'm sure
he is close by; he can enter
this hallway while you two
may talk, and then you may
speak your mind quite freely.
He will listen to what you say.
Then let fortune do the rest.
**Doña Leonor.** You put it all so neatly,
there seems to be nothing to fear;
even honor cannot doubt it,
when everything is clear.
Go now, find Don Luis.

*[Exit SIRENA*

**Doña Leonor.**                    Love,
I have opened up the gate,
yet being what I am,
I can control my passion.
Not levity but honor
is my porter at the gate,
and must be my protector.
But if honor fail, I stand alone,
and if I cannot persevere,
I know well how to die.
I am trembling; each step I hear
I think is Don Lope's.
Was that the wind or he approaching?
Is it listening, has it heard me?
How like fear itself, that sound!
Oh, how can a woman of my
reputation take such a risk?

*Enter SIRENA and DON LUIS, in the dark.*

**Sirena.** Leonor awaits you here.
**Don Luis.**                    God,
how often have I dreamed
of this moment, thinking

it never would come to pass.

**Doña Leonor.** Now you are in my house, Don Luis.
This is the occasion
you desired; say what you must
quickly, then go away.
I am so frightened of myself,
I feel as though my feet were chained
in ice; my own breathing
points a dagger at my heart,
and a rope around my neck.

**Don Luis.** Fair Leonor, unless you've chosen
to forget past joys and pleasures,
you must recall how in Toledo
once, our native city
I loved you dearly, from
the moment I first saw you
one early morning in the meadow,
where your presence adorned
that blossoming field; for the flowers
your hands had plucked, your lovely feet
restored. Now you must recall . . .

**Doña Leonor.**                                    Wait,
I shall be briefer. I recall
the days you used to haunt my street
and, despite my coldness,
sustained your faith and love
until I smiled at you at last.
For who would not succumb to tears
men weep when they truly are in love?
Thus favored, and with the night
as faithful go-between,
as well as with that letter
slipped through my lattice, you spoke
of marriage. But when you learned
that you'd received a captaincy
obliging you to serve the King,
you went away to Flanders.

**Don Luis.**                                    Yes,
and I'll tell you of that now.
I went off to battle
where a certain valiant
gentleman was killed; his name
was Don Luis Benavides,
and he came from Aragon.
Since our names were identical,
I was mistakenly reported
dead. How easily a lie's believed!
Returning to Toledo . . .

**Doña Leonor.** I can account for that

more simply. Lifeless, shocked,
benumbed, I wept my days away.
Although I might enlarge
upon my feelings then
and name such sorrows one by one,
I must stop here. In brief,
urged and finally convinced
by others, I was married
by proxy in Toledo
to Don Lope.

**Don Luis.**　　　On the road back home
I learned of this. Intending
to undo the marriage,
I hastened here, disguised
as a merchant, which was when
I saw and spoke to you
so ambiguously.

**Doña Leonor.** I was already married,
as I then informed you.
Why did you persist in coming here?

**Don Luis.** I came only to discover why
I had been so abused.
And if I can satisfy myself
that you have broken faith,
I shall return to Flanders
where a musket ball will
ultimately make good
a promise long delayed.

**Sirena.** Someone is coming up the stairs.

**Doña Leonor.** My God, what can I do?
This hallway is dark; as long
as you remain here all is well.
Since you are alone here
you can slip out, once whoever
it is has come inside.
But do not leave yet for Castile.
There will be occasion later
to finish what you have to say.

**Sirena.** I shall follow you, my lady.

*[Exeunt DOÑA LEONOR and SIRENA*

**Don Luis.** My bewilderment is suddenly
as deep as my unhappiness.
The hallway darkens, pulling in
the dismal shadows of the night.
Since I was never here before,
I cannot tell house from doorway.
My heart hangs heavy. Oh, Sirena
and Leonor, your fears

have left me witless in the dark.

*Enter DON JUAN, in the dark, who meets DON*
*LUIS; both draw their swords.*

**Don Juan.** At this late hour, and nobody's
lit the light But what is this?
Who's there? You won't answer?
**Don Luis.** [*aside*] I have found the door. Now I can
get out.

*[Exit DON LUIS, groping his way*
*through another door*

**Don Juan.**        Answer me at once or else
my unsheathed sword will answer for you.

*Enter DON LOPE, in the dark, and MANRIQUE.*

**Don Lope.** The sound of clashing swords,
and the room in total darkness!
**Don Juan.** I hear your footsteps now.
**Manrique.** I'll go and get a candle.

*[Exit MANRIQUE*

**Don Lope.** Now there's swordplay in the house,
I have reason to fear the worst.
**Don Juan.** I say it again, who are you?
**Don Lope.** Who dares ask my name?
**Don Juan.**                          Since you ask,
I am one whose sword will slit open
in your breast a thousand mouths.
**Doña Leonor.** [*offstage*] A light, quickly!

*Enter DOÑA LEONOR and SIRENA, and*
*MANRIQUE with a candle.*

**Don Lope.**                          Don Juan!
**Don Juan.** Don Lope!
**Doña Leonor.**            God preserve us!
**Don Lope.** What does all this mean?
**Don Juan.** As I was going through the hallway,
I saw a man go out that way.
**Doña Leonor.** It must have been a man attempting
to rob the house.
**Don Lope.**        A man?
**Don Juan.** Yes, and when I asked his name,
he did not say a word.
**Don Lope.** [*aside*] I must dissimulate
or else be thought the victim
of the very fear I scorn.
—Upon my word, I might easily
have killed you! It was I
who went out that door, Don Juan.

40

Since I did not recognize
your voice and thought some stranger
challenged me in my own house,
I was angry, lost patience,
and replied silently, with my sword.

**Sirena.** How close we must have been
to some terrible catastrophe!

**Don Juan.** But how can that have happened?
If the man I say I saw
was actually here,
then he could not have left
this hallway by the door
through which you came in.

**Don Lope.**                                    I say
I was that man.

**Don Juan.**             How strange!

**Don Lope.** [aside] How inept, how damaging
an inquisitive friend can be!
The wisest, most prudent man alive
must one day find his conscience
on the very tongue of such a friend.
—Since you take it as a certainty
a stranger's broken in,
I'll have you strictly guard that door
against his leaving, while I
proceed to search the house.

**Don Juan.** He shall never escape this way.
You may safely search the house.

**Don Lope.** Be sure to guard it closely.
Do not leave it for any reason.

                                                    [Exit DON JUAN

[aside] I must now act most cautiously,
and if I find my honor stained,
I'll be so coolly circumspect
that only in my deepest silence
will the world discover
any hint of my revenge.
—Here now, Manrique, light the way
for me.

**Manrique.** I don't dare; at least
I don't share your fondness for ghosts.

                    [DON LOPE attempts to enter a bedroom,
                         and DOÑA LEONOR stops him.]

**Doña Leonor.** Do not enter this room, my lord.
Trust me, all is safe inside.

**Don Lope.** [to MANRIQUE] Well, what are you afraid of?

**Manrique.** Of everything.

**Don Lope.** [to DOÑA LEONOR] Open it, I say.

[to MANRIQUE] And you now, begone. [aside] Misfortune
needs no further witnesses.

> [DON LOPE takes the light and goes in while
> MANRIQUE leaves the other way.]

**Doña Leonor.** Alas, Sirena, how cold
his anger is! Despair
bids me end my life here.
Don Lope will surely find
Don Luis concealed inside.
Don Lope has decided that
whoever left by the hallway door
entered my bedroom and is still there.
But why do I persist in wondering
what has happened? By now
Don Lope's found and spoken with him.
What shall I do? Escape, I cannot:
unhappy fear has chained my feet,
imprisoned me in cowardice.
Wretched, miserable confusion.

> Enter DON LUIS, his cloak hiding his face, sword drawn, and behind him
> DON LOPE, carrying the candle, his sword drawn.

**Don Lope.** Sir, do not conceal yourself.
**Don Luis.** Then, sir, put down your sword.
Once a man's your prisoner,
there's more harm done than valor shown
in the spilling of his blood.
My home is in Castile;
there, in a field, I killed
a man in fair combat:
the issue was a lady
and my jealousy. I fled
and sought asylum here
in Lisbon, since I was banished
from Castile for that offense.
I learned this morning that
the dead man's brother was lurking
in this neighborhood
where he was seeking, treacherously,
with the help of others,
to take me by surprise.
Thus forewarned, I was passing this house
when three men in your doorway sprang out
and assaulted me. Perceiving
that self-defense against three men
was futile (though one's courage may
sometimes surprise one), I escaped
by climbing up your stairway; and they,
because they saw I'd found

a refuge, or because the change
of circumstance made vengeance
seem more doubtful, in any case,
they did not follow me.
I stayed where I was, behind
the first closed door, waiting
till they departed; then
when I judged they were no longer
in the street and I was about
to venture out, I stumbled into
a man leaving the hallway.
"Who's there?" he shouted at me.
Supposing him to be one
of my assailants, I thought it
safer not to answer,
then fled from one room to another
till I found myself in here.
This, sir, is the reason
you have found me hidden
in your house. Now my life
is in your hands, take it.
For as I've told the truth,
and no one's virtue is at stake,
I can die happily, and sacrifice
my life, heart and soul,
to an honorable sentiment,
not to some infamous revenge.

**Don Lope.** [*aside*] How can one man harbor in himself
such diverse perplexities?
The substance of one's dread and fears,
the torments and the doubts!
By Heaven, as if it were not
enough already to be plagued
by his presence out of doors,
must I now encounter him
ensconced here in the house?
Suspicions, seal your lips;
and yours too, my agony;
for everything he says
may be quite true, but if not,
the time is not yet ripe
for extreme measures.
—My dear sir, I am glad my house
has served as your asylum
against such treachery.
Because you are a stranger here,
accept my hospitality.
One gentleman must support
another in his difficulties.

43

I can assure you of my help
on every occasion you
have need of it; my sword
is ready to do you service
against a multitude, and so
you need not turn your back again.
But now, that you may leave
the house quite secretly,
I'll indicate the way
to go, through the garden
and out by a hidden door . . .
I'll open it for you . . . I must
take proper precautions
so that the servants (who are
one's worst enemies at home)
won't know I found you here.
It will be most important
to satisfy them all on this.
For though surely nobody
would doubt a truth so evident
as yours, and though it convinces me
quite sufficiently, still,
who of us can flee from malice,
and who escape suspicion?
Who is free of rumor's tongue,
and who can defend himself
against malevolence?
For if it once should be believed . . .
No, what's belief? If I once imagined,
if I once thought that someone
had compromised my honor . . .
no, not even honor—let's say
my reputation, my renown;
and if the hateful syllable
were uttered by my least servant,
a slave, by Heaven, there's
no one's life I'd hesitate
to take, no amount of blood
I would not spill, no quantity
of souls I would not readily
dispatch; and each of them
I'd break in two, bringing
to light the hearts on which
the infamy was written.
Come, I will light the way
ahead of you.
**Don Luis.** [*aside*] My voice
freezes in my throat. What
a display of Portuguese pride!

*[Exeunt DON LOPE and DON LUIS*

*Enter DOÑA LEONOR and SIRENA.*

**Doña Leonor.** Things have turned out better
than I'd expected, Sirena.
But bad luck may only once
fail to justify one's darkest
expectations. I can speak now,
I can move my frozen feet.
Oh Sirena, I'm alive again,
and my soul's inside my body.

*Enter DON LOPE.*

**Don Lope.** Leonor.
**Doña Leonor.**          My lord, what do you
intend to do? Have you discovered
why he came here? Now you know
I was not to blame.
**Don Lope.**          Would I dare
think otherwise, who love you
and respect you? No, Leonor,
I only wish to ask that we agree
between ourselves now . . .
**Doña Leonor.**                    Did he not
say just now that the reason
he came here from Castile
had to do with someone's death?
Well, I, my lord, knew nothing of that.
**Don Lope.** You need not defend yourself,
Leonor; understand . . . see how
you mortify me. How, Leonor,
how could you have known of it?
But now let it suffice that he has
given us assurances,
and was not seen leaving here.
And you, Sirena, I would not
have you speak of what's occurred
among the three of us, not to
anyone, not even to Don Juan.

*Enter DON JUAN.*

**Don Juan.** *[aside]* Don Lope has delayed so long
I've grown somewhat concerned.
**Don Lope.** By God, Don Juan, that was
a fine idea of yours, urging me
to search the house, though I'm still certain
that the culprit was myself!
Here, take the candelabrum
for a while, and lead the way.
**Don Juan.** But why go on when I'm convinced

45

I was mistaken? I was wrong,
and I admit it now.
**Don Lope.** Still, we must be thorough;
let's search the house together now.
**Doña Leonor.** [*aside*] What remarkable prudence!
**Don Juan.** [*aside*] What courage and what pride!
**Sirena.** [*aside*] What despair!
**Don Lope.** [*aside*]         Thus must he
proceed who seeks revenge until
the moment's ripe: in sufferance,
silence, and dissimulation.

## ACT THREE

### *In the courtyard of the KING'S palace in Lisbon*

#### *Enter DON JUAN and MANRIQUE.*

**Don Juan.** Where is Don Lope?
**Manrique.**                When he went
inside the palace, he
left me here.
**Don Juan.** Go find him,
and say that I'm waiting to see him.

*[Exit MANRIQUE*

Now to rehearse alone
the dialogue that must ensue
between us, and the doubtful purpose
I pursue in making it
my duty to discuss the matter
of his reputation with a friend.
I feel I am as closely bound
to him as ever one man
has been to another.
At home, his constant guest,
using his estate as though
it were my own; and what is more,
he trusts me with his life and soul.
How can I ever be ungrateful
for that friendship, loyalty,
and trust? And how can I be silent
while I see his purest honor
trampled down and not give up
my life to aid his vengeance?
How can I coldly countenance
the rumor of that Castilian's
adoration of Leonor,
and while her reputation suffers

46

for it, plainly see her
encouraging the gallant—
see and hear all this while Don Lope
himself knows nothing of it?
No, that I can't abide.
Don Lope has but to say the word—
I'll shoulder his revenge,
and that Castilian dies today.
Even without such word, I can
dispatch the gentleman
skillfully and silently.
But will slander be avenged
if the arm that strikes it down
is not membered to the body
of the man who suffered it?
My frank advice to Don Lope
will be, "Do not ask the King
to join him, but stay at home."
But if he asks me why,
how shall I answer him?
This is the sorest point of all;
for to warn another
that his precious honor lies
in jeopardy is but to speak
the word that quits him of that honor.
What must a friend do then?
If I say nothing, I only add
to the offense, if I tell him,
I incarnate the offense, and I
offend him if I avenge it.
If indeed I've served him
as a true reflector of his
conscience, why can't I counsel him?
I see him coming now. He shan't
have reason to complain of me,
for he will now advise himself in
that which I would counsel him to do.

*Enter DON LOPE and MANRIQUE.*

**Don Lope.** Manrique, go back and say
that I am going to my
country house and there await
his word when the King is ready
to receive me.
**Manrique.** There's Don Juan,
who's come to speak with you.

*[Exit MANRIQUE*

**Don Lope.** *[aside]*              Ah,
what new trouble's brought him here?

47

—Yes, Don Juan, what brings you this way?
[*aside*] And so the coward's always
victimized by his own fears.
**Don Juan.** Dear friend, I've come to ask
for your assistance in clearing up
a disconcerting doubt of mine.
This is in strictest confidence.
**Don Lope.** [*aside*] I already know it deals
with some misfortune of my own.
—Tell me about it.
**Don Juan.** This concerns
a friend who's asked my help.
I seek advice in his behalf.
**Don Lope.** And the matter?
**Don Juan.** Two gentlemen
were playing cards one day when
some difference arose between them.
An argument ensued in the course
of which one man accused
the other of a lie.
In all the hubbub, the man
who was insulted did not catch
the insult, but a friend heard it
and others heard it too.
Because he is a loyal friend,
this doubt assails him now:
is he obliged to tell his friend,
straight out, he has been wronged,
who knows nothing of it?
Or should he stand by and let
the other's reputation suffer
while the insult goes unavenged?
If he conceals it, the wrong increases;
if he discloses it,
he violates the friendship.
What's better: speech or silence?
**Don Lope.** Let me consider this awhile.
[*aside*] Honor outmaneuvers me:
doubt deployed by doubt; this way
madness lies: compelled to speak
about my own condition
as though it were another's.
The question put by Don Juan's friend
clearly is his own, which means
he's seen enough to be aroused.
Shall I tell him? No, I cannot.
I have resolved on silence.
—Don Juan, I imagine I would say,
if my opinion were solicited

that a man cannot have suffered
insult and not know of it.
The guilt is totally his own
who suffers insult and dissimulates,
because he won't avenge it.
In a case so desperate,
the man at fault is not
the one who knows nothing
of the wrong that's been done him,
but he who knows and, in choosing
to be silent, conceals it.
As for myself, I'd say
that if a friend, like you
(being close as we two are),
came to tell me any such thing,
assuming or imagining
he could do so freely,
he'd be the first I would
avenge myself upon.
It would be too cruel a thing
to speak of face to face.
In fact, I cannot understand
at all how one man would have
the temerity to tell another,
"You have lost your honor."
That one's best friend should bring
such evil tidings—why, I say it
again: as God is my witness,
if I so much as dared tell myself
such a thing, I'd kill myself at once,
I who am myself my oldest friend.

**Don Juan.** Now I am instructed by you,
I can warn my friend his course
is silence. May God be with you.

*[Exit DON JUAN*

**Don Lope.** Who would doubt the pass I've reached when
an affair involving two calls for
a third to act as mediator?
And so Don Juan suspects that
Leonor intends to ruin me;
sensing what wrong's been done,
he perceives I must avenge it,
and the world perceives this too.
Well, honor, there's an end to it.
I must act at once and not
permit suspicion to yield
to credence, nor apprehension
to the evil it anticipates.
And before her inconstancy

49

achieves its basely wished for end,
I'll work out the strategy
by which revenge makes clear
the harsh reward of treachery.

*Enter the KING and his retinue.*

**King.** Since we intend to spend the night
in what the populace is pleased
to call the King's country house,
tell them we now depart from Lisbon.
Also tell the people to expect
processions where the most brilliantly
arrayed shall pass in full regalia.
Their shining plumes and iridescent hues
everywhere will vie with
flowering April and its sunbeams.

**Don Lope.** [*aside*] I shrink as I approach the King.
Tormented passion has so far
reduced me that I must imagine
the whole world knows my shame,
my grief, my cowardice.
—Accept my humble salutation, sire.

**King.** Ah, Don Lope, if only I might have
your stout sword beside me
there in Africa, how swiftly
I'd vanquish the haughtiest of Moors.

**Don Lope.** Then how can that sword be sheathed,
and I allow it to repose unused,
when yours, great sire, is drawn?
I shall join you in the war.
Sire, what reason can there be
on this occasion to detain me
here in Portugal?

**King.**                    Are you married?

**Don Lope.** I am, Your Majesty,
but my being married does not alter
the man I was and am.
And formerly my highest honor
thrived only on the highest deeds.

**King.** Being newly wed, how will your wife
like this?

**Don Lope.**    As a thing most honorable.
She'd feel that she has given you
the soldier in her husband, than whom
none nobler or more manly, great sire,
has ever fought upon your side.
If formerly I lent
my reputation to your cause,
I now offer it both hers and mine.

Being absent from my wife
will not conflict with my desire.
**King.** I believe you, but I queried you
because it seems to me unjust
you should separate so quickly
in this fashion. Though our present
enterprise is lofty, still, Don
Lope, in making it your cause you
may be leaving things amiss at home.

*[Exeunt the KING and his retinue*

**Don Lope.** Good Lord, what is this shadow passing
over me? Can my heart have rightly
heard the tale my senses tell?
Has some report of wrong done me
already reached the King?
How widely broadcast it must be
if its echoes reach me last.
If so, my misfortune
is immeasurable. My God,
I'd sooner have the punishment
which totally consumes the body
in one lightning stroke while the thunder
rolls insensibly behind me
than suffer the King's grave sentence
implying there is something amiss
at home. For now I suffer more
who must endure a lightning
even more intense, and rise again,
the phoenix of my grief,
from my own ashes. Such
mountains and stone obelisks
hurled down upon my back
now become my monument,
and I lie buried underneath it,
still alive. Yet all this weighs lightly,
far more lightly than the force
of insult that has crushed me down.
Honor, you are greatly in my debt.
Come closer, listen to me.
Why do you complain of me?
Tell me how I have offended you?
To that courage I inherited
have I not brought full measure
of my own, and by it lived my life
and scorned the greatest dangers?
Honor, since I would not subject you
to the slightest risk or fault,
when have I not been courteous
to the humble, friendly

51

to the gentleman, generous
to the poor, fellow comrade
to my soldiers? And as a husband
now, alas, how have I failed,
and of what am I to blame?
Was not the wife I chose
of noble blood and ancient stock?
Do I not love my wife?
Do I not respect her?
If I have been at fault
in none of these, and if
my conduct has not given rise
to viciousness of any sort,
whether out of ignorance
or malice, why am I exposed
to insult? Why? By what tribunal
must the innocent be so condemned?
Can there be punishment
without a crime, a trial
without an accusation read?
And penalty where there is no guilt?
Oh, the world's insane legalities!
That a man who has ever labored
in the cause of honor cannot know
if he has been insulted!
When the evil consequences
of another's actions
are visited upon me,
then never has the world misprized
virtue more. Again, I ask:
why is goodness less esteemed
than misdemeanor, in whose hands
its proud fortress is surrendered
so supinely, and merely
in response to the blandishments
of appetite? Who put honor
in a glass so fragile,
then, totally inept in physic,
made such crude experiments in
that retort? But let me now be brief.
An injured man will hurl
cries endlessly against
blind custom's cudgeling.
I cannot lessen them a whit,
and this is all men's fate.
I live to avenge, not mend them.
I'll join the King, and then,
returning another way,
when occasion beckons me

I'll strike, and thereby bring about
the world's most overt vengeance.
The King, Don Juan, and everyone
will know of it; then, oh God,
it shall be forever known
to all recorded time and fame
how a Portuguese defends his name.

[Exit DON LOPE

### On the seashore

*A clashing of swords offstage; then enter DON JUAN and
others fleeing from him, and exeunt.*

**Don Juan.** Cowards, I erased the insult
When I killed the man who uttered it.
**A Soldier.** Run for your lives! His sword is lightning!
*Enter DON JUAN and his antagonists.*

**Don Lope.** [*offstage*] Is that you, Don Juan?
I'm coming.
*Enter DON LOPE.*

**Another Soldier.** [*aside*] He has killed me.
**Don Juan.** [*returning*]                    With your support,
there is nothing in the world I fear.
**Don Lope.** They've escaped; tell me what's happened,
unless there's reason to pursue them.
**Don Juan.** Ah, Don Lope, my wound
gapes wide again; the insult
I once avenged and thought
was stricken out of mind,
now tears at me afresh.
Alas, I was deluded.
For simple vengeance has not served
to bury the offense.
When I left you last, Don Lope,
it was to come here to this
sea-beaten shore, having in mind
your purpose: the transfer
of your household to this country seat
against your imminent departure.
Happily arrived, I saw a group
of men conversing, and in passing
heard one address the others:
"There goes Don Juan de Silva."
Hearing my own name spoken
(the most readily perceived of words),
I soon overheard the rest.
And then another asked, "And who

is this man, Don Juan?" "But
have you never heard of him?"
replied the first. "He's the man
Don Manuel de Sosa
publicly insulted".
But this was intolerable,
and so I drew my sword and said,
"I am the man who killed his enemy
Don Manuel so swiftly, he found
no time for further words
after uttering the insult.
I'm the man who blotted out the wrong,
and not the man who suffered it.
With his blood I cleansed my honor."
On this I closed swords with them all;
they fled, I followed here, and they
escaped. All gossips are cowards;
instead of courage, they show their heels.
This, Don Lope, is my burden.
Would to God my daring equaled
my terrible despair;
I'd hurl myself into those waves
or end my life upon this sword,
and not let injury consume me.
"He is the man," they said,
"Don Manuel insulted," and not
"the man who blotted out the wrong."
Can one ever anticipate
offense And when it's been redressed,
has one not done enough?
It was not enough to put my life
in jeopardy, preferring
death with honor to life without it.
No, that was not enough.
For however much, however often,
a man of pride and daring
avenge the insult done him,
by so much and so often
does he publicize that insult.
For his vengeance must reveal
what the insult may conceal.

[Exit DON JUAN

**Don Lope.** "For his vengeance must reveal
    what the insult may conceal."
And so when I redress the wrong
    done me, I broadcast the offense.
Clearly, then, my vengeance will reveal
    what the insult may conceal.
And once I have straightforwardly

avenged myself, it must
mistakenly be said of me,
"There goes the man who was insulted,"
not, "the man who blotted out the wrong."
And when this hand of mine today
is bathed in blood, it will bespeak
the insult, since vengeance thus proclaims
what the wrong itself does not.
Then, by Heaven, I must not seek it
publicly, but seal its mouth instead.
Prudent vengeance calls for sufferance,
silence, and dissimulation.
Done secretly the deed elicits
greater honor, greater praise.
In silence my purpose
refines my instrument;
otherwise my vengeance but reveals
what the insult now conceals.
This happened to Don Juan,
after he regained his honor,
when the soldier said, "There's the man
who was insulted," not, "the man
who blotted out the wrong."
Then let my vengeance be a work
of such skill and forethought that the sun
itself will scarcely see it done.
And whoever now believes me wronged,
let him believe it still.
Meanwhile, until that most secret
of occasions beckons,
oh injured heart, be strong
in sufferance, silence, and
dissimulation. Boatman!

*Enter a BOATMAN.*

**Boatman.**                    Sir?
**Don Lope.** Have you a boat at hand?
**Boatman.** I shall surely have one for you, sir.
But at the moment, all the boats
are occupied, coming and going
all afternoon in the train of
King Sebastian (Heaven protect him),
who is moving to his country house.
**Don Lope.** Then see you have one ready for me;
I must be off to my own house.
**Boatman.** Must it be right away?
**Don Lope.**                    At once.
**Boatman.** I'll go to fetch one now.

*[Exit BOATMAN*

*Enter DON LUIS, reading a letter.*

**Don Luis** [*to himself*] I'll re-read this letter
which now commands my fate,
for the pleasure is redoubled
when experienced again.

[*reads*] "This evening the King goes to his country house; disguise
yourself among the people in his train, until occasion grant we meet, you
to finish your complaints, and I, my own defense. God keep
you.—Leonor"

Now, as luck would have it, there is
no boat to carry me across!
Great God, let fortune aid me now and
I'll never ask another favor.
**Don Lope.** [*aside*] The man reading that letter awaits
my vengeance. He doubtless reads
of my disgrace. How feverish
my honor is: hearing, seeing,
and believing nothing
but the pain that drives me.
**Don Luis.** [*aside*] That fellow is Don Lope.
**Don Lope.** [*aside*] I must give no sign of anger,
but rather smile at fury's prodding
while I suffer and dissimulate,
like the snake that wheedles and cajoles
while it swells its bitter gorge,
then bursts and spits its venom out.
— Sir, I must believe you hold
my offer in very low esteem,
having asked no favor of me yet
who wish so much to serve you.
I was so far taken by
your courtesy, your courage
and discretion, that I've searched
all Lisbon for you since,
hoping to enlist my sword
in your cause against any new
assault by your antagonists,
they who may so easily
encounter and outnumber you,
and while you least expect it,
kill you on this very spot.
**Don Luis.** And I in turn, Don Lope, know
the debt I owe you and am hoping
to repay; but as a stranger
here today, I doubt I'll have
the honor to enlist your aid.

Therefore, good sir, there is no need
to burden you with the affair
against my rivals in which
you would assist me. Aside
from that, I think we two are friends
enough that I may speak
to you quite openly of things.

**Don Lope.** Yes, I hope you may; but first,
be sure you know the risk you take;
for the friendship of a man aggrieved
is not a very stable thing.

**Don Luis.** Quite the contrary: I say,
and feel, once I am your friend,
of whom may I be surer,
unless it be my enemy?

**Don Lope.** The point's debatable, though
you're entitled to believe it
as you do, reasonably or not.
Keep your opinion, I'll keep mine.
But tell me, what brings you
to this place?

**Don Luis.**　　　　I must find
a boat to take me to the King's
country house.

**Don Lope.**　　　　You've come in time.
Trust me, I shall help you there.
The boat I've hired will soon be here.

**Don Luis.** Here the King extends such favor
to the populace, thousands
have crossed over, scarcely
leaving any boat to go by.
I'm eager to be one among
that animated crowd, for
I assume the occasion
is unprecedented.

**Don Lope.** Then you'll cross with me. [aside] And speed me
to my own occasion now.

**Don Luis.** [aside] Is there anyone can say
he has better luck than I?

**Don Lope.** [aside] Now he's crept into these hands
in which he soon must die.

**Don Luis.** [aside] And who should bring me on the scene
but her husband, as a go-between!

*Enter the BOATMAN.*

**Boatman.** The boat's at your disposal.

**Don Lope.** [to the BOATMAN] Board the boat yourself while I
wait for my servant here.
No, wait for him here yourself;

you'll know him when he comes.
Tell him we're inside the boat.
**Boatman.** Don't board her yet, there's no one
at the helm; a single mooring
holds her: she won't be too secure.
**Don Lope.** Go find my servant, and we'll
both await you in here.
**Don Luis.** [*aside*] How could I be luckier?
He leads me to the very spot
where I shall try his honor.
**Don Lope.** [*aside*] And so I lead him to the spot
where he shall die at last.

            [*Exeunt DON LUIS and DON LOPE*

**Boatman.** I suspect that servant won't
get here for years and years.
But what's this? The boat is gone,
the mooring's broken! They're in the hands
of God, unless He saves them,
they'll surely find their graves,
both of them, beneath the waves.

            [*Exit BOATMAN*

*Another part of the beach, within view of*
*DON LOPE'S country house.*

*Enter MANRIQUE and SIRENA*

**Manrique.** Here I stand, Sirena, transfixed
by your glance, enchanted and bewitched.
Perhaps you've wandered this beach
of yours to hear the song
the Siren sings out in the sea?
My sonnet here's most opportune:
heroic, grave, and quite discreet.
Listen, it's not importunate;
simply one of the great hoard
of sonnetry I promised you.

        [*MANRIQUE takes out a sheet of paper and reads.*]

"To a Green Ribbon," a sonnet:

    "Green ribbon with your neatly tucked-in end,
    You could have been the ribbon which that god
    (Ruling the fifth planet) steeped in blood
    So as to make the goddess Venus pregnant.
      Spring dips its brush into your coloring,
    For whom I carry through this labyrinth
    (As long as that made famous once in Corinth)
    My heart, blacker than the blackest ink.

Now let your hope conjoin with my fear,
So love may choose a green or yellow tint,
Guessing which one is phlegm and which is choler.
For since I paint myself in your own color,
It cannot be (harpoons won't make me flinch)
But that my hope is sure to stick much faster."

**Sirena.** Oh, what a beautiful sonnet
you've written! But do show it
to me, the ribbon, I mean—
to see if it's really green.
**Manrique.** [*aside*] I now recall, too well,
what happened to that ribbon.
Let's see: yes!—On a certain
day, Sirena, while strolling
by the Tagus, the idea came
to me: how the sweetness
of the river matched your beauty,
and my happiness as well.
To soothe my fondest hope
I brought the ribbon out;
but seeing it reminded me
of all your fickleness,
and all at once I wept on it,
and kissed it sighingly.
While I stood there thus engaged,
an eagle who had seen me bring
the ribbon to my lips, as though
I'd offered him a bite to eat,
descended from his boulder,
resolutely snatched the ribbon,
and alighted on his perch again.
Giddy with anxiety,
I made as if to scale the boulder
when I recalled I lacked a pot
to serve me as a helmet.
With this event your ribbon
faded out of human history.
That, Sirena, is the story
called "The Green, or Unripe, Ribbon."
**Sirena.** But hear me now recount
that story's epilogue.
Standing in a field one day,
I spied the selfsame eagle
flying by, who deciding
that the ribbon was no
bite to eat, promptly dropped it
not very far away;
I hurried to the spot

to discover what had fallen,
and found this ribbon draped
about the flowers; tell me
if it is the one you lost.

**Manrique.** What a sweet coincidence!

**Sirena.** My vengeance will be sweeter.

**Manrique.** Let's leave that for later; your mistress
is coming through the field.

*[Exit MANRIQUE*

*Enter DOÑA LEONOR.*

**Doña Leonor.** Sirena.

**Sirena.**     Madam.

**Doña Leonor.**       I am very
much distressed.

**Sirena.**     Do I know
the reason why?

**Doña Leonor.** You do;
but listen to what I say.
Ever since that saddest night,
heaped with such confusions,
while I stood by imagining
the house afire, like another Troy,
I've been absolved by everyone.
Don Juan is deceived still further,
Don Luis gone free, and Don Lope
reassured; since then I've come
to live here in this pleasant
country house, awaiting Don Lope's
departure, while nature
excellently paints this meadow
and adorns the lofty hill,
and never has Don Lope
honored me more. And so, Sirena,
I've come to lose the fear I bore
for my own self-respect.
And since I have emerged so well
from so harrowing a circumstance,
audacity now summons me
to act without restraint.
The danger's past and left
no hint of retribution.
And so it's come to this:
Don Lope is more fond of me
than ever; as if, supposing
he'd suspected some abuse before,
he so enjoys the sense
of being disabused
that he's turned it into love.

How many have loved another
in this fashion, how many
have become love's object
intensified by insult!
The wisest and most learned men
will still succumb to such
mistaken passion, and of all
women, the most judicious
and best loved will not recall
the substance of another's love
for her. Thus when I was loved by
Don Luis, I felt that I
disliked him; when that love
was guiltless, I seemed to fear it.
And now (what utter madness!),
I neither love my being loved
nor fear my guiltiness.
I began to love when I felt
I'd been deserted and offended.
Now my love is guilty,
I become more daring.
And while Don Lope himself
goes off on my behalf today
to join the King, I've written
Don Luis to visit me,
and give my love away at last,
for it belongs to him.

*Enter DON JUAN.*

**Don Juan.** [*aside*] How can a heart that suffers
such continual assaults
stand firm and not finally
succumb to any one of them!

**Doña Leonor.** What's this, Don Juan: you've come
without Don Lope?

**Don Juan.**          I could not wait
for him, though he said he'd come shortly,
before the sun sinks in the sea.

**Doña Leonor.** But now that time seems past;
pallid shadows creep across
the earth, and heavy clouds
hang in the murky sky.

**Don Juan.** Sudden irritation seized me.
A man fleeing from himself neither
waits nor cares to look behind.

**Don Luis.** [*offstage*] God save me!

**Doña Leonor.**          What pitiful cry
was that upon the wind?

**Don Juan.** I see no one here on land.

61

**Doña Leonor.** There against the waves I see
some vague shape moving toward us.
In this trembling twilight,
it is hard to recognize.
**Don Juan.** He is desperately attempting
to escape and now he seems
to lean toward us as if
imploring Heaven's aid.
Quickly, let us go down to him
and give him what support we can.

[*Exit DON JUAN*

**Don Lope.** [*offstage*] Alas, alas.
**Don Juan.** [*offstage*]        Stretch out your hand!
**Don Lope.** [*offstage*] My land, sweet earth of all mankind!

*DON JUAN returns, entering with DON LOPE, drenched,
and with a dagger in his hand.*

**Don Juan.** Who's this? Don Lope?
**Doña Leonor.**            Dear husband!
**Don Lope.** Merciful fate, that leads to
such a gracious haven as now
you hasten to extend me
in my weariness. Oh Leonor,
my treasure! I should not doubt
that Heaven, with its customary
grace, now showers me with happiness
to make up for so much misery.
My friend!
**Don Juan.**    What does all this mean?
**Don Lope.** This happiness of mine follows
the most pitiful of all events.
**Doña Leonor.** Since Heaven has heard my prayers
and brought you back alive,
I would not reproach good fortune,
as tragic custom does.
**Don Lope.** After speaking with the King, I looked
for you, but when I could not
find you, I hired a boat.
The boat was on the point of
moving off when I was hailed
by a gallant gentleman
whose name I scarcely knew,
though I believe it was
a certain Don Luis
de Benavides. He hastened
to explain he was a foreigner,
whose well-meaning boldness
therefore deserved to be excused,

and begged me to forgive
his asking to be taken
with me in the boat, since he
most eagerly desired
to see the populace
join in homage at King
Sebastian's country house. I was thus
obliged to make room for him.
He had scarcely come aboard—
the boat responding to the added
weight, though the boatman had not
yet boarded it—when the mooring,
already strained and rotted
by the sea, broke loose, assaulted by
a wave which rudely claimed it.
I could not ward off the blow,
although I seized the oars.
Then when strength deserted me,
we collapsed inside the boat,
prey to our anxieties
among the blue and thrashing waves:
at one moment raised aloft
the highest salty peaks, and at
the next, buried deep beneath
arched caverns in a sapphire
radiance. We were hurled at last
in this direction when,
just in sight of land lights,
the boat was split and swamped
with sea and sand. I could not save
the gallant gentleman, swept
beyond my reach by the blow that
wrecked us; and since he could not save
himself, he sank into a grave
and watery oblivion.

**Doña Leonor.** Alas!

[*She faints.*]

**Don Lope.**        Leonor, my wife
my treasure, you mar your loveliness.
Merciful God! Look, an icy
pallor slowly moves through
her translucent hands. Oh, Don Juan!
It was not her seeing me engulfed
by peril that mortifies
her soul; the hearts of women
do not succumb so easily
to the telling of sad tales.
Do help carry her to bed.

[*She is carried off by DON JUAN and SIRENA.*]

**Don Lope.** It well becomes a man
　　to silence insult, and even
　　seem to bury his revenge.
　　This way he comes eventually
　　to requite his wrongs, who
　　waits and suffers patiently.
　　Honor, we have pursued
　　our course assiduously,
　　and now silently repay
　　dissimulated insult
　　with dissimulated vengeance.
　　How well I grasped the chance
　　occasion offered when
　　I cut away the mooring
　　and took the oars in hand
　　to push us farther off
　　while pretending I meant
　　to draw us back to shore.
　　How well my plan succeeded,
　　for I killed the man (as this
　　dagger is my witness) intent
　　on my dishonor and disgrace,
　　and hurled him, a glassy monument,
　　upon his raging tomb.
　　How well I managed when I
　　crashed the boat against the shore,
　　for now the act lends credence
　　to my tale and so dissuades
　　suspicions of complicity.
　　Now that I have acted in
　　conformance with the law of honor
　　and killed the gallant first,
　　I must turn next to Leonor.
　　When the King beholds her blood
　　staining the sheets of that
　　still unviolated bed,
　　he cannot bid me stay behind
　　for anything amiss at home.
　　Tonight my vindication ends,
　　resolved most prudently and wisely.
　　Leonor, alas! Leonor,
　　as fair as she is false,
　　as unhappy as she's lovely,
　　my honor's fatal ruin.
　　Leonor, now asleep in sorrow
　　and subdued by anguish,
　　as though she had outwitted death
　　and left it baffled in the hands
　　of life, Leonor must die.

I shall entrust my secret only
to the elements, since
only they can share my silence.
There, to wind and water
I have yielded half my vengeance;
and here I now entrust to earth
and fire my sorrow's other half.
Tonight I must boldly burn
my own house down; first the bedroom
will be set afire, and when
the flames start up, in darkest daring
I shall strike Leonor dead—
then let it be surmised the fire
was her bloody. executioner.
From that blaze I'll snatch up again
the honor of my former
high renown, purified
of the alloy basely dulling it.
By experiment in such a
crucible, one extracts the gold
to which the lowly metal clung
that dimmed its glow and purity.
And so the sea was first to wash
away the stain of my disgrace;
and now the wind carries it away
where no one shall hear of it again.
Next, the earth must turn away from it,
and fire reduce it all to ashes.
This indeed is the fate of every
mortal breath which dares becloud
the sun; by water cleansed,
by earth interred, by wind borne off,
by fire totally consumed.

                                        [Exit DON LOPE.

*Enter the KING, the DUKE OF BERGANZA, and retinue.*

**Duke.** Because the sea believes it's caught
    another sun asleep
    within its realm, it gently
    etches stars upon the waves.
**King.** Duke, I chose to come by sea,
    and though I might have chosen land,
    it seemed to offer some delay
    and this way is closer.
    Besides, the waters seemed so sweetly
    beguiling that the sky itself,
    a blue Narcissus self-entranced,
    lingered fondly, silently above.
    I was right to come this way

where so many ships lie anchored,
their beacons like a thousand
burning comets flashing on
a thousand fluttering swans,
suggesting a kind of rivalry
between the ones who'd fly
by using oars and those
who'd row by using wings.

**Duke.** The night's so fresh and still, it
liberates every thing alive.

**King.** This vista is delightful, poised
halfway between the land and sea.
All those country houses
among the trees are so enchanting
they would rouse nymphs out of the sea,
who seem indeed to be approaching
now, obedient, in breathless
quietude. And meanwhile, we appear
to gaze upon a wandering forest
on a moving hill, for as we view
them from the sea, they stir
as if to wave farewell.
Farewell, my sweet beloved land.
I shall return, if my cause is just,
and you shall see me enter
next in victory and laurels
earned triumphantly upon
a thousand bloody fields,
my honor brightened by new fame,
the Church acclaimed by thousands more,
I trust . . .

[*Shouts offstage of "Fire! Fire!"*]
Duke, what cries are those I hear?

**Duke.** They are shouting, Fire; the cries appear
to come from the nearest country house.
If I'm not mistaken, that's Don
Lope's house bursting into flame.

**King.** I see it now: smoke and fire
gathering in one volcanic roar
spread clouds of spark and ash.
It seems to draw from everywhere,
like some gigantic furnace.
It appears impossible
anyone can be alive inside.
Come, let us go and see
if there is any way to fight it.

**Duke.** But sire, is this not rash?

**King.** No, Duke, a simple act of mercy.

*Enter DON JUAN, half naked.*

**Don Juan.** I must rescue Don Lope,
   though I am burnt to ashes.
   His bedroom is on fire.
**King.** Stop that man!
**Duke.**                    Madman, what
   can you be thinking of?
**Don Juan.** Of leaving the world some record
   of true friendship. Since the fire
   has drawn you here, you should know its cause.
   Oh, Your Majesty, no sooner
   had we found ourselves inside
   than suddenly, without warning,
   the fire burst forth, as if
   avenging its own violence.
   Don Lope and his wife are still
   inside; I must save them.

*Enter MANRIQUE.*

**Manrique.** Belching sparks like the devil
   in a play, I go flying
   from my house. Am I not this Troy's
   Aeneas? I must plunge this body
   in the sea, though burning
   harm me less than drinking water.

*Enter DON LOPE, half naked, and bearing*
*DOÑA LEONOR, dead, in his arms.*

**Don Lope.** Forgive me, merciful Heaven,
   for though I risked my life,
   hers slipped by, eluding me.
   Oh, Leonor!
**King.**              Is this Don Lope?
**Don Lope.** Yes, I am Don Lope, sire,
   if feeling, rather than this fire,
   has left me any trace of life
   by which to recognize you
   and address you. For now my
   heart and soul, plunged in
   this hideous catastrophe,
   this horror, this tragedy,
   lie smoldering in white ashes.
   This dead beauty, this flower
   frozen by so much fire,
   which only it would dare to touch
   because it envied her beauty's
   radiance, this, sire, was my wife:
   a woman noble, proud,
   honorable and chaste,

whose praise all the tongues of fame
will sing eternally. This is
the wife I loved so tenderly
that I preferred to lose her,
and never see her more, than find her,
to my great sorrow, as she appeared,
wrapped in heavy smoke and flames
and who, when all my courage sought
to save her, laid her life
down in these arms. Torment,
bitter agony, catastrophe!
This one consolation's left me:
I may freely serve you now,
my duties at home all ended.
I shall go with you to battle,
and there may end my life,
if indeed misfortune ever ends.
[*aside to* DON JUAN] And you, my valiant friend,
Don Juan, tell him who seeks
advice of you, how a man
must be avenged and not permit
a living soul to know of it;
for vengeance now no more reveals
what the offense no more conceals.
**King.** This has been a painful tragedy.
**Don Juan.** May it please Your Majesty
to hear me privately.
It befits the nature of this case
that you alone should know of it.
Wracked by his suspicions,
which soon became realities,
Don Lope prudently resolved
that *secret insult* must be met
by *secret vengeance*; so
he killed the gallant there
at sea, when they came together
in a boat alone. Thereby the secret
perished, first in water, then in fire;
since only he who knew the wrong
he suffered could avenge it.
**King.** In this most notable
of cases antiquity has known,
we have seen how secret insult
most requires secret vengeance.
**Don Juan.** This is a true history
of the great Don Lope
de Almeida; in our admiration
this tragicomedy is ended.

# DEVOTION TO THE CROSS

# (LA DEVOCIÓN DE LA CRUZ)

## Devotion to the Cross

The tyranny of honor is mitigated and momentarily transcended in **Devotion to the Cross**. With so harsh a principle to justify, one would expect Calderón to portray, as he does, exemplary subversions against it with scrupulous intensity. What happens here is what must happen in a mercy play: the thaumaturgy of religious faith upheld by a single belief succeeds, because it is part of a mightier machine, in toppling the ratiocinative machinery of the insult-vengeance formula. For this victory to occur, the case must be exceptional, and it is—and again, almost absurdly melodramatic, as both miracle and honor plays must be because they enforce the tension between a suprapersonal ideality and a violent renunciation.

Eusebio kills Lisardo, his friend, who goaded him into a duel for daring to court Julia, Lisardo's sister, without the permission of their father Curcio, an impoverished nobleman. Eusebio is presumed to lack the qualifications of nobility, though before killing Lisardo, he tells a long story about his miraculous existence as directly influenced by a holy cross, whose symbol was inscribed on his chest at birth. Before Lisardo dies, Eusebio carries him off to be shriven, and before the corpse is brought home, Eusebio begs Julia to escape with him instead of entering the convent as her father has ordered her to do. When Lisardo's death is announced, Julia cannot bring herself to hate Eusebio, though, respecting her wish, he agrees to leave her. Eusebio becomes the leader of a brigand gang, marauding the mountains and villages, killing and living off the spoils of his victims. One near-victim, the priest Alberto, is saved when a bullet is diverted by a holy book he wears against his chest. Eusebio permits him to go when Alberto agrees to confess him before he dies one day. Curcio, who has denounced Julia for being like her dead mother, now pursues Eusebio in the vicinity of the mountains where once, out of some unfounded jealousy, he struck at his wife Rosmira, who gave birth to twins at the foot of a cross. One child, Julia, and the mother were miraculously transported home while the other child disappeared. Meanwhile, Eusebio breaks into the convent and is about to rape Julia when he discovers that she also bears the sign of the cross on her breast. Eusebio flees from her in dread and bewilderment, and she follows behind, though he does not know this. She disguises herself as a man, leads a life of crime and murder, ultimately confronts Eusebio and is disarmed. Curcio's men find Eusebio and stab him, but before dying he is acknowledged by Curcio to be Julia's long-lost twin (and hence Lisardo's brother as well!) Alberto, the priest, returns and Eusebio revives long enough to be shriven. After he dies a second time, Julia reveals herself, confesses her sins, and, as she about to be struck by her father, embraces the cross at the foot of which Eusebio is lying, and both are borne upward to Heaven.

This dry, frenzied morality play, suppurating with immorality and incest, is more notable for the blow it delivers against the nobleman's overweening pride than for any religious exaltation it incidentally dramatizes. The wages of the father's sins are relentlessly visited upon his wife and children until Curcio's survival at the end seems an ironic piece of justice. But we must assume that Curcio's punishment is greater than theirs, since he is forced to suffer the holocaust of the insult-vengeance complex without any possibility of resolving it. A domestic tragedy, **Devotion to the Cross** shows up the moralistic cannibalism of the honor code in a patriarchal figure who endures like a ruined column standing in the shambles of the proud roof it once supported. In these shambles are the evidence of many hapless falls.

Calderonian drama is full of crucial falls; there are half a dozen plays, including **Life Is a Dream** and **The Surgeon of His Honor,** where the action is initiated with a horse. The action of **Devotion to the Cross** begins with a donkey fallen in a ditch, the first of six such falls involving Lisardo, Rosmira, Alberto, Eusebio, and Julia—not to mention the unspecified number of peasants who fall at the hands of Eusebio and Julia. The cause of the cross ascending at the end is obviously intended to answer for them all. All other causes in the play are earthbound, murderously honorbound and incestbound. Eusebio's devotion to the cross saves him from the authoritarian justice of his father, and his career, despite his crimes which, like Julia's, are consequences of original sin, parallels the symbolic career of the fallen Adam become the risen Christ by reenacting the incestuous crime in the garden (convent) where he seeks to be reunited with Julia—the female Eve, his other self. Otherwise, the spectacle of a seducer and his female partner being rewarded instead of punished would be less than meaningless—it would make a mockery of the laws of honor. How far one has come here from the fruitful Moorish conservatism of the harem, the domestic custom underlying the Spanish concept of honor (fear of assault on one's property being equivalent to fear of sexual assault from strangers), we can now judge by witnessing the desolation of an impoverished noble family brought on by the father's fearful pride and exaggerated idealism. Human pride, followed to its logical conclusion in a Spanish context, invariably leads to a personal *auto-da-fé*, an act of honorable murder in the name of a suprapersonal faith.

# DEVOTION TO THE CROSS

# (LA DEVOCIÓN DE LA CRUZ)

## DRAMATIS PERSONAE

| | |
|---|---|
| EUSEBIO | Captain of the highwaymen |
| CURCIO | An old man |
| LISARDO | Curcio's son |
| OTAVIO | Curcio's lieutenant |
| ALBERTO | A priest |
| CELIO | A highwayman |
| RICARDO | A highwayman |
| CHILINDRINA | A highwayman |
| GIL | A clownish peasant |
| BLAS | A peasant |
| TIRSO | A peasant |
| TORIBIO | A peasant |
| JULIA | A lady, daughter of Curcio |
| ARMINDA | Julia's maid |
| MENGA | A clownish peasant woman |
| Highwaymen | |
| Peasants | |
| Soldiers | |

*The scene is laid in SIENA and its surroundings.*

# DEVOTION TO THE CROSS

## ACT ONE

### *A hilly grove off the main road leading to Siena.*

**Menga.** [*offstage*] Look out, the donkey's slipping!

**Gil.** [*offstage*] Ho, you devil! Stop, you stupid ass!

**Menga.** [*offstage*] Now there, she's stuck; you didn't stop her.
Ho! Gee up!

**Gil.** [*offstage*] The devil take her!
No one to grab her tail, but thousands
like her who should be wearing one!

### *They enter.*

**Menga.** Gil, a nice mess you've made of it!

**Gil.** A nice mess *you've* made of it, Menga!
You're the one to blame, you were
riding her—you showed her where
the muck was to get stuck in,
and just to irritate me.

**Menga.** But I'm the one she threw!
It must be you who told her to.

**Gil.** Now how are we to get her out?

**Menga.** You mean you'd leave her in the mud?

**Gil.** It's no use: all my strength won't budge her.

**Menga.** Look, I'll pull her by the tail
while you pull her by the ears.

**Gil.** No, I have a better plan.
I'll just imitate the driver
of the coach that got stuck
in the mud the other day.
Two skinny nags were drawing it,
slinking among the other coaches
like some sort of wretched poor
relation down the street.
It lurched from curb to curb,
if not from door to door, as though
cursed, poor thing, by both its parents,
till it reeled into a wayside ditch
and stuck. Inside, the squire swore;
the coachman lashed his whip.
First by coaxing, then by force,
now by wheedling, now by threats,
they tried to move it out.
But the harder they worked on it,
the tighter it got stuck.

Since nothing would budge it,
a bag of barley was brought out
and placed just out of reach
of the half-starved horses,
who as they strained to reach it
tugged and pulled until at last
they dragged the coach out of the ditch.
Now we'll try this very trick ourselves.
**Menga.** Pooh! All your cock-and-bull stories
aren't worth a single candle.
**Gil.** Menga, I'll have you know I've got
a sharp eye; I'll spot the needle
in the haystack every time.
**Menga.** And because you are so clever
I'm the one must go to town
and see if I can find a neighbor
kind enough to help us now.
**Gil.** There you go, stubborn as ever!
**Menga.** Oh my poor, Godforsaken donkey!

*[Exit*

**Gil.** Oh you're the donkey of my heart,
the most respected ass in town.
Scrumptious in your choice of
company, and never one
to gad about, you prefer
the stable joys and a diet
of domesticity
to a life of labor out of doors.
Perhaps you're fickle, well,
even a little vain, but I swear
no one's ever caught you gaping
out the window at some jackass.
You have no tongue for flattery,
plain speaking is your specialty,
as when you say, "My mouth's my own."
And when you've had your fill,
I've often seen you turn
and give away the rest
to some beastly uninvited guest.

*[A noise offstage.]*

But what's that noise I hear?
Ah there, I see two men dismounting
and tying up their horses.
Now they're coming here. My, how pale
they look, and in the open fields
so early in the morning!
I'm sure they must have eaten mud
to look so constipated.

But what if they are highwaymen?
Now wouldn't that be something!
Well, whoever they may be,
I had better disappear.
They're coming very fast; they're here.

[*He withdraws.*]

*Enter LISARDO and EUSEBIO.*

**Lisardo.** This is far enough; I find
this spot, hidden by the bushes
from the road, most appropriate
for our present purposes.
Now, Eusebio, draw your sword!
Mine is drawn—no further word
need be wasted on such men as you.

**Eusebio.** Though there's sufficient cause
to bring me to this field, I still
would wish to understand your motives
in this matter. Tell me,
Lisardo, what have you against me?

**Lisardo.** I've more reasons than tongue can utter,
words can tell, or patience suffer,
reasons I would rather silence
and blot completely out of mind—
for an insult that's repeated
is thereby committed once again.
Have you ever seen these papers?

**Eusebio.** Throw them on the ground; I'll pick them up.

**Lisardo.** Here they are; take them. You're surprised.
Why do they disturb you?

**Eusebio.** Ah, the man is cursed, he's cursed indeed,
who confides the secrets
of his heart to pen and paper!
His writing's like a hurtled stone:
the hand that cast it forth is known,
but not on whom it may have fallen.

**Lisardo.** Then you recognize the letters?

**Eusebio.** They are all in my handwriting.
That I cannot deny .

**Lisardo.** Then you should know I am Lisardo,
son of Lisardo Curcio,
from Siena. My father
was a profligate who rapidly
consumed the great estate
his family had left him.
In so doing, he was heedless
of the straitened circumstances
to which his children were reduced.
And yet, although necessity

may beggar one's nobility,
it does not lessen in the least
the obligations one is born with.
Yet it would seem that Julia
(God knows the name is painful
to me now) must either
have ignored them or never
sensed their fullest meaning.
Still, Julia is my sister—
would to God she were another's!
You ought to know it is forbidden
to court a woman of her rank
with *billets-doux*, whispered flatteries,
and secret messages conveyed
by some infamous go-between.
But I do not wholly blame you;
I would have done the same,
I must admit, had any lady
given me the liberty.
The reason I do blame you
is that you are my friend,
and on that account are guiltier
for knowing where she was at fault.
As your wife—I surely can't believe
you'd dare to woo her otherwise . . .
and even at that, God knows
I'd sooner see her dead,
murdered by my own two hands,
than married to you—yet, as I say,
if you chose her as your wife,
the proper course would be
to make your wishes known, not to her
but to my father. That would be
the only thing to do.
Then my father would decide
whether you might have her,
though I think he would say no.
For in such a case as this,
an impoverished gentleman
who finds his fortune does not meet
the requirements of his rank
must see to it his maiden daughter,
rather than pollute his blood
by marriage, is taken off
in safety to a convent.
In all this, poverty's the culprit.
Accordingly, tomorrow, my sister
Julia will quickly take the veil,
whether she wishes to or not.

And since it does not suit a novice
to embrace the vestiges
of foolish love and vain desires,
I herewith return these letters
to you, determined not only
to get rid of them but of
their author too. So draw your sword,
for here and now one of us must die:
you, who will be kept from wooing her,
or I, who will not see you do it.
**Eusebio.** Hold, hold back your sword, Lisardo.
I have listened patiently
to your disparagement of me—
now hear my answer. My discourse
may be protracted beyond
reasonable endurance,
but since we two stand alone
on the point of mortal combat,
which leaves but one survivor,
lest Heaven choose to take my life,
listen to my wondrous story,
the marvels of my life,
which if I die must unhappily
be sealed in eternal silence.
I never knew who my father was,
though I do know that my first cradle
was planted at the foot of a cross,
and that my first pillow was a stone.
My birth was strange—so said the shepherds
who found me lying in a gully
here among these hills.
Three days, they say, they heard me
crying, but they could not reach
the isolated gorge I lay in
because they feared the wild beasts
pacing all around me,
who, yet, neither harmed nor touched me.
That surely must have been because
the cross protected me.
There, at last, a shepherd found me
while searching for a lost lamb
in the mountain fastnesses.
The shepherd carried me to the town
where Eusebio lived, who no doubt
was fated to be living there.
The shepherd told him of
the miracle of my birth,
and with Heaven's aid the tale
aroused his pity. Then

Eusebio had me taken
to his home, where I was reared
as if I were his son.
I am called Eusebio
of the Cross, a name combining
his with that of my first ally
and protector. The pursuit of arms
was my love, books and learning
were my pastime. Then when
Eusebio died, I
inherited his estate.
My destiny has been no less
miraculous than my birth,
hostile and unfriendly
but kind and merciful as well.
While still a babe in arms,
my fierce and savage nature
declared itself against my nurse.
That was when my infant gums,
surely with demonic cruelty,
tore the nipple off the tender breast
that fed me, and the nurse,
desperate with pain and blinded
by fury, threw me deep into
a well, unseen by anyone.
Attracted by the sound of laughter,
my rescuers descended
to the bottom where, they say,
they found me floating on the water
with my infant fingers crossed
softly on my infant lips.
Then again, one day when fire
broke out in our house, fiercely
barred the way, and made escape
impossible, I walked freely
through the flames, emerging
quite unscathed; while doubting
this was due to the fire's clemency,
I later learned that day had been
a holiday—the Day of the Cross.
Again, when I was scarcely
fifteen years of age, while sailing
on a ship to Rome, a heavy storm
drove us foundering toward
a jagged rock, and there the vessel,
split wide open, was splintered
in a thousand pieces. But lo!
I caught a heaving plank, and drifted
safely till I reached the shore.

The plank I'd caught was cruciform.
Then once among these mountains,
while traveling with a friend,
I came upon a cross where the road
divided in two separate ways.
I stopped to pray; my companion
went ahead. Having finished,
I hastened to catch up with him,
only to find him dead,
a bloody victim of the highwaymen.
Another day when I was fighting
in a duel and closely hemmed about,
my opponent struck one blow
which knocked me helpless to the ground.
While all assumed the wound
was mortal, close examination
showed only that the crushing sword
had nicked the cross I wore
around my neck, which thus
had rescued me from death.
Again, while I was hunting
high up in these craggy hills,
the sky grew dark and thickened,
and as though declaring fitful war
against the astonished earth,
hurled down its thunderbolts,
unleashed torrential rain, tilted
like lances, and poured hailstones down
like a barrage of bullet shot.
All sought shelter from the onslaught
under boughs and in the thickest copse.
Then a bolt of lightning struck,
like a dark comet driven
by the wind, and then and there
reduced the two companions
nearest me to heaps of ashes.
Blind and frenzied to distraction,
I turned around and saw a cross—
I believe the very one
that towered over me at birth,
and whose imprint is now pressed
upon my breast. By such means
Heaven has distinguished me
and variously brought to light
the symbol of some secret cause,
unrevealed as yet. Thus,
though I know nothing of
my origin, there is a force
that now impels me, an impulse

that ignites my spirit,
and a courage that informs me
I am worthy of your sister Julia.
Inherited nobility
is not superior to
nobility that's been acquired.
This much I know and have acquired,
and though I understand your cause
and could sufficiently repair
your grievance, a cold passion
blinds me; I cannot tolerate
your manner or your sharp rebuke.
Thus I offer no excuses
for my action nor admit
there's any basis for a quarrel.
And since I wish to marry Julia,
however much you may oppose me,
however high the walls that guard her,
however unapproachable
the convent where you'd hide her,
none shall be an obstacle to me.
And as Julia's held too good
to be my wife, she shall be
my mistress; so far am I impelled
by thwarted love and outraged patience
to punish your contempt and repair
the insult to my honor.

**Lisardo.** As long as this blade of mine can speak,
Eusebio, further speech is useless.

> [*They draw and fight, and LISARDO falls; he
> tries to rise but sinks again to the ground.*]

Alas, I am wounded.

**Eusebio.**                But not dead?

**Lisardo.** No, and while there's one breath left
in me, I'll . . . Oh, I cannot even
raise my legs!

**Eusebio.**        Nor can you raise your voice.

**Lisardo.** Please, let me be shriven
before I die!

**Eusebio.**      Die, you wretch!

**Lisardo.** Don't kill me, I beg you not to do it—
by the Cross Christ died on!

**Eusebio.** That word prevents this final thrust.
Arise, Lisardo. When you cry
for mercy by the Cross,
my arms grow limp, my anger
droops and dies. Up, I say.

**Lisardo.** I cannot rise. My life's blood
slowly drains away, and I think

my soul would swiftly follow after
if it knew which door, poised before
so many doors, it must go through.
**Eusebio.** Courage, then—I'll lift you in my arms.
There's a little hermitage nearby
where penitential friars live.
They will give you absolution
if you reach their doors alive.
**Lisardo.** For the mercy you have shown me,
I give you my word: If I am
worthy to be brought into
the holy fold of God, I shall pray
you do not die unshriven.

> [EUSEBIO lifts him up and carries him away. GIL
> emerges from his hiding place; after him enter
> TIRSO, BLAS, MENGA, and TORIBIO.]

**Gil.** Have you ever seen the likes of it?
Charity! Sure, it's wonderful,
but excuse me if I say this:
dispatch a chap—like that!—then hoist him
on your back? That's the limit!
**Toribio.** You say you left him here?
**Menga.** Yes, waiting with the ass.
**Tirso.** Look, he's standing there stock-still.
**Menga.** Gil, what are you gaping at?
**Gil.** Oh, Menga!
**Tirso.** What's up, what happened?
**Gil.** Oh, Tirso!
**Toribio.** What did you see? Speak up!
**Gil.** Oh, Toribio!
**Blas.** Say it, Gil. What's wrong?
Whatever is ailing you?
**Gil.** Oh, Blas, oh my dear friends!
I'm dumb as that donkey there.
He killed him, picked him up, this way,
on his shoulder, like an animal
he was going off to smoke and cure.
**Menga.** Who killed who?
**Gil.** How should I know?
**Tirso.** Who was killed?
**Gil.** I don't know who it was.
**Toribio.** Who picked him up?
**Gil.** How do I know who?
**Blas..** Who carried him off?
**Gil.** Whoever
you like. But if you'd really like
to know, come, everyone, follow me.
**Tirso.** Where are you taking us?

**Gil.** I don't know, but come anyway,
  they can't be very far away.

*[Exeunt omnes*

### A Room in CURCIO'S house in Siena

*Enter JULIA and ARMINDA.*

**Julia.** Let me weep awhile, Arminda.
  These are freedom's last few hours, and
  while I live there's no end to sorrow.
  Have you ever seen a gentle stream
  slowly descend to find repose
  in a valley? And then, even while
  the sweetest blossoms on the banks
  are scarcely moved by its downflow,
  suddenly the stream erupts, and floods
  them all in wildest turbulence.
  My grief and pain are such a stream:
  pent up so long within my breast,
  it now bursts forth in tears. Let me weep
  at my father's cruelty.
**Arminda.** But madam, take care . . .
**Julia.**                    To die of grief!
  What happier fate can I hope for?
  The grief that triumphs over life itself
  brings one to a glorious end.
  The grief that trickles out before
  life ends is only pitiful.
**Arminda.** What can have thrown you into
  such despair?
**Julia.**          Listen, Arminda dear:
  every letter of Eusebio's
  has been taken by Lisardo
  from my writing desk.
**Arminda.**                How did he know
  they were hidden there?
**Julia.**                    It was an
  accident—and my unhappy fate.
  When I saw him pacing
  so despondently about the house,
  I thought he might suspect me,
  but not that he already knew.
  Then he came to me; his face was pale.
  With an effort to be calm,
  he told me he had lost at cards, Arminda,
  and he wished to borrow
  a jewel of mine, which might help
  turn his luck. Willing as I was

for him to have it immediately,
he could not wait, but snatched the key
impulsively, and angrily
unlocked the drawer, where,
as soon as he had opened it,
he found all Eusebio's letters.
He eyed me once, then locked the drawer.
Without a single word, oh God!
he rushed out to find my father.
Then inside his room behind locked doors,
the two of them spoke loud and long—
to seal my fate, no doubt.
When they emerged and left the house,
they went, as Otavio told me
later, directly to the convent.
Now if everything they spoke of
has been accomplished by my father,
I have good reason for these tears;
what's more, if he means to force me
to forget Eusebio and become
a nun, I shall kill myself at once.

*Enter EUSEBIO.*

**Eusebio.** [*aside*] No one yet has ever dared,
however desperate his
situation, to seek asylum
in his victim's house. Before
she hears about Lisardo's death,
I must speak to Julia, and by some
device disarm fate's tyranny.
While still ignorant of my crime,
she may be swayed by love
to run away with me.
Later, when she learns about
her brother's unhappy end,
she will accept the deed of violence
since she no longer can prevent it.
—My lovely Julia!
**Julia.** What's this?
Have you come here?
**Eusebio.** My love for you
and my grim misfortune
impel me to take the risk.
**Julia.** But how did you get in the house?
What wild notion made you try it?
**Eusebio.** Like death itself, I fear no one.
**Julia.** But what is it you have in mind?
**Eusebio.** Julia, I have come at last
to bind you to me; with your consent,

83

our love is born anew
and all my hopes are crowned with glory.
I know how much your father
is offended by my suit.
He knows we love each other
and intends to change your state
tomorrow, and so destroy
my hope and joy with one fell stroke.
If I please you and you favor me,
if you ever loved me
and are sure you love me still,
Julia, come away with me!
It's clear that while you stay
you can't oppose your father's will.
Then come with me, and there will be
a thousand ways to cope with him.
Once you've left his house to be
with me, he must bow and make
a virtue of necessity.
I have many houses, and you'll
be safe in every one; I've servants
to defend you, all my wealth
to offer you, and my very soul
to spend adoring you.
If you would have me live, if your love
for me is true, you must be bold
and come away with me, or, to your
grief, see me slain before your eyes.

**Julia.** Eusebio, listen . . .

**Arminda.**                         Madam,
I hear my master coming.

**Julia.** Heaven help me.

**Eusebio.**                         Wherever I turn
misfortune follows me.

**Julia.** Can he get out now?

**Arminda.**                         No,
that's impossible now; they're
knocking at the door.

**Julia.**                         This is
terrible!

**Eusebio.** Insufferable!
What am I to do?

**Julia.**                 You must hide.

**Eusebio.** But where?

**Julia.**                         Here, inside this corridor.

**Arminda.** Quickly, I hear his footsteps.

*[EUSEBIO hides.]*

*Enter CURCIO, a venerable old man*

**Curcio.** Daughter, if you do not yield your heart
    and soul to that happiest and most
    coveted state that now awaits you,
    then you do not deserve
    the zealous care I have spent
    securing it for you. The matter
    is all settled; everything
    is ready. You have only
    to put on your radiant robe,
    and then become the bride of Christ.
    Imagine the joyous prospect
    as you move along today
    towards that holy marriage,
    the envy of all your friends.
    What do you say?
**Julia.** [*aside*] What can I do?
**Eusebio.** [*aside*] If she says yes to that,
    I shall kill myself at once.
**Julia.** [*aside*] I do not know what to say.
    —Sir, a father's authority
    precedes all others; it dominates
    one's life, but not one's liberty
    of conscience. Would it not have been
    much better, sir, had you made
    your wishes clear before,
    and also inquired into mine?
**Curcio.** No. Right or wrong, my will
    is all you need to know.
**Julia.** The only freedom proper to a child
    is the freedom to determine
    for himself his state in life.
    In this his free will should not be forced
    by the dictates of an impious fate.
    Give me a moment to decide, sir,
    and do not be surprised I ask this
    of you: to change one's way of life is
    no matter to be taken lightly.
**Curcio.** My decision will suffice, and that
    has been resolved. The matter's closed.
**Julia.** Since you're determined to live my life,
    take the very vows you'd have me take.
**Curcio.** Rebel, hold your tongue! Are you mad?
    I'll twist your braids around your neck,
    or else I'll rip that tongue of yours
    out of your mouth with my own hands
    before it cuts me to the quick again.
**Julia.** I defend my freedom, sir,

but not my life: take that now and end
my sorrow and your grief together.
The life you gave me I can only
offer back again; but you cannot
take my freedom, which is Heaven's gift.

**Curcio.** So at last I have the proof
of what I long suspected:
that your mother was dishonorable,
a woman who deceived me.
So you attack your father's honor,
whose luster, birth, nobility
the sun itself can never equal,
with all its radiance and light.

**Julia.** I do not understand you, sir;
therefore, I cannot reply.

**Curcio.** Arminda, step outside.

[Exit ARMINDA

The secret that has burned within me
these many years, though you may have
seen it lurking in my eyes, blind
passion has torn out of me at last.
To honor my ancient name, the Senate
in Siena once sent me
on a mission of fealty
to His Holiness the Pope
Urban Third. Your mother's
saintly reputation
was a byword both at home
and with all the Roman matrons.
Even now it seems impossible,
my sense of satisfaction in her
being so secure then, I can
utter any word against her.
Your mother stayed behind
while my embassy in Rome
kept me eight months away from home.
The issue was whether to award
Siena to the Pope or not.
The matter still unsettled (which,
may God resolve as He sees fit,
seems of little moment to me now),
I returned to Siena,
and found her . . . words fail me now,
my breath is choked, my spirit falters.
I say I found (I must be brave now!)
your mother nine months pregnant.
Her deceitful letters already
had informed me of this misfortune,
telling how on my departure

the prospect had seemed likely.
Yet I was so certain that
my honor had been stained,
I fell to brooding on the insult
till I imagined my disgrace.
I do not say that I believed it
as an accomplished fact,
though a man of noble blood
need not wait for proof; what he
imagines is sufficient.
Oh, the tyranny of honor
and its laws, the savage edict
of the world! What is the point
of all his misery
if a nobleman has nothing
but want of knowledge to excuse it?
The laws of honor lie, they lie!
How can a man raise mere suspicion
to the certainty of fact who has
no inkling of the truth? What law
proves the innocent is guilty?
And how does mere opinion prove
him culpable? There again
the law is false for calling
mere unhappiness dishonor,
that same law which inflexibly
imposes blame upon the victim
and the thief of honor, both.
And if the world's opinion
weighs against the innocent,
what choice has the guilty one but
to recognize it and be silent?
Wracked by such confusions,
I found no comfort at my table,
no respite on my bed at night.
Divided in myself, my heart
looked coldly down upon me,
my soul tyrannized over me.
And no matter how often
I reviewed the evidence
in your mother's favor and
recognized she might be innocent,
the fear of my disgrace obsessed me.
So, though at bottom realizing
she was chaste, I determined
to revenge myself, not against
your mother's misdemeanors
but against my own presentiments.
To pursue such vengeance in

closest secrecy, I made
arrangements for a fictitious
hunting party. Yes, the greatest
comforts a jealous man can know
are the fictions his mind invents.
We went up into the mountains,
and while the others guilelessly
enjoyed the hunt, I, with honeyed words
(how easily they sweeten
treachery, and delight
a lover's heart!) I led Rosmira,
your mother, off the path
through a winding copse. Amusing her
along the way, I reached
a lonely isolated cave
whose mouth the sun had never touched,
it was so hidden by nature's,
not to say by love's interlacing
thickets, trees, and boughs. And there,
where hardly any other
human foot has ever ventured,
the two of us, alone . . .

*Enter ARMINDA.*

**Arminda.** Sir, if your noble courage and
the fortitude of all your years
would only support you
at this unhappy moment,
such strength will see you through
a very heavy trial.
**Curcio.** What reason have you to force
this interruption on me?
**Arminda.** Sir . . .
**Curcio.**        Say it, quickly. Waiting
is much more painful.
**Julia.**              Why
are you so quiet? Speak!
**Arminda.** I cannot be the voice of sorrow
spelling out misfortune.
**Curcio.** Do not be afraid to say
what I no longer fear to hear.
**Arminda.** Oh, sir, Lisardo, . . .
**Eusebio.** [*aside*]        This
will be the end of me.
**Arminda.** . . . bathed in blood, is being carried here
upon a litter by four shepherds.
He is dead (my God!), killed in a duel.
Ah, here they come. Don't look, sir.
**Curcio.** Merciful Heavens! Are these torments

for my sins? Alas, alas.

> *Enter GIL, MENGA, TIRSO, BLAS, and TORIBIO bearing*
> *LISARDO, his face blood-smeared, on a litter.*

**Julia.** What violent monster spent
　its bloody wrath on that poor breast?
　What inhuman hand, maddened only
　by his innocence, washed itself
　in my brother's blood? Alas.
**Arminda.** Oh, mistress, don't . . .
**Blas.**　　　　　　　　　　Better
　not look at him.
**Curcio.**　　　　　Stand back.
**Tirso.** Sir, don't come any closer.
**Curcio.** Friends, I must. Upon my soul, I must.
　Let me gaze upon this cold body,
　now the sad repository
　of frozen veins, time's ruin,
　fate's impious corruption, the last
　reliquary of my sorrow.
　What tyrannous necessity,
　oh my son, raised you like a tragic
　monument in sand, only to be
　mourned in vain and shrouded round
　by my white hair? Oh tell me,
　friends, who killed my son, this boy
　who was all of life to me?
**Menga.** That, Gil will tell you; he was
　hidden in the shrubbery
　and saw your son fall wounded there.
**Curcio.** Tell me, then, my friend, who was it
　took his life away from me?
**Gil.** I only know the man was called
　Eusebio—the one that fought
　with him, I mean.
**Curcio.**　　　　　Eusebio?
　So he has robbed me of my life
　and honor both.
　[*to JULIA*]　　　Daughter, you may
　pardon him and say ambition
　goaded him to cruel extremes;
　or say he dreamed of chastest love
　but lacked the means to write of it,
　and so he had need to use your blood
　to pen his lascivious desires.
**Julia.** Sir . . .
**Curcio.**　　　Please spare me your customary
　insolence, but prepare at once
　to take religious vows, or else

prepare to leave your beauty here
and share Lisardo's early tomb.
Both of you at once, though differently,
must be buried now: Lisardo,
though a corpse, shall still live in my
memory; and you, though still alive,
shall be dead to me and all the world.
Prepare, then, for your burial.
You shall not escape; I'll lock this door.
Stay with him and learn that lesson well
which his death teaches you to share.

*[Exeunt CURCIO and the others*

*JULIA stands between LISARDO and EUSEBIO,*
*who enters from another door.*

**Julia.** Cruel Eusebio, each time
I try to speak, my breath
fails me, my spirit flags,
my voice grows dumb. Oh, I cannot,
I do not know how to speak to you.
All at once my righteous anger
is consumed by some strange sympathy.
Then I want to shut my eyes
to the innocent wet blood,
like pink carnations strewn
so lavishly upon this deathbed
and crying out for vengeance.
And in the tears streaming down your face
I even seem to find some reason
to forgive you. For only wounds
and tears seem true, and melt one's heart.
In the same breath my love rushes
to defend you, and my hate,
to punish you; in the throes
of these perplexities and passions,
I strive to vanquish all compassion,
then slowly sentiment undoes me.
Eusebio, is this the way
you'd bind me to you? Is this the way
you'd woo me, heap cruelties
upon me instead of tenderness?
When I eagerly awaited
my joyous wedding day,
you brought about these obsequies
for me to mourn. When I sought
to seal your happiness
and disobeyed my father,
you caused me to wear mourning
and not my wedding gown.

When I risked my life to make it
possible to marry you,
you offered me a tomb to lie in,
and not the marriage bed.
I proffered this hand, Eusebio,
scorning everyone who whispered
my honor had been lost; in return
you gave your hand, dripping
with my brother's blood. What happiness
can I find in your embrace
when, to reach your arms with all the life
my love embodies, I must first
stumble over this poor body
stilled to death? What will they say of me
who know I am forever wed
not only to the insult
but to the insulter too?
Even if I could forget so much,
each time I found your arms about me
the buried thought would spring to life
again. Then I—yes, I
who cherish you would turn
all love's tenderness and joy
to hateful wrath and cry for vengeance.
How could you bear to have me by you,
a heart in which two instincts clash,
now yearning for your punishment,
now desperate to prevent it?
I have said enough to show
that I forgive you, for I love you.
But you must never hope
to see or speak to me again.
Look, here is the window leading
to the garden; go now, escape.
Escape the peril that awaits you
if my father finds you here.
Go now, Eusebio, and forget me.
From this day forward I am lost to you,
lost forever, which is no more
than you clearly have desired.
Go then, all happiness attend you,
and may your felicity be such
that all its blessings are enjoyed
without forfeiture to sorrow.
I shall make my own life
a narrow prison cell, if not
the sepulcher in which my father
wishes to inter me.
I shall at least be free to mourn

misfortune, the severities
of fate, the bitter turns
now wrought by passion in rebellion,
my star-crossed life, and lament
my shattered love, whose dissembling hand
destroyed me but did not let me die
so that I might relive my every
sorrow, and in each forever die.

**Eusebio.** If, by chance, your hands
can wreak revenge more cruelly
than your words, I readily
submit myself to them.
My crime has led me here, a captive,
but love for you is my prison cell,
where all my faults are chains,
bonds that shake me to the soul;
conscience is my executioner,
and if your eyes are magistrates,
my doom is sealed, for the sentence
that I read in them is death.
If this be so, then Fame
must subsequently frame
this epitaph: "Here lies one
made victim by his love."
The reason is: my only crime
was loving you. I do not ask
your pardon; there is none
for so gross a deed as mine.
I only ask that you be swift now:
kill me and avenge yourself.
Here, take this dagger: pierce the heart
that so offends you, dispatch the soul
that so adores you, and thereby spill
your own heart's blood with mine.
But if you will not do it,
I'll cry out to let your father know
I'm here inside your chamber,
and let him take his vengeance now.

**Julia.** Come back! Grant me this last of all
requests I'll ever ask of you.

**Eusebio.** It is granted.

**Julia.**                 Then go, escape now
while there is time to save yourself.
You have your own estate,
and your servants will protect you.

**Eusebio.** I would do better staying here
without them, for as I live,
I never shall stop loving you,
nor will you be free of me,

even behind a convent wall.
**Julia.** Safeguard your own life now,
   I can well protect myself.
**Eusebio.** Shall I come back to see you?
**Julia.** No.
**Eusebio.**    Then there is no hope for me?
**Julia.** Do not expect it.
**Eusebio.**          And all
   because you now detest me so?
**Julia.** I have reason to detest you.
**Eusebio.** And to forget me too?
**Julia.** I do not know.
**Eusebio.**        When shall I see you?
**Julia.** Never again.
**Eusebio.**       Then what of the love
   we shared together in the past? . . .
**Julia.** Then what of the bloody corpse
   that stares at us this moment? . . .
   They're at the door; quickly, go!
**Eusebio.** I'll go, but only to obey you.
   Oh, but how can I and not come back?
**Julia.** Oh, but how can I let you?

*[A noise offstage. Exeunt at opposite doors.*
*Servants enter and carry off the body.*

## ACT TWO

*Shots are heard; enter RICARDO, CELIO, and EUSEBIO*
*as highwaymen, with harquebuses.*

**Ricardo.** That ball of lead went straight into
   his chest.
**Celio.**      And no shot ever left
   a tragic imprint more bloodily
   on such a tender flower.
**Eusebio.** Put a cross over him,
   and God have mercy on his soul.
**Ricardo.** Yes, and how's that for honor
   and devotion among thieves?

*[Exeunt RICARDO and CELIO*

**Eusebio.** Since ignoble fate has forced me
   to become the leader
   of these highwaymen, my crimes,
   like my griefs, grow infinite.
   And since I let it be believed
   Lisardo's death was caused by
   treachery, and not in fairness
   by a duel, my country's outrage
   knows no bounds and in its fury

adds to my despair so that
I am compelled to take the lives
of many men simply to save my own.
My lands and villas confiscated,
they have pressed so hard I am deprived
even of my daily sustenance,
which is why I must resort to force
and let no traveler pass
these mountain paths, unless
he forfeit his money and his life.

*Enter RICARDO and other highwaymen leading in
the old man, ALBERTO, as prisoner.*

**Ricardo.** I was looking at the fellow's wound
when—believe me, captain,
it's the strangest story.
**Eusebio.** Well, I'm waiting to be enlightened.
**Ricardo.** I found the shot embedded
in this book he carried against
his chest, and nothing broken through.
The fellow only fainted, and here
he is again, as sound as ever.
**Eusebio.** This is astonishing—strange indeed.
Who are you, old man, whom Heaven
so amazingly protects
with such prodigious miracles?
**Alberto.** Captain, I am the most fortunate,
though not the worthiest of men.
I had the honor to be made
a priest, and in Bologna spent
forty-four years teaching
sacred theology.
To reward my zealous study,
His Holiness offered me
the Bishopric of Trent.
But I was troubled in my heart;
seeing that I could give account
of every soul but mine,
I left behind my titles
and my honors, and shunning all
such worldly blandishments,
came to seek in solitude
the peace beyond illusion,
and live according to the naked
truth among these rocky wastes.
I was making my way to Rome
to ask the Pope's support in founding
a holy order of hermit monks
when your furious attack all but

cut short my life and destiny.
**Eusebio.** Tell me, what is this book you carry?
**Alberto.** The fruit of a lifetime's study.
**Eusebio.** Then what is it about?
**Alberto.**                          It concerns
   the true history of the Holy
   Tree divine on which the dying Christ
   in all His Glory triumphed over
   death. In short, the book is called
   "The Miracles of the Cross."
**Eusebio.** How well that flaming shot
   obeyed your text by turning
   stubborn lead softer than wax!
   God knows, I could wish my hand burned
   to a crisp before it dared fire
   any shot against these pure pages.
   Keep your money, life, and vestments,
   but let me have this book. Friends, see him
   safely on his way, then set him free.
**Alberto.** I shall pray to God for your
   enlightenment, that you may see
   the error of your ways.
**Eusebio.** If you wish me well, pray only
   that I do not die unshriven.
**Alberto.** I promise I shall be your
   intercessor in that pious hope.
   Your clemency has touched my heart,
   and now you have my word.
   that if you call me I shall come
   from my hermitage to confess you,
   wherever you may be.
   I am a priest, my name is Alberto.
**Eusebio.** Then I really have your promise?
**Alberto.** Here is my hand.
**Eusebio.**                          I humbly thank you.

*[Exit ALBERTO, accompanied by*
*RICARDO and the others*

*Enter CHILINDRINA, a highwayman.*

**Chilindrina.** I have climbed for miles through every
   mountain pass to find you.
**Eusebio.** And what's your news, my friend?
**Chilindrina.** Two reports—both quite bad.
**Eusebio.** I fear I know what you will say.
   Well, what are they?
**Chilindrina.**                The first is that—
   I wish I did not have to say it—
   Lisardo's father has been given . . .

**Eusebio.** Go ahead, I'm waiting.
**Chilindrina.** . . . permission by the state
  to capture you, alive or dead.
**Eusebio.** I fear your other news is worse.
  The sense of it already drains
  my heart and tramples on my soul.
  What has happened, tell me.
**Chilindrina.**                         Julia . . .
**Eusebio.** Then I was right. If you want
  to see me turn ill at once,
  you'll begin with Julia.
  You said Julia, did you not?
  Isn't that enough? Oh, how I curse
  the fate that made me love her.
  Well, then, you said Julia. Go on.
**Chilindrina.** She's in the convent as a novice.
**Eusebio.** God, I cannot bear it! To think
  that Heaven could exact its vengeance
  by such pangs of lost desires,
  such mouths full of ashen hopes,
  and then that I should come to feel
  this jealousy of the very
  Heaven she has left me for!
  Yet I, who in despair have come to
  live by murder and by robbery,
  I cannot be worse than I have been.
  Then here's to the final leap:
  let thought erupt in action
  as lightning hurls its thunderbolts
  Call Celio and Ricardo!
  [*aside*] This love will lead me to my grave!
**Chilindrina.** I'll call them.

                                                    [*Exit*

**Eusebio.**                         And tell them I'm waiting.
  I shall scale those convent walls.
  The grimmest consequence shan't stop me.
  To be lord and master over all
  her beauty, I shall force my way,
  driven by the tyranny of love,
  break into the cloister and
  violate those consecrated grounds.
  My desperation knows no bounds.
  And if love had not forced the issue,
  I'd do it simply for the pleasure
  of committing every crime at once.

                *Enter GIL and MENGA.*

**Menga.** It would be just our luck
  to stumble on him here.

**Gil.** But Menga, can't you see I'm with you?
  Forget that bungling bandolero.
  But if he comes, don't fuss. I have
  this sling and bludgeon handy—see?
**Menga.** Gil, it's only his mad pranks I fear,
  to be caught up in his clutches
  like that Sylvia who
  went uphill a maiden
  and came downhill a matron.
  Now that's no trifling matter.
**Gil.** Well, things might go even worse for me—
  because, you know, I'm still a virgin,
  and I might end up as a patron.

                      *[They notice EUSEBIO.]*

**Menga.** [*to EUSEBIO*] Oh, sir, be careful or you're done for!
  This is Eusebio's territory.
**Gil.** I wouldn't go too far that way, sir.
**Eusebio.** [*aside*] They do not recognize me.
  I shall play their little game awhile.
**Gil.** Would you have that bandit murder you?
**Eusebio.** [*aside*] They are only peasants.
  —How can I repay you for your
  good advice?
**Gil.**          Just run off
  and leave the bandit to himself.
**Menga.** If he catches you, sir,
  no matter what his mood may be
  or what you do or what you say,
  he'll kill you—just like that!
  Believe me, sir, and he'll stick
  a cross on top of you
  and think he's doing you a favor.

          *Enter RICARDO and CELIO.*

**Ricardo.** Where did you leave him?
**Celio.**                    Here.
**Gil.** [*to EUSEBIO*] Now there's a bandit. Run, I tell you.
**Ricardo.** What is it you wish, Eusebio?
**Gil.** Eusebio? Is that his name?
**Menga.**                 Yes.
**Eusebio.** I am Eusebio. What have you
  against me? Have you lost your tongues?
**Menga.** Gil, where's that sling and bludgeon?
**Gil.** The devil take them, and you too.
**Celio.** On a plain that skirts this mountain,
  just where it meets the sea, I saw
  a band of peasants climbing; they are
  fully armed and looking for you,

and will be here any moment now.
They are coming to carry out
Curcio's revenge. Determine
your strategy, call the men
together, and let us leave at once.
**Eusebio.** Yes, it is time we left this place.
There is much to do tonight.
The two of you come with me; I am
sure I have your strictest confidence.
**Ricardo.** So you do. In Heaven's name, I would
die at your side, when it comes to that.
**Eusebio.** Shepherds, your lives are spared solely
to convey a message to
my enemy. Tell Curcio
that together with these brave men
of mine my only wish is
to protect my life and not
deprive him of his own.
Tell him that he has no reason
to pursue me as he does.
It was not by foul means that I killed
Lisardo but in fair combat;
we fought man to man, on equal grounds,
and before he breathed his last
I carried him in my arms
to make sure that he was shriven—
an action worthy of some esteem.
But if Curcio is still bent
on vengeance, I shall know
how to defend myself.
[*To the highwaymen.*] Now make sure these two do not know
which path we take; blindfold them
and tie them to these tree trunks.
What they don't observe they can't report.
**Ricardo.** Here, I have some rope.
**Celio.**                              Tie them quickly.
**Gil.** They've trussed me up like Saint Sebastian.
**Menga.** And me like Saint Sebastiana.
Just as long as you don't kill me,
you may tie it tighter, if you wish.
**Gil.** Look here, sir: don't tie me up at all
and I swear I'm a dirty pimp
if I run away. And Menga here,
she'll swear the same thing too.
**Celio.** Now they're firmly tied.
**Eusebio.**                              So far,
so good. There'll be no moon tonight
and pitch dark everywhere.
Julia, though Heaven be your guardian,

I must enjoy you totally.

*[Exit, with his men*

**Gil.** Menga, what would they say who saw us
bound and blinkered here but that we are
a pair of thieves going to be
hanged or lynched?
**Menga.** Gil, move a little closer to me.
I cannot budge an inch.
**Gil.** Menga, come here and untie me first,
then I'll free you easily.
**Menga.** Since you're so insistent,
you should be the first to move.
**Gil.** How in the world is it possible
nobody's passing this way?
No muleteer mewling,
no traveler begging bread,
no student munching lunch,
not one pious nun at her beads?
On this great wide open road,
nobody's passing today.
Oh I can see, it's all my fault.

*[A voice is heard offstage.]*

**Voice.** There, I think I heard voices
in that direction. Come quickly!
**Gil.** You come in the nick of time, sir.
Now you can help us unravel
a knotty problem that's tied us down
on this spot for some time.
**Menga.** Sir, if you happen to be searching
these parts for some nice rope,
I have a good supply of it here.
**Gil.** Mine's better and stronger.
**Menga.** Women first! That's only
common courtesy.
**Gil.**               Don't stop
for courtesies; untie me first.

*Enter CURCIO, BLAS, TIRSO, and OTAVIO.*

**Tirso.** The voice I heard came from here.
**Gil.** You're getting warm.
**Tirso.**               Is that you, Gil?
**Gil.** Now you're hot as the devil.
Untie me, Tirso, then I'll tell you
all my troubles.
**Curcio.**          What's this?
**Menga.** Welcome, sir. You've come just in time
to punish a traitor.
**Curcio.** Who tied you up this way?

**Gil.** Who? Why, Eusebio, and in fact
    he told us to tell you . . . But what
    do I care what he told us!
    He just tied us up in one knot
    and left us.
**Tirso.** Well, don't complain.
    He seems to have been fairly lenient
    with you today.
**Blas.**                    Terribly lenient,
    leaving Menga behind for you here!
**Gil.** Oh, Tirso! I'm not complaining
    that he wasn't lenient.
**Tirso.**                         Why then?
**Gil.** You ask me why? Why, because
    he *did* leave her behind.
    When he took Anton's wife away,
    he kept her for six days,
    and when she sallied forth at last,
    we had a glorious feast on those
    hundred *reales* she brought back.
**Blas.** Yes, and when Bartolo married
    Catalina, wasn't she bearing
    a kid before six months were up,
    and didn't he strut around
    like a peacock crowing,
    "Can you beat that? What takes
    other women nine months to do,
    my little wife does in five!"
**Tirso.** There's no sense of honor there.
**Curcio.** Am I condemned to hear about
    all that villain's debaucheries?
    What a pass I've reached to come to this!
**Menga.** If you're thinking of putting an end
    to him, why even the women
    among us would take up arms
    against him, if you wish.
**Gil.** It's clear we're on his trail.
    This long procession of crosses, sir,
    point to all the men he's killed.
**Otavio.** We are in the most secluded spot
    in the mountain.
**Curcio.** [*aside*]        Heavens, it was here
    I witnessed that miraculous proof
    of innocence and chastity
    in one whose beauty I
    so frequently had wronged
    with my infamous suspicions.
**Otavio.** What new thought disturbs you now, sir?

**Curcio.** The tremors of a soul's disease,
    Otavio, a lifetime's grief
    and my disgrace, which since
    my tongue so stubbornly withholds
    can only be revealed
    in silent glances. Otavio,
    lead my followers away,
    for I must be alone a while
    to arraign myself and plead my case
    to Heaven.
**Otavio.**       All right, men: at ease.
    Break ranks!
**Blas.**          Break what?
**Tirso.**                What's he saying?
**Gil.** He says *at ease;* that means it's time
    to hunt for lice and fleas.

*[Exeunt all but CURCIO*

**Curcio.** Who has not some time felt the need,
    when sorrows weigh him down,
    to seek communion with himself
    rather than confide in others?
    The mind swarms, a dump of thoughts and
    notions heaped one upon another.
    Sighs and tears flow round them,
    like intermittent winds and waters,
    where I now stand alone
    on this wild crag seeking
    my self, my own companion, to lance
    the poisoned sac of all my ills with
    the scalpel of my sharpened wits.
    No bird, no tumbling fountain
    even, may hear my tale.
    Birds chatter, fountains murmur.
    Only these few gnarled trees will be
    my witnesses; they are dumb
    and pay no heed to passing things.
    These very peaks were once the stage
    whereon was played the strangest
    of moralities which time,
    with all its stock of dazzling shows
    that echo back to all
    antiquity, has yet produced.
    It concerned a woman's
    innocence and simple truth.
    Yes, but who can break the bonds
    of his suspicion long enough
    to see the truth that lies have stifled?
    Jealousy is the death of love.
    Neither the humblest nor

the loftiest of souls escapes
that fearful consequence.
And as I say, it was on this spot
that Rosmira and I . . . Is it
any wonder now that memory
should clutch my heart and freeze my voice?
Every leaf I see here startles me,
every stone here jars me,
every tree trunk crowds me,
every rock would seem to crush me,
every slope about to hurl me down.
All, all these have been an audience
to my infamous performance.
That time I drew my sword, and she,
so calm and so undaunted—as if
to prove that innocence
does not recoil before
the terrible exposure
of honor held in question—
she said, "Oh wait, wait, my husband,
my life is yours to take;
I cannot refuse to yield
that which is yours already.
I only ask to know the reason I
must die, then beg you to embrace me
as I die." To which I then replied:
"Like a viper you bear the seed
of your destruction in your womb.
The proof is that shameless birth
you now await. If I kill you,
I end your shame, scourging you
and your unborn angel too."
"If, by chance," she said, "husband,
if by any chance you honestly
believe my virtue slack, you are right
to kill me now. But by this Cross
rooted in the ground before me,
I swear I never knowingly
did you wrong or stained your honor,
and I trust the holy power
of the Cross to bear me out." I wish
then that I had thrown myself
at her feet and repented
while her shining eyes bespoke
her innocence of heart.
He who is all intent upon
an act of treachery
would do well to weigh his motives.
For once he openly declares himself,

and specifies his cause,
he must proceed to act upon it,
however much he wishes
to call back his declaration.
And so I raised my hand—
not because I disbelieved
her innocence, but to relieve my
mad and overnourished jealousy—
and slashed the air above her
angrily, as if inflicting
a thousand mortal wounds.
And there, at the Cross's foot,
I left her for dead; but when in my
distraction I fled home
I found her there, lovelier
than the golden dawn that daily
brings the infant sun alive.
There she lay with Julia in her arms,
reflecting Heaven's grace and beauty.
My joy was boundless, for Rosmira
had given birth that very afternoon
at the Cross where I had left her.
And as if to prove the miracle
the work of powerful
divinity, there for all the world
to see, upon the newborn infant's
breast a tiny cross was etched
in blood and fire. But oh that joy—
when even the child herself
seemed to gurgle with delight—
was tempered by the loss
of another infant left behind.
For as Rosmira later said,
she had felt in the agony
of labor she had borne two children;
then I . . .

*Enter OTAVIO.*

**Otavio.** A band of highwaymen
are passing through the valley, sir,
and before evening closes in,
it may be wise to overtake them.
Otherwise we'll lose track of them.
They know these mountains better
than we do.
**Curcio.**             Call our men
and let us proceed at once.

There'll be no peace or joy for me
until I have my revenge.

[*Exeunt*

### The outside of a convent

*Enter EUSEBIO, CELIO, and RICARDO.*

**Ricardo.** Quietly now; come bring the ladder
  and stand it here against the wall.
**Eusebio.** I'll be another Icarus,
  though I have no wings, another
  Phaëthon, and though I have no fire
  I'll scale the sun, if it lend me light,
  and climb straight to Heaven's firmament.
  Love makes a tyrant of me.
  When I have reached the top,
  remove the ladder and wait
  until I signal to you.
  Though I rise only to topple down,
  rise I must, and fall when
  I am scorned, then burn to ashes.
  Yet however grave the fall,
  I shall at least have known
  the glory of ascent.
**Ricardo.** What hinders you?
**Celio.**                    What obstacle
  impedes your proud ascent?
**Eusebio.** Did you see that livid flame
  flashing down on me?
**Ricardo.**                 Only
  your fancy, sir, born of fear.
**Eusebio.** What fear?
**Celio.**              Start up, then.
**Eusebio.**                          I'm going.
  Though a brace of lightning blind me,
  I shall penetrate that fire.
  The flames of hell won't stop me.

[*He climbs up and enters.*]

**Celio.** Now he's in.
**Ricardo.**            That must have been
  some hallucination come from
  a sense of horror at
  his own daring.
**Celio.**            Take the ladder down.
**Ricardo.** We'll have to wait here until dawn.
**Celio.** It's a daring thing he's done, all right—
  to break into a convent.

As for me, I'd rather spend the night
with my little peasant girl from town.
Well, there'll be time enough for that.

*[Exeunt*

### JULIA'S *cell inside the convent*

*Enter EUSEBIO.*

**Eusebio.** I have wandered all through this convent,
and so far, unobserved.
My fate has guided me past the narrow
open doorways of a thousand cells,
but Julia is nowhere to be found.
How far my doubtful hopes
have brought me! What stark forbidding
silence now surrounds me!
What a deep and deadly darkness!

*[He draws a curtain.]*

Ah, here's a light—another cell,
and Julia is in it. What stops me?
Is my courage now so faint
that words fail me entirely?
What keeps me? Why do I hesitate?
The more I doubt my impulse,
the more my boldness falters
and gives way to cowardice.
She seems lovelier than ever
in that humble robe she wears.
Modesty in women is
their essential beauty.
As her loveliness increases, lewd
desires stir me to possess it,
and with such strange intensity
that while her beauty rouses
all my passion, her modesty
fills me with respectful awe.
Julia! Ah, my Julia!
**Julia.**                         Who calls me?
Heavenly God, what is this I see?
Are you the phantom of desire
or the shadow of a dream?
**Eusebio.** Is the sight of me so appalling?
**Julia.** Who would not be startled, and wish
only to escape your presence?
**Eusebio.** No, Julia, stay.
**Julia.**                         Why do you
torment me, ghostly image,
specter of the mind which

the eye alone perceives?
Are you the fearful spokesman
of imagination come
to punish me? Are you not
the figure of illusion,
the portrait of some fantasy
transported here on the cold night air?

**Eusebio.** Julia, listen to me. I am
Eusebio, and quite alive,
who lie here at your feet.
If I were the image of your thought,
I would have been here with you always.

**Julia.** I only deceive myself again
by listening to you, and I know
that in the shame of my dishonor
I would prefer the false and ghostly
to the true and living Eusebio.
Here where every day I die
again in torments of a living death,
you come to me. What do you want?
I can scarcely breathe! What is
your purpose now? I am dying!
What object can you have?
I am afraid to hear of it!
Whatever fatal plan you have,
I do not want to know of it.
How can you have found me here?

**Eusebio.** The turbulence of love prevailed
against my own despair
and your severity.
Until you took the veil,
fond hopes still sustained me.
But once you passed inside these walls,
I kicked aside religious scruples
and the convent's sacred law.
Whether justified or not, I say
you are my accomplice in this act.
Spurred by passion and necessity,
I have forced my way in here.
But in the sight of Heaven,
I plead my cause is just.
Before you took religious vows,
you swore to be my wife.
Now you cannot pledge yourself
to both such lives at once.

**Julia.** I do not deny the bonds of love
which happily united us,
nor that sweet urgency
which prompted me to call you

my beloved spouse; all this,
I must admit, is true.
But in this holy sanctuary,
prompted by a higher law,
I have given both my word and hand
to be the bride of Christ.
I am His; what more have I
to do with you? Go, and leave me now,
you who cast a pall upon the world
by murder and by rape.
Go now, Eusebio, and forget me.
Your love is hopeless and insane.
Remember where you are, this holy place,
and let it fill your heart with horror.

**Eusebio.** The more you contradict me,
the more you kindle my desire.
Now that I have scaled these walls
and found you, some darker cause than love
goads me on. Submit to me
or I shall say you called me here
and have kept me hidden in your cell
these many days. I cannot bear it,
I am desperate, I'll shout: "Hear me! . . ."

**Julia.** No, be silent! Oh, Eusebio . . .
My God, listen to me . . .
I hear footsteps, the nuns
are on their way to chapel.
Heavens! What can I do now?
Shut the cell door, bar it.
Stay here now: one fear feeds
another, and the danger spreads.

**Eusebio.** How huge and heavy is my love!

**Julia.** How implacable is my fate!

### Outside the convent

### Enter RICARDO and CELIO.

**Ricardo.** Three o'clock. What's keeping him?

**Celio.** The lover sunken in his bliss,
Ricardo, is no night watchman
waiting for the sunrise.
I'll wager he thinks the dawn never
came so soon—today especially.

**Ricardo.** Yes, it always comes too soon
when passion's kindled, and too late
when it's been consummated.

**Celio.** Well, at any rate, I don't think
he's inside now yearning for the dawn.

**Ricardo.** But he's been in there two hours.

**Celio.** It wouldn't seem that much to him.

**Ricardo.** Yes, it's true: the hours of
your impatience set against
the hours of his pleasure.

**Celio.** Do you know, Ricardo, I suspect
that it was Julia after all
who summoned him to come.

**Ricardo.** Yes, I agree; otherwise, who'd have
the gall to break into a convent?

**Celio.** Ricardo, did you hear voices now?

**Ricardo.** Yes.

**Celio.**        Well, bring the ladder here.

*Enter JULIA and EUSEBIO above.*

**Eusebio.** Woman, go back.

**Julia.**               How can I?
I submitted to your desires.
You entreated me, your anguish
moved me, I relented.
Now I have flaunted Heaven twice:
first by disobeying God, then
by disobeying Him, my spouse.
Now you tear yourself away
and leave me, made hopeless
by your disdain, and by your scorn,
still waiting to be your wife.
Where are you going?

**Eusebio.**             Woman,
what do you want of me? Leave me.
I tore myself away because in your
embrace I felt the presence
of some strange divinity.
What it was I cannot say.
Your eyes were two fiery jets,
your sighs blew scorching flame.
Each word you spoke was a volcano,
each hair jagged as a lightning flash.
Each phrase you uttered sentenced me
to death; each caress tore
open the gates of hell.
All these omens rocked my brain
when I spied the livid cross
upon your breast. That sacred symbol
has been Heaven's prodigy,
which I cannot fail to venerate
despite my sinfulness.
For if hereafter I let it be
the witness of all my villainies,

how can I shamelessly
invoke it in moments of distress?
Stay here, Julia, in your cloistered
cell; I do not scorn you.
I adore you more than ever.
**Julia.** Oh, listen to me! Wait, Eusebio!
**Eusebio.** Here's the ladder.
**Julia.** No, stay!
Or take me with you.
**Eusebio.** I cannot.

[*He descends.*]

I must leave you here, and leave behind
all the joys I have so long awaited.
God help me, I am falling!

[*He falls.*]

**Ricardo.** What's happened?
**Eusebio.** There, there!
Don't you see that ball of fire with bolts
of lightning in its bloody fist?
Don't you see that lowering
red sky rolling toward me?
Where can I find refuge now
that Heaven rages over me?
Oh Cross Divine, this I promise you
and take this solemn vow
with strict attention to each word:
wheresoever I may find you,
I shall fall upon my knees
and pray devoutly, with all my heart.

[*He rises; exeunt EUSEBIO, CELIO, and
RICARDO. The ladder is left behind.*]

### JULIA, *alone, at a window*

**Julia.** I am alone, in my confusion
and perplexity. Ingrate, are these
your promises to me? Is this
the sum of what you called your love's mad
passion, or is it my love's madness?
How you persisted in your suit—
now by threats, now by promises,
now as lover, now as tyrant,
till I at last submitted to you.
But no sooner had you become
master of your pleasure
and my sorrow than you fled
before you had possessed me.
Now in escaping you have

vanquished me entirely.
Merciful Heaven, I am lost
and dead! Why does nature provide
the world with poisons when the venom
of contempt can kill so swiftly?
So his contempt will kill me,
since to make the torment worse
I must follow him who scorns me.
When has love been so perverse before?
When Eusebio wooed me, pled
with me and wept, I scorned him.
But now that he scorns me
I am impelled to seek his favor.
Such is woman's nature that
against her inclination
she withholds that pleasure
which she most delights to give.
And he does not love her well
who would overvalue her;
for when she's loved at such a rate,
she scorns him, and when she herself
is scorned, her love for him is strongest.
I would not care if he had ceased
to love me; it is his leaving me
which hurts. This is where he fell; then I
must fall there too and follow him.
But what is this? His ladder?
Yes, of course. But what can I
be thinking? Oh no, the dreadful
thought's too overwhelming.
Stop! Does not my creed tell me
that once I give assent in thought
I thereby commit the crime?
Did not Eusebio scale
these convent walls for me?
And did I not feel pleased
to see him run such risks
for my sake? Then why am I afraid?
What scruple holds me back?
If I leave now I do the very thing
Eusebio did when he entered;
and just as I was pleased with him,
he'll be pleased to see me too,
considering the risks I've taken
for his sake. Now I have assented,
I must take the blame. And if
the sin itself be so tremendous,
will enjoying it be any
less so? Since I have assented

and am fallen from the hand of God,
it is useless to suppose
I may be pardoned for committing
such a heinous crime. Then why wait?

*[She descends the ladder.]*

Now as I turn my hooded eyes
blindly on this dark immensity,
I find that my esteem for mankind,
honor, and my God is nothing
but an arid waste. Like an angel
flung from Heaven in my demonic
fall, I feel no stirring of
repentance. To return is hopeless.
I have left my sanctuary.
The night is dark and silent
and I am wrapped in fright.
I stumble down this murky path
as though headed toward the pitfall
of my crime. Where now? Where can I turn?
What must I do? The silence deepens,
horrors swarm about me; my blood
is frozen, my hair stands on end.
Conscience traces ghostly figures
on the air, and every echo
booms out my heavy doom.
The crime which briefly fed
my bloated pride now stalls
and shackles me in cowardice,
till I can scarcely drag
my heavy feet another step.
My back is sunken, as though
weighted with tremendous loads,
and I am stiff with cold.
No, I'll not go any farther.
There's the convent, I'll go back,
confess my sin, and pray
to be forgiven; faith teaches
there is nothing which the clemency
of Heaven cannot touch or reach:
all the sparkling constellations,
all the sands of all the oceans,
every atom, every mote upon
the air, and all these joined together,
are as nothing to the sins
which the good Lord God can pardon.
I hear footsteps! I'll hide back here
until they pass; then, unobserved,
I'll climb inside again.

*[She hides.]*

*Enter RICARDO and CELIO*

**Ricardo.** The ladder was forgotten in
    Eusebio's fright; I've come in time
    to take it so that it won't be seen
    at dawn leaning against this wall.

*[Exeunt, carrying the ladder between them*

**Julia.** They're gone, at last. Now I can climb
    inside unobserved. But where is it?
    Isn't this the wall it stood against?
    No, but surely it's over there.
    No, it's not here either. Good Lord!
    How am I to get inside?
    Ah, but I begin to understand
    the depths of my misfortune.
    This is a sign my way is barred,
    and thus when I would strive
    to creep back, a penitent,
    I am shown my cause is hopeless.
    Mercy is refused me.
    Now a woman doubly scorned,
    I shall perpetrate such
    desperate deeds even Heaven
    will be astounded, and the world
    will shudder at them till
    my perfidy outrages all time
    to come, and the deepest pits
    of hell shall stand agape
    with horror at my crimes.

## ACT THREE

### *On the mountain*

*Enter GIL, covered with crosses; a very large one is sewn on his breast.*

**Gil.** Here I go, at Menga's bidding,
    scouring the mountainside for firewood,
    and for my own protection
    I've concocted this stratagem.
    They say Eusebio loves crosses.
    Well, here I am, armed from head to foot
    with them. Oh, Lord—don't tell me!
    No sooner speak of the devil than
    there he is! I'm so frightened now,
    I can't budge an inch. Where do I hide?
    He hasn't seen me yet;
    maybe I can slip off there and freeze
    until he goes away. But what's this

I'm stuck to now? A bramble bush!
Oh, forget it, forget it. God,
these little thorns are prickly!
From the frying pan into the fire!
This is worse than a woman's
tongue-lashing, or a public
confession, or envying
the village idiot.

*Enter EUSEBIO.*

**Eusebio.** Where can I turn to now?
Life is burdensome and tedious,
but death never seems to come
to one who wearies of life.
Julia, how long ago it was
when marriage seemed so imminent, and
in your happy arms' embrace I dreamed
our sweet love's consummation.
Yet I turned away and left that joy
behind untouched, untasted.
It was not my fault I was driven
by the impulse of a higher power
whose cause prevailed against my will,
forbidding me to trespass on
the Cross—the Cross that I respect—
inscribed upon your breast,
and identically inscribed on mine.
Oh Julia, the two of us were born
subject to that sign, and thus I fear
the portents of a mystery
which only God can understand.

**Gil.** [*aside*] I can't stand it any longer;
I'm stung all over!

**Eusebio.**                    There is
someone in the bushes. Who's there?

**Gil.** [*aside*] Well, here's where I get tangled
in my snare.

**Eusebio.** [*aside*] A man tied to a tree,
and wearing a cross on his breast!
I must be true to my word and kneel.

**Gil.** Why do you kneel, Eusebio?
Are you saying your prayers, or what?
First you tie me up, then you pray
to me. I don't understand.

**Eusebio.** Who are you?

**Gil.**                              Gil. Don't you remember?
Ever since you tied me up here
with that message, I've been yelling out
my lungs but, just my luck,

nobody's yet come by to free me.

**Eusebio.** But this is not the place
I left you.

**Gil.**                That's true, sir.
The fact is, when I realized that
no one was passing by, I moved on,
still tied, from one tree to the next
until I reached this spot.
And that's the only reason
why it seems so strange to you.

                                        [*EUSEBIO frees him.*]

**Eusebio.** [*aside*] This simpleton may be of use
to me in my misfortune.
—Gil, I took a liking to you
when we met the other time.
So now let us be friends.

**Gil.**                            Fair enough,
and since we're friends, I'll never
go back home but follow you instead,
and we'll be highwaymen together.
They say the life's ideal—not a stitch
of work from one year to the next.

**Eusebio.** Good. You'll join me then.

        *Enter RICARDO and highwaymen leading JULIA in;*
        *she is dressed as a man, and her face is muffled.*

**Ricardo.**                          We caught
the prisoner at the crossroads
down below, and I thought
this one would amuse you.

**Eusebio.** Yes, that's fine, but first, look here:
we have a new recruit.

**Ricardo.**                    Who's he?

**Gil.** I'm Gil. Can't you see?

**Eusebio.**                        Though he may not
look it, this peasant knows every
landmark in these hills and plains,
and he will serve us as a guide.
What's more, he'll go down among
the enemy and be our trusty spy.
You may give him an harquebus
and a uniform meanwhile.

**Celio.**                        This way.

**Gil.** [*aside*] Oh, pity me! What do
I know of brigandry?

**Eusebio.** Who is this gentleman whose face
is muffled?

**Ricardo.**        He refuses to tell

his name or where he comes from except
in the presence of our captain.
**Eusebio.** Then it is time to reveal them;
you are in his presence now.
**Julia.** Are you the captain?
**Eusebio.** Yes.
**Julia.** [*aside*] My God!
**Eusebio.** Speak. Who are you, and why
have you come here?
**Julia.** I shall answer that
in private only.
**Eusebio.** Leave us a while.

[*Exeunt all but EUSEBIO and JULIA*

**Eusebio.** Now we are alone where only
silent trees and flowers eavesdrop
on your words. Remove the cloth
that hides your face and tell me—
who are you? Where do you come from?
What is your purpose here? Speak.
**Julia.** [*drawing her sword*] So you may know me and my purpose
both at once, draw your sword.
This is the only way to tell you
I am one who comes to take your life.
**Eusebio.** I shall draw, but only
to defend myself against
your rashness and my own suspicions.
Your voice is gentler than you pretend.
**Julia.** Coward, fight! Lift your sword,
and you will see how quickly death
relieves you of suspicions.
**Eusebio.** I'll fight, but not to injure you,
for I must protect myself
as well as you; otherwise,
if I kill you or you kill me,
I shall never know the reason
for this duel. Therefore, I beg you,
show your face.
**Julia.** Your point's well taken.
One's honor would not be
completely satisfied
unless the offender recognized
the vengeful hand which struck him down.

[*She reveals herself.*]

Do you know me now? What startles you?
Why do you stare at me?
**Eusebio.** Because
I still can only half believe
that you are standing here, and because

115

I cannot doubt that it is you,
your presence now appalls me.
**Julia.** Then you have surely recognized me.
**Eusebio.** Indeed, and as I look at you
I feel new confusions heaped
upon dismay. A moment ago
I would have given both my eyes away
to catch a glimpse of you.
Now I'd gladly pluck them out
not to see you here. You, Julia,
wandering through these mountains?
And dressed in men's clothing?
You commit a double sacrilege.
How did you come here all alone?
What prompted you?
**Julia.**                     Your scorn
and my despair prompted me.
You have yet to learn that a woman's
burning passion is swifter
than an arrow sprung from its bow,
more fiery than a shot of lead,
more sudden than a lightning bolt,
which is why I gloried in the crimes
I have committed until now—
and what is more, I would be glad
to do them all again.
I left the convent, fled into
the mountains, and there, because
a shepherd told me I had been
ill advised to take the path
I came by, and because I panicked
foolishly, I quickly reassured
him by stabbing him to death.
I killed him with the knife
he carried in his belt. That knife,
which proved so fine a
minister of death, I used again.
To relieve me in my weariness,
a traveler kindly made room
behind him on his horse.
I went along until we reached
the outskirts of a village;
and because he wished to lodge there
when my purpose was to flee again,
I killed him for his kindness
on the spot. Three days and nights
I wandered in the wilderness,
with nothing but wild roots and herbs
to eat and cold boulders for my bed

at night. When at last I came upon
a humble cottage, I remember
thinking how the thatched roof glistened
like a gold pavilion
to my quickened senses.
There, a shepherd and his wife
showered me with hospitality.
Their fare, though crude, was plentiful;
their simple board was good and clean.
Soon they dispelled my weariness
and hunger. And yet, on leaving them,
I resolved that they would never live
to tell pursuers, "Yes, she was
our guest." So I killed the gentle
shepherd when he came along
to guide me through the mountain;
then I returned and killed his wife.
But knowing that the dress I wore
would be incriminating, I now
concluded I must find a suit
of clothes. These, together with his sword,
were furnished by a hunter
whom I killed, along the way,
as he was sleeping. After
many such encounters,
surmounting every obstacle,
scorning every danger, and wreaking
havoc everywhere I went,
I came here at length to find you.

**Eusebio.** I listen to you, fascinated,
enchanted by your voice,
bewitched by everything you say,
although the sight of you
fills me with dread. Julia, please—
it is not that I despise you
but that I fear Heaven's
retribution looming over me.
This is why I turn away, and beg you
to go back now to your convent.
I live in such horror of that Cross.
I must avoid you.—What's that noise?

*Enter the highwaymen.*

**Ricardo.** Sir, prepare for their attack.
Curcio and his men have crossed
the highway and are climbing
toward you up the mountain.
All the villagers are roused
against you; more and more

117

are joining him—old men, women,
even children. They are coming
to avenge the murder of
Lisardo, and they swear to seize
and punish you for all the lives
you've taken, and then to bring you
as a prisoner, alive or dead,
to justice in Siena.
**Eusebio.** Julia, we'll speak together later.
Cover your face now, and come with me.
You must not be taken
by your father and your enemy.
Men, show your strength and courage now!
Remember, if you fail, they come
prepared to wipe us out
or take us prisoners.
Once we're captured, we'll find ourselves
in prison, our honor lost
and hounded by disgrace.
Knowing this, which of us would fear
to take the greater risk —
for honor and dear life?
Do not let them think we hesitate.
Forward, to the attack!
Fortune smiles upon audacity.
**Ricardo.** There's no need to get at them;
they're coming at us now.
**Eusebio.** Take up your arms, stand firm!
And, by Heaven, if I see
one of you retreat or run,
my sword will find that coward's heart
before it nicks the enemy.
**Curcio.** [*offstage*] I can see that wretch Eusebio
taking cover there among the crags,
but he cannot long defend
himself behind those boulders.
**Voices.** There they are! We see them now
from here, through the foliage.
**Julia.** To the attack!

[*Exit*

**Eusebio.**                Miserable
peasants! As Heaven is my witness,
it won't be long before your blood,
which stains these fields, will flow in torrents.
**Ricardo.** They're nothing but a pack of cowards!
**Curcio.** [*offstage*] Where are you hiding, Eusebio?
**Eusebio.** Hiding? I'm coming after you!

[*Exeunt omnes*

[*Shots are fired offstage.*]

### *Another part of the mountain; a stone cross*

*Offstage shouts; enter JULIA.*

**Julia.** Coming down the mountain,
  I had scarcely set foot in the fields
  when the air was torn with
  agonizing cries, the clash
  of companies of men in battle.
  The echoing guns choked my hearing;
  the glittering swords blinded my sight.
  But now—what is this I see?
  His troops dispersed and driven back,
  and Eusebio left to face
  the enemy alone. I'll go back,
  bring his men together, and try
  to rally them again in his
  defense. If I succeed,
  I shall grow monumental
  by his side become the terror
  of the world, the cutting shears of Fate,
  the fiery executioner
  of all their lives, the symbol
  of terrifying vengeance,
  the wonder of our age
  and all ages yet to come!

[*Exit*

*Enter GIL, as a highwayman.*

**Gil.** To save my skin, I became
  a novice highwayman.
  I'd scarcely done so when I found
  a bandit's life is full of danger.
  When I was a laborer,
  laborers were always being drubbed.
  Now that I'm a highwayman
  I'm still stuck on the losing side.
  Far from being miserly,
  I'm loaded down with misery.
  I am so unlucky
  that this has often struck me:
  If I turned Jew, I'd be the reason
  why all Jews are oppressed.

*Enter MENGA, BLAS, TIRSO, and other peasants.*

**Menga.** After them, they're running off!
**Blas.** Catch them, and don't let any one
  escape alive.

**Menga.**                    Look, there's one
who's crawled away to hide.
**Blas.** Kill the thief!
**Gil.**                    Oh, can't you
tell it's me?
**Menga.**         He's a highwayman—
I can tell it by his clothes.
**Gil.** Then my clothing is a liar
for deceiving you about me.
**Menga.** Thump him good and hard!
**Blas.**                                        Paste him down,
I say!
**Gil.**       I've been thumped and pasted down
enough; remember now . . .
**Tirso.**                    All we need
remember is that you're a brigand!
**Gil.** Look, for Heaven's sake, I'm Gil!
**Menga.** Gil? Well, why not say so
in the first place?
**Tirso.**                Yes, Gil,
why not tell us sooner?
**Gil.** First place! Sooner! When I said it's me,
that should have told you to begin with.
**Menga.** What are you doing here?
**Gil.**                                    Can't you see?
Just breaking the Fifth Commandment,
killing off more souls than a doctor
and a summer plague put together.
**Menga.** Where did you get that uniform?
**Gil.** It's the devil's; I killed one
and dressed up in his clothes.
**Menga.** But if you killed him in it,
how come the uniform's not bloody?
**Gil.** That's easy. The answer is
he died of fright.
**Menga.**                Come along now,
we're running all those brigands down.
They're nothing but a pack of cowards.
**Gil.** Now good riddance to this uniform,
though I catch my death of cold.

*[Exeunt omnes*

*Enter EUSEBIO and CURCIO, fighting.*

**Curcio.** We are alone at last. Heaven be
praised for granting me the power
to avenge myself upon you,
for not permitting someone else
the deed for me, or me

to see you slain by another's sword.

**Eusebio.** This time, Curcio, Heaven has not
frowned upon our meeting, so that if
you come in anger, you will return
in anger, punished for your pains.
I do not know what reverence
the sight of you instills in me,
but I know your suffering awes me
more than your sword; though your courage
might well daunt me, I confess it is
your white hairs alone which so
appall me that I fear
I have grown cowardly.

**Curcio.** Eusebio, I grant that
your appearance tempers overmuch
the grievous wrath I feel.
But I'll not have you so mistaken
as to think you fear these poor white hairs
while there's any valor left in me.
Come, lift up your sword and fight!
No lucky star or other omen
will suffice to turn me now
from the vengeance which I seek.
Lift up your sword!

**Eusebio.** I, afraid?
It would be rash of you to call that
fear which is simple reverence;
and truth to tell, the only
victory I seek is to fall
upon my knees and beg you
to forgive me; here at your feet
I lay this sword which has struck
so many hearts with fear.

**Curcio.** Eusebio, I will not
have you think that I could kill you
by taking such unfair advantage.
There's my sword.
[*aside*] And so I miss
the chance of killing him.
—Come, fight with your bare hands.

[*They close and struggle.*]

**Eusebio.** I do not know what influence
you cast upon my heart,
disabling wrath and vengeance
as tears well up in my eyes,
and I am so unnerved
I can only beg you
to revenge yourself and take my life.
Take it, sir, for I am vanquished.

I lay my life down at your feet.

**Curcio.** However just his cause, a nobleman
does not stain his sword upon
a vanquished enemy.
The better part of glory's gone
when victory is tinged
by such a victim's blood.

**Voices.** [*offstage*] They went this way.

**Curcio.**                                        My men are looking
for me. They have won the day, while yours
have fled the field in panic.
I want to spare your life: go now,
escape. I cannot stay the anger
of a vengeful peasant mob. Alone,
you cannot possibly survive.

**Eusebio.** I have never fled from any show
of force except your own,
which I truly fear. But once
this sword is in my fist again,
you will find that all the valor
which you paralyzed in me
will more than serve against your men.

*Enter OTAVIO and all the peasants.*

**Otavio.** From the deepest valley
to the highest crag, not a soul
among them's left alive except
Eusebio, who escaped.
I saw him running off at night . . .

**Eusebio.** Liar! Eusebio never
runs away.

**Otavio.**            Is this Eusebio?
Kill him!

**Eusebio.**     Come on, peasants, try it!

**Curcio.** Hold on, Otavio, wait!

**Otavio.** What is this, sir? You rallied us
before, and now you'd stop us?

**Blas.** And defend the man whose sword
destroyed your honor and good name?

**Gil.** And such a man—who coolly goes
about ravaging the countryside,
enjoying every maid and melon
on his way, and killing all the rest—
how can you defend him now?

**Otavio.**                                Sir, what
do you say? What can you be thinking?

**Curcio.** Wait, listen to me (oh bitter day!).
Would it not be better now
to take him to Siena?

Eusebio, if you surrender,
I promise, on my honor as a
nobleman, to help you all I can.
Even against my interests, I'll be
your advocate before the law.

**Eusebio.** I yield to Curcio, but not
to any court of law. Respect
for him would prompt me to surrender,
but to the law, only fear.
And there is nothing that I fear.

**Otavio.** Death to Eusebio!

**Curcio.**                    No, wait . . .

**Otavio.** Would you still defend him, and be
a traitor to your country too?

**Curcio.** I, a traitor? No—Eusebio,
forgive me, for if I am
suspected and insulted,
I am afraid that I shall have
to be the first to see you dead.

**Eusebio.** Stand aside, sir; otherwise
your presence will unnerve me,
and then your men, I know,
will use you as a shield against me.

*[Exeunt all the peasants and EUSEBIO, fighting*

**Curcio.** They are swarming after him.
No one can save you now,
Eusebio, even if
he shields you with his life.
There he goes, stumbling up that crag,
the victim of a thousand
bloody wounds. He is stepping back.
Oh, he has fallen down the valley.
I must run: his chilling blood cries out
to me so timidly. And if
his blood were not my own in part,
it would not beckon me,
nor would I hear it cry.

*[Exit CURCIO*

*[Having fallen headlong from the cliff, Eusebio is*
*seen, lying at the foot of the Cross.]*

**Eusebio.** Fallen from the highest cliff, I see
my fitful life must here ebb away
where there is no earth to bury me.
Guilt pricks at me and goads my soul,
yet not remorsefully
for this departing life of mine,
but only for some way
I may atone for all my crimes

with something more than this,
my one small life. Soon the vengeful mob
will come to take me, but since they'll
never take me while I'm still alive,
I must die fighting. Though I would
rather crawl away and pray for
Heaven's mercy, this Cross towering
in my path would seem to urge
that my pursuers only seek
my instant death while it
offers me eternal life.
Oh Tree, where Heaven chose to hang
the one true fruit to ransom man
for his first forbidden mouthful!
Oh flower of paradise regained!
Rainbow light that spanned the Flood
and thus pledged peace to all mankind!
Oh fruitful vine: the harp of yet
another David; and the tablets
of another Moses:
Here I am, a sinner seeking grace.
What was given you to do
must be rendered to me too.
Had I been the only sinner
in the world, God would have died
for me alone. You are my own Cross,
for God never would have suffered death
upon you were it not
for all my crimes. Oh Holy Cross,
from the very first my most ardent
prayer has ever been that never
would you let me die unshriven.
I shall not be the first thief
who by your grace, within your arms,
was taken unto God. Now I,
the second thief, who lie repenting
in your arms, I beg you to bestow
on me that redemption
granted to a former thief.
You too, Lisardo, whom I held
dying in my arms, though I could
have killed you instantly—
I saw to your confession
in good time, before the mortal coils
unbound you. And now, with my own
dying breath I summon you
and that old man, and beg you both,
take pity on me. See, Lisardo,
I am dying! Alberto, listen,

I am calling to you.
              *Enter CURCIO.*

**Curcio.** He must have fallen here somewhere.
**Eusebio.** If you have come to take my life,
    there is very little left of it,
    and that no longer in my keeping.
**Curcio.** Oh, the sight of so much blood
    would blanch a statue made of bronze.
    Give up your sword, Eusebio.
**Eusebio.** To whom?
**Curcio.**          To Curcio.
**Eusebio.**              Here it is,

                              *[Giving it to him.]*

    and I yield myself to you as well;
    forgive me for the injury
    of that first crime against you . . .
    I cannot speak, for I've a wound
    that swallows up the breath of life
    and floods my soul with dread and fear.
**Curcio.** What can I do? Is there
    no human remedy for this?
**Eusebio.** My sick soul needs the medicine
    of God, I think.
**Curcio.**            Where is your wound?
**Eusebio.** Here, in my chest.
**Curcio.**                Let me place
    my hand there and see if I can feel
    your breathing. Alas, I fear the worst!

        *[He uncovers the wound and sees the Cross.]*

    What is this sign, so fair and so
    divine, which stirs me to the roots
    of my whole being?
**Eusebio.**            The escutcheon
    I inherited from this Cross,
    at whose foot I was born.
    That is all I know about
    my origin. I do not blame
    my father for denying me
    a cradle. He must have sensed
    the evil that was in me.
    Yes, I was born here.
**Curcio.**            And here
    is where grief contends with joy,
    pleasure locks with pain, twin
    burdens of a fate both glad
    and impious. Oh, my son!
    The pride and pain of finding you!
    You are indeed my son,

Eusebio. All these signs
have proved it and justly overwhelm
my heart to mourn you on your deathbed.
Every word you say confirms
my premonitions. On this very
spot where I found you, your mother
once abandoned you; and here,
where I once sinned against her,
Heaven's wrath descends upon me.
More and more this place brings
confirmation of my guilt.
Yet what stronger proof is there
when I find the Cross inscribed
upon your breast the same as Julia's?
By this sign Heaven wrought
a mystery that was sealed
upon the two of you here at birth.
Eusebio. My breath is failing, father.
Farewell! An icy shroud numbs
my body; death flies swiftly down
to choke the words of my reply,
the life to greet you with,
the heart that would obey you.
There, the heavy stroke is fallen,
the last rigor seizes me.
Alberto!
Curcio.      How I hated him
alive, now how I grieve his death!
Eusebio. Alberto, come!
Curcio.                    How cruel
his struggle, and how futile!
Eusebio. Alberto! Alberto!

[*He dies.*]

Curcio. That terrible convulsion
snuffed out his final breath.
Let me begin to count each grief
by these white hairs.

[*He tears his hair.*]

                *Enter BLAS.*

Blas.                    Sir, it is useless
to complain. Your courage has always
been equal to the worst misfortune.
Curcio. It was never tried so much
as it is now. The fury of
my scalding tears would burn
this mountain down. Heavenly God,
I cannot bear this bitter grief!

126

*Enter OTAVIO.*

**Otavio.** Curcio, fate pummels you today
   with the cruelest blows of all.
   Heaven knows how sad I am
   to tell you this.

**Curcio.**          What is it?

**Otavio.** Julia has fled the convent.

**Curcio.** In my wildest dreams, could I ever
   frame so horrible a sentence or
   imagine this stroke of pain it brings?
   No, it goes beyond belief.
   This poor cold corpse, Otavio,
   this thing you see was once my son.
   Consider, should not any one
   of these adversities suffice
   to kill me? Heavens, let me be
   patient, or else crush out this
   savagely tormented life of mine!

*Enter GIL and peasants.*

**Gil.** Sir!

**Curcio.**   What new sorrow do you bring?

**Gil.** The bandits we routed
   now rally to attack again,
   led on by some fighting devil
   out of hell—a man who keeps his name
   and face a secret, even from them.

**Curcio.** Now my griefs are legion,
   the worst seem little more than jests.
   Take up this broken body
   of Eusebio's, and lay it
   mournfully aside till there is time
   to build an honorable
   sepulcher from which his ashen gaze
   may contemplate my tears.

**Tirso.** What? How can you think of burying
   a man in holy ground who died
   beyond the pale of Church and God?

**Blas.** For anyone like that, a grave here
   in the wilderness is good enough.

**Curcio.** Oh, villainous revenge!
   Are you still so outraged
   you must strike at him beyond the grave?

                       *[Exit CURCIO, weeping*

**Blas.** He was a fiend. Let wild beasts
   and carrion be his grave.

**Voice.** That's too good for him. Let's throw him
   off the cliff and watch him land

in pieces.
**Tirso.**      No, we'd better move him
now and cover him with branches.

*[They place the body of EUSEBIO*
*under the branches.]*

But night is falling in its murky
shroud; so Gil, you stay here and guard
the body on this height since yours
is the only voice loud enough to
reach us when the bandits climb uphill.

*[Exeunt omnes, except GIL*

**Gil.** They're very calm about it all!
They put Eusebio away
and leave me here alone
to watch him overnight.
Eusebio, sir, remember please
how you and I were such good friends.
What was that? Am I dreaming
or is that an army down there
coming up to get me?

*Enter ALBERTO.*

**Alberto.** Returning now from Rome,
I find I have lost my way again,
here beneath the silent twilit sky.
This is where Eusebio spared
my life, and I fear the peril
of encountering his men.
**Eusebio.** Alberto!
**Alberto.**           Whose breathless voice
is this I hear quavering out
the syllables of my name?
**Eusebio.** Alberto!
**Alberto.**           Again it calls me.
It seemed to come from here, now I must
find it.
**Gil.**      God Almighty!
It's Eusebio. I think
my hair's standing on its end.
**Eusebio.** Alberto!
**Alberto.**           That sounds closer.
Whose voice repeats my name
upon the fleeting wind? Tell me,
who are you?
**Eusebio.**      I am Eusebio.
Come closer here, Alberto,
and remove these branches
that cover me. Do not fear me.

128

**Alberto.** I am not afraid.

[*Uncovering him.*]

**Gil.** But I am.

**Alberto.** Now I have uncovered you,
    tell me, in the Name of God,
    what is it you wish me to do?

**Eusebio.** Through Him, Alberto, my faith
    summoned you to hear my
    confessional before I die.
    I have been dead some while
    but my spirit, severed from this
    useless body by the savage stroke
    of death, remained within my corpse.

[*He rises.*]

    Come close, Alberto, let me confess
    my sins, more numerous than all
    the grains of sand beneath the sea
    and all the atoms of the sun.
    Yet still more powerful than all
    of these in Heaven is
    my devotion to the Cross!

**Alberto.** Every penance I have given
    sinners till this day, I offer you.
    May they somewhat assuage
    the heavy burdens of your conscience.

[*Exeunt ALBERTO and EUSEBIO*

*Enter JULIA and the highwaymen from the other side.*

**Gil.** Almighty God, there he goes,
    walking off! And to make this plain as
    day, the sun shoots down its last few rays.
    I am bursting to tell the news!

**Julia.** Now that victory and sleep
    have put them off their guard,
    we can take them by surprise.

**A Highwayman.** If you want to ambush them, we must
    lie in wait in here, for they
    are coming now this way.

*Enter CURCIO and the peasants.*

**Curcio.** Grief has not yet put an end to me
    and my adversities; it must be
    I am made, past endurance,
    to bear them all forever.

**Gil.** People stream in from everywhere . . .
    Let me be the first to tell you all
    the most amazing miracle
    this world has ever seen.
    Where only now Eusebio

lay dead, a corpse, he suddenly
arose, calling loudly for a priest.
But why bother putting into words
what all of you can plainly see?
There, look at how devoutly
he is praying on his knees.

*[EUSEBIO is shown kneeling before ALBERTO,*
*who is confessing him.]*

**Curcio.** My son! Oh Lord Divine,
  what a miracle you have wrought?
**Julia.** Who has ever seen a more
  astounding sight?
**Curcio.**           Look, just as
  that saintly elder made the sign
  of absolution over him,
  Eusebio fell dead at his feet,
  a corpse again.

*[ALBERTO approaches.]*

**Alberto.** Of all the wonders of this world,
  let my voice extol the greatest
  it will ever know: Heaven kept
  Eusebio's soul in his
  dead body till he could confess
  his sins. By this sign the Lord
  reveals how much He esteems
  devotion to the Cross.
**Curcio.** My dearest son! You were not
  so wretched or forsaken
  after all, when in your tragic death
  you merit so much glory.
  Now if only Julia
  would recognize her crime.
**Julia.** God help me! What is this I hear,
  what ominous revelation?
  Can it be that I who was
  Eusebio's lover
  was his sister too? Then let
  my father and the whole wide world,
  let everybody know about
  my crimes. My perversions hound
  and overwhelm me, but I shall be
  the first to shout them out.
  Let every man alive be told
  that I am Julia, Julia
  the criminal, and of all
  the infamous women ever born,
  the worst. Henceforth my penances
  will be as public as the sins
  I have confessed. I go now to beg

forgiveness of the world for the vile
example I have given it,
and pray that God forgive
the crime of all my life.

**Curcio.** Monster of every wickedness,
I shall kill you with my own two hands,
and have you die as violently
as you have lived.

**Julia.** Oh Cross Divine,
save me now. I pledge my word to you
I shall atone beneath your sign
and be born again to a new life.
Farewell!

> [*As CURCIO is about to strike her, she embraces the Cross,*
> *which is EUSEBIO'S sepulcher, and it rises heavenward.*]

**Alberto.** Another miracle!

**Curcio.** And with this wondrous close,
the author happily concludes
*Devotion to the Cross.*

# THE MAYOR OF ZALAMEA

# (EL ALCALDE DE ZALAMEA)

## The Mayor of Zalamea

In **The Mayor of Zalamea**, a play based on a historical situation, the strictures of honor seem to have been relaxed to allow for an amplification of the code so that its *sui generis* structure may be challenged from within. This happens when the sexual assault on a peasant girl by a nobleman, who is also the captain of a regimental company, alters absolute caste justice and simultaneously elevates peasant justice long enough to incriminate the one and exonerate the other. To put this another way: the act of vengeance receives public and judicial cognizance and is officially sanctioned by the King so that the prestige of honor, though upheld by a peasant, is reaffirmed without victimizing the revenger. Hence the insulted man gains a real, not merely illusory, satisfaction in the end. This satisfaction is even imparted through the play's original title: **El garrote más bien dado (The Best Garroting Ever Executed.)**

What happens is so forthright that one may easily miss the subversive attack that is being leveled against the autocratic honor principle. Pedro Crespo, a rich farmer, is preparing quarters in his home for the captain, Don Álvaro, when the latter manages to burst in on Crespo's daughter, Isabel, who has agreeably moved to an upstairs room during the brief stay of the troops in town. The field commander, Don Lope de Figueroa, arrives in time to stop the quarrel between Crespo and the captain. Smitten by the peasant girl he formerly scorned, the captain abducts Isabel after Don Lope has left the house with Crespo's son Juan, now his orderly. When Crespo interferes, the captain's men bind him to a tree in the nearby forest where Isabel has been raped. Juan, meanwhile, has wounded the captain, who is returned to town to have his wound treated. When Isabel releases Crespo and they return to town, he learns that he has been selected mayor of Zalamea; he then orders the arrest of Don Álvaro and the accomplices. In a private interview, Crespo offers the captain all his wealth and estate if Don Álvaro will marry Isabel and repair the insult. When Don Álvaro refuses, Crespo has him jailed. Don Lope returns to punish the mayor for imprisoning a nobleman, but Crespo refuses to release the captain. A show of force between the troops and the peasants is imminent when the King arrives, hears Crespo's legal defense, is shown the captain garroted in his cell, and concludes the play by honoring the peasant with the permanent mayoralty of Zalamea. Crespo's personal cause, enunciated early in the play ("My life and property I render / to the King; but honor is / the heritage of my soul, / and my soul belongs to God alone.") has been thoroughly vindicated.

But something more than a democratic principle is involved. A humane view of life emerges that is totally different from anything appearing in the conventional honor play. From the beginning the play teems with animation: the expostulations of the braggart soldier Rebolledo and the camp follower ballad-singer La Chispa; the posturings of the impoverished nobleman Don Mendo and his satiric servant Nuño; the intermingling of soldiers and peasantry; the small-town garden scene on a late August night; and the humorous exchanges between Crespo and the gout-ridden commander Don Lope. From these vital elements arises a pastoral ethic countervailing the austere and darkly marauding incursions of the aristocratic seducer and the exactions of the military caste. The spirit of Zalamea, typified by the bold and independent-minded Crespo, reminds us of the ancient organization of the Roman municipalia, the autonomous Spanish town with its own mandates guaranteed by imperial authority. Abetting this qualification is Crespo's diligent husbandry as a cultivator of the land, his concern for the harvest and the small world of the town where his efforts have been rewarded. When pitted against the ephemeral, warbound soldiery who intrude upon it, this small world reveals his own positive and abiding values. These are the values which the King implicitly vindicates at the end by approving Crespo's actions. Ultimately, they are the only values which can heal the rift in the divided and conscience-driven agent of the autocratic honor code.

# THE MAYOR OF ZALAMEA

# (EL ALCALDE DE ZALAMEA)

## DRAMATIS PERSONAE

| | |
|---|---|
| PHILIP II | King of Spain |
| DON LOPE DE FIGUEROA | Commander in chief |
| DON ÁLVARO DE ATAIDE | Captain |
| A SERGEANT | |
| LA CHISPA, | A camp follower |
| REBOLLEDO | A soldier, La Chispa's sweetheart |
| PEDRO CRESPO | An old farmer, later the Mayor |
| JUAN | Pedro Crespo's son |
| ISABEL | Pedro Crespo's daughter |
| INÉS | Isabel's cousin |
| DON MENDO | An hidalgo |
| NUÑO | Don Mendo's servant |
| A CLERK | |
| Soldiers | |
| A Drummer | |
| Farmers | |
| Attendants | |

*The scene is laid in ZALAMEA and its outskirts.*

## ACT ONE

### *A field near Zalamea*

*Enter REBOLLEDO, LA CHISPA, and Soldiers.*

**Rebolledo.** I say, damn his bloody hide
    for forcing us to march
    this way from town to town
    without a break!
**All.**               Hear, hear!
**Rebolledo.** What are we now a pack
    of wandering gypsies? Must we
    traipse around to hell and gone
    behind a wrapped-up flag,
    thanking our lucky stars
    if the drum's . . .
**1st Soldier.** He's off again!
**Robolledo.**            . . . stopped banging for a while just because
    it hasn't split our heads yet?
**2nd Soldier.** Don't let it get you down.
    You'll forget your aching back, I guess,
    soon as we get to town.
**Rebolledo.** To town? I'm dead beat now!
    Even if I get there half alive,
    God knows if we'll have billets.
    Suddenly the Mayor's Council
    will pop up to reassure
    the Commissary they'll give us
    everything we need—if we move on.
    First he'll tell them, "No, impossible!
    The men are all fagged out."
    But if the Council slip
    a little something in his pocket,
    he'll add, "Men, we can't stop here.
    I've got orders we must push on now."
    Then we poor foot-slogging fools obey,
    snap to the order, making him
    rich as any cloistered monk, and me
    as poor as any begging friar.
    Well! I swear to God, when we get
    to Zalamea this afternoon
    and they make us march straight through
    on some damn excuse, they'll go
    without me. I'll put it to you straight:
    it won't be the first time in my life
    I've turned and gone—over the hill.
**1st Soldier.** No, and you won't be the first wretched

common soldier to pay for it
with his life; especially now
that Don Lope de Figueroa
commands the regiment.
Though he's praised and famous
for his valor in the field,
he's also the most ruthless
and hardest-swearing man alive.
He'd sentence his best friend
to death without bothering
to give him a fair trial.

**Rebolledo.** You've all heard what he said?
Well, I'm still game: I'll desert.

**2nd Soldier.** How can any soldier boast of it?

**Rebolledo.** It's all the same to me, and if
it weren't for this poor wench here
who shadows me . . .

**La Chispa.**                          As for me,
Sir Rebolledo, don't give it
another thought; as you know,
I was born with hair on my chest,
so to speak—so your qualms about me
are insulting. I'm here to serve for
honor's sake, and suffer for it too.
Otherwise it's clear I wouldn't
for the world have left that Magistrate
and his groaning board, where at the end
of every month a thousand gifts
pour in, since he's one of those
who hold a monthly open house.
But as I'd rather march and suffer
right along with Rebolledo,
and never burden him, what's this
he says about his having
qualms and doubts about me?

**Rebolledo.** In Heaven's name, my girl,
you're the crown of womankind!

**2nd Soldier.** It's true, she is. Three cheers for Chispa!

**Rebolledo.** And three cheers again, if she'll
take the curse off this march,
up the hill and down again,
with a rousing song or ballad.

**La Chispa.** Here are the castanets
to answer that summons, sir.

**Rebolledo.** I'll be a party to it,
if every chap here will agree
to pass judgment on this trial.

**1st Soldier.** That's well said, by Heaven!

*[REBOLLEDO and LA CHISPA sing.]*

**La Chispa.** *Ti-teeri-ti-teeri-ti-teers,*
*I'm queen of the balladeers.*
**Rebolledo.** *Ti-tari-ti-turri-ti-teevs,*
*I'm king of the thugs and thieves.*
**La Chispa.** *Let officers go overseas,*
*And fight the war on their knees.*
**Rebolledo.** *And kill all the Arabs they please,*
*Who aren't my enemies.*
**La Chispa.** *Just fill up the oven with meat,*
*And make sure I've plenty to eat.*
**Rebolledo.** *Kill a chicken or two, yessiree,*
*But keep mutton away from me.*
**1st Soldier.** Wait ! I'm sorry to stop the singing
and the happy din it makes
as we go along, but I've just
caught sight of that tower,
which must be where we halt.
**Rebolledo.** Then that's Zalamea?
**La Chispa.** The belfry says so, plain enough.
Our song must end, but don't be sad:
there'll be many a chance
to pick it up again.
I love to sing, and where
other women burst into tears
over any little trifle
I myself burst into song.
So I've hundreds yet to sing.
**Rebolledo.** Let's stop right here now and wait
until the sergeant brings the order:
we either enter in formation
or else break ranks.
**1st Soldier.** That's him coming now
alone; and the captain's
waiting right behind him.

*Enter the CAPTAIN and the SERGEANT.*

**Captain.** Men, I have good news: we stay here now
in billets until Don Lope
and his troops arrive from Llerena.
The order of the day's come up
to wait in readiness
and not take up the march
to Guadalupe till
the regiment is reunited.
Then Don Lope joins us here.
Meanwhile you all can have
several days of well-earned rest.
**Rebolledo.** That's good news, all right!

**All.** Three cheers for the captain!
**Captain.** Your quarters are all arranged.
Soon as he gets the word,
the Commissary will assign you
each a billet.
**La Chispa.** I swear to God,
before the day is over
I'll find out for myself
why that gang of thugs ended with:
*Kill a chicken or two, yessiree,*
*But keep mutton away from me.*

[*Exeunt omnes*

### A street in Zalamea

#### The CAPTAIN, the SERGEANT

**Captain.** Sergeant, have you found my billet?
You know where I'm to stay?
**Sergeant.** Yes, sir.
**Captain.**                And where is it?
**Sergeant.** It's at a farmer's house,
the richest man in town.
They say he's proud as a peacock,
vain and full of pomp and circumstance,
like the royal prince of old León.
**Captain.** Well, if he's a wealthy peasant
he's entitled to be vain.
**Sergeant.** And they say he's got the finest house
in town, though I must confess
the reason why I chose it for you
has little to do with that
but much more with another fact:
there's not a girl in Zalamea
lovelier than . . .
**Captain.**             Go on.
**Sergeant.**                  . . . his daughter.
**Captain.** Well, whatever pride and beauty
she may have, she'd still be
nothing more to me than a peasant
with her dirty hands and feet.
**Sergeant.** Then you'd be the only man alive
to say so.
**Captain.** And your reason, fool?
**Sergeant.** Do you know a better way
to pass the time of day—I mean
if you happen not to be in love
and simply wanting some diversion—
than to woo a simple farmer's

140

daughter, and she so dumb
she can't tell yes from no?
**Captain.** There's something I never could abide—
no, not even for a moment:
unless the woman's neat and trim
and has the wit to bring it off
in the way she dresses,
she's not for me.
**Sergeant.**          As for me, sir,
any woman's right who comes my way.
Suppose we go now—by God, I mean
to have a turn or two at her.
**Captain.** Now do you really want to know
which of us is right ? Say the beauty
I adore goes by. What do I say?
"There goes my lady love!" Of course.
Not "There goes my peasant love!"
So if the beauty I would call
"my lady love" is nothing but
a peasant girl, it follows that I
take the name of lady quite in vain.
Now what's that noise?
**Sergeant.**              Why, some chap
just dismounted at the corner
from a scrawny nag that looks
like Rocinante. The chap himself's
so stiff and spare you'd think
he were another Don Quixote—
the one Cervantes wrote about.
**Captain.**  Look at that amazing face!
**Sergeant.** Sir, it's time we were on our way.
**Captain.** Sergeant, first bring my clothing
to the house; then come back
and let me know you've done so.

                                              [*Exeunt*

### *Enter DON MENDO and NUÑO.*

**Don Mendo.** How's my dapple-gray steed?
**Nuño.** He's so fagged out, he can't raise a hoof.
**Don Mendo.** Come, come, did you tell the groom
to walk him up and down a bit?
**Nuño.** Without feed? Hm, that's food for thought.
**Don Mendo.** There's nothing like a little walk
to freshen up a tired horse.
**Nuño.** I'd say a little barley'd do it.
**Don Mendo.** And what about the hounds?
Are you sure they're all unleashed?
**Nuño.** Yes, and they're delighted,
though I know the butcher isn't.

**Don Mendo.** That's enough! It's three o'clock;
   I'll have my toothpick and my gloves.
**Nuño.** What if someone guesses
   your toothpick's just a ruse?
**Don Mendo.** If anyone should dare suspect
   I haven't lunched on pheasant,
   I'd say he lied in his throat
   and I'd cut him down right here—
   or anywhere else.
**Nuño.**             I'd rather see
   you cut my hunger down
   than bother with a stranger.
   I'm your servant, after all.
**Don Mendo.** That's a lot of nonsense!
   Tell me now: did the soldiers
   come to town this afternoon?
**Nuño.** Yes, sir.
**Don Mendo.**    I pity the poor peasants.
   They were expecting paying guests.
**Nuño.** There are others I pity more
   for expecting no guests at all.
**Don Mendo.** Who?
**Nuño.**           The gentle folk. But
   don't let that worry you.
   No one would think of lodging soldiers
   in the home of some hidalgo.
   And do you know the reason why?
**Don Mendo.** No, why?
**Nuño.**               Because they'd starve to death.
**Don Mendo.** Heaven rest my father's soul,
   my good sire who, at his going hence,
   left me his mighty patent
   of nobility, blazoned o'er
   in blue and gold, attesting
   to my ancient lineage.
**Nuño.** Heavens, if he'd only put
   something of that gold aside!
**Don Mendo.** Yet, when I consider it—
   and now I must speak honestly—
   there is no need to thank him
   for my noble birth. I would never
   have allowed anyone but
   a nobleman to beget me
   in my mother's womb, however much
   another might insist.
**Nuño.** Quite a job to draw the line there.
**Don Mendo.** On the contrary: quite simple.
**Nuño.** How, sir?

**Don Mendo.**     Knowing nothing
of philosophy, you miss
the first principles, of course.
**Nuño.** That's right, I do, sir; and since
I eat with you, I miss desserts
together with first courses.
In fact, your table at the moment
smacks a bit of Heaven,
having no beginning, middle,
or final course whatever.
**Don Mendo.** That's not the sense in which
I've used the word; but you should know
that when we're born our substance
is the food which our parents ate.
**Nuño.** You mean to say your parents ate?
That trait was lost in you.
**Don Mendo.** The food they ate becomes
our very flesh and blood.
And so if my father
had been eating onions,
the instant the odor struck me
I would have cried out, "Stop!
you've no right to make me
out of slops like that!"
**Nuño.**     Well,
now I see it's true . . .
**Don Mendo.**    What's true?
**Nuño.**       . . . that hunger sharpens wit.
**Don Mendo.** Rogue! How dare you say I'm hungry!
**Nuño.** Don't be angry, sir, because if
you aren't hungry, you might well be.
After all, it's three o'clock,
and we've enough saliva,
you and I, to wash away the stains
of fuller's earth in potter's clay.
**Don Mendo.** What of it? And besides,
is that a reason why I should be
hungry? Let peasants be hungry!
I'm different. A nobleman
has no need of food.
**Nuño.**     Ah,
if I were only a nobleman!
**Don Mendo.** And now, no more of this.
We're on the street where Isabel lives.
**Nuño.** If you're so wrapped up in devotion,
why not ask her father
for her hand in marriage?
That way you'd kill two birds with one stone:

you'd get three meals a day
and he'd have noblemen for grandsons.
**Don Mendo.** Nuño, let's have no more of that.
Am I to get down on my hands
and knees for a bit of cash and let
a man of common stock
become my father-in-law?
**Nuño.** Well, I used to think it was
important to have a simple
commoner for one's father-in-law,
though it's often said such men are traps
to gobble up a son-in-law.
But if you do not mean to marry her,
why go through the motions of
professing your undying love?
**Don Mendo.** Aren't there nunneries enough
where I can drop her if she bores me,
without my marrying the girl?
Now go see if you can find her.
**Nuño.** But if Pedro Crespo happens
to see me, I'm afraid . . .
**Don Mendo.** You're my servant—how can anyone
possibly harm you? Therefore,
follow your master's orders.
**Nuño.** That I will, although I never sit
at table with him.
**Don Mendo.**              Proverbs!
What else does one expect of servants?
**Nuño.** Ah, now you'll owe me something
for the news: she's coming to
the window with Inés, her cousin.
**Don Mendo.** Go tell her she's the sun
come forth, diamond-crowned, again,
from an early morning sky
now dawning in the afternoon.

*ISABEL and INÉS at the window*

**Inés.** Good Lord, cousin: do come and look
out the window, and see the soldiers
marching into town.
**Isabel.**              Don't ask me
to stand at the window
while that man is on the street.
Inés, you know how much
the sight of him annoys me.
**Inés.** But think of all the trouble that
he takes to woo and honor you.
**Isabel.** I'm no happier on that account.
**Inés.** I think you're wrong to take it sadly.

**Isabel.** How would you have me take it?
**Inés.**                                          Lightly.
**Isabel.** Take my own displeasure lightly?
**Don Mendo.** [*approaching the window*]
    As I am a gentleman, I swear
    (and my oath's unbreakable)
    there was no dawn today until
    this moment. But why should I wonder
    at it, or even that the day
    should dawn again to greet in you
    its dazzling twin aurora?
**Isabel.** Now I've told you many times,
    Don Mendo, all the pretty speeches
    and fine frenzied lover's compliments
    you deliver here, day after day
    at my window, are simply wasted.
**Don Mendo.** If lovely women only knew
    how much anger, cruelty, and
    sheer disdain enhanced their beauty,
    they'd waste no time applying
    any paint but indignation.
    I swear you're beautiful.
    Come, come, pile on your anger,
    for I'll have more of it.
**Isabel.** Since anger won't convince you,
    Don Mendo, this will. Inés, come in
    and shut the window in his face.

                                                                    [*Exit*

**Inés.** Sir Knight Errant, thou who must
    forever champion thyself in jousts
    of self-defense since thou canst not
    easily endure a rival,
    may thy love itself suffice thee.

                                                                    [*Exit*

**Don Mendo.** Inés . . . So, Nuño, beauty must
    always win the day.
**Nuño.**                            And may I add,
    born beggars are born losers.

                    *Enter PEDRO CRESPO, and then JUAN CRESPO.*

**Crespo.** [*aside*] I can never walk up or down
this street of mine without spotting
    that little country squire taking
    the breeze—always with a face so long!
**Nuño.** [*aside to his master*] Here's Pedro Crespo coming.
**Don Mendo.** Let's turn the other way;
    he's such a mean-mouthed commoner.

*Enter JUAN CRESPO.*

**Juan.** [*aside*] I never come here without
    finding this phantom in the doorway,
    in plumes and gloves, and bold as brass!
**Nuño.** [*aside to his master*] Now here comes Crespo's son.
**Don Mendo.** Don't let it worry or upset you.
**Crespo.** [*aside*] Now here's Juanito.
**Juan.** [*aside*]                    And there's father.
**Don Mendo.** [*aside to NUÑO*] Pretend.
        [*to CRESPO*] Pedro Crespo, my good man.
    God be with you.
**Crespo.** And with you.

                    [*Exeunt DON MENDO and NUÑO*

*PEDRO CRESPO and JUAN*

**Crespo.** [*aside*] The fellow persists too much;
    one day I'll see to it he feels it
    where it really hurts.
**Juan.** [*aside*] Some day he'll really get me mad.
    Greetings, father, where have you been?
**Crespo.** At the threshing floors. This afternoon
    I went to see the fields all richly
    heaped in piles with sheaves of grain.
    They looked like mounds of purest gold
    as I approached them, and the grain
    so precious it could only be
    assayed in Heaven. The breeze
    flows gently over them, the fork lifts
    grain to one side while chaff falls
    to the other; even here it seems
    the meek make way before the strong.
    I pray God grant me leave
    to bring it safely to the granary
    before a squall flings it far away
    or a whirlwind lays it all to waste.
    And you, what have you been doing?
**Juan.** I don't know how to say it
    without annoying you.
    This afternoon I placed two bets
    at bowls and lost them both.
**Crespo.** There's nothing wrong, if you covered them.
**Juan.** But I didn't; I had no money.
    So I was just coming
    to ask you, sir . . .
**Crespo.**            Well, listen to me
    before you speak. There are two things
    you must never do: promise what
    you can't accomplish, and bet more

than what you have on hand.
Then if by chance you lose
you don't lose your reputation too.
**Juan.** Advice that fits you to a *T*.
Let me, out of filial piety,
offer this: never give a man
advice who's just run out of cash.
**Crespo.** Excellent, you won that round!

[*Exeunt*

### The courtyard and entrance of PEDRO CRESPO'S house

#### Enter CRESPO, JUAN, and the SERGEANT.

**Sergeant.** Does Pedro Crespo live here?
**Crespo.** Is there something you would have him do?
**Sergeant.** Take these clothes belonging to
Don Álvaro de Ataide,
the captain of the company that's
just arrived this afternoon
to bivouac in Zalamea.
**Crespo.** Enough, that's all I need to know.
My home and all I own are God's; next,
the King's and all his officers.
And while the captain's room is readied,
you may leave his clothing here,
then go and tell him everything
awaits his pleasure and his coming.
**Sergeant.** Then he will come at once.

[*Exit*

#### CRESPO and JUAN.

**Juan.** You're a wealthy man—how can you
subject yourself to playing host
to guests like these?
**Crespo.**                     Well, how
can I avoid it or beg off?
**Juan.** By purchasing a patent
of nobility.
**Crespo.**          Tell me,
but truly now, is there anyone
who doesn't know, however pure
my ancestry, that I'm a simple
commoner? No, of course not!
Well then, what use is there
in purchasing a patent from the King
if I cannot buy the noble blood
to go with it? Would I be taken
for a better man than I am now?

147

That's ridiculous. Then what would
they say of me? That I've become
a gentleman by virtue of five
or six thousand silver pieces.
Well, that's money for you, not honor.
No one can ever purchase honor.
Here's the plainest little story
to illustrate my point.
Suppose a man's been bald for ages,
then finally gets himself a wig.
According to his neighbors,
has he stopped being bald?
Not at all. When they see it they say,
"The old so-and-so looks good
in that new wig!" But what's he gained?
Though they cannot see his bald spot,
everyone knows he still has it.

**Juan.** He's got rid of certain nuisances,
improved his situation,
and repaired the ravages
of wind and frost and sun.

**Crespo.** I can do without such wiggish
honor which only calls attention
to what I lack by hiding it.
My parents and theirs before them
all were peasants; I trust my children
accept their lot.—Now call your sister.

**Juan.** Here she comes.

Enter ISABEL and INÉS.

**Crespo.** Daughter, the King our sovereign lord
(may God protect him all his life),
is on his way to Lisbon, there
to claim the crown which properly
belongs to him. This is why
the troops and the artillery
are moving forward now, and with them
the famous Flanders Regiment
under Don Lope, a man they call
the Spanish Mars. Soldiers
will soon arrive to stay here.
It is essential that they do not
see you here. And so, my dear,
you will go at once and occupy
the attic rooms in which
I used to stay.

**Isabel.**          I was on my way
just now to ask for your permission
to do that very thing. I know

that staying here below
would only mean listening
to a stream of endless nonsense.
When Inés and I withdraw
into the attic, nobody,
not even the sun itself,
will know our whereabouts today.

**Crespo.** God bless you. Meanwhile, Juanito,
stay here to receive our guests
while I rummage through the house for
the wherewithal to entertain them.

[*Exit*

**Isabel.** Come, Inés.
**Inés.**                    Yes, cousin, let us go.
But I think it just absurd to put
a woman under lock and key when
safe's the last thing she wants to be.

[*Exeunt ISABEL and INÉS*

*Enter the CAPTAIN and the SERGEANT.*

**Sergeant.** This is the house, sir.
**Captain.**                    Well,
see to it my things are brought up
from the bivouac at once.
**Sergeant.** [*aside to the CAPTAIN*] I want to be the first to have
a go at the peasant girl.

[*Exit*

**Juan.** Welcome to our house, sir. It is
our great good fortune to have
a noble gentleman like you
honor it. [*aside*] How bold and trim he looks!
What I wouldn't give to wear
that uniform!
**Captain.**          My compliments.
**Juan.** Forgive these makeshift arrangements.
My father would wish this house
had been a castle for your sake.
He has gone to look after
your supper, something quite special.
Meanwhile I shall see to it
your room is ready.
**Captain.**                    I
appreciate your kind attention.
**Juan.** You have only to command me.

[*Exit*

*The CAPTAIN and the SERGEANT*

**Captain.** Well now, sergeant, have you seen

your peasant girl?

**Sergeant.** By Heaven,
I've looked everywhere—in the kitchen,
in the bedroom—but I've still
to find out where she is.

**Captain.** That country bumpkin must have stowed her
off somewhere.

**Sergeant.** I did ask the maid
about her, and she said
the girl's father locked her
in an attic room with strict orders
not to show herself at all down here.
It seems he's quite suspicious.

**Captain.** Show me a commoner who isn't.
Now perhaps if she were here
and quite available,
I wouldn't care two pins about her.
But just because the old man's
locked her up, so help me, he's made me
want to force my way up there.

**Sergeant.** But what excuse have we
to get inside, sir, without
arousing their suspicion?

**Captain.** By sheer doggedness I'll find
some pretext to dig her out.

**Sergeant.** It doesn't have to be
a clever pretext; that won't
matter much as long as it succeeds.
And that might make it all the more
appreciated.

**Captain.** I have it now.
Listen.

**Sergeant.** Fine, what is it?

**Captain.** Now, you'll pretend . . . No, that won't do.
[*He sees REBOLLEDO coming.*] Now here's that soldier;
He's cleverer and a better blind
for the little plan I have in mind.

*Enter REBOLLEDO and LA CHISPA.*

**Rebolledo.** [*to LA CHISPA*] That's the reason why I've come
to see the captain—to find out
if I've any luck left.

**La Chispa.** Well, then,
ingratiate yourself with him.
After all, the idea is not
completely mad or scatterbrained.

**Rebolledo.** Lend me a bit of sanity
and wit.

**La Chispa.** You're welcome to

the long and short of it.

**Rebolledo.** Wait here for me while I speak to him.
[*advancing*] I've come, sir, to beg of you . . .

**Captain.** By Heaven, I've grown to like
this Rebolledo; he's full of bounce
and wit. I'll help him all I can.

**Sergeant.** Yes, he's a fine soldier.

**Captain.**                                   Well,
how are things? What can I do for you?

**Rebolledo.** Sir, I've lost whatever money
I have, have had, and will have,
and hereby take the pauper's oath
to cover present, past, and future.
So may it please you, sir, to ask
the ensign to advance me a little
something over and beyond my pay
to defray the costs of running . . .

**Captain.** Say it—of running what?

**Rebolledo.** A little table game of bowls
I am a man burdened by debt,
but still a man of honor.

**Captain.** Your point's well taken. The ensign
will know my pleasure in this matter.

**La Chispa.** [*aside*] Hurrah for the captain!
Oh, I can't wait till everyone
calls me Mistress of the Bowling Game!

**Rebolledo.** I'm off to give him that message.

**Captain.** Wait, a word before you go.
I shall need your help to carry out
a little plan I have in mind,
and so, I hope, relieve myself
of certain doubts.

**Rebolledo.**                     But what's
all the hesitation?
No sooner said than done!

**Captain.** Now listen to me. I plan
to go up to that attic room
and see if there's a certain person
living there who has been trying
to escape detection.

**Rebolledo.**                     Well, then,
why not go up at once?

**Captain.** I'd rather not attempt it
without a good excuse.
There now, let's pretend we're quarreling,
and you're forced to flee upstairs.
I'm angry, then; I draw my sword.
You're so frightened that you burst in

upon the hidden person
I am looking for up there.
**Rebolledo.** Fine! Now I know the score.
**La Chispa.** [*aside*] Rebolledo and the captain
are getting on so famously,
I'm sure to be the Mistress
of the Bowling Game.
**Rebolledo.** [*raising his voice*] By God!
Am I to be denied
the same allowance freely given
a thief, a sniveling coward
and a scoundrel? And I, a man
of honor, get nothing for my pains?
**La Chispa.** [*aside*] The deal was sealed, and now
he opens his trap!
**Captain.** What, are you addressing me this way?
**Rebolledo.** Since I'm right, can't I get angry?
**Captain.** No, and don't you dare speak of it
to me. Just be grateful now
that I've forgiven you.
**Rebolledo.** Sir, you're captain here, so mum's the word,
I guess. And yet, by God,
if I were captain for a while . . .
**Captain.** [*grasping his sword*] Yes, what would you have done to me?
**La Chispa.** Stop, Sir! [*aside*] I'm sure he'll kill him now.
**Rebolledo.** I'd have you mend your speech a bit.
**Captain.** What's kept me from killing
this cheeky beggar on the spot?

[*Draws his sword.*]

**Rebolledo.** I withdraw, in deference to your rank.
**Captain.** That won't help; You're a dead man now.
**La Chispa.** What a mess he made of it!
**Sergeant.** Easy, Sir!
**La Chispa.**          Stop!
**Sergeant.**                    Wait, hold on!
**La Chispa.** Good-bye Mistress of the Bowling Game.
[*The CAPTAIN runs off after REBOLLEDO, and the*
*SERGEANT, behind the CAPTAIN; enter JUAN,*
*with drawn sword, followed by his father.*]

*JUAN, CRESPO, and LA CHISPA.*

**Juan.** To the rescue, everybody!
**Crespo.** What's going on here?
**Juan.**                    How did it
get started?
**La Chispa.**     The captain drew his sword
against a soldier, then bounded
up those stairs behind him.

**Crespo.** Of all the nasty tricks of fate!

**La Chispa.** After him, everyone!

**Juan.** [*aside*] It was a pointless gesture,
hiding my cousin and my sister.

*A room upstairs in the same house*

*REBOLLEDO, fleeing, meets ISABEL and INÉS;*
*the CAPTAIN and the SERGEANT follow.*

**Rebolledo.** Fairest ladies, since a temple
has always been a place of refuge,
let this, which is love's shrine,
now become my sanctuary.

**Isabel.** Who forces you to flee this way?

**Inés.** And what's your excuse for entering?

**Isabel.** Who is it that's coming after you?

*Enter the CAPTAIN and the SERGEANT.*

**Captain.** It's I, by God, who mean to kill
that beggar, if he thinks . . .

**Isabel.** Sir, control yourself, if only
for the reason that he came
to beg for refuge here.
Gentlemen like yourself
are duty-bound to honor
womankind, if not because
they're individuals,
then because they're women.
As a gentleman, let that
suffice you now.

**Captain.**                  Your beauty
is the only sanctuary
through which he may escape my wrath.
In consequence, I spare his life.
But consider how ill-advised
you'd be in such a case as this
to take a human life yourself
while you'd have me refrain.

**Isabel.** If, sir, your courtesy
has now indebted us to you
for life, do not move so quickly
to endanger such a mortal balance.
I beg of you to spare this man,
but do not seek to claim of me
that debt for which I am obliged.

**Captain.** The rare perfection of your beauty
is twin to your intelligence.
And I discern how now in you

153

both grace and wit conjoin
to pledge their single troth.

> *Enter CRESPO and JUAN with drawn swords;*
> *LA CHISPA is behind them.*

**Crespo.** What's this, sir? Expecting in my fear
to find you killing a man,
I find you're . . .
**Isabel.** [*aside*]       Heaven help me!
**Crespo.** . . . simply flirting with a woman.
You're a nobleman, no doubt of that:
you quickly forget your anger.
**Captain.** A man whose birth saddles him
with obligations must uphold them.
Because of my esteem for this lady,
I overcame my wrath.
**Crespo.** Sir, my daughter Isabel's
a peasant girl, not a lady.
**Juan.** [*aside*] By Heaven, all this was nothing
but a trick to get inside!
It discomfits me no end
that they should think they've hoodwinked me.
This can't go on. [*aloud*] Captain,
had you considered this,
you might have better understood
how much my father wished to serve you,
and prevented this affront to him.
**Crespo.** Boy, who's asked you to meddle here?
And what affront's there been?
If the soldier angered him,
was the captain not obliged
to follow him? My daughter deeply
appreciates the favor shown
in pardoning the man, and I
the esteem which he has shown her.
**Captain.** There clearly could have been
no other issue, and so be
more careful of the words you use.
**Juan.** I have been most careful.
**Crespo.** How is it you speak to him that way?
**Captain.** Since you are present, I shan't
chastise the boy again.
**Crespo.** Hold on, captain. Chastising
my son's my own affair, not yours.
**Juan.** And I'll take it from my father,
but from no one else.
**Captain.**               What
would you do about it?

**Juan.** I'd stake my life on my good name.
**Captain.** And what can a good name mean
    to a peasant?
**Juan.**            As much as it does
    to you, who wouldn't be a captain
    if there were no peasants.
**Captain.** By God, this insolence
    is insufferable!
**Crespo.**           Look here,
    to get at him you go through me.

                                    *[They strike swords.]*

**Rebolledo.** In God's name, Chispa, there's going
    to be a brawl!
**La Chispa.** *[shouting]* Guards, this way!
**Rebolledo.** Don Lope! *[aside]* Here's trouble coming!

    *Enter DON LOPE, in an elegant uniform and carrying his*
         *baton; SOLDIERS and a DRUMMER.*

**Don Lope.** What's all this about? I've just arrived,
    and must the first thing I come up
    against be a squabble?
**Captain.** *[aside]*          And what a rotten time
    for him to come!
**Crespo.** *[aside]* That shaveling of mine,
    by Jove, held his own against them all!
**Don Lope.** What's up here? What happened?
    Now, speak up, by God, or I'll throw
    the whole pack of you, man, woman, and child,
    out the window! Did I have to
    drag myself up here, game leg and all
    (the devil take it!), and still
    not hear a word from anyone
    to tell me why?
**Crespo.**           It's nothing
    at all, sir.
**Don Lope.** Speak up now, the truth!
**Captain.** Well, the fact is I'm billeted
    in this house, and one of the soldiers . . .
**Don Lope.** Go on.
**Captain.**          . . . forced me to draw my sword.
    I chased him up here, and followed
    when he entered the room
    these peasant girls were in.
    Then their father and brother,
    or whatever they are, were riled
    because I'd broken in.
**Don Lope.** Then I've come in the nick of time
    to settle everything. Now tell me,

who was the soldier who forced
his captain to draw his sword?
**Rebolledo.** [*aside*] Am I supposed to take
the brunt of this for all of them?
**Isabel.** This was the man who first broke in.
**Don Lope.** Give him the rope treatment, twice.
**Rebolledo.** Treatment? How will I be treated, sir?
**Don Lope.** With a rope, like that.
**Rebolledo.**                              I'm not a man
who's used to being treated so.
**La Chispa.** [*aside*] Now they're sure to cripple him for me.
**Captain.** [*aside*] Keep your mouth shut, Rebolledo.
I'll see you get off scot-free.
**Rebolledo.** [*aside to the Captain*]
How can I? If I keep still
they'll tie my arms behind
and treat me like a criminal.
[*aloud*] The captain ordered me
to sham a quarrel so he'd have
a good excuse to break in here.
**Crespo.** Now you can see that we were
justified.
**Don Lope.** But not enough
to warrant exposing this town
to the danger of being razed.
All right now, sound the drum,
and let the guard round up all troops.
Everyone today's confined
to quarters, on penalty of death.
As for you, Captain, I discharge you
from your duties here, and likewise
you, sir, from further discomfiture.
And to satisfy you both meanwhile,
Captain, find other lodgings.
I'll set up quarters in this house
myself, and stop here till we march
to Guadalupe to meet the King.
**Captain.** Sir, your wishes are my strictest
orders.

                    *[Exeunt the CAPTAIN, SOLDIERS, and LA CHISPA*

**Crespo.**     You may leave us, now.

                         *[Exeunt ISABEL, INÉS, and JUAN*

                    *CRESPO and DON LOPE*

**Crespo.** Sir, I thank you heartily
for your gracious intervention.
It has saved me from the consequence
of suffering a fatal loss.

**Don Lope.** How do you mean—suffering
a fatal loss?
**Crespo.**            The result
of killing a man against whom
I bore no grudge at all.
**Don Lope.** In God's name, you know that
he's a captain, don't you?
**Crespo.** In God's name, yes, and even if
he were a general, I'd kill
the man who sullied my good name.
**Don Lope.** Sullied or not, should anyone
so much as touch the cuff
of the lowest soldier here,
I'd hang him, as Heaven is my judge!
**Crespo.** Should anyone so much as breathe
a syllable against my honor,
I'd hang him too, as Heaven
is my judge!
**Don Lope.**        Don't you know
you're duty-bound, because of who
you are, to lend your services?
**Crespo.** Of my estate, but not my honor.
My life and property I render
to the King; but honor is
the heritage of my soul,
and my soul belongs to God alone.
**Don Lope.** By Heaven, there seems to be
some truth in what you're saying!
**Crespo.** Yes, by Heaven, and I've always
said so.
**Don Lope.**  I'm very tired,
and this devilish leg of mine
cries out it needs some rest.
**Crespo.** Well, and who'd say no to that?
Here's this devilish bed of mine
all ready for you.
**Don Lope.**              And did you
get it from the devil all made up?
**Crespo.** Of course.
**Don Lope.**              Then I'll unmake it now.
I'm worn out enough, by God.
**Crespo.** Use it then, by God.
**Don Lope.** [*aside*]              This chap's
a stubborn one, all right,
and maybe he'll outswear me.
**Crespo.** [*aside*] Don Lope's hard as nails:
we won't get on at all.

## ACT TWO

### *A street*

#### *Enter DON MENDO and NUÑO.*

**Don Mendo.** Who told you all this?
**Nuño.**                                  Ginesa,
  her maid—she told me everything.
**Don Mendo.** So the upshot of the quarrel
  in her house, whether sham
  or genuine, is that the Captain
  has begun to court my Isabel!
**Nuño.** It turns out he stays at home
  just about as little as we do.
  They say he sticks to her door
  all day long, and every hour
  on the dot he sends in a note.
  His messenger's a wretched little
  private who trots in and out with them.
**Don Mendo.** Enough!! That's more poison,
  far more poison, than one heart
  can imbibe.
**Nuño.**           Especially when
  one's resistance is so low
  he has no stomach for it.
**Don Mendo.** Nuño, let's be serious
  a moment.
**Nuño.**          Ah, God help me,
  if I could only joke about this!
**Don Mendo.** And how does she take to him?
**Nuño.** Just as she takes to you,
  for Isabel's a goddess in her way:
  aloof and beautiful she shines on high,
  unmoved by vaporings profane.
**Don Mendo.** God bring you better news!

*[With this exclamation, he slaps NUÑO across the face]*

**Nuño.** And you a beak of broken teeth!
  You've knocked out two of mine.
  Go on, knock them all out, if you like.
  They're not much use, they've nothing
  now to chew on anyhow. Here comes
  the Captain.
**Don Mendo.**    If I thought less of
  Isabel and her reputation,
  by Heaven, I'd kill him on the spot!

**Nuño.** [*aside*] Less of your own head, you mean.

**Don Mendo.** I'll get behind here, and listen in.
  Come on, get in here with me.

*Enter the CAPTAIN, the SERGEANT, and REBOLLEDO.*

**Captain.** This fire and passion which I feel
  are not the pangs of love alone
  but a fixed idea, a madness,
  a raging inner fury.

**Rebolledo.**         Oh, sir!
  You should never have set eyes
  on that lovely peasant girl.
  She's driven you to distraction!

**Captain.** What did the servant tell you?

**Rebolledo.** Don't you know it well enough by now?

**Don Mendo.** [*aside to NUÑO*] I must act at once! Now while night
  begins to cast its darkling shade,
  and before discretion bids me
  take a tamer course, go and bring
  my arms.

**Nuño.**         Come now, what other arms
  do you possess, sir, than those
  portrayed in your escutcheon
  on the tile that's framed above your door?

**Don Mendo.** For purposes such as this,
  I imagine there are some pieces
  in my ancestral armory
  which I can don.

**Nuño.** Let us go then,
  before the Captain hears us.

                                        [*Exeunt*

*The CAPTAIN, the SERGEANT, and REBOLLEDO*

**Captain.** Not even the slightest word
  of recognition from her!
  How can a mere peasant girl presume
  to stand upon her virtue
  as though she were a lady!

**Sergeant.** Such girls aren't smitten, sir,
  with gentlemen like you.
  It would take some bumpkin
  of her own class, wooing her
  accordingly, to make her
  turn her head. Besides, your courtship's
  not very opportune. Since you leave
  tomorrow, how can you expect
  a woman to respond and give herself
  to you within a single day?

**Captain.** Within a day the sun sheds light

and fades away; kingdoms fall and rise
within a day. In one day,
the proudest building lies in ruin;
in a day a losing battle's won.
An ocean storms and stills within a day;
in a day a man is born and dies.
And so within a day my love,
like a planet, may come to know
both dark and light, and like an empire,
pain and joy; like a forest,
men and beasts; like an ocean,
peace and storm; as in a battle,
victory and defeat; and as
master of all my faculties
and senses, know life and death.
And so, having come to know within
one day an age of love's torment,
why may it not still grant me time
to know its bliss? Is joy so much
more sluggish to be born than pain?

**Sergeant.** But you've seen her only once.
Is this the pass it's brought you to?

**Captain.** Having seen her once, what better
reason is there for seeing her
again? The slightest spark will
at once burst into flame;
a sulphurous abyss will all at once
heave up a furious volcano.
All at once a bolt of lightning
consumes whatever's in its way;
and all at once the sleeping cannon
spews forth its deadly horrors.
Is it any wonder then that love,
a fire four times more intense?
containing flame and cannon shot,
volcano and the lightning bolt,
should terrify and scorch,
wound and lay one low, all at once?

**Sergeant.** Weren't you the one who said peasant
girls can never be attractive?

**Captain.** Overconfidence was precisely
my undoing. The man aware
of danger finds protection
in forewarning; the man who runs
a risk is the man who's all cocksure:
danger takes him by surprise.
The girl I thought would be another
peasant wench turned out to be
a goddess. Does it not follow then

that danger overcame me
through my very inadvertency?
In all my life I've never seen
such perfect beauty, such utter
loveliness. Ah, Rebolledo,
there is nothing I would not do
to get another glimpse of her!

**Rebolledo.** There's a soldier in our company
who can sing superbly;
then there's La Chispa, keeper
of my bowling game, and she
can dance and bawl out ballads
like no one else alive.
Look now, suppose we have a revel, sir,
and serenade your Isabel
beneath her window; in that way,
Captain, you can see her,
even speak to her as well.

**Captain.** But there's Don Lope; I wouldn't like
to wake him.

**Rebolledo.**       Don Lope? With that leg
of his, when does he ever sleep?
Besides, Captain, if you went along
disguised among the troops,
and any question rose,
we'd take the blame, not you.

**Captain.** Though this lead to worse complexity,
love's anguish must endure it all.
We'll all meet here tonight;
meanwhile let no one know
I've anything to do with it.
Ah, Isabel, my love for you
grows costlier and hazardous.

[*Exeunt the CAPTAIN and the SERGEANT*

*LA CHISPA and REBOLLEDO.*

**La Chispa.** [*offstage*] Take that!
**Rebolledo.**                    La Chispa, what's going on?
**La Chispa.** There, the wretch has got his face slashed
for his pains.
**Rebolledo.** What was all the row
about?
**La Chispa.** He had the gall to try
and cheat me of my due; he kept me
watching odd and even numbers
for an hour and a half
while he maneuvered. I got sick
of it and cut him up with this.

[*She shows the dagger.*]

While he's getting stitched up
at the barber's, let's go
to the guard room and I'll tell you
all about it.
**Rebolledo.** A fine time to have
a row when I've come about
a revel!
**La Chispa.** Well, what's one got to do
with the other? My castanets, sir—
here! Now what is it we sing?
**Rebolledo.** Not till tonight, and then the music's
got to be more formal. Come now,
don't straggle, we're off to the guard room.
**La Chispa.** My name is made, ah worldly fame!
La Chispa's Mistress of the Bowling Game.

*[Exeunt*

*A downstairs room in CRESPO'S house, with a view and
an exit on the garden. A window on one side.*

*DON LOPE and CRESPO.*

**Crespo.** [*offstage*] Set the table for Don Lope
in this veranda; it's cooler here.
—You'll find dinner here much more
enjoyable. After all,
there's not much in the way
of recompense for August days
except the evenings.
**Don Lope.**                  Indeed,
this bower's most pleasant now.
**Crespo.** It's just a bit of garden which
my daughter finds agreeable.
Sit down, sir. Here the tender breeze
that stirs the gentle leaves
within the trellised bower
murmurs in a crowd of voices
to the cadence of the fountain,
a zither silvery and pearled,
with pebbly strings where chords are struck
across its golden frets.
Pardon us, sir, if our music
is simply instrumental,
unaccompanied by singers
and their song for your further pleasure.
Our sole performers here are
warbling birds who will not sing at night,
nor may I force them to.
But do sit down and let the scene

divert you from your pain.
**Don Lope.** Nothing will—it nags and nags,
and makes relaxing quite
impossible. God help me!
**Crespo.** Indeed, sir, I hope He will.
**Don Lope.** And give me patience to endure it.
Sit down, Crespo.
**Crespo.**          Thank you, I am fine.
**Don Lope.** Do sit down.
**Crespo.**          Since you give me leave,
I shall obey you, sir—
but excuse the liberty
I take in doing so.

[*He sits down.*]

**Don Lope.** Do you know what I've been thinking?
That yesterday you must have let
your temper get the best of you.
**Crespo.** No, it never gets the best of me.
**Don Lope.** Then how was it that yesterday
you sat down without waiting
to be asked by me, and even took
the finest chair?
**Crespo.**          Because you didn't
ask me to. And today, because
you did, I preferred not to.
Courtesy nods to courtesy.
**Don Lope.** Yesterday you were full of hissing
oaths, b'gods and b'heavenses.
Today you're pleasant, gentler,
and much more circumspect.
**Crespo.** Sir, I always answer as I'm
spoken to; yesterday I was
compelled to use the tone
which you applied to me. I take it
as a prudent policy
to pray with him who prays,
and swear at him who swears at me.
I am all things to all men.
And so it happened that all last night
could not sleep a wink for thinking
of your lame leg. When I arose
this morning both my legs were lame.
Not knowing which it was that pained you,
the right one or the left, I managed
to ache in both of mine. I wish
you'd tell me which it is
so that I may reduce
the pain to only one.

**Don Lope.** I've good reason to complain.
  Do you know, in thirty years
  of wartime service out in Flanders,
  through winter frost and scorching
  summer heat, I've never taken leave
  nor have I known what it is to be
  a single hour without pain?
**Crespo.** May the good Lord give you patience!
**Don Lope.** What would I do with it?
**Crespo.** Then do without it.
**Don Lope.**                 Let it steer clear
  of me, or let a pack of devils
  come and make away with me
  and patience altogether!
**Crespo.** If you say so. But if they don't,
  it will be because they're not inclined
  to do good deeds.
**Don Lope.**            Oh, God!
  God Almighty! God!
**Crespo.**           May He
  keep you in His grace—and me.
**Don Lope.** Good Lord, it's killing me!
**Crespo.** Good Lord, I'm sorry for you!

        *Enter JUAN, bringing in the table.*

**Juan.** Here's the table for you.
**Don Lope.** How is it my own servants
  are not waiting on us?
**Crespo.** I beg your pardon, sir,
  but my instructions were
  they need not bring provisions
  nor wait upon you here.
  Thank God, I am sure you won't lack
  for anything while you are my guest.
**Don Lope.** Well, since my servants aren't here,
  please ask your daughter to come
  and dine with me.
**Crespo.**            Juan, go and call
  your sister in at once.

                        *[Exit Juan*

**Don Lope.** On that score, my ailment
  places me above suspicion.
**Crespo.** Even if your health were as sound
  as I could wish it, I would not be
  suspicious of you. You belittle
  my affection for you; nothing of
  the sort disturbs me. The reason
  I'd kept my daughter from coming down

here was simply to protect her
from being subject to crude,
impertinent remarks. If all
soldiers were gentlemen like yourself,
she'd have been the first to wait on you.
**Don Lope.** [*aside*] What a wily chap this peasant is,
or else he's naturally astute!

*Enter JUAN, INÉS, and ISABEL.*

**Isabel.** Sir, what is it you'd have me do?
**Crespo.** Don Lope wishes to honor us.
It's he who's called you in.
**Isabel.** Your humble servant, sir.
**Don Lope.** But I wish to serve you.
[*aside*] What remarkable beauty!
—I should like you to dine with me.
**Isabel.** It would be better if we two
served you your dinner.
**Don Lope.**                     Be seated.
**Crespo.** Sit down. Do as Don Lope says.
**Isabel.** There's virtue in obedience.
                    [*They are seated. Guitar music from offstage.*]
**Don Lope.** What's that?
**Crespo.**                     They're playing and singing
outside—some of your soldiers
strolling along the street.
**Don Lope.** War's a pretty grim business—
hard to put up with without
a little relaxation.
Yes, a soldier's life is rather strict;
he's got to have some time off
to loosen up a bit.
**Juan.** Still, it's a wonderful life.
**Don Lope.** You'd take to it quite willingly?
**Juan.** I would, sir, if I could spend it
at the side of Your Excellency.

*Sounds of REBOLLEDO and SOLDIERS offstage.*

**A Soldier.** [*offstage*] We'd do better singing right here.
**Rebolledo.** [*offstage*] Sing some lines for Isabel.
To make sure that she's awake
throw a pebble at her window.
                    [*Sound of a pebble against a window.*
**Crespo.** The music's aimed at someone's window;
let's wait and see.
**A Voice.** [*offstage*]
          *Rosemary buds, so blue today,*
               *Isabel, my dear,*

> *Tomorrow will be turned to honey,*
> *just like you, my dear.*

**Don Lope.** [*aside*] Ah, the music's fine, but throwing stones
   another matter, and then pitching
   these ditties at the house
   where I am staying! . . . Well
   I'll let it pass for Crespo's
   and the girl's sake.—What nonsense!
**Crespo.** Just boys, boys. [*aside*] If it weren't for
   Don Lope, I'd see to it that they . . .
**Juan.** [*aside*] If I could get that old buckler down
   that hangs in Don Lope's room . . .

                               [*Starting to leave.*]

**Crespo.** Where are you off to, young man?
**Juan.** To see to it they bring the dinner.
**Crespo.** There are servants there to see to that.
**Soldiers.** [*singing offstage*] Oh Isabel, wake up, wake up!
**Isabel.** [*aside*] Good Lord, what have I done
   to deserve this?
**Don Lope.** This wretched thing's
   intolerable—I won't stand for it!

                               [*He knocks over the table.*]

**Crespo.** I'll say it's intolerable!

                               [*He knocks over his chair.*]

**Don Lope.** [*aside*] My impatience carried me away
   —tell me, isn't it incredible
   how much one leg can ache?
**Crespo.** That's exactly what I meant.
**Don Lope.** When you knocked the chair over,
   I thought you'd something else in mind . . .
**Crespo.** I had nothing closer to knock down
   when you upset the table . . .
   [*aside*] Oh honor, let me endure this!
**Don Lope.** [*aside*] If I were on that street right now!
   —Well, I don't want any dinner now.
   Leave me.
**Crespo.**      As you wish, sir.
**Don Lope.** God be with you, madam.
**Isabel.** And with you, sir.
**Don Lope.** [*aside*]         My room's right off
   the front door, isn't it? And isn't
   there some sort of buckler in it?
**Crespo.** [*aside*] Can't I take my trusty sword
   and go out the back way?
**Don Lope.** Good night.
**Crespo.**              Good night to you, sir.
   [*aside*] First I'll lock the children in.

**Don Lope.** [*aside*] I'll wait till the house is quiet.
**Isabel.** [*aside*] Heavens, how badly the two of them
    conceal the thing that troubles them!
**Inés.** [*aside*] Each pretends so poorly
    for one another's sake!
**Crespo.** See here young man! . . .
**Juan.**                    Yes, Father?
**Crespo.** Your bedroom's over there.

                                     *[Exeunt*

### The street outside

*The CAPTAIN, the SERGEANT, LA CHISPA and REBOLLEDO*
*with guitars, and the SOLDIERS.*

**Rebolledo.** We're better off right here.
    This spot's more convenient.
    Now, everyone to his place.
**La Chispa.** Now the music again?
**Robolledo.**                    Yes.
**La Chispa.** Ah, this is right down my alley.
**Captain.** But she's not even left
    one window ajar!
**Robolledo.**          They'll hear it
    pretty well inside anyhow.
**La Chispa.** Wait!
**Rebolledo.** I suppose I'll pay for this!
    Let's wait and see who's coming.
**La Chispa.** What's the matter? Don't you see
    it's just that little knight in armor?

          *Enter DON MENDO with an old shield, and NUÑO.*

**Don Mendo.** [*aside to NUÑO*] Can you make out what's going on?
**Nuño.** Not much, though I can hear it clearly.
**Don Mendo.** Oh God, who can possibly
    endure this?
**Nuño.**       I can.
**Don Mendo.**         Perhaps
    Isabel will open her window.
**Nuño.** Well, perhaps she will.
**Don Mendo.**                No, she won't, fool!
**Nuño.** Well, then she won't.
**Don Mendo.**             Ah, my jealous heart,
    cruel pain! I could easily slash
    and scatter them all right now,
    but I must hide my grief
    until it's clear what part she's played
    in all this perfidy.

**Nuño.**                     Well, then,
    let's sit down a while.
**Don Mendo.**                     Good,
    from here I shan't be recognized.
**Rebolledo.** Well, now the chap is sitting down,
    unless he means to crawl about and groan
    like some poor soul in limbo suffering
    the blows he caught behind his shield.
    [*to LA CHISPA*] Open up and sing!
**La Chispa.**                          It's coming
    to me now.
**Rebolledo.** Let's have a song so fresh
    it makes the blood run cold.
**La Chispa.** Yes, indeed!

    *DON LOPE and CRESPO enter, armed, from opposite sides of the stage.*

**La Chispa.** [*singing*]
            There once was a certain Sampayo,
                As natty a chap as you'll find,
            Bursting with gypsy bravado
                To melt you and rob you blind.
            He found his sweetheart Chillona
                One day, the day was . . .
**Rebolledo.** Let's not mention
    the day of the week; everyone knows
    it was on a blue Monday
    when the moon shows lovers its horns.
**La Chispa.**
            He came, as I say, on Chillona,
                With the sun sinking fast out of sight.
            She was drinking a pint with that fella
                Named Garlo—both looking quite tight.
            Garlo's sword was like greased lightning
                When he decided to fight.
            So he whisked off his cloak, and whipping
                The thing to his left and his right . . .
**Crespo.** You mean like this!
**Don Lope.**                     Like this, no doubt!
        [*DON LOPE and CRESPO thrust at the SOLDIERS, at DON
            MENDO and NUÑO, and rout them all; DON LOPE returns.*]
    They've all scampered away,
    except for that one over there.

                                                    [*CRESPO returns.*]

**Crespo.** [*aside*] Here's someone who's left behind.
    No doubt a soldier.
**Don Lope.** [*aside*] And this one won't get off
    until his blood flows like wine.
**Crespo.** [*aside*] And I won't let up on this one

until I drive him up the street.
**Don Lope.** Now get going, like the others!
**Crespo.** Try it yourself, you're better at it!

*[They fight.]*

**Don Lope.** *[aside]* By God, the chap's handy with that blade!
**Crespo.** *[aside]* This chap fights well, by God!

*Enter JUAN, with a drawn sword.*

**Juan.** *[aside]* Now, by Heaven, let me get at him!
—I'm here, sir, at your side.
**Don Lope.** Is that you, Pedro Crespo?
**Crespo.** Yes, it's me. Is that Don Lope?
**Don Lope.** Yes, indeed. But didn't you say
you weren't going outside? What's
the meaning of your little exploit?
**Crespo.** My excuse and my reply must be:
I've done exactly what you've done.
**Don Lope.** But this was my affair, not yours.
**Crespo.** Well, I won't keep it a secret:
I left the house to join the fight,
and to keep you company.

*Enter the Soldiers and the CAPTAIN.*

**Soldier.** *[offstage]* Let's join ranks and mop up these peasants.
Look there!

*[Appearing onstage.]*

**Don Lope.**      Where are you off to? Halt!
What's this uproar all about?
**Captain.** The men were strolling in the street,
strumming along a bit and singing
(not really making a commotion),
when they got into an argument,
and I've come to put a stop to it.
**Don Lope.** Don Álvaro, I know you've shown
good sense. The town's been in
a fairly nasty mood today
and I'd like to keep from using
any stricter measures.
Now the dawn's come up, my orders are
to take your company out
of Zalamea, and keep them out
of town all day so there won't be
any further trouble here.
Once that's done, I don't want to hear
of things like this again,
and if I do, by God, I'll settle
their hash personally,
with the end of this blade!
**Captain.** I give you my word: the company

169

will be out of town this morning.
[aside] My lovely Isabel,
you shall be the death of me!

**Crespo.** [aside] Don Lope's hard as nails:
we'll get on together after all.

**Don Lope.** Come along with me now; don't let me
catch you wandering off alone.

[Exeunt

*Enter DON MENDO, and NUÑO wounded.*

**Don Mendo.** Well, Nuño, how is your wound?

**Nuño.** If it were slighter than it is,
I'd still say it's most unwelcome
and might have spared me its company.

**Don Mendo.** I have never felt such pain
or anguish in all my days.

**Nuño.** Me either.

**Don Mendo.**      Now I've a right
to be angry. He gave you
quite an ugly blow there on the head,
did he not?

**Nuño.**      It throbs down to my toes.

[Drumbeats offstage.]

**Don Mendo.** What's that?

**Nuño.** The troops are going off now.

**Don Mendo.** That's music to my ears: I won't be
jealous of the Captain any more.

**Nuño.** He'll be gone, at least all day.

*On one side of the stage, the CAPTAIN and the SERGEANT;
on the other, DON MENDO and NUÑO.*

**Captain.** Sergeant, keep the troops marching
until nightfall; and then,
as the gleaming beacon's quenched
in the cold spindrift of our Spanish
ocean sea, I'll await you
on that hill, and from there today
proceed to find my life and love
when death engulfs the sun.

**Sergeant.** [aside to the CAPTAIN] Shhh! There goes that town character.

**Don Mendo.** [aside to NUÑO] Courage, Nuño; don't be so thin-skinned!

**Nuño.** Is there a choice, then? Could I be stout?

[Exeunt DON MENDO and NUÑO

**Captain.** I must steal back to town.
I've already bribed her maid,
and so, with luck perhaps,
I may yet speak to her again,
my fatal enchantress. I hope

my gifts will pave the way.
**Sergeant.** Well, sir, if you must go back,
be sure to take a good escort.
You can't trust those peasants now.
**Captain.** Right. Go pick some men to come along
with me.
**Sergeant.**     I'll do anything you wish.
But what if you happen to meet
Don Lope on the way? . . .
**Captain.** Love has vanquished fear, in this
and every other way.
On leaving Don Lope before,
I discovered he is due
in Guadalupe to inspect
the Regiment today,
because the King, who's on his way,
is expected momentarily.
**Sergeant.** Your orders shall be carried out
at once, sir.

                                                    *[Exit*

**Captain.** Remember now,
my life hangs on a thread.
                *Enter REBOLLEDO and LA CHISPA.*
**Rebolledo.** Sir, I've good news for you.
**Captain.** To what effect, Rebolledo?
**Rebolledo.** Oh, I think it's very good.
Wait until you hear this . . .
**Captain.** I'm waiting.
**Rebolledo.**                Well, simply this:
you've one enemy less to be
concerned about.
**Captain.**                Who's that? Be quick now.
**Rebolledo.** That chap, Isabel's brother.
Don Lope asked his father for him;
the father has agreed to it, and now
the chap's to serve with Don Lope.
I came across him in the street:
all got up so fine and dashing,
the farmboy manner not rubbed off yet,
and the soldier in him
just breaking into bud.
Well, now we've just the old man
to worry about.
**Captain.**            So far so good,
and even better if her maid
comes through who's fed my hope
I'll speak with Isabel tonight.

**Rebolledo.** And I'm sure you will, sir.
**Captain.** I'll be going back along this road;
    meanwhile my duty's to attend
    the troops just marching off.
    You two will be my escort; stand by.

                                        *[Exit*

**Rebolledo.** We two? That's a mighty skimpy
    escort; even if there were four
    of us, or six or eight, God knows
    that would still be few enough.
**La Chispa.** Talk about *your* having to go back!
    Now what about me? What am I
    to do, and how safe will I be
    if I meet that chap whose face I slashed?
**Rebolledo.** But what am I to do with you?
    Are you ready to come along?
**La Chispa.** Yes, indeed! Ready, willing, and able!
**Rebolledo.** Fine. Then there'll be a uniform
    for you—the extra one
    the captain's page was using
    and left behind here.
**La Chispa.**                 Well, then
    I'll step into it and take his place.
**Rebolledo.** Come on, there's the color guard.
**La Chispa.** Now it dawns on me! How's that song go
    I've been singing all along?
        *"A soldier's love lasts but an hour."*

                                          *[Exeunt*

        *Enter DON LOPE, CRESPO and JUAN.*

**Don Lope.** My deepest gratitude to you
    for many things, but above all
    for giving up your son today
    to join me as a soldier. Accept
    my heartfelt thanks and my esteem.
**Crespo.** I give him up to you
    to be your orderly.
**Don Lope.** I take him with me as a friend.
    I'm partial to his energy
    and spirit and to his feeling
    for the military life.
**Juan.** I shall be your faithful servant,
    always. You'll see, sir. And I shall do
    my best to heed every word you say.
**Crespo.** But I beg you, sir, to make
    allowance if he doesn't quite
    come up to snuff. In this crude
    academy of country life,

where our best books are plow and harrow,
shovel, hoe, and pitchfork,
he's learned nothing of those fine manners
and age-old civilities
which only living in
great mansions can teach one.
**Don Lope.** Now the heat of the sun's somewhat
abated, I'll take my leave.
**Juan.** Sir, let me see to your litter first.

*[Exit*

*Enter ISABEL and INÉS.*

**Isabel.** Are you going, sir, without
bidding farewell to one
who's wished so much to serve you?
**Don Lope.** I would never leave before
I'd kissed your hand, nor before
I'd begged your pardon for my boldness
in presenting you with something
meriting your forgiveness.
In this the gift is nothing,
the giving everything.
I hope you will accept this poor
medallion; though set in richest
diamonds, it grows dull in your hands.
Yet wear it round your neck, I beg you,
as a souvenir from me.
**Isabel.** I'd be very sorry if you thought
this most generous of gifts
were a payment for your stay here.
For that honor we are in debt
to you, and not you to us.
**Don Lope.**                          No,
not as payment but as a token
of my affection.
**Isabel.**                  Only
then, sir, do I accept it.
Let me commend my brother to you;
he is fortunate indeed to merit
service as your orderly.
**Don Lope.** I assure you once again: do not
concern yourself about his safety.
He shall be close to me, my dear.

*Enter JUAN.*

**Juan.** Your litter is ready, sir.
**Don Lope.** God keep you all.
**Crespo.**                          And you too, sir.
**Don Lope.** Ah, Pedro Crespo, you're a fine chap!

**Crespo.** Ah, Don Lope, and you're a brave one!
**Don Lope.** Who'd have thought that first day
   we spotted one another here
   that we'd become such bosom friends?
**Crespo.** I would, sir, if I'd known then,
   when I first heard you speak,
   that you were . . . [*while DON LOPE is leaving*]
**Don Lope.**        Well, out with it now!
**Crespo.** . . . such a fine, warmhearted old bully!

                                    *[Exit DON LOPE*

          *CRESPO, JUAN, ISABEL, and INÉS*

**Crespo.** While Don Lope is getting ready,
   listen Juan, to what I have
   to tell you, in the presence of
   your cousin and your sister.
   By the grace of God, my son,
   your lineage is as pure
   as golden sunlight, though
   you come of peasant stock.
   Remember both these things:
   the first, so that you won't
   allow your natural pride,
   through lack of confidence,
   to stifle prudent judgment
   by which you may aspire
   to make something more of yourself;
   nor forget the second, so that
   you won't be so puffed up
   you become something less
   than what you are. Be equally
   aware of both endowments:
   employ them with all humility.
   Being humble, you'll be more likely
   to conform with right opinion,
   whereby you'll find yourself forgiven
   where prouder men are soon accused.
   Think how many men succeed
   in erasing some personal
   defect through their humility;
   then think how many, having
   no defects whatever, acquire
   them because they lack humility.
   Be courteous in every way,
   be generous and good-natured.
   A hand that's quick to doff a cap
   and offer cash makes many friends,
   but all the gold the sun observes
   heaved up in the Indies

and wafted hither overseas
is less precious than the general
esteem a man is held in by
his fellows. Don't speak ill of women;
even the most abject of them
is worthy, I assure you,
of all possible respect.
Were we not all born of women?
Fight only when you have just cause.
Now when I see those in our towns
who teach the use of foils, I often
tell myself: "Their schools leave
something wanting, it seems to me.
The chap they teach to duel with so much
fervor, skill, and gallantry
should be instructed first
as to why—not how—he fights.
And I believe if there were only
one fencing master prepared
to teach the why and wherefore
of the duel, we'd all entrust
our sons to such a man."
To this advice I add the money
to defray expenses for your journey
and to buy your several uniforms
when you reach your quarters.
Now with Don Lope's benefactions
and my blessings, I pray God
I shall see you soon again.
Farewell, my son. Words fail me.
**Juan.** I shall take every word you say to
heart, and remember them forever.
Father, your hand—and sister,
your embrace. Now I must be off
to catch up with Don Lope, my lord.
**Isabel.** If my arms could only hold you back!
**Juan.** Cousin, farewell.
**Inés.**                    My tears
can only speak for me.
Farewell.
**Crespo.**     Go now, quickly.
Your presence only makes me wish
to keep you here. Remember
all I've told you.
**Juan.**                  God bless you.
**Crespo.** God keep you and protect you.

*[Exit JUAN*

*CRESPO, ISABEL, and INÉS*

**Isabel.** How cruel of you to let him go!
**Crespo.** [*aside*] Now he's no longer here,
  words come more easily again.
  —What would I have done with him at home?
  He'd be a lazy good-for-nothing
  all his life. Let him serve his King.
**Isabel.** I'm so sorry he had to leave
  at night.
**Crespo.**       In summertime
  traveling at night's a pleasure,
  no job at all. Besides,
  he's due to catch up with Don Lope
  as soon as possible.
  [*aside*] Ah, the boy's leaving is hard to take;
  outwardly I must be braver.
**Isabel.** Come, father, let us go indoors.
**Inés.** Now the soldiers have gone away,
  why not stay a little longer
  in the doorway and enjoy the breeze
  that's just sprung up. Soon the neighbors
  will be passing by here.
**Crespo.** [*aside*] It's true, I can't go in now.
  Out here at least I can imagine
  Juan is that white speck I see
  far down the road.—Inés, bring out
  a chair for me, here beside the door.
**Inés.** Here's a little bench.
**Isabel.**                    They say
  this afternoon the town
  elected new officials.
**Crespo.**                    Yes,
  that's customary here in August.

*[He sits down.]*

*Enter the CAPTAIN, the SERGEANT, REBOLLEDO, LA CHISPA,
and the SOLDIERS, their faces muffled in their capes.*

**Captain.** [*aside to his men*] Quietly, quietly now.
  You, Rebolledo, go on
  ahead and tell the maid
  I'm waiting outside in the street.
**Rebolledo.** I'm going. But what's this I see—
  there are people in the doorway!
**Sergeant.** One of them is Isabel, I think:
  see, the one whose face is now
  reflected in the moonlight.
**Captain.** Yes, it's she! I know it
  instinctively, without the moonlight.

We've come in good time. Now that we're here,
we must be absolutely fearless;
then everything will turn out
as we planned.
**Sergeant.**      Can you still
take a word of advice?
**Captain.**            No.
**Sergeant.** Well, then, don't; go right ahead
and do what you wish.
**Captain.**            I must get
to her there, and then boldly
carry her off. Meanwhile,
use your swords to keep them back.
**Sergeant.** We've come this far with you;
we'll do exactly as you say, sir.
**Captain.** And remember our rendezvous
is in the woods nearby, just off
the road to the right.
**Rebolledo.**            La Chispa?
**La Chispa.** Yes?
**Rebolledo.**      Hold on to these capes.
**La Chispa.**                        Oh, well.
In fighting you're safest, I suppose,
if you stand guard on the clothes.
Though this is said about swimming.
**Captain.** I must get there first.
**Crespo.**                  Well,
that was a pleasant interval,
but it's time we went inside.
**Captain.** [*aside to his men*]
Men, this is it now; let's go.

> [*The SOLDIERS burst in, restraining
> CRESPO and INÉS, and seize ISABEL.*]

**Isabel.** Let me go, villain ! What does this mean, sir?
**Captain.** Mean? Love's frenzy and
delirium is what it means!

> [*He carries her off.*]

**Isabel.** [*offstage*] Villain, let me go!
**Crespo.**                  Cowards!
**Isabel.** [*offstage*] Father, father!
**Inés.** [*aside*]            I'll slip away now.

> [*Exit*

**Crespo.** Damned traitors! You dare do this to me
because you see that I'm unarmed!
You rogues! You cowards!

**Rebolledo.**                    Out of my way,
or take this final blow and die!

[*Exeunt kidnapers*

**Crespo.** Go ahead! What use is there
in living now my honor's dead?
Oh, if I only had a sword!
There's no point in running after them
unarmed, and if I dashed inside
to get my sword, they'd soon be
out of sight. Ill luck has it—
what am I to do? I must lose,
whatever way I choose.

*Enter INÉS, with a sword.*

**Inés.** Here is your sword now.
**Crespo.**                    Ah,
you've brought it just in time.
Now I have this sword to follow them,
my honor is restored.

[*Exeunt*

### In an open field

*CRESPO is fighting with the SERGEANT, REBOLLEDO,
and the SOLDIERS; the voice of ISABEL.*

**Crespo.** Cowards! Dogs! Release the daughter
you have stolen from me!
I'll free her, or else die in the attempt.
**Sergeant.** It's useless: you're outnumbered.
**Crespo.** The injuries you've done me
are legion; they'll fight for me . . .

[*He falls.*]

**Rebolledo.** Finish him off!
**Sergeant.**                    No, let him live.
It's bad enough for him
he's lost his honor. Better
tie him up and leave him in the woods
where he won't attract attention.
**Isabel.** [*offstage*] Oh Father, help me!
**Crespo.**                    Dearest daughter!
**Rebolledo.** Drag him off, as you say!
**Crespo.** Oh, my daughter, only
my sighs can follow you now!

[*He is carried away.*]

*ISABEL and CRESPO enter offstage; then, enter JUAN.*

**Isabel.** [*offstage*] Oh, my God!
**Juan.** [*entering*]          What sad cry is that?

**Crespo.** [*offstage*] Oh, my God!
**Juan.**                          The moan is human!
  My horse was galloping so fast
  when we came into these woods
  that he stumbled and both of us
  went down. Now I can't see where he went
  through the thickets. Someone is weeping
  here—and there, someone else is groaning
  in great misery. I hear
  both voices but can't tell where they are,
  they're so muffled. Two human voices
  invoke my aid with equal
  urgency. One of them's a man's,
  the other, a woman's.
  I shall help her first, and this way
  obey my father twice:
  "Respect all women, and fight
  only when you have just cause."
  So now to help this woman,
  then have just cause to fight.

## ACT THREE

### *In a forest*

### *ISABEL, weeping.*

**Isabel.** Oh, never let the glorious day
  touch my eyes again nor waken me
  to know my shame beneath its shade!
  Oh morning star, harbinger of so
  many fleeting planets, stay and give
  no quarter to the dawn which now
  invades thy bluest canopy.
  Let it not erase thy quiet face
  with dewy smiles and tears.
  But as I fear this must come to pass,
  admit no smile at all, dissolve
  in tears. Now, sun, thou greatest star
  of all, delay, hold back,
  and linger yet a while below,
  in the ocean of cold foam.
  Let night for once protract
  its hushed and trembling empery,
  and thus, attentive to my prayer,
  assert thy majesty by will
  and not by sheer necessity.
  Why shouldst thou wish to rise and witness
  in the tale of my calamity

the vilest, most terrible
enormity, the maddest violence
that Heaven ever hoped to publish
on the shame of all mankind?
But alas, thou art cruelly
despotic, for despite my pleas
to stay thee, I detect thy face
now rising luminous beyond
those hills. Alas, must I contend
with thy wrathful gaze now fixed upon
my extinct honor while so many
wretched ills, such horrible
adversities pursue me?
What am I to do? Where shall I go?
If my errant feet turn homeward,
I intensify the injury
against my poor dear father,
whose only joy and fortune
was to see his purest honor
mirrored in my own, once white and chaste
as is the moon, now so sadly palled
and, to my shame, totally eclipsed.
But if respect for him and my own
tormented fear prevent my going
home, I thereby invite the world
to name me as accomplice
to my own disgrace, and by so blind
an inadvertency let
innocence attest to slander.
How wrong I was, how wrong
of me to flee my brother!
It would have been much better
had I told him of my plight, and so
moved his proud wrath to kill me.
I must cry out now; let him return,
furious and vengeful, to kill me.
Let the echo of my voice
clarify these mutterings,
and by repeating them proclaim . . .

CRESPO and ISABEL

**Crespo.** [*offstage*] Come back now and finish me.
　　Come, be merciful and kill me.
　　It is no kindness to allow
　　a man so wretched as I am to live.
**Isabel.** Whose voice is this, so thick
　　and broken? I cannot make it out.
**Crespo.** [*offstage*] Kill me, I say. Oh, that
　　I might urge you to be so kind!

**Isabel.** Heavenly God! Here is another
who yearns to die, another so
miserable he lives against his will.

[*She parts the foliage and
discovers CRESPO, bound.*]

Ah, what do these eyes of mine behold?
**Crespo.** Whoever you are, so timidly
approaching through the wood,
for pity's sake, come here and kill me.
Heavens! who is this I see?
**Isabel.** And both hands bound up behind you
to this heavy oak . . .
**Crespo.**                     And her voice
so sweet, so heavenly . . .
**Isabel.**                     Father!
**Crespo.** Ah, Isabel my dear.
**Isabel.** My own dear father!
**Crespo.**                     Come closer.
Here. Good, now untie me.
**Isabel.** I dare not do it. Once my hands
untie the bonds that grip you now,
I shall never have the courage,
Father, to tell the story
of my grief, recounting
all my sorrows to you.
Once your hands are freed, and you find
strength regained but honor lost,
your revenge entails my death.
Sooner than have you learn of it
through someone else, I must tell
my wretched story to you now.
**Crespo.** No more of this, Isabel my dear.
You need not say another word.
There are often tales that tell themselves;
they need not be spoken.
**Isabel.** There are many things you must be told
which even as I mention them
can hardly fail to move you
to revenge before you've heard them all.
Only last night I sat
in perfect safety, sheltered
by your reverend love and all
the promise which it held in store
for me; then all at once they fell
upon us, those muffled villains
whose only law is that honor
must succumb to force; and so
they carried me away. I think

of them only as ravenous wolves
who steal inside the fold
and snatch away the suckling lamb.
There the Captain, the wretched
ingrate, who on the very day
he came to lodge with us
brought with him such unheard of,
such unspeakable discord
(full of guile and treachery,
outbursts and violence),
the Captain plunged ahead, seized me
in his arms while his cohorts, those
other rogues of his, protected him.
He brought me to this dense dark forest,
the haunt he'd chosen near the town.
When are such dim retreats not used to
perpetrate the vilest infamies?
There I found myself, incredulous,
half-crazed, when even the sound
of your voice trailing behind me
disappeared. The words you shouted
one by one faded in the distance,
dispersed upon the wind.
Then what were words became
the merest sounds, and finally
not even sounds but simply
the muffled echoes of alarms
scattered through the air, as when
trumpet sounds have died away and
one still hears the ringing afterward,
but not the notes themselves.
Then when that villain sensed there was
no one following behind him
and no one to defend me
(for now the moon itself withdrew,
cold and vengefully behind dark clouds,
the very light it borrows
from the sun), he attempted, to my
eternal sorrow, to justify
his guilty love with grievous lies.
Who'd not be shaken with disgust
by the patent effrontery
that converts the crudest
violence to tender love?
Beware of him, I say beware
the man who seeks forcibly
to win a woman's heart:
he cannot see nor understand
that love's victory is not

in snatching up the spoils
but in securing the affection
of the loveliness that's treasured.
When desire seeks to gain
such loveliness dishonorably,
by force, it then becomes
a lust for beauty that is dead.
How I pled with him and wept—at first
spoke humbly, then cold and cuttingly.
But all in vain. And then
(now let my voice grow dumb),
the arrogance (and grieving cease),
the insolence (let my heart moan),
the impudence (let my eyes shed tears),
brutality (rumor shut its ears),
cruelty (and breath fail to tell it),
and shamelessness (and I wear mourning) . . .
But what words cannot express
my gestures and emotions may.
I hide my face in shame.
I weep tears of bitter outrage.
I wring my hands in anguish.
Rage has cracked my heart. You know
my meaning there are no words
to utter it. Enough to say
my cries, so wearily
repeated on the wind, no longer
begged for help but justice.
Dawn came, and lit my way, I heard
the branches rustle; I turned to look
and saw my brother standing there.
Heavenly God! When, oh bitter fate,
was such favor ever shown
so quickly to one in misery?
In the uncertain morning light,
while only dimly visible,
he swiftly guessed my plight
without needing to be told.
Sorrow's looks are lynx-eyed:
they penetrate at a glance.
Wordlessly he drew his sword, the one
you'd girded round him that same day.
Then the Captain, recognizing now
that someone had at last come
to my aid, replied with his sharp blade.
They closed and fought, thrust and parried.
But while they fought relentlessly,
in my grief and fear I recognized
that my brother would not know

if I was or was not
guilty of complicity.
And so, not to risk my life before
I could explain the circumstance,
I turned into the forest's
tangled underbrush and fled.
And yet, not completely, Father;
for it was also my desire
to know what would ensue behind me
that prompted me to turn and watch them,
screened behind a latticework of vines.
Soon I saw my brother wound
the Captain, who stumbled backward; and
just as Juan prepared to follow through
the Captain's men, who had been searching
for him, burst in, furious
to avenge him. At first, Juan stood
his ground, then saw himself outnumbered
and swiftly disappeared.
They resolved to aid their officer
rather than pursue his assailant.
Heedless of his crime, they lifted up
the Captain and brought him back
to town, deciding that the safest
course, however hazardous,
would be the most expedient.
When I considered how one's worst fears
increase, and link by link are forged
to one another, I ran off
blindly, confused and stumbling
in distraction, and unguided
wandered dimly through woods and fields
and undergrowth until
I reached your side, where
having told my bitter tale at last,
I lie prostrate at your feet
awaiting the stroke of death.
Now you know my grievous story,
summon up your courage, take your sword
and end my life. Do it boldly
as my own hands untie your bonds.

[*She unties his bonds.*]

Bind this cord around my neck
and choke my wretched life out.
I am your dishonored daughter.
Now you are free, kill me
and thereby let the world
commending you say this: "To resurrect
his honor, he took his daughter's life."

**Crespo.** Stand up, Isabel, my child. No,
  do not kneel before me on the ground.
  If it were not for such torments
  and afflictions, all our sufferings
  would go unrewarded, and all
  our joys quickly turn to ashes.
  This is the lot of man,
  and we must gird ourselves
  to bear it deep within our hearts.
  Come, Isabel, let us go home
  quickly now; the boy's in danger
  and we must make every effort
  to find out where he is
  and bring him back in safety.
**Isabel** [*aside*] Oh, stars above, does this show
  true concern or simply caution?
**Crespo.**                      Come.

                                           [*Exeunt*

### A street leading into town.

#### CRESPO and ISABEL

**Crespo.** As sure as there's a God above,
  that Captain's been driven back here
  just to get his wound attended to,
  and I suspect before he's through
  he'll wish he died of it
  and spared himself the thousand
  and one wounds in store for him.
  By God, I shan't rest till I see him
  dead! Come, come child, we're almost home.

#### Enter the TOWN CLERK.

**Clerk.** Ah, Master Pedro Crespo,
  I've good news for you.
**Crespo.**                  Yes, clerk—
  good news of what?
**Clerk.**                You were selected
  Mayor of the town today,
  and to mark your debut in office
  you've two important functions
  to perform now. The first concerns
  the King, who is expected to arrive
  either today or tomorrow;
  the second concerns the Captain
  who with his company was
  billeted in town here yesterday.
  Some of his men have brought him back

in secret; he needs urgent treatment,
for he's been wounded, though he
refuses to declare who did it.
If this can be established,
there will have to be a trial.

Crespo. [aside] Just when my honor was to be
avenged, the staff of magistrate
is thrust into my hands!
How can I exceed the law myself
when I am committed to the role
of keeping others within its bounds?
But such matters need further
mulling over.—I am extremely
grateful to the Council
for the honor they've bestowed on me.

Clerk.. Let us proceed to the Town Hall
and your official installation,
after which you may look further
into these affairs.

Crespo.                Come along, then.
[to ISABEL] You'll go directly home.

Isabel. Heaven preserve me! Should I not go
with you now?

Crespo.                Child, now your father's
mayor here, he'll see to it
there'll be justice done you.

                                        [Exeunt omnes

### The CAPTAIN's lodging

*The CAPTAIN, wounded, wearing a bandage; the SERGEANT.*

Captain. Why, there's nothing to this wound at all.
Why did you have to bring me back here?

Sergeant. Who could tell it was so slight
before we had it looked at?
Now that we know you're perfectly
all right, we must consider there is
further danger to life and limb
since you had the wound patched up.
But think how much worse off you would be
if you'd been left to bleed to death.

Captain. Well, it's wrong to stay here any
longer now that I've been treated.
Let's get out before the word
goes round we're here. Are the others
waiting outside?

Sergeant.                They are.

Captain. Only a swift escape will save us

from running into all those peasants.
Once they discover I am here, we'll
have to fight our way out barehanded.

*Enter REBOLLEDO.*

**Rebolledo.** The officers of the law are here.
**Captain.** Civilian law! What's that to me?
**Rebolledo.** I only said they've just arrived.
**Captain.** Good, I could wish for nothing better.
Since they've found me out, there's no need
to worry now about the townsfolk.
The law obliges them
to turn me over to
a military court, and there,
although the case is awkward,
I'll be perfectly safe.
**Rebolledo.** The peasant's probably
registered some complaint.
**Captain.** That very thought's occurred to me.

*Enter the CLERK and FARMERS.*

**Crespo.** [*offstage*] Lock the doors! Don't let any soldier
out of here, and if any
tries to leave, kill him.
**Captain.**                What right
have you to be here? [*aside*] Good Lord!
Now what's this I see?

*Enter PEDRO CRESPO with his magistrate's staff
and flanked by FARMERS.*

**Crespo.**                    And why not?
As magistrate, I think I have
sufficient reason to be here.
**Captain.** If you look into this,
I believe you'll find that
a civilian judge (though you've been one
only for a day or so)
has no jurisdiction over me.
**Crespo.** My word, sir—do calm yourself!
I've come here with but one concern,
and that's a matter, if
you don't mind, for your ears only.
**Captain.** [*to the SERGEANT and REBOLLEDO*] You may
leave us now.
**Crespo.** [*to the FARMERS*] Yes, and you too.
[*aside to the CLERK*] Watch those soldiers carefully.
**Clerk.** Yes, indeed.

*[Exeunt FARMERS, the SERGEANT,
REBOLLEDO, and the CLERK*

CRESPO and the CAPTAIN

**Crespo.** Having used the authority
of my office to avail myself
of your attention, I lay
this staff aside, so, [*putting his staff aside*] and speak
to you simply as one man to
another, unburdening his heart.
We're quite alone now, Don Álvaro.
Let us both speak more candidly,
but yet not utterly permit
our deepest feelings, locked up
in the dungeons of our hearts,
to break at once the bars of silence.
I am an honest man
and, as Heaven is my witness,
despite the drawbacks of my humble
origin, I have never had
the slightest reason to regret
the station I was born in.
My fellow townsmen have never failed
to treat me respectfully. The town
church and Council have even thought me
worth honoring. I've been blessed
with a considerable estate
and, I thank Providence, there's no man
wealthier in all this district.
I have raised my daughter,
if I may say so, to be modest,
virtuous, and universally
esteemed—as was her mother,
God bless her soul in Paradise.
I think it will suffice, sir,
to prove the truth of what I've said
if I add that though I'm rich,
nobody here resents me,
and though I'm frank and unassuming,
nobody uses or insults me.
Odd, perhaps, especially
considering we live
in a small community,
where our only fault is prying
into one another's business—
and I could wish to God, sir,
it would only stop at that!
There is, of course, my daughter . . .
She is most attractive—
your own infatuation
will attest to that . . . although,
in saying so, perhaps I should

more stringently deplore it,
since that was her undoing.
But I shall not now pour all
the poison into a single cup;
let some of it remain
to test our fortitude.
We cannot leave everything to time,
sir; we must do something to conceal
its cracks, its imperfections.
One such crack, as you can see, gapes
so wide I cannot hope to mend it,
however hard I try.
If I might keep it hidden,
buried in my heart's deep core,
God knows I'd have no need to come
to you. I'd learn to bear it if
only I might hear nothing further
said of it. Well, then: to redress
so manifest a wrong,
to seek some way of righting
the insult done to me,
is not to look for remedies
but for revenge. So, having cast
about, this way and that,
I have hit upon one recourse—
and one only—that satisfies me,
and should not displease you much.
That's to have you take over
all my property at once,
and unconditionally.
Not a penny will I ask
for my own sustenance or my son's
(whom I shall bring here to beseech
forgiveness at your feet).
On the contrary: we'll be content
to beg out on the street
if there is no other way
to sustain ourselves. What's more:
if you decide you wish
to brand us as slaves and sell us
immediately, you may add
those proceeds to the dowry
I have offered you. Repair
the damage you have done
to my good name. I cannot think
that doing so will detract
one whit from your honor, sir.
For what your sons may lose in
quality by being my grandsons,

they'll make up by that prestige to which
being your sons would entitle them.
As they say, and truly, in Castile,
"It's the stallion that redeems the mare."

*[He kneels.]*

Look, on my knees, and by
an old man's tears that even
seem to melt the snowy beard
they fall on, I beg you. What is it
I beg? Only to restore
the honor you deprived me of.
And though that honor is my own,
I beg for its return so humbly
it must appear I beg for yours.
You know that I can seize it from you
forcibly, but I would have you
yield it willingly instead.

**Captain.** Tiresome old man, you've babbled on
until you've worn my patience out.
You can count your lucky stars
I've spared your lives so far—
you and that son of yours.
And you ought to know you owe your luck
to Isabel and her beauty.
As for your threat of using force
to retrieve your honor,
that moves me very little.
And when it comes to legal matters—
you've no authority over me.

**Crespo.** You mean my misery does not
affect you?

**Captain.**            An old man's like
a woman or a child: his fears
are easily dissolved in tears.

**Crespo.** For all my wretchedness, you've not
a single word of sympathy?

**Captain.** What more sympathy do you need?
I have spared your life.

**Crespo.**                        Look, sir:
I am down upon my knees.
I beg you to restore my honor.

**Captain.** How tiresome can you be?

**Crespo.**                        Look, sir:
I am Mayor of this town.

**Captain.** I am not subject to
your jurisdiction—only
to a military court's.

**Crespo.** Is that all you have to say?

**Captain.** That's it, you tedious old babbler!

**Crespo.** Is there no remedy at all?

**Captain.** Yes, indeed. The best remedy
for you is silence.

**Crespo.**                  Nothing else?

**Captain.**                               No.

**Crespo.** Then, by God, I swear you'll pay
for all this dearly. Ho, there, come in!

[*He rises, picking up his staff.*]

FARMERS, CRESPO, and the CAPTAIN

**Farmer.** [*offstage*] Sir!

**Captain.** [*aside*]        What are these peasants up to?

*Enter the FARMERS.*

**Farmer.** What are your orders, sir?

**Crespo.**                               I
order you to arrest the Captain.

**Captain.** Indeed! You know you're acting rashly.
You cannot arrest someone like me,
an officer of the King.

**Crespo.**                  We'll see.
But you either leave this place as
my prisoner or as a corpse.

**Captain.** I warn you I am a captain,
and quite alive and in commission.

**Crespo.** Well, what do you take me for—
a dead mayor, out of commission?
Surrender, you're in my custody.

**Captain.** Since I cannot defend myself,
I have no other choice.
I shall complain of your insult
to the King.

**Crespo.**        And I'll complain to him
of yours. It's good he's in
this vicinity: he can listen
to us both. And incidentally,
better leave your sword.

**Captain.**                  You have no right . . .

**Crespo.** Why not, since you'll be in jail?

**Captain.** Now treat it with due respect . . .

**Crespo.** Right you are! I heartily agree.
Take him to his cell, with due respect.
Then, with due respect, shackle him.
With due respect, see to it
he does not communicate
with any of the soldiers.
Then put the other two in jail
as well, and, as it befits their case,

keep them duly separated
so that afterward, with due respect,
they may each of them submit
their sworn depositions,
whereupon if any two of them
evidence their culpability,
by God, I'll hang them one and all
at once—with due respect.

**Captain.** Oh, these peasants drunk with power!

[*The CAPTAIN is led away by the FARMERS.*]

*REBOLLEDO, LA CHISPA, the CLERK, and CRESPO*

**Clerk.** The page and this soldier here
were finally apprehended.
The other one got away.

**Crespo.** That's the rascal who sings; a little
stretching of the voice box
and he'll never sing again.

**Rebolledo.** Since when is it a crime to sing, sir?

**Crespo.** Singing's fine, I'm sure. In fact,
I've a little instrument here
to improve your singing. Make up
your mind now, and tell . . .

**Rebolledo.**                    Tell what?

**Crespo.** All about last night . . .

**Rebolledo.**                    Your daughter
knows more about that than I do.

**Crespo.** Otherwise you die.

**La Chispa.** [*aside to REBOLLEDO*] Don t
admit a thing! Deny it all,
and if you do you'll be the hero
of a ballad I'll make up and sing.

**Crespo.** Later you'll be obliged to sing
a little too.

**La Chispa.** You can't torture me.

**Crespo.** Why not, may I ask?

**La Chispa.**                    It's a
pretty well accepted thing.
And there's no law against it.

**Crespo.** What alibi have you?

**La Chispa.** A great big one.

**Crespo.**                    What is it? Speak up.

**La Chispa.** I'm pregnant.

**Crespo.**                    And bold as brass, I see!
This is the last straw! Aren't you
the captain's groom?

**La Chispa.**          Not at all, sir:
I'm nearer to another's bridle.

**Crespo.** I want your testimony—both of you.
   Now make up your minds to tell me
   all you know.
**La Chispa.** Of course we'll tell you
   all we know—and even more.
   That's much better than being dead.
**Crespo.** It will save you from the rack, at least.
**La Chispa.** If it does, by Heaven, I was born
   to sing, and so I'll sing
   as I have never sung before!
[*She sings.*]
     *"Now since they want to torture me . . ."*
**Rebolledo.** [*singing*] *"What do you think they'll do to me?"*
**Crespo.** What's all this?
**La Chispa.**            Just tuning up now—
   then we'll go right on to sing.

                                  [*Exeunt omnes*

#### A room in Crespo's house

**Juan.** After wounding that villain
   in the forest and turning back
   when all his henchmen came,
   I've scoured the woods, slashing
   every thicket, but in vain.
   My sister has disappeared.
   Since I have returned to town,
   I am resolved to tell my father
   everything, here and now.
   God in Heaven, I shall learn
   from him what must be done
   to restore my honor and my life.

       *Enter INÉS and ISABEL, downcast; JUAN.*

**Inés.** You grieve and sigh so heavily,
   my dear, your suffering
   is like a living death.
**Isabel.** Inés, who told you I find my life
   anything but odious?
**Juan.** I'll tell my father . . . [*aside*] Alas,
   that's Isabel! It's plain as day.
   What am I waiting for?

                              [*He draws his dagger.*]

**Inés.** Cousin!
**Isabel.**         Brother! What do you mean
   to do?
**Juan.** Avenge the life and honor
   which you compromised today.

**Isabel.** But wait . . .

**Juan.** In Heaven's name, I'll see you dead first.

*Enter CRESPO and the FARMERS.*

**Crespo.** What's this?

**Juan.** This is to expiate
a terrible offense, to avenge
a heinous crime, and punish . . .

**Crespo.** Enough, enough. You were wrong
to come here and so rashly . . .

**Juan.** But what's this I see?

**Crespo.** . . . present yourself
before me now, having just wounded
a captain in the forest.

**Juan.** I attacked him, sir, but
my cause was just: your own honor
was at stake . . .

**Crespo.** That's enough now, Juan.
Here, arrest him—take him off
to prison.

**Juan.** Father! Is this the way
to treat your own flesh and blood?

**Crespo.** I wouldn't hesitate to treat
my father this way, if I had to.
[*aside*] I do it to save his life,
but it will probably be taken
as the oddest piece of justice
ever wrought!

**Juan.** Let me at least explain
why I first attacked the Captain,
then tried to kill my sister.

**Crespo.** I know all about that now, but
knowing personally about it
won't do at all. I must be
officially apprised of it
as Mayor, and then investigate
the evidence. Until your guilt,
if any, has been duly proven
at the trial, I must see to it
that you're detained. [*aside*] I'll find a way
to clear him.

**Juan.** Your object is
utterly incomprehensible.
You arrest a man and strip him
of his honor for attempting
to restore your own, while you
protect the very culprit
who relieved you of it.

*[He is taken off in custody.]*

*CRESPO, ISABEL, and INÉS*

**Crespo.** Come, Isabel, go in and sign
   your name to the complaint you lodged
   against the man who injured you.
**Isabel.** You who wished to keep that grievous
   insult secret, how can you now
   persuade yourself to publish it?
   If you cannot manage
   to avenge it, at least try
   to say nothing more about it.
**Crespo.** No, I cannot treat the matter now
   in any other way. As Mayor
   I can no longer satisfy,
   as I might wish to do
   in private, an attack
   against my honor.

*[Exit ISABEL*

               Now, Inés,
   bring that staff inside; since he's refused
   to make personal amends for this,
   he'll learn how hard the law can be.

*[Exit INÉS*

**Don Lope.** [*offstage*] Stop! Stop!
**Crespo.**                What's that? Now who,
   who in the world is shouting
   as he dismounts outside? And who's this
   coming in?

*Enter DON LOPE and SOLDIERS.*

**Don Lope.** Ah, Pedro Crespo!
   Here I am again. I wasn't
   very far along the way when
   a most alarming piece of news
   brought me back to town. I wouldn't think
   of stopping elsewhere, Pedro,
   since you and I are such good friends.
**Crespo.** God bless you, Don Lope. Your presence
   always does me honor here.
**Don Lope.** I miss your son; I wonder that
   he has not joined me as yet.
**Crespo.** I shall readily tell you why,
   but first, sir, I hope you'll let me
   know the news that brought you back.
   You seem desperately disturbed, sir.
**Don Lope.** It's the most disgraceful thing
   you can possibly imagine,
   the most confounded, harebrained
   nonsense anyone could think of!

Why, listening to that sergeant
who overtook me on the road . . .
I tell you, I won't, I can't . . .
I could burst with rage . . .

**Crespo.**                          Indeed, sir!

**Don Lope.** Well, some little jackass
of a mayor here threw the Captain
into jail. I swear to you,
this blasted leg of mine
never shook me as it did today;
otherwise I'd have been here
on the spot a long time ago
and have done that mayor in. Sweet
Jesus, I'll flog that rogue to death!

**Crespo.** Then I think you've come in vain
because that mayor won't let himself
be flogged.

**Don Lope.**        Then he'll get it willy-
nilly.

**Crespo.**    That seems very drastic,
and I can tell you there's no one
in the world who wouldn't say so.
Do you know why he seized the Captain?

**Don Lope.** No, I don't; whatever the reason,
the injured party must look
to me for justice, and if
beheading is what's called for,
I know a bit about that too.

**Crespo.** I'm afraid you do not understand,
Sir, the functions of a mayor
in a town.

**Don Lope.**    What else can he be
but another country bumpkin?

**Crespo.** A country bumpkin he may be,
but once his mind's made up
the prisoner deserves
garroting, I swear he'll do it.

**Don Lope.** And I swear he won't! Perhaps
you'd like to see whether
he gets away with it or not.
Well, just tell me where to find him.

**Crespo.** He lives quite close by.

**Don Lope.**                          Come now,
tell me who this mayor is.

**Crespo.**                          Myself.

**Don Lope.** By God, I suspected it!

**Crespo.** By God, I've just told you so!

**Don Lope.** Now, Crespo, I meant exactly

what I said.
**Crespo.**          Now, Don Lope,
I meant exactly what I said.
**Don Lope.** I've come to take the prisoner
away and punish his keeper.
**Crespo.** And I'll keep the prisoner right here
for all the wrongs he's done us.
**Don Lope.** Don't you understand he is
an officer of the King
and I'm his judge?
**Crespo.** Don't you understand
he broke into this house
and snatched my daughter from me?
**Don Lope.** Don't you know I'm sole arbiter
in any case?
**Crespo.**          Don't you know
he ravished my daughter in the woods?
**Don Lope.** Do you know how much greater
my authority is than yours?
**Crespo.** Do you know how much I pleaded
with him first and he refused me,
which left no other course than this?
**Don Lope.** No matter how you argue it,
you've trespassed on my authority.
**Crespo.** He's trespassed on my good name,
which is beyond your authority.
**Don Lope.** I assure you I'll settle that account;
he'll be made to pay for it in full.
**Crespo.** I've never left to someone else
what I can do myself.
**Don Lope.** I tell you once for all:
the prisoner is mine.
**Crespo.** I am drawing up the evidence
of this trial right here.
**Don Lope.**                    What evidence?
**Crespo.** Certain papers I am gathering
from witnesses to support the case.
**Don Lope.** I am going straight to your jail now
and take him away.
**Crespo.**                    I cannot
prevent your going there,
but remember this: my orders are—
shoot anyone who's caught approaching.
**Don Lope.** I am fairly well accustomed
to the threat of bullets,
but there's no point to risking
anything in this little fray
of ours. You there, soldier!

Run as fast as your legs
will carry you, and inform
all the companies lately
billeted here and on the march
today to return directly here
in battle formation,
all muskets and cannons loaded
and ready to be fired.
**Soldier.** Sir, there's no need to summon them.
The troops have heard what happened here,
and they're in town already.
**Don Lope.** Then, by Heaven, let's see whether
I get the prisoner now or not!
**Crespo.** Then, by Heaven, before that happens,
I mean to do what must be done!

*[Exeunt omnes*

### Inside the prison

*[DON LOPE, the CLERK, SOLDIERS, CRESPO
are all heard offstage. The sound of drums.]*

**Don Lope.** Men, here's the prison where
the Captain's being held.
If they refuse to let him go,
set fire to the place at once;
burn it to the ground. If they resist,
burn down the town—all of it.
**Clerk.** Let them set fire to the jail;
he's beyond their help now.
**Soldiers.** Death to the peasants!
**Crespo.**                    What's death?
Come now, is that all?
**Don Lope.**              They've got
reinforcements now. Go at it, men!
Break the jail down; smash the door!

*Enter the SOLDIERS and DON LOPE on one side; the KING, his retinue,
CRESPO, and the FARMERS on the other.*

**King.** What is going on here? Is this
the way to greet your King?
**Don Lope.**                    This, Sire,
is the most insolent piece
of peasant villainy
that has ever been reported.
You may take my word for it,
Your Majesty, had you reached
this town a moment later,
your progress here would have been marked

by row on row of blazing houses.

**King.** What has happened here?

**Don Lope.**                    The Mayor
has imprisoned a captain
and refuses to release him
at my command.

**King.**              Who is this mayor?

**Crespo.** I.

**King.**      And what have you to offer
in defense?

**Crespo.**        This evidence,
by which the crime is proven
conclusively, and the death sentence
clearly called for. The girl
was abducted, then ravished
in a lonely wood, the culprit
refused to marry her,
despite her father's earnest plea
and offer to forgive him.

**Don Lope.** This man is the Mayor
and the girl's father as well.

**Crespo.** It does not matter one way
or the other; if any stranger
brought the same complaint, would he not
deserve to have like justice done him?
Of course he would; then why
should I not treat my daughter's case
as I would any stranger's?
Besides, I've put my own son
in prison, which should show
I'm impartial to the issue
where the family tie's concerned.
Here, let Your Majesty himself
decide if the trial was fair,
or if anyone can say that
malice has misled me,
if I have suborned a witness,
beyond the facts I have given you.
And if so, I shall pay for it with my life.

**King.**                              The verdict
is justified. However,
you have no authority
to execute it; that's a matter
for another court's decision
and jurisdiction. And so,
you must release the prisoner.

**Crespo.** I can hardly do that now,
Your Majesty. We have only
one tribunal here, which executes

whatever verdict has been passed.
And so the sentence in this case
has already been carried out.
**King.** What's that you say?
**Crespo.**                    If you doubt my word,
Sire, turn this way and look.
That's the Captain there.

[*A door is opened and the CAPTAIN
is revealed, garroted in a chair.*]

**King.**                    You've dared do that?
**Crespo.** You yourself have said the verdict
was justified; I cannot then
have been far wrong to do it.
**King.** Why did you not leave this for
the military court to decide?
**Crespo.** All royal justice, Sire, is contained
in one body with many hands.
What difference can it make then,
if one arm of justice perform
the job intended for some other
arm? What harm's been done
if some detail is slighted
in accomplishing the broader
purpose which justice must serve?
**King.** Well, suppose I grant you that.
But how is it you did not behead
the prisoner as he deserved,
being a captain and a nobleman?
**Crespo.** I am sorry you should doubt me
on that score, Your Majesty.
In these parts the noblemen
are so well behaved, it happens
our executioner never learned
how to go about beheading
anyone. In any case,
that scruple should properly concern
the dead man—it's within
his jurisdiction, one might say;
but since he's not complained yet,
I trust others need not be concerned.
**King.** Don Lope, the deed is done.
The execution was fully
justified; to deviate
in some particular
is unimportant so long as
justice is upheld in principle.
Let no soldier stay behind now;
order all to march at once.
We must reach Portugal without

another moment of delay.
[*to CRESPO*] And you are hereby appointed
permanent Mayor of this town.
**Crespo.** Sire, only you would know
how to honor justice so completely.

                       *[Exit the KING, with his retinue*

**Don Lope.** You can thank your stars His Majesty
arrived here when he did.
**Crespo.** Even if he hadn't come,
by Heaven, there still would not have been
any other way to settle this.
**Don Lope.** Wouldn't it have been better
if you'd consulted me
and released the prisoner?
Then he would have been compelled to mend
your daughter's reputation
by marrying her.
**Crespo.**             She has chosen
to enter a convent now
where she will be the bride of one
who cares nothing for the differences
in social origin among us.
**Don Lope.** Well, let's have the other prisoners.
**Crespo.** Bring them out at once.

                             *[Exit the CLERK*

      *DON LOPE, CRESPO, SOLDIERS, FARMERS;*
      *REBOLLEDO, LA CHISPA; later JUAN*

**Don Lope.**                 I see your son's
still missing. Now that he's a soldier
he cannot be detained in prison.
**Crespo.** Sir, he must be punished
for disrespect; he attacked
his captain, though it's true
he was obliged to do so
since his honor was at stake.
Still, he might have found some other way.
**Don Lope.** Pedro Crespo, never mind that.
Call him in.
**Crespo.**      Here he is.

          *Enter JUAN.*

**Juan.** I humbly thank you, sir. I am
your devoted servant always.
**Rebolledo.** I don't think I'll ever want
to sing another note again.
**La Chispa.** As for me, I think I will—
every time I see the image

                        201

of that rack before my eyes.
**Crespo.** With which our author says
this true history now ends.
For its errors, pardon us, dear friends.

# THE PHANTOM LADY

# (LA DAMA DUENDE)

## The Phantom Lady

The ameliorative principles and virtues noted in **The Mayor of Zalamea** are closely articulated in **The Phantom Lady**, the most charming of Calderón's cape-and-sword comedies. The pastoral ethic which allows for a triumph of bottom dog over top dog in **The Mayor of Zalamea** provides for a more conclusive victory in the comedy. For here, the romantic heroine, otherwise so dismally sacrificed in the honor plays, invades the scene and, by her imaginative stratagems, asserts her right to act freely as a woman in love. But her liberty and successful strategy are all the more remarkable when viewed in a tangle of *enredos*—shadowy complications, mischievous deceptions, appearances turning into realities, matters of fact turning into clinkers and dust. All this is initiated and managed by Doña Angela, the young widow immured in her brothers' house, who maneuvers a mystery by means of a movable glass panel separating her apartment from that of her brother's guest, the gallant Don Manuel.

Closely guarded at home, where she is, in effect, "wedlocked to a brace of brothers," Angela has slipped out of the house to see the shows at the palace grounds. There she is observed and pursued by her libertine brother, Don Luis, who does not recognize her because she is veiled. Appealing for help to a stranger, Don Manuel, she is able to reach home safely while Don Manuel intercepts Don Luis. As they duel, the other brother, Don Juan, appears, recognizes Don Manuel as his friend and guest, and takes him home. A raging Don Luis is doomed to be frustrated at every turn; the more he is frustrated, the more prurient he becomes, turning from his sister to Beatriz, his brother's sweetheart, and back again, unconsciously, to his sister. Like Don Alvaro in **The Mayor**, Lisardo in **Devotion**, and Don Luis and Don Juan in **Secret Vengeance**, he is a type of morose, honorbound intruder who incites the insult-vengeance complex. As the honor spokesman in the play, he thereby masks the strong incestuous drive which Don Manuel, Angela's lover, must thwart. Because he has liberated her imagination, Don Manuel becomes the object of her wakened curiosity: the erotic Prince Charming, (not the bestial male aggressor she fled from in Don Luis), who arrives to rouse her sleeping womanhood. Against the defects of her brother's erotic anarchy are the clearly enumerated virtues in Don Manuel: self-sacrifice, discretion, courage, gentlemanly honor. Believing him to possess these virtues, Angela can feel safe with him, safe from rude assault. In reciprocating, she can feel free to perform her womanly role by using her will and imagination to endow him with the instinctive gifts of love. These are the very gifts which Calderón's honor victims, subdued by rape (Isabel in **The Mayor**), incestuous attack (Julia in **Secret Vengeance**), are unnaturally prevented from bestowing. They are the gifts of a woman's realistic love for a man, framed by the pastoral virtues and unhampered by the paternalistic strictures of the honor code.

Don Manuel and his superstitious servant, Cosme, are inducted into a mystery created by Angela, in the guise of a phantom lady, whose purpose is to convert the rule of honor into the rule of love. She is the sometimes veiled and hidden priestess of the new rule, accompanied by her servants and Doña Beatriz. Don Manuel is the initiate whose faith must be tested by various trials; these will indicate his fitness to serve and eventually marry the lady. Cosme, whose faith is being challenged on a lower level, is also involved, and such involvement is deepened by his close relationship to a master whom he typically serves as an alter ego—as an instigator and guide through the mystery, but also as a threat and a challenge to his rational mind. As the representatives of the rule of honor, the repressive principle, Don Luis and Don Juan are the antagonists and Doña Angela's keepers within the walls of the house. But Don Juan is distinguished from the rapacious Don Luis on several counts, the most notable being that, as Doña Beatriz's favored lover, his autocratic rule is tempered significantly by Doña Angela's cause of love. For his part, Don Luis is the unconscious assailant on his sister's honor, the marauder and homicidal force perpetuating the old rule, who must constantly disrupt Angela's love rites. In such a situation the fear of dishonor and the enticements of incest spring up together in the same breast. But one must remember that when his suspicions are aroused, Don Juan himself acts no differently from his brother, and in this sense with regard to Angela, "wedlocked to a brace of brothers", he is also an antagonist of the new rule.

If the developments of the mystery are thus mythotypical, they also parallel the standard devices in Calderón's vengeance plays where the man-with-a-cause is sequestered inside his own consciousness, his movements and strategies swaddled in secrecy, and his growing knowledge and purpose isolate him from all antagonists until he is ready to strike. But since Doña Angela, the principal agent here, is a woman-with-a-cause, and because the ethos she acts in is the social ethos of comedy instead of tragedy, she shares her knowledge and purpose with female accomplices, who help her to penetrate her isolation, go through doors and walls, and light up the darkness. When the play ends, the irrational, in the double form of phantom lady and imaginary devil, has been given its due. The incest threat flickering across the anxious face of honor has been put down, and, for once in Calderón, the rites of love have superseded the bleak honor formula that induces the insult-vengeance complex with all its disastrous consequences.

# THE PHANTOM LADY

# (LA DAMA DUENDE)

## DRAMATIS PERSONAE

| | |
|---|---|
| DON MANUEL | |
| DON JUAN | Don Manuel's friend |
| DON LUIS | Brother of Don Juan |
| COSME | Clownish servant to Don Manuel |
| RODRIGO | Servant to Don Luis |
| DOÑA ANGELA | Sister of Don Juan and Don Luis |
| DOÑA BEATRIZ | Doña Angela's cousin |
| ISABEL | Maid to Doña Angela |
| CLARA | Maid to Doña Beatriz |
| Servants | |

*The scene is laid in MADRID.*

# ACT ONE

### *A street*

*Enter DON MANUEL and COSME, dressed as travelers.*

**Don Manuel.** We've come an hour late and missed
    the grand festivities Madrid
    is celebrating in honor
    of Prince Balthazar's christening.
**Cosme.** As far as that's concerned, things often
    went awry before because
    someone lost an hour more or less.
    If Pyramus had reached the fountain
    an hour earlier, he wouldn't
    have discovered Thisbe dead there.
    But the berries didn't leave a stain,
    you know, for according to
    the poets that tragedy
    was written with blackberry juice.
    If Tarquin had delayed an hour,
    Lucretia would have found seclusion,
    and our classic authors would never
    know—unless they turned vicariates
    before a court of law—whether it
    really was a case of rape or not.
    If Hero had spent an hour
    considering the wisdom
    of leaping from her tower,
    I'm certain she never would have
    done it, in which case the good Doctor
    Mira de Amescua
    would have been excused from offering
    the theatre such a finely
    executed play, and likewise,
    the Amarylis Company,
    from playing it so credibly
    that even the acrobat at
    Carnival—which corresponds to Lent—
    was more than once observed
    to lose his head applauding it.
    But as we've missed the grand
    festivities, let's not also come
    an hour late to our lodging, or else,
    like the Moorish hero of romance,
    we'll find ourselves outside the gate.
    Besides, I'm curious to see this
    friend of yours, whose regal

hospitality awaits us—
God knows how or why—just when
we need it most, like two
knight-errants being feted
for the tournaments.
**Don Manuel.**                  You mean Don Juan
of Toledo; Cosme, he is my
dearest friend, and so zealous
in professing our amity
as to challenge any of
the closest friendships, celebrated
down the ages, in antiquity.
We went to school together,
and later followed the career
of arms; we were comrades in the field
at Piedmont. When the Duke of Feria
honored me as captain
in the infantry, I made Don Juan
my color guard. As field ensign
he was badly wounded
in a skirmish, and it was I
who nursed him in my tent.
Thus he has always felt that,
next to God, he owes his life to me.
I refrain from mentioning
certain other obligations—
all quite trivial, of course.
A gentleman does not discuss
such matters. In that regard,
the Academy portrays
a wealthy matron turning her back
upon her own benefaction,
thus showing the discretion
of one not wishing to be
reminded of her gift.
When, in brief, he heard that
I was coming to Madrid
in order to accept
His Majesty's preferment
for service to the Crown,
Don Juan, wishing to acknowledge his
gratitude on various counts,
insisted I take up lodging at
his house during our sojourn here.
And though his letter I received
in Burgos indicated
how to find his street and house,
I did not think it fitting
to ask about such matters

while we rode along the way.
That is why I left our bags
and horses at the inn, and how,
in coming here, I noticed
the celebration and everyone
in gala costume. Learning
of the holiday, I resolved
to catch a glimpse of it,
which is why we've been delayed . . .

*Enter DOÑA ANGELA and ISABEL, both veiled*
*and dressed in long skirts.*

**Doña Angela.** Sir, if you are the gentleman
your manner and attire indicate,
defend a woman urgently
in need of your protection.
My very life and honor are
at stake if I am overtaken
by that hidalgo at my heels.
By all that's sacred, I implore you:
save a noblewoman from
coming to grief; then someday, perhaps,
she will . . . Farewell. Alas,
I must run or I am lost.

*[Exeunt DOÑA ANGELA and ISABEL in great haste*

**Cosme.** Was that a lady or a whirlwind?
**Don Manuel.** How very strange!
**Cosme.**                                    What will you do?
**Don Manuel.** What a question! As a man
of honor, what else can I do
but defend the lady
from misfortune and disgrace?
No doubt the man in question
is her husband.
**Cosme.**                      And how
do you propose to stop him?
**Don Manuel.** By some stratagem or other,
but if that won't do it,
I shall have to use my sword,
and no further questions asked.
**Cosme.** If you're looking for a stratagem,
leave that to me: I've got one ready.
I'll use this letter from a friend
recommending me to one in town.

*Enter DON LUIS and RODRIGO, his servant.*

**Don Luis.** I must discover who she is,
if only because she's so intent
upon avoiding me.

**Rodrigo.** Overtake her, and you'll find out.

> [COSME *approaches while*
> DON MANUEL *withdraws.*]

**Cosme.** Sir, pardon my temerity,
   but may I ask Your Grace
   if he will kindly help me read
   the address written on this letter?
**Don Luis.** I've no patience for such stuff now.
**Cosme.** [*detaining him*] Well, if it's patience you lack,
   I've plenty. I'll give you half of mine.
**Don Luis.** Out of my way!
**Don Manuel.** [*aside*] How long and straight this street is!
   And there she is: still in sight.
**Cosme.** Be so good, sir . . .
**Don Luis.**                    By God,
   if you pester me any more
   I'll break your head! . . .
**Cosme.**                    Well, then,
   I'll pester you a little less.
**Don Luis.** This is insufferable.
   Get out of here!

> [*Beats him.*]

**Don Manuel.** [*aside*] I must intervene,
   throw caution to the winds,
   and face up to him.—Sir,
   that's my servant you're knocking about.
   I should like to know how
   he has offended you to warrant
   such ill treatment.
**Don Luis.**                    I never deign
   to satisfy a man who questions
   any act of mine. Good day!
**Don Manuel.** If I decide such satisfaction
   is in order, you may be sure
   your arrogance will not persuade me
   to depart without it.
   The question I put to you—
   namely, in what manner
   were you injured or offended—
   deserves a much more civil answer.
   Now, it would seem to me
   to be an insult to the Spanish Court
   if a stranger in Madrid
   were forced to teach the gentlemen
   who live here better manners.
**Don Luis.** How dare you think I need be taught . . .
**Don Manuel.** Hold your tongue, and let your sword
   reply.

[*They draw swords.*]

**Don Luis.**     You put it well.
**Cosme.**                         Oh, how lustily
  they take to fighting.
**Rodrigo.**                     Come now,
  let's see your sword.
**Cosme.**                     Since mine
  is still a blushing virgin
  whom no one's spoken for as yet,
  I cannot expose her
  to public view.

      *Enter DOÑA BEATRIZ, who tries to hold back DON*
             *JUAN; and CLARA, her servant.*

**Don Juan.**                   Beatriz,
  let me go.
**Doña Beatriz.** You must not do it.
**Don Juan.**                             Look,
  it's my brother he is fighting with!
**Doña Beatriz.** Gracious me!
**Don Juan.** [*to DON LUIS*] I'm at your side.
**Don Luis.** Hold on, there, Don Juan. Stop!
  Your support has hindered me;
  it makes me out a coward.
  Noble stranger, you will understand
  how one who had just cause to cross swords
  with you in single combat
  must now, in being seconded,
  either withdraw or else be taken
  for a craven coward. Go your way,
  sir. My sense of honor
  disallows my taking
  unfair advantage of any man,
  especially of one who shows
  such spirit and such valor.
  God be with you.
**Don Manuel.**         I appreciate
  your gracious courtesy.
  But if, by chance, you are troubled
  by any scruple later,
  you may count on finding me
  whenever you desire.
**Don Luis.** My respects to you, sir.
**Don Manuel.** And mine to you.
**Don Juan.**                         What's this
  I see and hear? Don Manuel!
**Don Manuel.** Don Juan!
**Don Juan.**                     My heart is full of doubt,

211

buffeted by fear and joy.
I cannot understand the cause
of such violent disagreement
between my brother and
my bosom friend.

**Don Luis.**　　　It was simply
that this gentleman took
his servant's side, whose impertinence
provoked me; and that's all
there was to it.

**Don Juan.**　　　In that event,
I trust that I am free at last
to embrace my friend, Don Manuel,
our noble and eagerly awaited
guest. Having fought as equals,
may you henceforth become
the faster friends for it;
you know each other's valor now.
Your hand!

**Don Manuel.** Before I shake your hand,
may I say how much I admire
Don Luis for his bravery.
I am at your service, sir.

**Don Luis.** I am proud to be your friend,
and am only sorry that I failed
to recognize you, though
your skillful sword should certainly
have told me who you are at once.

**Don Manuel.** Yours might have warned me, having
left this wound upon my hand.

**Don Luis.** Ah, I would rather have been wounded
a thousand times instead!

**Cosme.** So, now they fight with powder puffs!

**Don Juan.** A wound? We must have it dressed at once!
Stay here, Don Luis, and see
Doña Beatriz to her carriage.
Give her my apologies for this
unseemly haste. Come, Don Manuel,
I shall take you to my house—
more properly, your own—
and make sure your wound is dressed.

**Don Manuel.** Oh, it's nothing at all.

**Don Juan.** Please come at once.

**Don Manuel.** [*aside*]　　　How annoying
to be welcomed to Madrid in blood!

**Don Luis.** [*aside*] How tiresome to lose the
opportunity of finding out
who that lady was!

**Cosme.** [*aside*]    How
  appropriate! It serves my master
  right for playing Don Quixote
  to every passing Dulcinea!

> [*Exeunt DON JUAN, DON MANUEL, and COSME,*
> *while DON LUIS joins DOÑA BEATRIZ,*
> *who has been waiting nearby*

**Don Luis.** Now the storm is past and gone,
  I entreat you, madam, to allow
  the tinctured hue of roses
  once again to warm those cheeks made wan
  and desolate by the onset
  of so much icy apprehension.
**Doña Beatriz.** Where is Don Juan?
**Don Luis.**                    He begs
  your indulgence. Certain
  obligations and his
  solicitude for a wounded
  friend compelled him to depart at once.
**Doña Beatriz.** Wounded? Alas, is Don Juan wounded?
**Don Luis.** No, madam, not Don Juan.
  If my brother had been wounded,
  I would not be standing here
  so calmly. Do not be alarmed,
  for it seems to me unjust that
  when my brother feels no pain at all
  we two should be suffering
  with sorrow and anxiety.
  My sorrow's cause is seeing you
  too much overcome, too deeply
  sensible to some imagined harm
  which penetrates more cruelly
  than any actual wound.
**Doña Beatriz.** Don Luis: I am of course obliged
  to you for these compliments,
  granting that they mean to show
  your heart, and are all your own.
  But you should know I cannot
  otherwise respond to them:
  they address the stars, which may comply,
  but no mortal woman surely.
  If I seem to take your words
  so lightly, that's because the Court
  commonly regards nothing else
  so highly. Therefore, be grateful
  for my frankness, which is, at least,
  as rare a thing as you will find
  these days at Court. Good day, sir.

[Exit with CLARA

**Don Luis.** Good day, madam. Everything I do
    goes wrong, Rodrigo. If I see
    a lively woman passing by
    and try to know her better, some fool
    or duel comes up to stop me—and
    which of them is worse I do not know.
    If I am fighting, then my brother
    must rush in, and my antagonist
    turns out to be his bosom friend.
    If he suddenly departs,
    and I am left to soothe his mistress
    with apologies, she proceeds
    to treat me like a dog. And so:
    the veiled lady runs away from me;
    the meddling fool stops to drive me mad;
    the stranger attacks me;
    and my brother leads him off
    to be our noble guest at home,
    while a second lady leaves me
    writhing in her scorn. I've had
    a heap of sorry luck indeed.
**Rodrigo.** Do you care to know which
    of all those slights I think
    has pained you most?
**Don Luis.**                 You wouldn't know.
**Rodrigo.** Well, isn't it that you are jealous
    of your brother's winning Beatriz?
**Don Luis.** No, you're quite mistaken.
**Rodrigo.** What is it, then?
**Don Luis.**              If I must speak
    candidly—and this I say
    in strictest confidence—
    what pains me most of all
    is my brother's heedlessness.
    Consider it, Rodrigo:
    he brings a gay young gentleman
    to stay with us at home where,
    as you know, my lovely sister lives,
    who though she is a recent widow
    still is under age. Scarcely a soul
    knows of her presence there, she lives
    in such seclusion. At that
    the only visitor she sees
    is Beatriz, whom we allow
    because she is our cousin.
**Rodrigo.** Yes, I know that Doña Angela
    came secretly to live here

in Madrid. Her husband's death,
while Collector of the Royal Ports,
left a large deficit of funds
still owing to the Crown; meanwhile,
as she hopes to settle this affair,
she is living in strict seclusion
under your brother's roof
and his close surveillance.
This being the case, sir, remember
that the situation which forbids
her seeing anyone
will not be threatened by the presence
of Don Manuel at home.
Indeed, sir, since he will not know
she's even there, what harm is done
in his staying at the house?
Besides, special pains were taken
to make the door to his apartment
lead into the street. Then,
to conceal the second doorway,
which leads into the other rooms,
while allowing for its later use,
a paneling of glass mirrors
has been installed in that space.
And the panel's been designed
so that no one would suspect
there'd ever been another door there.

**Don Luis.** And do you suppose all this
will reassure me? Such precautions
only double my uneasiness,
for what you tell me, in effect,
is that the only thing now standing
as bulwark to my sister's honor
is a frame of glass a single blow
will shatter in a thousand pieces.

*[Exeunt*

### DOÑA ANGELA's apartment in DON JUAN's house

#### Enter DOÑA ANGELA and ISABEL.

**Doña Angela.** Here, Isabel, give me back
my widow's hood, worse luck!
And wrap me up again
in that black shroud; as cruel fate
will have it, I must be buried
in this way, alive.

**Isabel.**                     Put them on
quickly. If your brother entered now

215

with any reason to suspect you,
your dress would tell him at a glance
you were the one he met today
at the palace.
**Doña Angela.**    Heaven help me!
The two of them will be
the death of me. They have cooped me up
behind these walls where I can scarcely
see the light of day, and when night falls
my aching heart is fit to burst
this dungeon—here where the fickle moon
herself, imitating me,
can never boast she saw me mourn
my turn of fortune. Imprisoned here,
what freedom have I gained in
widowhood when my husband's death
releases me simply
to be wedlocked to a brace
of brothers? And then, if I happen
to go out, in perfect innocence,
to see the plays which everyone
in town's been flocking to,
authority decrees that though
I go there veiled, it's as if
I'd just committed murder. My luck's
so miserable and so unfair!
**Isabel.** But madam, it should not seem so strange
to you. After all, your brothers,
considering your youth, your charm,
and your vivacity, must take
precautions to protect you.
For such attractions are just
calculated to arouse some crime
of passion, especially here
at Court. For don't I cross myself
a thousand times a day in passing
those blossoming young widows?
There they go, flouncing down the street,
pretending they're so prim and chaste,
so holier-than-thou, you know,
when all they really care about
is showing off their latest gown.
Yet let them once take off their toques
and those airs of being so devout,
and they'll go bouncing off agog,
from one young fellow to another,
like a football. But madam, let's drop
this subject for a while; instead,
let's discuss the gallant stranger

whom you begged to be your champion
and in whose keeping you recently
deposited your honor.
**Doña Angela.** Why, Isabel, that's just the thing—
you seem to read my mind.
My one concern is what he must
have thought of me, for when
I heard the sound of clashing swords
behind me, I wondered, Isabel—
though you may think this fanciful—
whether he was not after all
so far taken by my pleas
that he was forced to draw his sword
on my account. I was mad
to urge him on so; but then, how can
a woman, scared to death, ever stop
to weigh the consequences?
**Isabel.** I do not know if you
incited him, but I do know
that afterward your brother
stopped pursuing us.
**Doña Angela.**              Wait, someone's there!

*Enter DON LUIS.*

**Don Luis.** Angela!
**Doña Angela.**        Why, brother,
you seem so upset. What's happened?
Is anything the matter?
**Don Luis.** Everything's the matter
when one's honor is at stake.
**Doña Angela.** *[aside]* Good Lord, now it's out—he saw me!
**Don Luis.** I am concerned because
your honor is so lightly treated
in this house.
**Doña Angela.**        Is there reason
for you to think so? What troubles you?
**Don Luis.** The worst of it, Angela, is
that when I come to see you, I am
no less vexed than I was
before I came.
**Isabel.** *[aside]* This is it now!
**Doña Angela.** But brother, how can I possibly
have offended you? Consider . . .
**Don Luis.** You are the cause, and when I look
at you . . .
**Doña Angela.** Oh, dear me!
**Don Luis.**                . . . .Angela,
I realize how little
my brother thinks of you.

**Doña Angela.** That is true.

**Don Luis.** For see how he now adds new sorrows
to those which brought you to Madrid.
And so I was not so wrong
in turning my annoyance with
Don Juan against his guest and friend
whom, out of some presentiment,
I wounded in a duel today.

**Doña Angela.** Indeed? How did that happen?

**Don Luis.** Well, sister: this afternoon
I walked to the palace grounds,
up to the stage reserved
for the public performances.
A flock of carriages
and gentlemen were crowded
all around, and it was there I found
a number of my friends conversing
with a lady in a veil,
whose wit they all seemed to relish
and admire. But I had no sooner
joined them than the lady grew silent.
And though someone begged her to explain
why my presence should have struck her dumb,
she would not say another word.
This appeared so odd to me
that I moved closer, thinking
I might know the lady—but in vain.
She only wound the veil about her
more securely, turned, and fled.
To determine who she was,
I followed her. And as she ran,
she turned continually to glance
behind at me, as if in utter
terror; yet her dismay
simply spurred my curiosity.
I continued in this way
until some stranger stopped me;
as I discovered later, it was
the servant of our present guest.
The fellow asked me to read
some letter; I said that I was
in a hurry, though I suspected
he meant to stop me purposely,
for I had seen the lady
speak to him in passing.
His persistence angered me, and I
told him—I can't remember what.
But at that point our guest came up,
looking fierce and military,

to defend his servant. Well,
we drew our swords and went at it.
That's all there was, although
it might have been much worse.
**Doña Angela.** I declare! To think that wicked
woman led you into such a trap!
Why, of all the shameless, conniving
wenches who . . . I'll wager
she did not even know you,
and only ran away
to make you follow her.
Now this is why I've often warned you,
as you recall, not to lose
your head over hussies whose
only thought is how to wreck men's lives.
**Don Luis.** How did you spend your afternoon?
**Doña Angela.** I spent it here at home,
and entertained myself by weeping.
**Don Luis.** Did our brother come to see you?
**Doña Angela.** He has not been here since morning.
**Don Luis.** I cannot tolerate his neglect
of you.
**Doña Angela.** Well, you had better not
be vexed, and finally accept
the situation. Remember,
he is our elder brother
whom we count on for our keep.
**Don Luis.** If you can reconcile yourself,
I shall have to do the same,
since it is only on your account
that I've been vexed. And now
that you've advised me of your feelings
in the matter, I shall go
to see him, and even pay
my compliments to his friend.

*[Exit*

**Isabel.** Well, madam, what have you to say
to everything that's going on here?
After suffering such a fright,
you have the very gentleman
who saved your life, and was even
wounded for it, lodged here now under
this very roof!
**Doña Angela.** I suspected
as much, Isabel. The moment
my brother mentioned the quarrel,
I gathered that the wounded man
was to be our guest. And yet,

I can scarcely bring myself
to believe the story. It seems
so incredible that a stranger
just arriving in Madrid
should instantly find himself
enjoined to save a lady's life,
then be wounded by her brother,
only to become her other
brother's house guest. Strange, though
not impossible—and yet
I shan't believe it's happened
till I see it with these eyes.

**Isabel.** If that's the way you feel,
I know how to satisfy your doubts.
You can have a look at him—
a good one, and even something more.

**Doña Angela.** Isabel, you are mad. How can I
see the gentleman when his room's
so far away from mine?

**Isabel.** There is a passage between the two.
Don't look so alarmed.

**Doña Angela.**                  It's not because
I wish to see him, but simply
out of curiosity . . . Tell me,
how can this be? I heard you well,
But don't believe a word you say.

**Isabel.** Did you know your brother's had
a paneling of mirrors made
to hide the inner guest room door?

**Doña Angela.** Oh, I think I understand you now.
What you are saying is that
we can bore a hole behind the door
and manage then to see
our guest through it.

**Isabel.**                  I think
we can manage much more than that.

**Doña Angela.** Tell me.

**Isabel.**                  Well, as I say, your brother
has built a movable panel
to shut off and conceal the door
leading this way to the garden.
The panel is movable so that
it may be easily removed,
and the door, later be replaced.
And though made of glass mirrors,
it may now be moved at will.
I discovered this myself
in cleaning up the guest room.
I had a ladder propped against it

when the paneling gave way.
Before I knew it, ladder,
paneling, and I, all at once,
went tumbling to the floor.
When I replaced the frame,
I left it hanging somewhat ajar,
so that now anyone who'd like to,
madam, can go in and out.

**Doña Angela.** Doing that would be quite rash,
thought we might discuss it.
Suppose then, Isabel, I'd some idea
I wished to get into that room.
I unhinge the panel from this side.
Now, could one also do the same if
one were standing on the other side?

**Isabel.** Why, yes—exactly! But just
to make quite sure no one else
can move it, we must fit two nails
in place, which only we
would know about, for prying loose.

**Doña Angela.** Now tell the servant when he comes
to light the candles and prepares
the bedroom for our guest,
to come back here and let you know
if the gentleman has left the house.
I'm sure his wound was slight
and won't keep him in bed.

**Isabel.** Gracious, madam, do you really
mean to go inside?

**Doña Angela.**          I have
the foolish notion that
I must discover if this man
is indeed the one who saved my life.
For if he spilled his blood on my behalf,
as his wound would testify,
I shall do everything I can
to show my gratitude—provided
I may do so without the fear
of being apprehended.
Come, Isabel, I must inspect
the panel; and if I can really
get into his room without
his knowing I am there at all,
I shall repay him for his kindness.

**Isabel.** Indeed, that would be a tale to tell.
But what if he should tell it?

**Doña Angela.** That he will not do, Isabel.
He has proved himself a gentleman,
a man whose courage is only equaled

by his sense of honor
and discretion. From the very first,
his noble qualities touched my heart.
Bold and chivalrous, gallant, prudent—
why, I do not for a moment doubt
that a man so liberally endowed,
could possibly expose me.
So many fine qualities
would never have been wasted
on a man who babbles all he knows.

*[Exeunt*

*DON MANUEL'S apartment; a movable glass panel hooked in
place is visible; also a brazier, and so forth.*

*Enter DON JUAN, DON MANUEL, and a servant with lit candles;
DON LUIS and another servant follow.*

**Don Juan.** You must lie down, I tell you.
**Don Manuel.** Ah, Don Juan, it's nothing but a scratch,
like the memory of a lady's
ribbon dropped by chance and forgotten
long ago.
**Don Juan.**     Thank goodness it's no worse
than that. I could never
forgive myself had I gained
the pleasure of your company
at the cost of any injury
to you, particularly since
it was my brother who wounded you,
however innocently.
**Don Manuel.** No, he's a gentleman. I envy him
his pluck and swordsmanship,
and could wish for nothing better
than to be his most devoted friend.

*Enter DON LUIS and a servant who is carrying his belt
and scabbard with the sword in it.*

**Don Luis.** I am your humble servant, sir,
one who still grieves the injury
he has caused you; do let me
repair it now. You must take this
from me; I can no longer bear
this instrument which wounded you.
It cannot please me nor be
of further service to me, and so
I must discharge it as a master
would some tiresome unruly servant.
Therefore I place this miscreant sword

here at your feet to beg forgiveness
for itself and for its master.
Take it, and if your cause requires
vengeance, turn it on its master.

**Don Manuel.** As once your valor, now
your courtesy has conquered me.
I accept your sword and will wear it
always at my side where it will
teach me how to be courageous.
My life henceforth will be immune
to danger, for I am confident
your noble gift contains the power
to repel it, as I myself
have recent cause to know.

**Don Juan.** Since Don Luis has shown me
how to prize a guest, I shall feel
remiss until you have received
some further gift from me.

**Don Manuel.** How will I ever repay
such favors when you rival
one another in showering me
with kindness?

*Enter COSME, burdened with baggage.*

**Cosme.**                  May an army
of devils straight out of hell
sweep me up like a squadron
of fiery dragons on high
and tear me to pieces meanwhile,
as the wrath of God, for good
and sufficient reasons, declares
they must do till all eternity,
if I wouldn't rather live
ungalled in Galicia,
or even in Asturias, than here
at Court in the capital.

**Don Manuel.** Now, check yourself . . .

**Cosme.**                              Let this baggage
check itself.

**Don Juan.**      What do you mean?

**Cosme.** I mean what I say. Any man
who makes up to his enemy
is nothing but a villain.

**Don Luis.** Hold on now. What enemy?

**Cosme.** The fountain, of course. The water
in that wretched fountain.

**Don Manuel.** Is that enough to throw you off?

**Cosme.** There I was, stumbling along the street
under that load of baggage,

when suddenly I tripped against
the foot of a fountain and fell,
pell-mell, hook, line, and sinker,
as they say, straight into
the muddy drain. Now the stuff's not
fit to bring into a decent house.

**Don Manuel.** All right, then—off with you.
You're drunk.

**Cosme.**              If I were really drunk,
I wouldn't half mind being dunked
in water. Once I read a book
about a thousand flowing fountains,
and the water had the power to change
itself into every sort of shape
and form. So I wouldn't be surprised
if the water I was soaked in
had suddenly been changed to wine.

**Don Manuel.** Once he opens up his mouth,
there's no stopping him.

**Don Juan.**                    The fellow's
humor is oddly fluent.

**Don Luis.** There's only one thing I want to know.
If you can read, as your reference
to that fountain book would indicate,
how is it you pestered me to read
that letter? And why so silent now?

**Cosme.** Because I can read books, not letters.

**Don Luis.** A smooth reply, indeed.

**Don Manuel.** Gentlemen, please pay no attention
to him. As you'll discover,
he is simply a buffoon.

**Cosme.** I'm proud to say my jests are legion,
and you're welcome to them, gentlemen.

**Don Manuel.** I must pay a visit
this afternoon, while there's still time.

**Don Juan.** I shall be expecting you at supper.

**Don Manuel.** Cosme, unpack the bags
and lay out my clothing,
but make sure you clean them first.

**Don Juan.** Here's the key to your rooms,
if you wish to lock the door.
I've a master key myself,
which I sometimes use when I return
home late. There are no other keys,
however, and no other door
to get in by. [*aside*] Now that's clear.
—if you leave yours in the lock,
the servants will come in daily

and attend to your apartment.

*[Exeunt omnes, except COSME*

**Cosme.** First things first—so now for a look at
my own private little stock.
It's time we got together, you
and I, to reckon up how much
we pilfered on the road.
At the inns they don't look after
every little item the way
they do at home, where one is always
pinching pennies like a drudge.
There's more elbow room at those inns,
where a chap can really turn his hand
to some advantage—not just standing
there akimbo, but busy working
in his neighbor's pocket.

*[He opens a traveling bag and takes out a purse.]*

There you are, my dear, my precious joy:
you've come into your own!
You started out this morning
thin as any untried maiden;
now you swell and bulge like a wench
that's nine months gone. Should I
count the money? No, that would be
a waste of time; after all, it's not
as though I'd just sold my master's
flock of sheep and had to figure out
the sum, down to the last
wretched little penny.
Whatever it comes to, that's it.
So. Here's my master's traveling bag.
I ought to open it at once
and lay out all his clothes. Why? Because
that's just what he ordered me to do.
But will I do it simply because
he wants it done at once? No.
There's no reason why a master's word
should interfere with what his servant
actually does. Now then,
I've every reason in the world
to go out and find some nice
worshipful little shrine
where I can get a drop or two
to slake this awful thirsty soul
of mine. How'd you like that, Cosme?
Ah, I'd love it! Well then, Cosme,
hurry along; pleasure
before business, you know—
especially where the first's your own

and the other is your master's.

[*Exit*

*DOÑA ANGELA and ISABEL enter by unhinging the glass panel.*

**Isabel.** This is the room; you see, it's empty.
As Rodrigo said, the gentleman's
gone out with your brothers.
**Doña Angela.** I never would have dared come here
otherwise.
**Isabel.**            Do you agree there's
no difficulty getting in?
**Doña Angela.** Yes, Isabel. I was so wrong
to doubt it. Why, there's nothing to it.
The panel moves so easily,
we can go in and out this way
without the slightest fear
of being seen by anyone.
**Isabel.** Now tell me why we've come here.
**Doña Angela.** Why, only to go back again.
When two women get together
and decide upon some mischief,
the thing's as good as done
once they've talked it over.
Since you proposed this to me
and I've come, there seems no reason
why we should come again—
except that if he really is
the gallant gentleman who boldly
risked his life to save me,
I still think, as I have told you,
I owe him something for his kindness.
**Isabel.** See how nicely your brother
furnished this apartment. That's
the gallant's sword upon the desk.
**Doña Angela.** Come here, Isabel. Isn't this
my writing box?
**Isabel.**                  It was your brother's
whim to put it there. He said
the gentleman needed such
materials for writing,
together with Lord knows how many
different books which I brought in.
**Doña Angela.** Two traveling bags are on the floor.
**Isabel.** And opened too, madam. Shall we look
and see what's inside of them?
**Doña Angela.** Yes, let's do that. I'm dying to see
the clothes and finery he's brought.
**Isabel.** A soldier and petitioner

wouldn't have much finery to bring.

[*After discussing the articles in question, they*
*fling them one after the other around the room.*]

**Doña Angela.** What's that?
**Isabel.**                                   A bundle of papers.
**Doña Angela.** Are they love letters?
**Isabel.**                                   No, madam.
I think they're legal briefs of some sort.
They're sewn together and quite heavy.
**Doña Angela.** They'd be light enough if some woman
had written them. Put them back.
**Isabel.** Here is some of his linen.
**Doña Angela.** Is it scented?
**Isabel.**                         It has the scent
of being clean.
**Doña Angela.** That's the sweetest
scent of all.
**Isabel.**          It also has
three other qualities: it's white
and soft and very fine. But madam,
what do you make of all
the instruments inside this case?
**Doña Angela.** Let me see. Ah, this one seems to be
a tooth-puller; those are tweezers;
and that's a curling iron
for his forelocks, and another
for his mustache.
**Isabel.**               Item:
hairbrush and comb. Gracious,
but this guest of ours has come
so well equipped he hasn't left
a shoelast out.
**Doña Angela.** How's that?
**Isabel.** Look, I'm holding it in my hand.
**Doña Angela.** Is there anything else?
**Isabel.**                                   Oh yes,
madam: another bundle
of papers. These do look more like
love letters.
**Doña Angela.** Give them to me.
Yes, this is a woman's handwriting.
But there's something more to it than that.
Wait, it's a portrait.
**Isabel.**                    What
fascinates you?
**Doña Angela.**        The sight
of beauty, which even
in a picture is intriguing.

**Isabel.** I'd say you look disappointed
  at having found it.
**Doña Angela.**         How silly
  you are! That's enough looking for now.
**Isabel.** What will you do next?
**Doña Angela.**              Write him a note.
  Take the portrait with you.

                                       *[She sits down to write.]*

**Isabel.** I'll look into his servant's
  traveling bag meanwhile. Ah,
  here's money, and quite heavy, too.
  Oh, but how mean of him!
  It's full of wretched coppers,
  plebeian money, and no royal
  gold or silver. I know what.
  I'll play a trick on him;
  I'll take the money out
  and fill the lackey's bag with charcoal.
  [*to the audience*] You'll say, "Where the devil
  did that woman find the stuff?"
  But you didn't notice, did you,
  that the month's November and there's
  a little brazier in this room?

                          *[She empties the money out of the*
                          *purse and fills it with charcoal.]*

**Doña Angela.** There, the letter's finished.
  Where do you think I ought to leave it
  so that my brother, if he happens
  to come in, won't see it?
**Isabel.** There, by the pillow, under
  the coverlet. He's sure to find it
  when he goes to bed, and yet no one
  will discover it till then.
**Doña Angela.** An excellent idea! Here,
  put it in there now, and pick up
  all these things.
**Isabel.**          Oh, but there's someone
  at the door!
**Doña Angela.** Then leave them here,
  just as they are and let's go back.
  Isabel, quick!
**Isabel.**         Open, sesame!

                        *[Exeunt through the panel,*
                      *which is left intact as before*

*Enter COSME.*

**Cosme.** Well, now I've served myself,
  I won't niggle any more about
  serving my master, gratis. What's this!

Who's been tossing our things around?
You'd think there'd been an auction here.
Hell's bells! They've made a flea market
of our stuff. Is anybody here?
Good Lord, nobody! Or at least
if anyone is here,
he's not in any mood to say so.
In that case, I'll say this much for him:
he must know I'm not the sort of man
who likes an idle babbler.
Well, be that as it may,
the truth is, here I stand
trembling like a leaf. But come
to think of it, why should I be?
As long as that baggage juggler's left
my purse intact, let him return and
juggle all the rest until he bursts.
Oh, but what's this I see? Good God!

[*Examining the purse.*]

He's turned my money into charcoal!
Goblin, ghost, or sprite, whatever
you are or happen to be,
you can do what you like
with this money you've left,
but what in the world can you want
with that money I filched?

Enter DON MANUEL, DON JUAN, DON LUIS.

**Don Juan.** What are you shouting about?
**Don Luis.** What's the matter?
**Don Manuel.**                    What's happened to you?
   Speak.
**Cosme.**     Oh, this is a fine little game
   you play! But sir, if you must
   keep a sprite in your house,
   why invite us to share its quarters?
   I was only gone for a moment
   but when I returned, look what I found:
   all our clothing scattered about,
   as though it had been up for auction.
**Don Juan.** Is anything missing?
**Cosme.**                          No, only
   the money I had in this purse
   of mine was turned into charcoal.
**Don Luis.** I see what you're driving at now.
**Don Manuel.** What sort of stupid joke is this?
   How gross and how ridiculous!
**Don Juan.** How lame and how impertinent!
**Cosme.** By God, I tell you it's no joke!

**Don Manuel.** Silence, I say! This is
  just like you—always the same.
**Cosme.** Very well, sir, but one of the ways
  I'm the same is that I don't take leave
  of my senses all of a sudden.
**Don Juan.** I bid you good night, Don Manuel,
  and trust my ghostly lodger
  will not disturb your sleep.
  But do inform your servant
  that he must improve his wit.

                                          *[Exit*

**Don Luis.** It is fortunate you are
  valiant, sir, since everywhere you go
  you are forced to draw your sword
  to settle every quarrel
  this fool must get you into.

                                          *[Exit*

**Don Manuel.** Do you see what they take me for
  because of you? Well, I must be
  an idiot to tolerate it!
  It never fails—wherever we are,
  your behavior exposes me
  to ridicule like this.
**Cosme.** But we're alone, sir. How can you
  suppose I still want to pull your leg?
  Besides, there wouldn't be much fun
  in tripping up one's lord and master
  when no one's there to laugh at it.
  The devil take me if I lied
  in saying someone, whoever
  it was, came in when I went out,
  and played this trick on us.
**Don Manuel.** Don't think you'll get out of it
  by repeating that foolish tale.
  Come, pick up all this stuff you dropped,
  and then prepare for bed.
**Cosme.**                Sir,
  sell me for a galley slave if . . .
**Don Manuel.** Silence! You've said enough.
  Another word and I'll break your head!

                            *[He goes into the alcove.]*

**Cosme.** If you did, no one would be
  sorrier than I. Well, well,
  so it's back you go again,
  one by one, into the bags.
  God, how I wish these toggeries
  had sense enough to answer
  to a bugle call; then they'd all

fall in at once.

                          *[DON MANUEL returns with a sheet of paper.]*

**Don Manuel.** Bring a light, Cosme.

**Cosme.** What's up, sir? Have you stumbled
  on anyone in there?

**Don Manuel.**          I found
  this sealed letter, Cosme,
  when I was opening the bed.
  It was lying by my pillow,
  underneath the coverlet.
  But stranger still is this inscription
  on the envelope.

**Cosme.**         And who's it to?

**Don Manuel.** To me, but put so oddly.

**Cosme.** What does it say?

**Don Manuel.**          I don't know what
  to make of it. *[He reads.]* "Do not touch me,
  anyone; I am meant
  for Don Manuel alone."

**Cosme.** God help you, sir, now that
  you must believe me! Stop,
  don't open it until
  you have it exorcised!

**Don Manuel.** It wasn't fear that stopped me
  but surprise. Two different things, Cosme.         *[He reads.]*

"Your well-being is a matter of some concern to me, who count myself
responsible for putting it in jeopardy. With gratitude and regret, I beg you
to advise me if you are well or not, and how I best may serve you. To inform
me further of such matters, leave your reply exactly in the place where you
found this letter. Remember: secrecy is all-important, for on the day you
breathe a word of this to either of your friends, my life and honor
immediately are forfeit."

**Cosme.** Isn't that astonishing?

**Don Manuel.**                What's
  astonishing?

**Cosme.**         Aren't you surprised?

**Don Manuel.** On the contrary: this letter
  simply reaffirms something
  I'd already suspected.

**Cosme.** How's that?

**Don Manuel.**        It's quite clear, Cosme,
  that the veiled lady whom we found
  so blindly fearful in her flight
  from Don Luis must be his mistress,
  for since he is a bachelor,
  I suppose she cannot be his wife.

If that's the case, all surprises
end at once, for then the lady
would naturally have free access
to her lover's house.

**Cosme.**                     So far, so good;
that's neatly reasoned out,
but my fears go much further.
Suppose she is his mistress
(and incidentally, sir,
congratulations, since now
she smiles at you), how could she
possibly have known beforehand
what was to happen on the street
so that she'd have the letter written
and waiting for you here?

**Don Manuel.** She could have had it written later,
after seeing me, then had
her servant bring it here.

**Cosme.** Yes, the servant might have brought it,
but how would he have got in here
if nobody has stepped inside
this room all the while that I've been here?

**Don Manuel.** There was time enough for doing that
before we came.

**Cosme.**              Very well.
Writing the letter's only one thing,
but how do you account for
the scattering around of all
our traveling bags and clothes?

**Don Manuel.** Go see if the windows are closed.

**Cosme.** Barred and bolted, sir.

**Don Manuel.**                      It's puzzling.
Now I'm flooded with new suspicions.

**Cosme.** About what?

**Don Manuel.**        I can't say exactly.

**Cosme.** Well, what do you intend to do?

**Don Manuel.** Oh, I shall answer her, of course,
but in such a manner that
there'll be no question of
her having pierced my armor
with apprehension or surprise.
For as long as we engage
in correspondence, I am sure
some occasion will arise
when we discover who the person
is who brings and takes the letters.

**Cosme.** And we're not to breathe a word of this
to either of our hosts?

**Don Manuel.**                    Of course not.
  How could I possibly betray
  the woman who confides in me?
**Cosme.** Then you'd rather betray the man
  you think is her lover?
**Don Manuel.**                    No indeed;
  all I know is this: I can
  proceed honorably
  only if I do not betray her.
**Cosme.** No, sir; there's more to this
  than you believe. I'm convinced of that
  in spite of everything you say.
**Don Manuel.** Exactly what convinces you?
**Cosme.** You can see for yourself:
  letters and things going in and out
  of this place, and still, you,
  with all your brains, cannot explain
  how such things happen. What
  would you believe?
**Don Manuel.**                    Simply
  that someone with wit and skill
  has found an entrance and an exit
  to this room, and some way
  of opening and concealing it,
  which we as yet have not discovered.
  And I'd rather lose all my brains
  at once, Cosme, than believe
  some supernatural thing
  has had a hand in this.
**Cosme.** Did you ever hear of sprites?
**Don Manuel.** No one's ever seen them.
**Cosme.** Household spirits?
**Don Manuel.**                    Pure fantasy.
**Cosme.** Witches?
**Don Manuel.**      Even more so.
**Cosme.** Sorceresses?
**Don Manuel.**                Utter nonsense.
**Cosme.** Succubuses?
**Don Manuel.**            No.
**Cosme.**                        Enchantresses?
**Don Manuel.** Hardly.
**Cosme.**                  Magicians?
**Don Manuel.**                          Tomfoolery.
**Cosme.** Necromancers?
**Don Manuel.**                  Preposterous.
**Cosme.** Energumens?
**Don Manuel.**            You're mad!
**Cosme.** Aha! Here's where I get you:

233

what about devils?
**Don Manuel.** They can't write
letters without a notary.
**Cosme.** Are there souls in Purgatory?
**Don Manuel.** Who write me love letters, you mean?
How utterly stupid can you be?
Go away, you're tiresome.
**Cosme.** All right, but what will you do?
**Don Manuel.** Stay up day and night and never
blink an eye until I solve
this mystery, in spite of every
ghost and goblin in the universe.
**Cosme.** As for me, I still maintain
some sort of devil's at the bottom
of it all; and he can fetch
and carry letters, among
other things, as quick as
anyone would puff tobacco smoke.

## ACT TWO

### DOÑA ANGELA's apartment

*Enter DOÑA ANGELA, DOÑA BEATRIZ, and ISABEL.*

**Doña Beatriz.** What a remarkable story!
**Doña Angela.** Remarkable? Just wait
until you hear the end of it.
Now, where were we?
**Doña Beatriz.** You were saying
you entered his apartment
through the panel, and that
this was more easily accomplished
than you were ready to believe;
then you left a letter for him,
and the next day found his answer there.
**Doña Angela.** Yes, and I must also tell you
I've never read anything so elegant
or so gallantly expressed.
His style is gay and high-flown, both,
much as the knights of old would write
on similar occasions.
Here's the letter, Beatriz;
tell me if you do not find it
absolutely charming.

*[She reads.]*

"Beauteous Damozel: Whoever thou art, in thy compassion for this poor
ardent knight, whose afflicted heart thou wouldst mercifully assuage, I beg

of thee, reveal to me where I may go to seek that arrant knave, that pagan miscreant, who to his infamy holds thee now in thrall, so that I, now recovered from my recent wounds, may sally forth beneath the standard of thine honor once again, and thus engage him to the death in extraordinary combat; for, depend upon it, such death were sweeter far than life to thy devoted champion. May the giver of all light preserve thee, and not forsake me. —The Knight of the Phantom Lady."

**Doña Beatriz.** Why, bless me, the writing's excellent,
   and the words so exactly fitting
   to the spirit of the adventure.
**Doña Angela.** I really expected his letter
   would be full of the gravest doubts and
   consternation, but since I find him
   so receptive I shall continue
   the exchange in the same fashion.
   And so, in my reply to him,
   I'll say . . .
**Doña Beatriz.** Wait, say nothing more;
   here comes Don Juan, your brother.
**Doña Angela.** Now he'll come in, the model lover,
   all truth and constancy,
   so joyous to see you, Beatriz,
   and speak with you in his own house.
**Doña Beatriz.** Well, to tell you the truth,
   I shan't take it amiss.

*Enter DON JUAN.*

**Don Juan.** As the common proverb has it,
   there is nothing quite so ill
   but that some good must come of it.
   I see this now confirmed in that
   all my happiness proceeds
   from your misfortunes. I refer,
   my lovely Beatriz,
   to that unhappy difference
   between your father and yourself
   which brought you, sad and vexed,
   to find refuge in our house.
   Though I should be sorry
   to discover happiness
   in the very circumstance
   which pains you, the pleasure
   of your present company
   has silenced all compunctions.
   The effects of love, you see,
   are so subtly various
   that the reason for your sorrow
   becomes the substance of my joy,

and in this is like the asp
whose bite discharges both the venom
and the antidote to cure it.
In brief, you are most welcome,
and though our hospitality
leaves something wanting, there is
this compensation: that you are
Beatriz, the happy sunlight,
who have come here to dwell
with Angela, our angel.

**Doña Beatriz.** Your greetings and condolences
are so graciously commingled,
I do not know what I can say.
It's true I've come because my father
is displeased with me. But you
must take the blame for that.
When he learned I'd spoken
at my balcony last night
to some gentleman (not knowing
the gentleman was you) he promptly
sent me here, while he cools his rage,
to stay with my cousin,
in whose virtue my father has
the highest confidence.
This much I'll tell you, but only this:
I can value my misfortunes too.
For like you I've come to see that
love's effects are subtly various,
and in this are like the sun
whose bounteous rays wither up
one flower at the very moment
they create another. So now
as with a single ray
love strikes against my heart,
it both withers up a sorrow
and gives birth to that joy
I find in being welcomed here.
In this your house is like
the jeweled firmament,
affording ample refuge
to a jealous sun as well
as to a certain angel.

**Doña Angela.** It seems a profitable day
for lovers, and even I receive
a windfall merely by standing
here between the gusts of
overwhelming compliments.

**Don Juan.** Sister, do you know what I think?
To punish me for the inconvenience

which my guest has caused you,
you have retaliated
by keeping this lady here
as a guest of yours.
**Doña Angela.** Quite right;
I've done it simply to put you to
the trouble of entertaining her.
**Don Juan.** I welcome such happy punishment.

*[He turns to leave.]*

**Doña Beatriz.** What's this, Don Juan? Where are you going?
**Don Juan.** Only to arrange for your further
comfort here. Beatriz, you know
that nothing else would make me leave you.
**Doña Angela.** Let him go.
**Don Juan.**                    Well, till later.

*[Exit*

**Doña Angela.** Yes, the good Lord only knows
what troubles Don Juan's guest has caused me.
Troubles enough to last me
all my life, but no less so, I see,
thank God, than those Don Juan
now suffers because of you;
so that guest for guest I'd say
the two of us are even.
**Doña Beatriz.** The only reason I can stand
for your sending him away
is that I'm curious
to know how your story ends.
**Doña Angela.** Well then, I won't tax your patience.
Letters have been flying thick and fast
between us ever since, and his,
at least, so admirably
ingenious, half jesting
and half serious, I've never
seen the likes of them before.
**Doña Beatriz.** And what do you suppose
he thinks of you?
**Doña Angela.**          That I am most
certainly Don Luis' mistress,
because I've been in hiding
and because, as he imagines,
I have another key
to his apartment.
**Doña Beatriz.**          There is
only one thing puzzling me.
**Doña Angela.** And what is that?
**Doña Beatriz.**                    Knowing that
someone must be bringing

all those letters back and forth,
how is it he has not found you out—
indeed, not yet caught you in the act?
**Doña Angela.** It's really very simple.
I have a servant posted
near his door whose job it is
to tell us when the coast is clear.
Then Isabel can get into
his rooms, knowing no one's in them.
Even now, my dear, the servant
has been waiting out there all day long
to give us word when everything
is safe, but we've heard nothing yet.
And that reminds me, Isabel,
be sure you get the basket to him
when you have the chance to do it.
**Doña Beatriz.** Another question: how can you think
the man so clever when he hasn't
even shown the simple wit to
find out where your secret panel is?
**Doña Angela.** Have you ever heard the story
of Columbus and the egg?
Well, the wisest men alive
had exhausted all their wits
endeavoring to set the egg
upright on a jasper table when
Columbus came along, gave the egg
a simple tap, and solved the problem
once for all. The greatest
difficulties solve themselves
once you know the simple answer.
**Doña Beatriz.** Another question, if you please.
**Doña Angela.** Oh, do ask it.
**Doña Beatriz.**                    What do you suppose
you'll gain by all this foolish nonsense?
**Doña Angela.** I don't know. I might say, of course,
to show our guest my gratitude
or while away the weary hours
I am doomed to spend in solitude,
but I confess there's more to it
than that. At first, I was prompted
by my silly curiosity,
but now that has turned to jealousy.
There's a portrait of a woman
in his room I yearn to see again.
And I'm determined to go in
and take it, just as soon as
I can do so. Indeed,
I don't know how to put it,

but I am equally determined
I must see and speak to him
in person.
**Doña Beatriz.** And tell him who you are?
**Doña Angela.** Oh no, Heaven forbid! But even
if I did, I would not think him
capable of revealing it
or indulging in such treachery
where his host and friend's concerned.
I'm sure the very thought
that I may be the mistress
of Don Luis has already
made him fearful and uneasy,
and explains the reason why
he writes me in so guarded
and overwrought a manner.
But I would never be so crude
as to tell him who I am.
**Doña Beatriz.**                    Well then,
how is he to meet you face to face?
**Doña Angela.** Now listen, this will be the most
remarkable device of all:
I shall walk straight into his room,
with no danger of his seeing me;
then he'll walk into mine,
but not know where he is.
**Isabel.** According to the script, insert
the other brother's name at this point
in the margin, for here comes
Don Luis.
**Doña Angela.** You'll hear all
about this later on.
**Doña Beatriz.** How differently the stars
influence our characters! For in
two men of equal gifts and merits
exist such inequalities of
disposition that what pleases us
in one annoys us in the other.
Come now, Angela, I want
no words with Don Luis.

*[They turn to leave.]*

### Enter DON LUIS

**Don Luis.** Why leave so suddenly?
**Doña Beatriz.** Simply because you have appeared.
**Don Luis.** Then when I enter you withdraw
the loveliest, pure light from which
the sun itself has learned to shine.
Am I then the lowering night?

If so, let your loveliness forgive
my boldness and discourtesy
for detaining you a while,
since I cannot ask your person
to indulge a presence
which it would refuse. Knowing
your severity, I must
unhappily forego the impulse
to ascribe any note of favor
to the merest courtesy.
I also know, of course, how little
my wildest love is capable
of rousing from your scorn
a single spark of hope.
Yet on that account precisely,
my love for you increases
as if it would retaliate
against your rigorous disdain.
The more you torment me,
the more I glory in my state;
the more you would abhor me,
the more my passion for you grows.
Say that you complain of this,
say that the same intensity
of passion in us (my love, your hate)
merely drives us to extremes.
Very well, then: teach me how to hate,
or I shall teach you how to love.
Let me learn severity from you,
unless you'd have me teach you kindness.
Let me learn all you know of harshness;
I'll teach you simple tenderness;
your contempt or my affection,
your neglect or my constancy.
And yet, however much you sought
to steep us both in profane
cruelty, the deity of love,
whom I have glorified,
still would elevate us, you and I,
in token of my faithfulness.
**Doña Beatriz.** You manage to complain
so eloquently, I feel
I should requite you for your pains.
But I cannot bring myself
to do so, simply because
it happens to be you.
**Don Luis.** I warn you, if you persist
in treating me so coldly,
I too know something of the language

of disdain.

**Doña Beatriz.** Very well, then: use it.
Perhaps your eloquent disdain
will cure your ill-bred disposition.

[*DON LUIS stops her as she is about to leave.*]

**Don Luis.** Listen to me: if this is your
revenge, you must suffer it with me.

**Doña Beatriz.** I've no intention to. Good Heavens,
Cousin, can't you stop him?

[*Exit*

**Doña Angela.** What little self-respect you have
to ask for such humiliation!

**Don Luis.** Oh, Sister! What am I to do?

**Doña Angela.** Forget your foolish passion.
To love someone who hates you
is an ordeal worse than death.

[*Exit with Isabel*

**Don Luis.** [*addressing the absent DOÑA ANGELA*]
Forget her when my heart is choked
with rage? Impossible! Who could?
First let her be kind to me,
then I'll forget her, gladly.
But after she insults me? Never!
The wisest man alive, no less
than I, would tell you this:
kindness is easily forgotten,
since it never sticks or sinks
so deeply as an insult.

*Enter RODRIGO.*

**Rodrigo.** Where have you been?

**Don Luis.**                    I don't know.

**Rodrigo.** You seem so sad; can you tell me why?

**Don Luis.** I was speaking with Doña Beatriz.

**Rodrigo.** Say no more. Her answer's
written on your face. But where was that?
I haven't seen her here at all.

**Don Luis.** The vixen's come here as my sister's
guest for a few days—as if
one guest already were not enough
to drive me mad. My family
is purposely conspiring
against me. They invite
a different person every day,
just to torment me: first
Don Manuel, and now Beatriz.
Heaven must have brought
all my suspicions home to roost;

241

I cannot understand it
otherwise.

**Rodrigo.**     Look, here comes
Don Manuel. He'll hear you.

*Enter DON MANUEL.*

**Don Manuel.** [*aside*] Why should such strange things happen
only to me? Good Lord,
how can I proceed, undetected,
to discover if this woman
really is the mistress of
Don Luis, or what secret
strategy she uses
to bring off her intrigue?

**Don Luis.** Well, Don Manuel.

**Don Manuel.**                              Ah, Don Luis.

**Don Luis.** And where have you been, sir?

**Don Manuel.** At the Palace.

**Don Luis.**                              Pardon me;
it was gross of me to ask
a man of your affairs
where he goes and where he comes from.
It should be obvious
all paths lead to Court as surely
as all rays do to Heaven.

**Don Manuel.** If my visits were restricted to
the Palace I'd feel much easier.
But the nature of my business
now requires further action.
I find His Majesty removed
his Court this afternoon
to the Escorial, which means
I must make haste to follow him
there tonight with my dispatches.
And this matter cannot be delayed.

**Don Luis.** If I may be of service, sir,
in whatever way at all, you need
only say the word, you know.

**Don Manuel.** I am much obliged to you.

**Don Luis.** It is no mere courtesy,
I assure you.

**Don Manuel.** I am certain
you have my interests at heart.

**Don Luis.** [*aside*] Yes, indeed—and the sooner I am
rid of you the better.

**Don Manuel.** But it would be unfair of me
to infringe upon the time
of so fine a gallant as yourself.
Surely you must now be engaged

in much pleasanter pursuits
than this tedious affair
you offer to support me in.

**Don Luis.** Had you heard me speaking with
Rodrigo when you came in,
you would never think so.

**Don Manuel.**                    Do you mean
I am mistaken?

**Don Luis.**          Yes, indeed;
though I'm presently involved
with a lovely lady, it is
only in bitterness,
not gratitude, for she is
utterly determined to treat me
with contempt.

**Don Manuel.**       I did not imagine
you could think yourself so helpless.

**Don Luis.** I am doomed to love a lady
as wholly cruel as she is
beautiful.

**Don Manuel.** You are joking, surely.

**Don Luis.** I wish to God I were.
But my unhappy fate is such
that this beauty flies from me
as the glorious daylight flies
the fall of night, and her scorching rays
consume me. Would you care to know
how miserable a man can be?
Lately, when I followed her,
torn by love and jealousy,
she bade another person intervene
to stop me. Consider
how completely she detests me,
for where others use a go-between
to achieve fonder proximity,
she uses one to flee from me.

*[Exeunt DON LUIS and RODRIGO*

**Don Manuel.** What further evidence do I need?
A woman who fled the sight of him
and had to have another person
stop him! This refers to me and her.
Well, at least I've cleared up one doubt.
If it's true she is that lady,
then she cannot be his fiancée:
he would not have her living
in his house if she detested him.
But here's an even crueler doubt:
if she is not his mistress

and does not live here in the house,
how can she correspond with me?
Ah, so one mystery ends
only to give way to another.
What am I to do or think?
I am more confused than ever. God
help me, for there's a woman in it!

*Enter COSME.*

**Cosme.** What's become of the phantom, sir?
Perhaps you've seen him hereabouts
again? Please say no, sir,
and I'll be overjoyed.

**Don Manuel.**                    Lower
your voice.

**Cosme.**          Because I've lots of work
to do in our rooms, but can't go in.

**Don Manuel.** Well, what's the matter?

**Cosme.**                                          I'm frightened.

**Don Manuel.** Is it becoming in a man
to be afraid?

**Cosme.**          No indeed, sir;
it's not at all becoming!
But here's a man afraid because
it's warranted.

**Don Manuel.**      No more nonsense now.
Go and fetch a light. I've several
things to write and papers to arrange
before we leave Madrid tonight.

**Cosme.** Yes, I'm sure, and the reason why
you change the subject is that
you're every bit as scared of spooks
as I am.

**Don Manuel.** I've told you once before
I do not share your interest
in that subject, and when you speak
of it my mind wanders
to more important matters.
And now, of course, I'm wasting
precious time. Light the candle while
I go to say good-by to Don Juan.

                                                            *[Exit*

**Cosme.** Yes, I'll do that, by all means;
it's time to light a candle
for that phantom; he'd be annoyed
if we left him in the dark.
There ought to be one here.
I'll light it in that lamp there
where the wick is dying down.

Now, let's be very cautious!
Well, here goes, I'm on my way—
and my heart pounding like a drum.

                                                    [Exit

### Don Manuel's apartment

*Enter ISABEL through the panel, carrying a basket.*

**Isabel.** They've gone out, just as the servant
    said they have. Now to put
    this basket full of linen
    in the right place. Oh, gracious me!
    It's so ghastly dark here at night,
    I'm afraid of my own footsteps.
    Good God, I'm all atremble!
    I must be the first phantom
    to put its trust in God.
    Oh, now I can't find the panel.
    How can that be? In all this darkness
    and confusion, I've lost my sense
    of where things are. I don't know where
    I'm standing or even where
    the table is. Heavens,
    what will I do now? If I can't
    get out and they find me here,
    the jig is up and everything
    is ruined. I'm shaking like a leaf!
    Worse yet, I think there's someone
    at the door. He's opening it.
    He's carrying a candle.
    It's all over now, I'm done for!
    There's nowhere I can hide
    and no way to get out.

*Enter COSME with a light.*

**Cosme.** Oh, phantom, please sir: I hope you are
    a well-bred phantom who perhaps
    are used to such devotions;
    I humbly beg of you, count me out
    of all those tricks you'd like to play.
    Here are four good reasons why:
    First, because I know why myself;

                        [*As he advances, ISABEL follows close
                            behind him so that he won't see her.*]

    second, you know why yourself;
    third, as they say, "a word
    to the wise . . ."; and fourth, because
    I know these old verses:

> *Oh Phantom Lady, Phantom Lady,*
> *Have pity on me please,*
> *I'm just a poor lad, all alone,*
> *And quaking in the knees.*

**Isabel.** [*aside*] Now, thanks to the light,
  I can make out where I am again,
  and he hasn't noticed me as yet.
  If I could only manage
  to blow out the candle,
  I'd surely get out of here
  while he is trying to relight it.
  He may hear me, but won't see me,
  and that's the lesser of two evils.

**Cosme.** Fear plucks me like an instrument!

**Isabel.** [*aside*] And here's the tune it plays.

                    [*She strikes him and blows out the light.*]

**Cosme.** Oh, my God, I've been killed!
Call a priest! Confession!

**Isabel.**            Now
  I can escape!

              *Enter DON MANUEL.*

**Don Manuel.** What's going on here?
  Cosme! What are you doing
  in the dark?

**Cosme.**          The phantom's
  snuffed us out—the candle and me both.

**Don Manuel.** Fear puts such nonsense in your head.

**Cosme.** In my neck, you mean!

**Isabel.**                 Oh,
  if I could only find the panel!

**Don Manuel.** Who's this here?

              [*ISABEL runs into DON MANUEL,*
                 *who catches hold of the basket.*]

**Isabel.**               Worse luck! Now
  I must deal with the master.

**Don Manuel.** Bring the light, Cosme. I've got hold
  of him, whoever it is.

**Cosme.** Well, don't let go.

**Don Manuel.**            I won't.
  Fetch that candle now.

**Cosme.**           Hold him tight.

                        [*Exit*

**Isabel.** [*aside*] He's got hold of the basket.
  I'll leave it in his hands.
  Now there's the panel. Good-by.

           [*Exit, leaving him with the basket*

**Don Manuel.** Whoever you are, you'd better

be still until the light's brought in.
If not, by God, I'll run you through
with this sword! But I'm only grabbing
the air now, and nothing alive
but this linen and something
very light. What can it be?
Good God, I'm at a total loss.

*Enter COSME with a candle.*

**Cosme.** Now we'll see the spook
  by candlelight. But what's become
  of him? I thought you'd caught him.
  What happened, sir?
**Don Manuel.**           What can I tell you?
  He left me with this basket and fled.
**Cosme.** Well, what have you to say to all this?
  You yourself just told me
  that you'd got hold of him,
  and here he's vanished into thin air.
**Don Manuel.** All I can say is that the person
  who makes it his business to get in
  and out of this room was somehow
  shut in here tonight, and to find
  his way out, doused your light,
  left me this basket, and escaped.
**Cosme.** Which way?
**Don Manuel.**          Through that door.
**Cosme.** You'll drive me out of my mind!
  Good God, I saw him myself,
  in the twinkle of an eye,
  when he nearly pounded me to death
  and the candle was just going out.
**Don Manuel.** Well, then, how did he look?
**Cosme.** He looked like a huge friar,
  and he had on an enormous cowl,
  which is why I believe
  he was a Capuchin ghost.
**Don Manuel.** Fear can make you see anything!
  Well, give me the candle
  and we'll see what the good friar's
  brought us. Pick up the basket.
**Cosme.** Me? Touch baskets the devil's been at?
**Don Manuel.** Come on, pick it up.
**Cosme.**                Oh, sir,
  my hands are all greasy
  with tallow, and I'd soil
  that nice taffeta covering.
  Better leave it on the floor.
**Don Manuel.** It's full of fresh linen

and a letter. Let's see
how discreet your friar can be.

[*He reads.*]

"During the short period you have been living in this house, there has not
been time enough to provide you with much linen; as it is made up, it will
be brought to you. Concerning what you have said about Don Luis and
myself, your notion that I am his mistress is, I assure you, not only untrue
but can never ever be true. I shall tell you more about this when I see you,
which will be very soon. Heaven protect you."

    This is a good, baptized phantom.
It commends me to God.
**Cosme.**               See, sir?
I told you it's a Capuchin.
**Don Manuel.** It's very late. Pack the bags
and secure those papers in a pouch.
They contain all the reason
for our going. Meanwhile,
I'll write an answer to my phantom.
         [*He hands the papers to COSME, who puts them
            on a chair, and DON MANUEL starts writing.*]
**Cosme.** I'll put them right here now,
so they'll be close at hand
and then I shan't forget them.
But still, sir, I'd like to pause
just long enough to ask you this:
Do you still believe that phantoms
don't exist?
**Don Manuel.**    What utter nonsense!
**Cosme.** Nonsense, is it? When you yourself
have seen all the evidence,
how gifts are thrust into your hands
out of thin air, and still you're doubtful?
But perhaps it's just as well you are,
since you benefit by all
that happens while I who have no doubts
am being constantly deprived.
**Don Manuel.** In what way?
**Cosme.**             I'll prove it, in this way:
when our clothes are scattered all about,
the sight can only make you laugh,
but I must pick them up and set them
right again, which takes some doing.
While letters suddenly appear for you
and your witty answer's carried back,
my money's stolen and my purse
is filled instead with clinkers.
You get sweetmeats brought to you

which like a monk you gobble up
while I, who cannot touch them, stand by,
grow thin, and suffer like a pimp.
Where you get fine collars, handkerchiefs,
and shirts, I only get the shivers
for listening and observing
what goes on about me.
If we happen to arrive here
almost at the same time,
you get a basket full
of nice soft linen, while I get
a monstrous whack on the back
of my head, enough to make me
cough my brains out. You, sir,
get all the pleasure and the profit;
I get all the punishment and pain.
It's just as if that spook
were treating you with silken gloves
and me with iron claws.
So the least that you can do
is to permit me to believe
what I believe; I get drained
and purified by suffering,
which is a state denied to those
like you, who refuse to see the things
that pass before their very eyes.

**Don Manuel.** Pack the bags and come along;
I'll wait for you in Don Juan's
rooms.

**Cosme.**　　But what's there left to pack?
The Court's in mourning, and all you need
to take along is your black cape.

**Don Manuel.** Shut the door and lock it;
take the key. If someone wishes
to get in meanwhile, Don Juan
will have the other key.
—I'm perplexed at leaving now,
not knowing what's behind
these strange occurrences,
or, indeed, which matter
is more pressing. Well,
one involves my family honor
and estate, and the other
some passing divertissement.
They are really two extremes,
and obviously where honor
is concerned, it must precede
every other consideration.

*[Exeunt*

*Doña Angela's apartment*

*Enter DOÑA ANGELA, DOÑA BEATRIZ, and ISABEL.*

**Doña Angela.** And that's what happened to you?
**Isabel.** Yes, I could have sworn the jig was up,
    because if I'd been found there, madam,
    that would have been the end
    of everything, but as I've said, I
    was lucky, escaping when I did
**Doña Angela.** How extraordinary!
**Doña Beatriz.**                                    And now
    he's sure to be more puzzled
    than ever, finding the basket
    in his hand and no trace
    of anyone anywhere!
**Doña Angela.** And after all this, if I can
    manage that interview with him
    in the way I've indicated,
    he'll surely go out of his mind.
**Doña Beatriz.** At this rate Angela, the sanest
    man alive would be completely stumped.
    Imagine his wanting to find you
    and not knowing where, and then
    meeting a beautiful woman
    who's rich and elegant besides,
    and not knowing who she is or where
    she comes from (all of this
    according to your little plan),
    and finally, being led
    blindfolded in and out of the room
    so that he isn't sure where he is!
    Oh, who could possibly stand it?
**Doña Angela.** Everything's ready, and if you
    had not been here, he'd have come
    to see me for the first time
    this very night.
**Doña Beatriz.** Don't you trust me
    to keep your pretty secret?
**Doña Angela.** Oh, Cousin, I do; that's not
    what I mean. It's simply that
    your presence here keeps my brothers
    in the house; they're so in love with you,
    they burn with starry-eyed devotion,
    and while they do, they're in my way
    and I can't risk doing anything.

*Enter DON LUIS behind the arras.*

**Don Luis.** [*aside*] God, how can I hide my feelings?
    How can I rein in my thoughts, drive back
    my tongue, and bridle my emotions?
    Although I have not done so yet,
    I must at least begin to try to
    check my passion and collect myself.
**Doña Beatriz.** I shall tell you how indeed
    you may arrange these matters
    so that although I'm present I
    shan't become unwanted company.
    For I wouldn't want to go away
    and miss what happens.
**Doña Angela.**                    Well then,
    what do you suggest?
**Don Luis.** [*aside*] What is it
    they're whispering? It is as if
    they had only one voice between them.
**Doña Beatriz.** We'll pretend my father's sent for me
    and while your brothers think I've left,
    we'll manage things so that
    I really stay behind here . . .
**Don Luis.** [*aside*] Heavens, what is she plotting
    against me now?
**Doña Beatriz.**        . . . so I can watch
    what happens, secretly,
    and meanwhile not be in your way.
**Don Luis.** [*aside*] My unlucky star, what's this I hear?
**Doña Beatriz.** You've no idea how much I'd like that!
**Doña Angela.** But then what could we say
    if they saw you here again?
**Doña Beatriz.** Well, why should that surprise you?
    Don't we have brains enough to think
    of some other little stratagem?
**Don Luis.** [*aside*] I'm sure you have. The more I hear
    of this, the more I feel old griefs
    and torments welling up within me.
**Doña Beatriz.** And that is how, my dear,
    unknown to anyone,
    I shall secretly await the end
    of your remarkable affair.
    For when I'm out of sight
    and everyone has gone to bed,
    I am sure that he can safely slip
    into your room from his,
    and not give rise to any scandal.
**Don Luis.** [*aside*] Ah, now I understand it all,
    only too well. Coward that I am,
    I'll die bravely yet. Though my brother

more happily deserves her,
I am consumed by jealousy.
So she desires some occasion
to delight him, and while she plans
to meet him secretly in here,
I grovel in humiliation.
To achieve their secret end
without arousing my suspicions,
those two enemies of mine
are plotting to deceive me.
Well, if this is what they wish,
by God, I'll see to it
their little tryst is broken up.
Let her hide then, no matter where;
I'll discover some excuse to search
the house, from room to room. Oh,
I'll do it thoroughly and boldly
till I find her. This passion
burning in my heart must break out.
I have no other choice; the last
resort of jealousy is to ruin
the happiness of others.
Saints alive, support me now!
Since I am torn apart by love,
I must die of jealousy.

_[Exit_

**Doña Angela.** Fine, then it's all arranged: tomorrow
we will say you've gone away.

*Enter DON JUAN.*

**Don Juan.** Sister! And my lovely Beatriz.
**Doña Beatriz.** We have missed you all this while.
**Don Juan.** Madam, while your words do so much
to magnify my fortune's star,
by contrast they appear to dim
the sunlight of your favor
toward my humble person;
and thus grown jealous of myself,
I distrust my happiness.
For it seems impossible my love
should merit so much of your concern,
and while I am engulfed in such
a tender trap (the object
both of envy and of love), I must
both pity and distrust myself.
**Doña Beatriz.** I would never think of questioning
so flattering a compliment,
Don Juan, except of someone
who has delayed his visit

and forgotten me. For of someone
of that sort I must believe that
he was elsewhere better entertained.
So it would seem more fitting
to distrust his dalliance there,
and pitiful to see him lose
the beauteous object which
delighted him. There is, you see,
a certain syllogism proving
how one might pity and distrust
himself at once.

**Don Juan.**        If it would not
offend us both, I could attempt
to satisfy you, Beatriz,
by saying that the person
who detained me was my guest,
Don Manuel, with whom
I had until this moment
been engaged before he left
Madrid tonight.

**Doña Angela.** Oh, good gracious.

**Don Juan.** Sister, why is that so startling?

**Doña Angela.** Good news may be as startling as bad.

**Don Juan.** Then I'm sorry if you take it so,
for there's more to it you will not like:
Don Manuel returns tomorrow.

**Doña Angela.** [*aside*] And so my dying hope revives.
—I was surprised only because
the source of so much turbulence
at home should disappear so quickly.

**Don Juan.** I cannot understand why
you found it troublesome at all.
Yet you and Don Luis appear
to be annoyed only, as it seems,
because the presence of our guest
gives me so much pleasure.

**Doña Angela.** I might easily say more to that
but shan't, and that's because
I wouldn't dream of interfering
in the game of love; as anyone
should know, I'd only be
a nuisance where three's a crowd,
for lovers' blandishments, like tricks
at cards, are more slyly interchanged
between a twosome pure and simple.
[*aside to ISABEL*] Come with me, Isabel.
I must carry off that portrait
tonight. While the coast is clear,
I can do that more easily.

Make sure you have the candle ready,
and we can go in unobserved.
I take it as an insult
that a gentleman who corresponds
with me should keep the portrait
of another woman.

*[Exeunt DOÑA ANGELA and ISABEL*

**Doña Beatriz.** I doubt your protestations are as
pure and weighty as you make them seem.
**Don Juan.** Then to prove to you I am sincere,
I'll weigh each one until they're clear.
May I proceed?
**Doña Beatriz.**      Why, yes indeed!
**Don Juan.** Then listen to me carefully.

Fair Beatriz, I swear my faith's so true,
My love's so firm, my deep regard's so rare,
That if I tried to bury love's desire
I'd find, despite myself, I must love you.
This then is my condition: if decree
Bade me forget you, I'd forget you clear—
That I might choose to love you, made more dear
In consequence of this than formerly.
Who's bound to love his mistress only when
He can't forget her is not bound by love.
Deprived of will, he cannot love her then.
I can't forget you, lovely Beatriz,
And regret to see my star so satisfied
To achieve the victory of your love.

**Doña Beatriz.**

If will is all you need to make your choice,
And eyes like fitful stars to give consent,
It seems to me your precepts both are spent
Upon uncertainties, nay, mere caprice.
Therefore, I must distrust your courtesies;
The impossible is what my faith must bend,
And if my will fell short of such intent,
Good grief! I'd view it with distinct surprise.
And as for that brief moment's lapse, aimed at
Forgetfulness so I might love you dearer,
I fear all fondness would evaporate.
And thus I find I cannot but deplore
Forgetfulness, for while I'd be engaged
In that, I wouldn't love you any more.

*[Exeunt*

*A street*

*Enter COSME, running, and DON MANUEL, chasing him.*

**Don Manuel.** Good God! If I didn't think . . .

**Cosme.** That's it, sir, do stop and think.

**Don Manuel.** . . . how degrading it would be
   to strike you . . .

**Cosme.**          Consider
   how faithfully I've served you
   and that a good Christian's not to blame
   if he's got a bad memory.

**Don Manuel.** Who'd have any patience with you,
   tell me who, when you forget
   the very thing that's most important,
   which I clearly ordered you to bring.

**Cosme.** Yes, that's just why I forgot it—
   because it *was* so important.
   If it hadn't been, how could I
   forget it? Hell's bells, it was
   my taking such special pains
   that made me put those papers
   carefully aside. So it was
   being thoughtful caused all the mischief.
   Otherwise I would not have packed them
   separately, and they'd have been here
   now with all our other things.

**Don Manuel.** At least it's fortunate you thought
   of them while we are still en route.

**Cosme.** I was worried there was something wrong,
   but didn't know just what.
   I thought it must be something foolish
   till it dawned on me—like that!
   And then I knew it had to do
   with all that fuss about
   remembering to bring those papers.

**Don Manuel.** Tell the boy to tie the mules
   and wait for us, there's no point
   in our making any noise
   and rousing the family.
   They must be fast asleep by now.
   Since I have the key, I can get in
   and find the papers without
   disturbing anyone.

                       *[Exit COSME, who returns at once*

**Cosme.** I've told the boy to wait.
   Now consider, sir, it would be

a very bad mistake to think
of doing this without a light.
You cannot possibly avoid
making some noise without one;
and if we do not get a light
from Don Juan's apartment,
how are we to find a thing?

**Don Manuel.** How tiresome you are!
Are you suggesting that I shout
and wake Don Juan? Can't you conceive,
you simpleton, you clumsy fool,
we've got to make our way
by groping in the dark and find
the papers where you left them?

**Cosme.** That's not what I'm afraid of. Of course,
I know I left them on the table
and can find them in the dark.

**Don Manuel.** Now open the door, at once.

**Cosme.** What bothers me is that I won't know
where the spook has hidden them.
Indeed, when have I ever put
anything down there and not found it
lying somewhere else again?

**Don Manuel.** There'll be time enough to ask for
candles if the papers aren't there.
Until then, I shall not rouse
our gracious host to whom
we owe so much already.

*[Exeunt DON MANUEL and COSME*

### DON MANUEL's apartment

*Enter DOÑA ANGELA and ISABEL through the panel.*

**Doña Angela.** Isabel, everyone's retired
and sunk in sleep that steals
half their lives away. Now our guest
has left, I must carry off
the portrait I saw here last time.

**Isabel.** Gently now, let's not make a sound.

**Doña Angela.** Go back and bolt my chamber door.
I'll stay here till you return.
I shan't take any further risks.

**Isabel.** Be sure and wait for me here.

*[Exit ISABEL, closing the panel behind her*

*Enter DON MANUEL and COSME in the dark.*

**Cosme.** [*whispering to his master in the doorway*] It's open, sir.

256

**Don Manuel.** Step lightly.
 Any noise heard coming from this room
 would throw the house into a turmoil.
**Cosme.** Would you believe it? I'm not afraid.
 At least that spook might have
 the decency to light a candle
 for us now.
**Doña Angela.** I may as well take out
 the candle I brought along.
 No one will see it now.

> [*At the opposite end of the room from DON
> MANUEL and COSME, she lights the
> candle in a lantern she has brought.*]

**Cosme.** [*aside to his master*] No sooner said than done!
 That spook was never so obliging.
 See, sir, how fond he is of you?
 When you appear now, a light is lit;
 when I appeared before,
 he snuffed out mine.
**Don Manuel.**                God help me, but this
 is really supernatural!
 Suddenly a light appears—
 it's just not human!
**Cosme.**                Aha,
 and so you finally admit
 that I was right.
**Don Manuel.** I'm petrified!
 I'm for getting out of here.
**Cosme.** So, you're only human after all.
 You're scared.
**Doña Angela.** I see the table there,
 and there are papers lying on it.
**Cosme.** It's moving toward the table.
**Don Manuel.** Good God! Can I believe my eyes?
 How can I take all this in?
**Cosme.** Do you notice how it leads us on
 to the very thing we came for,
 and yet we can't make out who
 it is carrying that light?
**Doña Angela.**

> [*She takes the candle out of the lantern, puts it into a
> candlestick on the table, pulls up a chair and sits
> down, with her back towards them.*]

 I'll put the light here now
 and go through these papers.
**Don Manuel.** Hold on! Everything comes clear now
 in the candlelight. I have

never seen such perfect beauty
in all my life. God in Heaven,
what am I to make of this?
Wonders seem to spring up
Hydra-headed all about me.
What in the world shall I do?

**Cosme.** She surely takes her own sweet time.
Now she's moved the chair.

**Don Manuel.**                    The hand of God
has never drawn a creature
half so beautiful before.

**Cosme.** True enough: there's nothing earthly
to her.

**Don Manuel.** Her lustrous eyes
outshine the candlelight.

**Cosme.** I'd say her eyes are lamps
like Lucifer's that fell from Heaven.

**Don Manuel.** Her radiant hair glints like sunlight.

**Cosme.** Also stolen from above, no doubt.

**Don Manuel.** Her curls, a diadem of stars.

**Cosme.** She very likely swooped them up
and brought them here as well,
from Paradise, Limbo, or Hell.

**Don Manuel.** I never saw such utter loveliness!

**Cosme.** I'll wager you wouldn't say so
if you could see her feet;
the likes of her are always sure
to have a pair of cloven hooves.

**Don Manuel.** Wondrous beauty, angel fair!

**Cosme.** Yes, it's as I say: an infernal
angel, cursed in the hoof.

**Don Manuel.** I wonder what she means to do
with all my papers.

**Cosme.**                    I would guess
she simply wants to go through them
and find the things you're looking for,
just to be saving you the trouble.
Oh, she's a helpful little devil.

**Don Manuel.** God only knows what I should do.
I've never thought myself a coward
till this moment.

**Cosme.**                    Unlike me,
who always have.

**Don Manuel.** I feel as though
my feet were bound in icy chains,
my hair, standing on its ends,
and every breath I draw,

like a dagger thrust straight
to the heart, or like a rope
tightened round my throat.
Must I go on like this, a prey
to my own fears? No, by Heaven,
I'll break this spell, I will!

[*He moves forward and seizes her arm.*]

Angel, woman, or devil,
I swear you won't slip by me this time!

**Doña Angela.** [*aside*] Good God, I'm lost! He didn't
go away—he just pretended to.
And now he's outwitted me.

**Cosme.** In God's Name (that should bring
a devil to its knees), tell us . . .

**Doña Angela.** [*aside*] But I'll brazen it through.

**Cosme.** . . . who thou art and what it is
thou seekest here.

**Doña Angela.** Most noble
Don Manuel Enríquez:
an enormous treasure lies in store
for thee. Therefore, unhand me,
come no closer, under pain
of forfeiting the very fortune
Heaven has reserved for thee,
in token of so favorable
a destiny and its
immutable decrees.
It was I who wrote to thee
this evening, and in that letter,
foreseeing this occasion,
promised we two soon would meet.
Since I have kept my word and come,
as now thou seest me, in the most
tangible of human forms
I could have chosen, depart in peace
and leave me. For the time
is not yet come when thou may'st fairly
seek to learn more concerning me.
Tomorrow thou shalt know all. Meanwhile,
forbear to breathe a word of this
to anyone, or thou shalt lose
thy greatest treasure. Go in peace.

**Cosme.** Well, sir, what is it you're waiting for?
She's told us twice we're free to go
in peace.

**Don Manuel.** [*aside*] By God, I am ashamed
such idle fears deluded me.
Now that I've regained my sanity,
I must get to the bottom

of this mystery once for all.
—Lady, whomsoever thou art
(and I cannot bring myself
to think thou art anything
less tangible), I am resolved,
by all that's sacred, to discover
thy name, by what means thou camest here,
and with what intent. And I shall not
wait another day for such
enlightenment. Speak as a devil,
if thou art one, or as a woman,
if such thou art. If thou art
the very devil, my valor
will not flinch or quail at any threat
or menace thou canst utter.
I know well enough that whilst thy shape
remains corporeal,
thou art no devil, but a woman.

**Cosme.** It's one and the same.

**Doña Angela.**                     Forbear
to touch me, or lose thy joy at once.

**Cosme.** This devil gives you good advice.
    Don't touch her; she's not a harp
    or lute or rebeck.

**Don Manuel.**            Indeed,
    we'll let my sword decide this.
    Art thou a spirit? Then

                                      [*drawing his sword*]

    though this blade penetrate,
    it cannot do thee harm.

**Doña Angela.** Mercy me! Drop your sword,
    your cruel, bloodthirsty arm.
    How can you kill a poor unhappy
    woman? I confess that's all I am.
    If it is a crime to love someone,
    it is surely not so heinous
    as to deserve such punishment.
    Please, do not stain or tarnish
    with my blood the roset
    of your sword.

**Don Manuel.**       Tell me who you are.

**Doña Angela.** It seems at last I'm forced to do so,
    and thereby call a halt to all
    my fancies' fond designs,
    the purity of my desire,
    the sweet and earnest pledge of love.
    But, sir, we are now in mortal
    danger if we're seen or overheard.
    I am much more than you take me for.

So let me entreat you, sir,
lest we be discovered here,
secure that door and the entrance
to the alcove also.
Then, if anyone should happen by,
our light will not be visible.
**Don Manuel.** Go, Cosme, bring the candle
so we can bolt the doors.
It's a woman now, you see,
and not a phantom.
**Cosme.**                     But didn't I
admit they're one and the same?

> *[Exeunt DON MANUEL and COSME*

**Doña Angela.** Gracious, Isabel has shut
the panel on the other side,
and now there's no way out.
I'm obliged to tell our guest the truth.
I've been caught red-handed in his room.

> *Enter ISABEL, through the panel.*

**Isabel.** Hist, hist, madam! Your brother
is asking for you.
**Doña Angela.**        In the nick
of time! Come now, and be sure
you shut the panel behind us.
Ah, my love, you must entertain
your doubts a little longer.

> *[Exeunt DOÑA ANGELA and ISABEL through
> the panel just as DON MANUEL
> and COSME enter the room*

**Don Manuel.** Now the doors have all been bolted,
madam, you may proceed to tell . . .
But what's this? Where is she?
**Cosme.** How should I know?
**Don Manuel.**                         Perhaps
she's gone into the alcove. Go ahead
and look.
**Cosme.**     It would be discourteous
of me to walk ahead of you.
**Don Manuel.** I'll search this place from top
to bottom. Hand me that light, I say.
**Cosme.** Oh, but you're welcome to it.

> *[DON MANUEL seizes the candle, goes into
> the alcove and returns again.]*

**Don Manuel.** No luck—how cruel!
**Cosme.**                         This time, at least,
you cannot say she went out the door.
**Don Manuel.** Well, how did she get out?

**Cosme.** That's beyond me, sir. But do you see?
It's just as I've always said:
she's a phantom, not a woman.
**Don Manuel.** By God, I'll search through every nook
and cranny in this apartment.
Surely there's an opening behind
some picture frame on those walls
or a trapdoor of some sort
underneath those carpets—
perhaps an archway through the ceiling!
**Cosme.** The only thing that I can think of
is that large mirror.
**Don Manuel.** No, it's clear
there's nothing there but one large surface
made of smaller panes of glass.
We must look elsewhere.
**Cosme.**                                    Sir,
I've always been averse to prying.
**Don Manuel.** I am still convinced she is no phantom.
She had sense enough to fear death.
**Cosme.** She also had another sense by which
she could foretell we'd be obliged
to come back here tonight and see her.
**Don Manuel.** There was something ghostly in the way
she suddenly appeared
in that fantastic light,
but there was also something human
in the way that she avoided
being seen and touched—
something mortal in her fear,
something feminine in her distrust.
Yet she simply came apart
like an illusion, and
like a spirit vanished in the air.
By God, if I gave this matter
any further thought, who knows,
who knows if I could any longer
separate credulity from doubt.
**Cosme.** It's all quite clear to me.
**Don Manuel.**                                    What?
**Cosme.** That the lady is the devil.
But there's nothing unusual
about it: when women are such devils
all year round, I wouldn't blame
the devil if he turned woman
to get even with them once for all.

## ACT THREE

### DOÑA ANGELA's *apartment*

*Enter DON MANUEL in the dark, being led by ISABEL.*

**Isabel.** Wait here in this room, sir;
  my mistress will see you shortly.

*[Exit, closing the door behind her*

**Don Manuel.** Well, this time I've not been tricked.
  Did you lock the door? She did.
  The suspense is more than I can bear!
  I found this note awaiting me when
  I returned from the Escorial;
  it was written by the same
  bewitching pilgrim, that wondrous
  beauty who last night lit the light
  but still keeps me in the dark.
  Yet her words are very tender:
  "If you would dare," she writes,
  "to come and see me, you must go
  out this evening with your servant
  until you reach the graveyard"
  (that's the odd part!) "behind
  the Church of Saint Sebastian,
  where two men will be waiting for you
  with a sedan chair." And she
  was serious. I was brought there,
  stumbled about, and lost my bearings
  totally. Then I found myself
  before a grisly-looking doorway, and
  went through it full of grim forebodings.
  In pitch darkness I found a woman
  (or so she seemed) waiting there alone.
  And without a word she led me
  from one room to another.
  I said nothing, heard nothing,
  saw nothing. I only groped my way
  behind her till I came here.
  Ah, now I see a light glimmering
  through the keyhole.

*[Looking through the keyhole.]*

        Ah, love, at last
you've conquered me; there's the lady now.
The risks were all worth taking.
What a magnificent house!
What an exquisite table!
And what lovely women! Look

how elegant they are!
How they glitter as they walk!
Such complete magnificence!

       *[The door is opened, and several ladies enter carrying*
       *napkins, sweetmeats, and water, curtseying as they*
       *pass DOÑA ANGELA, who is seated*
       *elegantly dressed, before them.]*

**Doña Angela.** *[aside to DOÑA BEATRIZ]*
Since my brothers assume you've gone home,
you'll be safe and sound here.
There'll be no excuse for their intruding,
and nothing at all for you to fear
while you stay here with me.
**Doña Beatriz.** *[aside to DOÑA ANGELA]* And what's my
role to be?
**Doña Angela.** *[aside to DOÑA BEATRIZ]* First, you'll be
my servant;
then you may withdraw and watch
everything that happens later.
*[to DON MANUEL]*
Are you weary of waiting for me?
**Don Manuel.** Not in the least, madam.
Whoever would await the dawn
knows full well that he must fret away
the cold and dismal night, by which he
is the more rewarded for his pains;
indeed, the longer he must wait,
the more surely will he
appreciate the day.
Yet I hardly think I need have
suffered through such darkness
had I known how much dazzling light
your beauty held in store.
For now I realize the splendor
of your all-pervading radiance
would not be dimmed by any
of the deepest shades of night.
Madam, you are the day itself
and have no need for sun to rise.
The night flies, madam, before the dawn's
sweet smiling promise, it will shine,
and yet will not illuminate.
Then when dawn gives way to morning,
its niggard rays illuminate,
and yet they will not burn.
Then morning light gives way
to the very sun itself,
and only such a sun
can shine, illuminate, and burn.

Dawn, if it would shine, must send night
packing, and morning, in its turn,
merely follow in the tracks of dawn,
if it would illuminate.
But where the all-pervading sun
defies them both, you in turn
defy the very sun,
which is why I say I need not
have suffered through the cold night darkness
had I known your sun of suns
would now arise to crown the day.

**Doña Angela.** Although I'm grateful to you, sir,
for such a pretty speech, I am
afraid your flattery's excessive
and rather questionable.
We do not dwell in Heaven's mansion
where the noblest passion
is so stormily expressed it would
reduce a tempest to exhaustion.
We live in this poor humble house
where such exaggerations
as you offer sound suspicious.
Do not compare me to the dawn
whose fixed smile I do not share,
for I am not frequently so blissful.
Nor am I like the early morning
light in shedding pearly tears;
I hope you have not found me weeping.
Nor can I like the sun divide
the light of truth I love
into so many parts.
And so, although I cannot say
exactly what I'm like,
I only know I'm not the dawn,
the morning, or the sun of day.
At least I cannot think I am
the sunlight all aglow,
or weeping like a stream.
In sum, my dear Don Manuel,
the only thing I'd have you say
of me is that I've always been
and am a woman, and you are
the only man I have ever asked
to visit me in private.

**Don Manuel.** But that comes to very little,
madam, for though I've come to see you
finally, I might say your
indulgence gives me more grounds
for regret than pleasure.

Indeed, you have offended me.

**Doña Angela.** *I*, offended *you*, sir?

**Don Manuel.** Yes, because you do not trust me
    well enough to tell me who you are.

**Doña Angela.** That is the one thing I beg you
    not to ask of me, for I cannot
    possibly enlighten you.
    If you wish to visit me,
    you may do so only
    on condition you do not seek
    to know or ask my name.
    I can only tell you this now:
    Accept me as something enigmatic,
    for I am not what I appear
    to be nor does my appearance now
    belie the person that I am.
    So long as I remain in hiding,
    you may see me, and I see you;
    but once you satisfy
    your curiosity and learn my name,
    you shan't be fond of me again,
    though I continue fond of you.
    When death has limned the features,
    what one sees is not a portrait.
    The life descried in one light
    is transfigured when it appears
    in any other. The same is true
    of Love, the painter, for whom I sit
    portrayed in double light,
    which is why I fear that what you
    delight to see in me at present
    is but one aspect of me, and that
    perhaps you will detest me when
    you come to see me in the other.
    All that I can tell you now
    which matters to me is that
    your notion about my being
    the mistress of Don Luis
    was utterly mistaken.
    You have my word, there is no ground
    for any such suspicion.

**Don Manuel.** Then, madam, what drove you
    to escape from him?

**Doña Angela.**          It may be
    my reputation was at stake,
    something I risked losing if I were
    recognized by Don Luis.

**Don Manuel.** Well, then, tell me at least
    how you managed to enter this house?

**Doña Angela.** I cannot tell you that just yet—
  another troublesome detail.
**Doña Beatriz.** [*aside*] That's my cue to enter graciously.
  The sweetmeats and iced water are served.
  Will Your Excellency observe
  if there is anything . . .

> [*The ladies come forward with napkins,*
> *water, trays of sweets.*]

**Doña Angela.** How gauche, how impertinent of you!
  Idiot! Whom are you addressing
  as Your Excellency? Is this
  the way you would deceive
  Don Manuel to make him think
  I am a lady of some rank?
**Doña Beatriz.** Indeed, I did not mean . . .
**Don Manuel.** [*aside*] There, that was a slip, enough to lift
  the irksome veil on all my doubts.
  Now I know she is a noblewoman,
  which is why she's so intent
  on cloaking her identity;
  and so, it was her money
  that devised and kept her secret
  plan in motion all this while.

> [*The voice of DON JUAN is heard;*
> *general consternation ensues.*]

**Don Juan** [*offstage*] Isabel, open this door.
**Doña Angela** [*aside*] Good Heavens! Who's knocking?
**Isabel.** I shall die!
**Doña Beatriz.** [*aside*] I am frozen stiff!
**Don Manuel.** [*aside*] God preserve me, my troubles
  aren't over yet.
**Doña Angela.**     That's
  my father at the door, sir.
**Don Manuel.**                What am I to do?
**Doña Angela.**                          You must go
  and hide somewhere out of sight.
  Isabel, take the gentleman
  to that other apartment—you know
  which—and see to it he's well hidden.
  Do you understand?
**Isabel.**                Perfectly.
  Come along, sir—at once.
**Don Juan.** [*offstage*] Won't you ever open this door?
**Don Manuel.** So help me, there goes my life,
  and my honor too, in one fell swoop.

> [*Exeunt DON MANUEL and ISABEL*

**Don Juan.** [*offstage*] Very well, I'll smash the door in.
**Doña Angela.** You might step into the entry,

Beatriz; they mustn't find you here.

[*Exit DOÑA BEATRIZ*

*Enter DON JUAN.*

**Doña Angela.** Now what brings you to my room
    at this hour of the night,
    and making such an uproar too?
**Don Juan.** Angela, first you answer me:
    what do you mean by wearing
    such a dress?
**Doña Angela.**    As my grief and sorrow
    require me to wear deep mourning
    constantly, I imagined I might
    lift my heavy spirits by donning
    these fineries for a change.
**Don Juan.** I don't doubt it. Though a woman's grief
    invariably is cured
    once she's decked herself in fineries
    and then convalesces with her jewels,
    in your case I find such
    consolations quite indecorous.
**Doña Angela.** Why should it matter if I change
    my gown, when no one comes to see me?
**Don Juan.** Tell me, has Beatriz gone home?
**Doña Angela.** Yes, her father's thought it wiser
    to cool his anger and has now
    made up with her.
**Don Juan.**    That is all
    I wished to know. Now perhaps
    I can see and talk to her tonight.
    Good night, but remember,
    that frippery is not for you.

[*Exit*

**Doña Angela.** Good night to you—and good riddance.

*Enter DOÑA BEATRIZ.*

**Doña Angela.** Beatriz, bolt that door.
**Doña Beatriz.** We've got out of that impasse
    very nicely. Now your brother's off
    to look for me.
**Doña Angela.**    Before we rouse
    anyone else and Don Manuel
    comes out to look for me,
    let's retire to that little room
    where no one will disturb us.
**Doña Beatriz.** If everything turns out the way
    you planned it, you'll really earn
    the title *Phantom Lady.*

[*Exeunt*

### DON MANUEL's *apartment*

*Enter DON MANUEL and ISABEL in the dark, through the panel.*

**Isabel.** You must stay here now, sir;
and be careful not to make a sound—
someone's sure to hear you.
**Don Manuel.** I'll be still as marble.
**Isabel.** Dear God, let me stop trembling
so I can shut this panel tight.

*[Exit*

**Don Manuel.** Lord, what risks a man takes
who dares intrude inside a house
where he can never know or sense
the pitfalls that await him,
the dangers lurking all around him.
So here I am, in some stranger's house,
and the owner a member
of the nobility—at least
she's called Your Excellency—
and this place, so far away
from Don Juan's house, is full of
ominous and flitting shadows.
What's that now? Someone on the other
side is opening the door. Yes,
and now he's coming in here.

*Enter COSME.*

**Cosme.** Thank God I can get into
my room tonight so handily [*groping*]
and not be frightened, though I come
and go without a light; but since
my lord the phantom seized my master,
what in the world would he want with me?

*[Running into DON MANUEL]*

Oh-oh, there *is* something he wants.
Who's that? Who is it?
**Don Manuel.**                     Be still,
I tell you, whoever you are,
or I'll run you through with this sword.
**Cosme.** I'll be mum as a poor relative
sitting at a rich man's table.
**Don Manuel.** [*aside*] This must be a servant
who happened to come by.
I'll try to get him to tell me
where I am.—Come now, whose house
is this, and who is the owner?
**Cosme.** Sir, the house and owner both

269

belong to Satan, because there is
a lady living here who's called
the Phantom Lady, and she's
the very devil.
**Don Manuel.** And who are you?
**Cosme.** An attendant, or you might say
a serving man; I'm a subject
and a slave, and I don't know
how or why I stand it,
but I have been bewitched.
**Don Manuel.** And who's your master?
**Cosme.**                                   A madman,
a fool, a meddlesome idiot,
a perfect ass, and hopelessly
in love with that lady.
**Don Manuel.** And what's his name?
**Cosme.**                                   Don Manuel
Enríquez.
**Don Manuel.** In God's Name!
**Cosme.** As for me, my name's Cosme
Catiboratos.
**Don Manuel.**   Cosme,
is that you? How did you get in?
It's your master. Tell me.
did you follow behind my sedan?
And did you come in, like me,
to hide in this apartment?
**Cosme.** A nice little game you're playing!
Tell me, how did you get here?
Weren't you the brave chap who sallied
forth alone to that distant churchyard?
Then how did you get back so soon?
And how in the world did you
get in here when I had the key
to the apartment all this time?
**Don Manuel.** Now you tell me: what apartment
are we in?
**Cosme.**      If it isn't yours,
it must surely be the devil's.
**Don Manuel.** You lie in your throat! Only
a moment ago I was far away
from here, in quite a different house.
**Cosme.** Well, then the devil's had a hand
in it, because what I've told you
is nothing but the honest truth.
**Don Manuel.** You'll drive me out of my mind.
**Cosme.** Do you need further proof? Just step
through that doorway to the alcove,

and see if you don't recognize the place.
**Don Manuel.** A good idea. I'll go and see.

[Exit

**Cosme.** [*to the audience*] Ah, ladies and gentlemen:
when shall we be done
with all this sham and muddle?

Enter ISABEL, through the panel.

**Isabel.** [*aside*] Now that Don Juan's returned,
I must get Don Manuel away
so that he won't be found here.
—Hist, sir, hist.
**Cosme.**                Oh, worse and worse: those *hists*
go straight to my sciatica!
**Isabel.** My master's gone to bed, sir.
**Cosme.** [*aside*] What master's that?

Enter DON MANUEL.

**Don Manuel.**                        Yes, this is my
apartment, no doubt of it.
**Isabel.** Is that you?
**Cosme.** Yes, it's me.
**Isabel.** Then come along with me.
**Don Manuel.** You were perfectly right.
**Isabel.** Don't be afraid. I won't mislead you.
**Cosme.** Oh, please, sir: the phantom
is towing me away.

[ISABEL takes COSME by the hand<br>and leads him through the panel.

**Don Manuel.** Won't we ever get to the bottom
of this mystery? You don't answer.
What a blockhead you are!
Cosme, Cosme! Good Lord,
there's nothing but the four walls now.
Wasn't I just speaking with him?
Where did he disappear to
suddenly? Wasn't he just here?
I really must be going mad.
Still, it's clear somebody else came in
from somewhere; I must find out
how and where. I'll hide in this alcove
and wait there patiently
till I can determine
who this wondrous Phantom Lady is.

[Exit

### *DOÑA ANGELA's apartment*

*Enter all the ladies, one with lit candles, another with assorted trays, and still another with a pitcher of water.*

**Doña Angela.** Now my brother's left to search for you
and Isabel's gone off to bring
Don Manuel from his room,
everything's in readiness.
He'll find this collation waiting
when he comes. Let us all
prepare to take our places.
**Doña Beatriz.** I've never seen the likes of this
in all my life.
**Doña Angela.**    Is he coming?
**Servant.**                    Yes.
I hear his footsteps now.

*Enter ISABEL, leading COSME by the hand.*

**Cosme.** Poor me, where am I going?
This joke's gone far enough.
But no . . . now I'm gazing at
a swarm of perfect beauties!
Am I really Cosme, or am I
Amadis of Gaul? Just little
Cosme, or Belianis of Greece?
**Isabel.** He's coming in. But what's this I see?
Sir!
**Cosme.** [*aside*] Now I'm sure I am bewitched.
My soul's about to leave my body.
**Doña Angela.** What's the meaning of this, Isabel?
**Isabel.** [*aside to her mistress*] Madam, I went back to where I'd left
Don Manuel and brought his servant
here by some mistake.
**Doña Angela.**          Don't gild
the truth; you've made a mess of it.
**Isabel.** It was dark.
**Doña Angela.**       Goodness me,
now it will all come out.
**Doña Beatriz.** [*aside*] Never mind, Angela.
This is even better. —Cosme.
**Cosme.** Damiana.
**Doña Beatriz.**     Come closer.
**Cosme.** I'm happy here.
**Doña Angela.**        Come, come.
You needn't be frightened.
**Cosme.** Frightened? A brave man like me?
**Doña Angela.** Then why stand so far away?

[*He advances toward them.*]

**Cosme.** [*aside*] There's no hanging back where
    a point of honor has been made.
    —Whenever there's respect you'll find
    some awe and fear mixed in with it,
    though Lucifer himself
    would hardly frighten me
    if he were dressed up as a lady.
    And he surely tried it once:
    brewing up a little stratagem,
    he slipped into some petticoats
    and a whalebone corset.
    For who but the devil himself
    could have invented such stuff?
    Well, that's just how he appeared,
    disguised as some wealthy, fair
    young damsel, before a shepherd.
    No sooner did the shepherd clap eyes
    on her than his heart was swept
    by flames of love. After the shepherd
    enjoyed the devil-lady,
    the devil changed shape, becoming
    something horrible and ugly
    and then he raised his voice:
    "Miserable creature," he said,
    "do you see the sort of beauty,
    all dressed up from wig to toes,
    that you have fallen for?
    Despair now: you have knowingly
    committed mortal sin."
    Well, the shepherd, less contrite
    than he was before he had enjoyed
    the lady, told the devil off:
    "Oh, vain and insubstantial shade!
    if you really wish to drive a wretch
    like me to despair, come again
    tomorrow morning, dressed up
    as you were before. You'll find me
    no less loving or obliging
    than I was just now. And be
    the devil, if you wish,
    because however horrible
    you are, a woman's just a woman
    in a dress."
**Doña Angela.** Collect yourself.
    Here, take a sweetmeat and some water.
    Fright sometimes brings on thirst.
**Cosme.** I'm not thirsty, though.
**Doña Beatriz.**                 Come here.

You've two hundred leagues to go, you know,
before you can get home again.
**Cosme.** Heavens, what's that noise?

[*Someone calling*]

**Doña Angela.**                              Is there
someone calling?
**Doña Beatriz.** Yes, indeed.
**Isabel.** [*aside*] How awful!
**Doña Angela.** [*aside*]            Gracious me!
**Don Luis.** [*offstage*] Isabel.
**Doña Beatriz.** [*aside*]            Good Heavens!
**Don Luis.** [*offstage*] Open this door!
**Doña Angela.** [*aside*]                        I've a brother
for every shock.
**Isabel.**                  And this the worst
of all.
**Doña Beatriz.** I'm going to hide.

[*Exit*

**Cosme.** [*aside*] That must be the honest-to-goodness
Phantom.
**Isabel.** [*to COSME*] Come with me.
**Cosme.**                              By all means.

[*Exeunt ISABEL and COSME*

*The door opens; enter DON LUIS.*

**Doña Angela.** What are you doing here
in my apartment?
**Don Luis.**                My own distress
compels me to disturb
the happiness of others.
I know that Beatriz is back;
I saw her sedan chair here lately
in the house, and I also know
my brother's somewhere hereabout.
**Doña Angela.** Well, what is it you wish?
**Don Luis.** I heard footsteps overhead, and thought
there must be visitors upstairs;
I came up only to make sure
I was mistaken.

[*He raises a portiere and finds BEATRIZ.*]

                        Is that you,
Beatriz?

[*BEATRIZ returns.*]

**Doña Beatriz.** Yes, it's me.
I had to come back. My father grew
annoyed again, and he's still angry.
**Don Luis.** You both seem quite confused here.
What extraordinary mischief's

274

going on with all these glasses,
plates, and sweetmeats?
**Doña Angela.**                    Are you simply
asking us to tell you how women
Entertain themselves when they're alone?

                    [*ISABEL and COSME make a sound at the panel.*]

**Don Luis.** Now that noise, how do you explain it?
**Doña Angela.** [*aside*] I think I'll die!
**Don Luis.**                    By God,
there *is* someone lurking there!
I only hope it's not my brother
hiding from me in this fashion.

                                        [*Takes a lit candle.*]

Merciful Heavens! The foolish
jealousy love planted in my heart
which drove me here to interfere
now gives way to insult.
Yet I must take this candle,
however rashly, and if light
uncovers everything,
light my way to honor lost.

                                                    [*Exit*

**Doña Angela.** Oh, Beatriz, we're lost
if they should meet!
**Doña Beatriz.**              You needn't worry;
once Isabel gets him to his
master's room, you can be sure
that Don Luis won't find out
about the secret panel.
**Doña Angela.** But, as luck would have it, what if
Isabel is so confused
she forgets to bolt the panel,
and then he follows her straight through?
**Doña Beatriz.** Well, then you'd better think
of finding refuge somewhere.
**Doña Angela.** I'll take advantage of your father,
just as he has of me.
Fate has turned the tables now:
if one sorrow brought you to my house,
another leads me home to yours.

                    [*Exeunt DOÑA ANGELA and DOÑA BEATRIZ*

### DON MANUEL'S apartment

*Enter ISABEL, COSME, DON MANUEL; later DON LUIS.*

**Isabel.** Get in, quickly.

                                                    *Exit*

**Don Manuel.**                I hear someone
in the entryway again.

            *Enter DON LUIS, with a lit candle.*

**Don Luis.** [*aside*] I can make out the figure
of a man there. By God!
**Cosme.** This looks bad.
**Don Luis.**              How does this panel come
to be ajar?
**Cosme.** Oh-oh, there's a light.
Here's where that table I found
will come in handy.

                     [*He crawls under the table.*]

**Don Manuel.** It's time to settle this at once.

                    [*He puts his hand on his sword.*

**Don Luis.** Don Manuel!
**Don Manuel.**             Don Luis!
What's this all about? I've never
been so mystified before!
**Cosme.** [*aside*] Well, just listen to him admit it!
I could have said so a thousand times.
**Don Luis.** Villain! You do not deserve the name
of gentleman! Traitor, ungrateful
wretch, you who would violate
the friendship and hospitality
of this house! You who would trifle
so shamelessly with the honor
of a man who has trusted
and befriended you!

                     [*Draws his sword.*]

            Since you dare
be so offensive, draw
your miserable sword and fight.
**Don Manuel.** Yes, I shall draw, but only
to defend myself. Can you really
be addressing me? I am
bewildered, and can hardly believe
my senses. Yet you cannot kill me,
though you try; a lifetime spent
in overcoming cruel misfortunes
has made me invulnerable;
nor can your sword, if this be
your intent, unhinge a life
already injured to the quick
by your accusations,
for however capable
your strong right arm may be,
the sorrow which your words inflict
is stronger—indeed, is mortal.

**Don Luis.** Soft replies will not stop me now;
only your sword will do that.
**Don Manuel.**                    At least
stop long enough to tell me, Don
Luis: Is there no other way
I can satisfy you in this?
**Don Luis.** After what you've done, how can you
speak of any other recourse?
Did you not use the secret panel
to enter that wanton's rooms?
Is there any satisfying
such an insult?
**Don Manuel.** Don Luis,
I would gladly suffer you to run
my body through a thousand times
if I so much as knew that there was
such a panel or that it opened
on anyone's apartment.
**Don Luis.** Then what were you doing here alone
without a light?
**Don Manuel.** [*aside*] What shall I tell him?
—I was waiting for my servant.
**Don Luis.** When I myself saw you hiding here?
Shall I doubt my own two eyes?
**Don Manuel.** Yes, for sight is more deceptive
than any other sense.
**Don Luis.** And if my eyes deceived me,
did my ears deceive me too?
**Don Manuel.** Yes, they did.
**Don Luis.**                    They all lie, then,
while only you can tell the truth,
and still it was you alone who . . .
**Don Manuel.** Stop there, or I'll cut you down
before you say another word, or
even think it, or imagine it.
If you want daring, I'm your man.
I've borne enough, for friendship's sake.
If we must come to blows,
let's do it properly. First, we'll
share this light between us, equally;
then, you bolt that door through which
you rashly entered, while I fasten
this other one. Now I'll throw this key
upon the floor. Whoever survives
can pick it up and flee.
**Don Luis.** I'll shut off the entrance
through this panel by placing
the table against it. Then no one

can possibly get in.

[*Lifting the table, he finds COSME.*]

**Cosme.** [*aside*] Well, the jig is up.

**Don Luis.** .                     Who's this here?

**Don Manuel.** Oh, my unhappy stars!

**Cosme.**                     No one's here.

**Don Luis.** Look here, Don Manuel. Isn't this
   the servant you were waiting for?

**Don Manuel.** There's no point in discussing that now.
   My cause is just; you may think
   whatever you wish. Once our swords
   are drawn, only one of us will live
   to boast about it.

**Don Luis.**          I'm for you, then.
   Why are you delaying?

**Don Manuel.** You presume too much. I am
   considering what to do about
   my servant; if I throw him out,
   he'll go for help; if I let him stay,
   that puts you to a disadvantage
   since he's sure to come to my aid.

**Cosme.** I won't, if it's inconvenient.

**Don Luis.** There's a door to that alcove.
   If you shut him up inside,
   we'll be on equal terms again.

**Don Manuel.** A good idea. Get in and stay there.

**Cosme.** What's all this to-do about
   keeping me out of the fight,
   when my not fighting
   is a foregone conclusion?

[*Exit

**Don Manuel.** Now we're alone at last.

**Don Luis.** Well then, let's go to it.

[*They fight.*]

**Don Manuel.** I have never seen a swordsman
   with a steadier wrist!

**Don Luis.** I have never seen a swordsman
   with a stronger thrust!

[*The sword is knocked out of his hand.*]
   You've disarmed me.
I'm defenseless now.

**Don Manuel.** That's the merest
   accident, and no aspersion on
   your valor. Go find another sword.

**Don Luis.** You are courteous as well as brave.
   [*aside*] My luck! What shall I do
   in this emergency?

He has robbed me of my honor
but lets me live when he has
vanquished me. One way or the other,
I must find some excuse
to resolve this question and
determine what it is I owe him.
**Don Manuel.** Are you going for your sword?
**Don Luis.** Yes, and if you will wait for me,
I shall return with it at once.
**Don Manuel.** Sooner or later, when you come,
I shall be waiting.
**Don Luis.** God keep you,
Don Manuel.
**Don Manuel.** And you, Don Luis.

*[Exit DON LUIS*

**Don Manuel.** Meanwhile I'll lock the door
and keep the key so that no one
can get in and find me here.
What illusions and confusions
go tumbling through my head!
How right I was to think
there was a secret door
where she got in, and that the lady
was his mistress after all!
Indeed, everything's turned out as I
imagined it. But then, our worst
imaginings often come true.

*[COSME peeps out over the doorway.]*

**Cosme.** Oh, sir! For pity's sake,
now that you're alone, let me
out of here. I'm afraid that phantom
will creep into this narrow place—
which is no bigger than its own
four walls—and haggling and squabbling,
one way or the other,
will carry me off at last.
**Don Manuel.** Yes, I'll open it for you.
I am so weary of my own
absurd reflections, I can even
be impervious to you.

*[DON MANUEL opens the door and enters
the room behind which COSME is shut up.]*

*Enter DOÑA ANGELA, veiled and in stocking feet, while
DON JUAN stands in the doorway.*

**Don Juan.** You'll stay right here until I find out
why you left the house, dressed as you are,
and at this hour of the night.

Ungrateful wretch, I shall not let you
enter your apartment till
I have satisfied myself
on this account by asking your maid
without giving you the chance to meddle.
[aside] Since she'll be left in Don Manuel's
apartment, I must post a servant
at the house door to warn him not
to come inside here when he returns.

[Exit

**Doña Angela.** How miserable I am.
One by one the doors are closed
against me. Now there's no way out.

Enter DON MANUEL and COSME.

**Cosme.** Let's go quickly.
**Don Manuel.**                What are you
afraid of now?
**Cosme.**           That that woman
is the devil and she's not finished
with me yet.
**Don Manuel.**    But we know now
who she is; and we know the panel
is shut off by a table
while the door itself is locked.
So where do you suppose
she can get in?
**Cosme.**            Wherever
she's a mind to.
**Don Manuel.** You're mad.

[COSME spies DOÑA ANGELA.]

**Cosme.** Lord God, save me, save me!
**Don Manuel.** What is it?
**Cosme.**                     The unmentionable one's
got in here, pretty as you please.
**Don Manuel.** What are you, woman, a shade
or some illusion sent here
to destroy me? Tell me,
how did you get in?
**Doña Angela.**        Don Manuel . . .
**Don Manuel.** Tell me.
**Doña Angela.**           Then listen patiently.
Don Luis knocked at my door
in great excitement, rushed in
wildly, checked himself,
seemed to overcome his
agitation, paused, spoke calmly;
then turned and rushed out blindly,

searched the house, ran through every room
until he found you, after which
the only sound I heard
was the clash and clatter of your swords.
Aware that two men were locked behind
closed doors, both grimly silent while their
swords proclaimed their quarrel,
one to prove his valor, the other,
his reputation, and knowing
such an issue must terminate
in the death of one or the other,
half dead myself, I fled the house.
There outside, the cold and silent night
became the pallid image of
my former happiness.
I found myself wandering
aimlessly, falling and stumbling,
and all my sluggish senses
muffled in the silken prison
of my clothes. Confused, alone,
and terrified, my errant steps
led me roundabout to some dim
familiar threshold, to the haven,
as it turned out later,
of my former cell, and not
the refuge or the sanctuary
which I sought. But where, indeed,
does any poor unhappy wretch
find refuge? Still, Heaven forges
our misfortunes, link by link,
so carefully, that on that very
threshold stood Don Juan—Don Juan,
my brother . . . At first, I forbore,
then vainly I delayed, to tell him
who I was, though knowing that
my hesitation put us both
in certain jeopardy. Still,
who would think silence in a woman
could be dangerous? Yet it was
precisely this, my being silent
and a woman, which nearly
finished me. For, as I say,
there he stood—good God! waiting in
the doorway just as I arrived—
like a frozen volcano
or an alp on fire. There,
in the dim moonlight he caught
the sudden gleam and flash of jewels
around my neck—not, by any means,

the first time that such baubles
have betrayed a woman. And there
he heard the rustle of my skirts—
nor, there again, was it the first time
a woman's dress gave her away.
He mistook me for his mistress,
to whom he flew directly,
as a moth would toward the flame
it would be consumed by,
the mere ghost of his lustrous star.
Who would suppose a gallant, wracked
by jealousy, should so utterly
mistake his own adverse destiny
as not to know that jealousy
would be. his fixed and awful fate?
He tried in vain to speak,
but deepest feeling's always mute.
At last his quaking voice,
which quickly blurred the words
his tongue would utter just
as they reached his lips, inquired
why he had been made to suffer
such an insult. I tried to answer,
but, as I've said, deep emotion
silenced me. I could not say a word.
Perhaps it was because I sought
to color the guilt I felt
that fears came surging up
to cloak my reason. It always
follows that when one must seek
excuses for one's innocence,
they never come, or if they do,
arrive too late, so that
the very crime one would deny
asserts itself more flagrantly.
"Get inside," he said. "My sister
is a wanton, and the first to stain
the honor of our ancient name.
I shall leave you under lock and key,
and while you're safely hidden,
I'll deliberate upon
the wisest course to follow
in redressing this insult."
Whereupon he locked me in here
to nurse my griefs, until,
as luck would have it, you appeared,
to lighten them. To love you
I became a phantom in my own house.
To honor you, I became

the living tomb of my own secret.
Indeed, I could not tell you that
I loved you nor how much
I respected you for fear
that any open declaration
would jeopardize your presence
as our guest, compelling you
to quit the house at once.
I only sought your favor
because I loved you and because
I feared to lose you. My only thought
was keeping you, to cherish
and obey you all my life, to wed
my soul with yours, and so all
my desire was to serve you,
as now my plea is but
to urge you to support me
in my pressing need: in effect,
to save me, comfort and protect me.

**Don Manuel.** [*aside*] All my troubles seem to rise up
Hydra-headed from dead ashes.
What am I to do, sunk in this deep
abyss, this human labyrinth
of myself? She is the sister
of Don Luis, and not his mistress,
as I thought. Heavens, if I was
so squeamish about crossing him
in love, what can I do now
that his honor is involved?
What an awful impasse!
She's his sister: if I try
to free her and defend her
with my blood, or let my sword
underscore her innocence,
I thereby compound my guilt,
for that's to say that I've betrayed
him as a guest in his own house.
If I plead my innocence
by implicating her, then that's
to say she was the guilty one,
which my sense of honor won't allow.
Then what am I supposed to do?
If I reject her, I'm a villain.
If I defend her, a thankless guest;
and fiendishly inhuman
if I yield her to her brother.
Say I decide to protect her:
that makes me a false friend;
and if I free her, I violate

a noble trust; if I don't free her,
I violate the noblest love.
Whichever way I turn, I'm in
the wrong. So I'll die fighting.
[*to DOÑA ANGELA*]
Madam, have no fear. I am a
gentleman; you shall be protected.

[*There is a knocking at the door.*]

**Cosme.** Sir, there's someone knocking.
**Don Manuel.** It's Don Luis, who went to fetch
a sword. Let him in.
**Doña Angela.**          Dear me,
my brother!
**Don Manuel.** There is nothing
to fear. I shall defend you
gallantly. Now stand behind me.

[*DOÑA ANGELA moves behind DON
MANUEL while COSME opens the door.*]

*Enter DON LUIS.*

**Don Luis.** I've come back. But what's this?
Oh, you traitress!

[*Seeing DOÑA ANGELA, he draws his sword.*]

**Don Manuel.** Sheathe your sword,
Don Luis. In this room, where I've been
awaiting your return, this lady
entered—by what means I did not know.
She informs me she is your sister.
But you have my word, as a
gentleman, that I did not know
of it before. It should suffice
to say that not knowing who she was,
though I could have been mistaken,
I spoke to her. At the risk of
my own life and soul, I must
conduct her now to safety
before we can resume our duel
behind locked doors and avoid
a further scandal. Having freed her,
I shall return here to take up
our quarrel. To one who would sustain
his reputation, the cause of honor
and his sword are his most vital
possessions. Just as I
permitted you to leave this room
to fetch another sword, permit me
now to leave in order to fulfill
the debt I owe my honor.
**Don Luis.** I went to get my sword, but only

to bring it here that I might lay it
at your feet, and so acknowledge
your generous behavior.
But since you've given me new grounds
for argument, I must pick it up
again. This lady is my sister.
No man in my presence shall lead her
from this house who is not her husband.
Therefore, if you insist on
taking her away, you must first
agree to marry her. Once
I have your word to this effect,
you may take her, then return
for the further disposition
of this matter, if you wish.

**Don Manuel.** I shall return, but instructed
by your prudence and honesty,
only to throw myself
upon your mercy—thus.

**Don Luis.** You must not kneel. Rise.

**Don Manuel.** Further,
in fulfillment of my sworn vow,
I now take your sister's hand.

*Enter DOÑA BEATRIZ and DON JUAN.*

**Don Juan.** If all that's lacking is her
guardian to give the bride away,
I'm here to do so. I was about
to enter when I heard voices
in the room where I had left
my sister in some displeasure.
So let me enter it again
to give you both my blessings.

**Doña Beatriz.** If congratulations to you both
are now in order, perhaps
we others ought not be omitted.

**Don Juan.** Why, Beatriz, have you come back
to grace this house?

**Doña Beatriz.** I never left it.
I'll explain this to you later.

**Don Juan.** Well, let us take advantage of
this occasion, which so clearly
bids us insure our happiness.

**Cosme.** Thank goodness, the Phantom Lady's
cleared things up.
[*to DON MANUEL*]
Tell me, sir, was I mad
or what?

**Don Manuel.** So long as you're not mad now,

you may marry Isabel today.
**Cosme.** That would only prove I'm really mad.
    Besides, I can't.
**Don Manuel.** And why not?
**Cosme.** Because the good time usually
    wasted on such nonsense
    would be much better spent now
    beseeching this audience
    to pardon our mistakes,
    and to say: our author humbly
    thanks you for your kind indulgence.

# LIFE IS A DREAM

# (LA VIDA ES SUEÑO)

## Life Is a Dream

**La vida es sueño** is Calderón's best-known play, and also the most universally celebrated in the history of the Spanish theatre. Its main theme, the transience of human life, ancient as man himself, is proverbial in the schoolchildren's round ending with "Merrily, merrily, merrily, merrily,/ Life is but a dream." The theme has been traced to earliest Oriental philosophy and religion, to the Taoist ethic and Buddhist thought, to echoing passages in Job, Isaiah, and Ecclesiastes, to Heraclitus, Plato, and Roman Stoicism, and finally to Christian ethics and apologetics—the tradition closest to Calderón's thinking as a deeply religious seventeenth-century man in a militant Catholic country whose empire had begun to dissolve.

Besides the subject of life's ephemerality, the play employs at least three other traditional ideas and motifs: the myth of the hero as a lost or sequestered child; the legend of man overcoming the auguries of fate based on an adverse reading of the stars; the legend of the drugged and transported sleeper.

The first publication of **La vida es sueño** was edited by Don José Calderón, the playwright's brother, who put it at the head of a collection of twelve plays in **Primera parte de comedias de Don Pedro Calderón de la Barca** (1636). Another, though defective, edition appeared in an anthology published the same year in Zaragoza. Two further editions of Don José's collection appeared in 1640; a spurious printing was put out by another editor around 1670; and still another (from which most Spanish texts of the play have since been derived) appeared in 1685, edited by Don Juan de Vera Tassis y Villaroel, who claimed the title of "best friend" to Don Pedro. Two modern editions of the play are by Professor A. E. Sloman (Manchester, 1961) and by Professor E. E. Hesse (New York, 1961).

Before our age of scholarly books and articles, the surest index to a literary work's readability was the foreign adaptations and translations it received. Angel Valbuena Briones, in his **Perspectiva crítica** (Madrid, 1965), lists five such seventeenth-century appearances, including one in Dutch and one in Italian during the year of the play's first publication, 1636. Another Dutch translation appeared in 1647, and a second Italian one in 1664. The score and libretto of a German opera based on the play were printed in Hamburg in 1693. Several French and further Italian versions appeared in the early eighteenth century; from then on until about 1870 more than seventeen German adaptations, operas, and translations came into existence, confirming the fact that Calderón's **Life Is a Dream** was most popular in the country where Romanticism first began in Europe. The first translation in English (by Malcolm Cowan) appeared in 1830, and an early Russian one in 1861.

Until fairly recently the play in English translation was best known through Edward Fitzgerald's free adaptation ("better the live dog than the dead lion"); its main virtue over the other and much "closer" nineteenth-century version by Reverend Dem F. MacCarthy is that Fitzgerald's is mostly readable. Among half a dozen contemporary translations are two by English poets, Roy Campbell (in **The Classic Theatre, III**, ed. E. Bentley, New York, 1959) and Kathleen Raine (London, 1968).

The appeal of **Life Is a Dream** can never be wholly accounted for. From one point of view it seems incomplete, even fragmentary, like Marlowe's **Doctor Faustus**. From another, the play powerfully condenses in its enacted metaphor of living-and-dreaming an overwhelming perception about life's worth together with man's failure to make much of it. The play is many-faceted: it keeps changing as one holds it up to scrutiny so that its real theme seems impossible to pin down. It has the appeal of a mystery, but one in which the living energy that makes up the mystery is withheld, and while being withheld gets transformed into something different from the rigid terms and structure meant to contain it. Though following a straightforward dramatic pattern and the clearly stated and often repeated idea framed in the title, the play's meanings are not reducible, as they are often made to seem, to a few neat exempla about the turnings of fate and religious belief. The meanings grow, they shift their ground; they multiply with each reading. It is what happens in all great literary works: for a moment we behold the full and clear design, only to note immediately beneath it the baffling multiplicity of effects raying out beyond, into so many intimately related ideas we cannot even begin to name them.

In this play, honor is seen in its broadest possible sense as related to the whole of life, interwoven with the very substance and meaning of life. The title implies the question, Is life worth living? By a further implication, if honor is an illusion, so is life, and if this is true, how does one cope with such a vast and fearful discovery?

Another related and basic problem is the question of how to deal with the violent and secret crimes of the older generation. Since Rosaura as well as Segismundo have been dishonored by their fathers, how can they redress their personal grievances without rupturing the relationship of one generation with the next, the succession of life itself? The old myths stir beneath the surface: Zeus dethroned Cronus (as Calderón fully showed in **La estatua de Promoteo — The Statue of Prometheus**); Zeus raped Leda as a swan and Europa as a bull; Aeneas abandoned Dido. All the actions pertain here to the sexual crimes of worldly men as fathers and lovers. Clotaldo raped and abandoned Violante, Rosaura's mother, and the rapist Duke Astolfo abandoned Rosaura. In political terms, Segismundo will swear to overcome his father and trample on his beard; Rosaura and Segismundo both have good cause to seek vengeance. They have been brutalized. Rosaura has been raped, deprived of her sexual honor, and rejected as a woman, without explanation. And, as far as he knows, also without explanation, Segismundo has been spiritually assaulted, deprived of his liberty, his free will, his honor as a man, and left since birth in a prison tower, like his father's guilty rotting dream. Deprived of his power as a man and as a prince, Segismundo has also been left ignorant of the existence of women, of love, of social communion.

To regain her honor (since there is no one to act for her), Rosaura must pretend to be a man—dress and act like one—so that she may have the sexual and political freedom needed to force the issue. To redress his grievances, Segismundo must seek power by revolution, imitate a tyrant in order to dethrone one, so that when he triumphs he can accomplish these things: rectify the misuse of power and the power proper to him as a man and as a prince; destroy the opposing vision: his father's self-rotting dream.

No other course is possible since, as the situation of the play poses, even if *la vida es sueño, vida infama no es vida*— a life disgraced is no life at all.

Segismundo must be twice awakened and have Rosaura's help before he attains to consciousness. So, too, Rosaura, in order to restore her honor as a woman, cannot finally act as a man; when her father fails her she can only seek Segismundo's help. He, in turn, is thus forced to confront her as a libidinous object and then to recognize that if he were to overmaster and take her as a woman, the act would be a violation of the sort she is now doubly seeking to redress: her father's rape and abandonment of her mother, and Astolfo's rape and abandonment of herself. She must serve Segismundo as a benign influence, a test and a guide, not as his sexual partner.

Theirs is a strange relationship. It seems that the similarity and common urgency of their grievances have set up something like an incest barrier between them. Perhaps it is not so much a relationship as a brief series of crucial "learning" confrontations. She arrives to bring him a new sense of the world of which he has been deprived since birth. Her beauty and her light are essentialized in her name: the spirit of the rose (*rose aura*) and a series of dawns (*auroras*, her name anagrammed). Beholding her beauty and person as the gifts they are, he instinctively wishes to possess them. He must learn that he can have her only as one who identifies his life's struggle for him and as someone who then must share a mission with him.

Vibrations of attraction and repulsion based on the incest taboo are actually featured in other Calderón plays—**Devotion to the Cross** and **The Crown of Absalom**—in which the incest barrier is dramatically broken down. In any case, one reason to stress the unconscious motif here is that the strong cause which Segismundo shares with Rosaura against brutalization is usually scanted in favor of discussions about techniques and metaphysics in the play. It is not often seen that the mysterious interdependence between Rosaura and Segismundo has directly to do with the moral realism of their claims in a male-dominated, autocratic society. They need each other not only to regain their womanhood and manhood, respectively, but also because what they have to face is an extremely adverse and unpromising set of circumstances, not least because they are going against the rule of custom and law as represented by the guilty, well-meaning, and unjust men: Basilio, the King; Clotaldo, his chief counselor and Rosaura's father; and Astolfo, the Duke. And so the act of restoring the human integer of magnanimity in the face of its thorough brutalization by well-intentioned, civilized men is nothing short of saintly. And this is what Segismundo proceeds to do. Though **Life Is a Dream** is Calderón's best-known play, it is not, like his *auto* of the same title, a religious drama, but a drama of the discovery of moral imagination. It is aligned with a variety of other plays such as **Devotion to the Cross, The Wonder-Working Magician, The Mayor of Zalamea**, and **The Phantom Lady** by its persistent exploration of the humane virtues of clemency, love, and magnanimity, held up against the combative principle of the strict honor code—the power drive, vengeance, absolute law. In **Life Is a Dream**, perhaps uniquely among Calderón plays, a metaphysical problem is supported, not by appeals to faith or insistence on ideality, but by the proofs of experience itself. For the virtue of magnanimity to emerge in Segismundo it must be shown to overcome the lesser virtues which breed the brutalization of experience—false pride, rape, murder and perverted sexuality. By implication the play is a criticism of inflexible rule, of self-deceptive authoritarianism masquerading as benevolent justice.

Appropriate to such criticism are Calderón's disclosures of the life of impulse which underlies the motivations of his characters. Such disclosures often lead typically to a formula whereby compulsive action, moral desperation, and distraught behavior must issue from sidetracked and guilty consciences: the pursuit of vengeance and the expression of doubt from the fear of infidelity, perverted love, and incest. But from this and other examples of his psychological realism, we see that Calderón at his best is never merely a preacher or an upholder of an abstract morality. He essentializes in order to identify; he dramatizes in order to characterize; and he particularizes experience in order to show the relationship of misguided motives to the espousing of false ideals and the necessity of earned perception for the attainment of practicable ideals. This still seems a lesson worth having.

# LIFE IS A DREAM

# LA VIDA ES SUEÑO

## Dramatis Personae

| | |
|---|---|
| BASILIO | King of Poland |
| SEGISMUNDO | Prince |
| ASTOLFO | Duke of Muscovy |
| CLOTALDO | An old man |
| CLARÍN | A clownish servant |
| ESTRELLA | Princess |
| ROSAURA | A lady |
| Soldiers | |
| Guards | |
| Musicians | |
| Retinue | |
| Servants | |
| Ladies | |

*The setting of the play is the Polish court, a fortress tower nearby, and an open battlefield.*

# Act One

*On one side, mountain crags; on the other, a tower, with*
*SEGISMUNDO'S cell at the base. The door facing the audience, is half*
*open. The action begins at dusk.*

*Enter ROSAURA, dressed as a man, at the top of a crag and descends to level*
*ground; CLARÍN enters behind her.*

**Rosaura.** Where have you thrown me, mad horse,
half griffin? You rage like a storm,
then flicker like lightning
outspeeding light, off in a flash
like a fish without scales,
or a white featherless bird
in headlong flight. Beast, there's not
one natural instinct in you—
tearing your mouth to hurl
and drag yourself through
this labyrinth of tangled rocks!
So stick to these heights like
that fallen sun-driver Phaëthon,
and be a hero to all
the wild animals, while I,
desperate and blind, scramble down
these rugged, twisting, barren crags
where there is no way but what the laws
of destiny set down for me,
here where the wrinkled cliffs
glower at the sun. Poland,
you greet this stranger harshly,
writing her entry in blood
on your sands; she hardly arrives
before hardship arrives.
Look where I am—doesn't this prove it?
But when was pity ever showered
on anyone in misery?
**Clarín.** Say any two, including me.
Misery needs company.
Besides, if it was the two of us
who left our country searching
for adventure, surely
the same two arrived here,
hard luck, crazy falls down crags
and all; so why shouldn't I complain
if in sharing all the pain,
I don't get half the credit?
**Rosaura.** I fail to mention you

in my complaints, Clarín,
because I do not like
depriving you of the right
and consolation to voice your own.
As some philosopher has put it,
there's so much satisfaction
in complaining that troubles
should be cultivated
so we may complain of them.
**Clarín.** Philosopher? He was
a drunken old graybeard.
Someone should have whacked him good and hard
to give him something to complain of.
Well, madame, what are we to do now,
alone and stranded without a horse,
at this late hour on a barren slope,
as the sun is setting?
**Rosaura.** Who'd imagine such strange things
could happen? But if my eyes
do not deceive me and this is not
a fantasy, a trick
of failing daylight, I seem to see
a building there.
**Clarín.** My hopes deceive me,
or else I see what you see.
**Rosaura.** Standing there amid huge bare rocks,
there's a crude fortress tower, so small
it barely reaches daylight,
and so roughly made among
so many crags and boulders that when
the dying sunlight touches it,
it looks like just another rock
fallen down the mountain side.
**Clarín.** Let's move closer, madame.
We've stared enough; it's better letting
them who live there exercise
their hospitality.
**Rosaura.** The front door
stands open to . . . what is it,
a mausoleum? And pitch darkness
comes crawling out as though
the night itself were born inside.

[*The sound of chains is heard.*]

**Clarín.** Good Heavens, what's that I hear?
**Rosaura.** I'm a solid block of ice and fire!
**Clarín.** It's just a bit of rattling chain.
Destroy me if it's not the ghost
of a galley slave. Would I
be so scared otherwise?

**Segismundo.** [*within*] Oh misery and wretchedness!
**Rosaura.** Whose unhappy voice was that? Now
  I've more suffering to contend with.
**Clarín.** And I, more nightmares.
**Rosaura.**                        Clarín . . .
**Clarín.** Madame . . .
**Rosaura.**               This is desolating.
  Let's leave this enchanted tower.
**Clarín.** When it comes to that, I haven't
  got the strength to run away.
**Rosaura.** Isn't that tiny light
  like someone's dying breath
  or some faintly flickering star
  whose pulsing, darting rays
  make that dark room even darker
  in its wavering glow?
  Yes, and even from here
  I can make out by its reflection
  a murky prison cell, a tomb
  for some still living carcass.
  But even more astonishing,
  there's a man lying there
  in heavy chains, wearing
  animal skins, whose only
  company is that tiny light.
  So, since we cannot run away,
  let's listen and find out
  what his misfortunes are about.

      *The door swings open and SEGISMUNDO appears in the*
      *tower light in chains, wearing animal skins.*

**Segismundo.** Heavens above, I cry to you,
  in misery and wretchedness,
  what crime against you did I commit
  by being born, to deserve
  this treatment from you?—although
  I understand my being born
  is crime enough, and warrants
  your sternest judgment, since
  the greatest sin of man
  is his being born at all.
  But to ease my mind I only want
  to know what worse offense was mine,
  aside from being born, to call
  for this, my greater punishment.
  Are not all others born as I was?
  And, if so, what freedom do they have
  which I have never known?
  A bird is born, fine-feathered

in all its unimagined beauty,
but scarcely does it sprout
that small bouquet of plumage
when its wings cut through the halls of air,
scorning safety in the sheltered nest.
Why should I, whose soul is greater
than a bird's, enjoy less liberty?
A brute is born, its hide all covered
in brightly painted motley,
which, thanks to nature's brush, is lovely
as the sky in star-strewn panoply,
till learning man's cruel need
to lunge and pounce on prey
when it becomes a monster
in a labyrinth. Then why should I,
with instincts higher than a brute's,
enjoy less liberty?
A fish is born, and never breathes,
spawned in weed and slime;
then, while still a tiny skiff of scales
sets itself against the waves,
and twists and darts in all directions,
trying out as much immensity
as the frigid sea womb will permit.
Why should I, with greater freedom
of the will, enjoy less liberty?
A stream is born and freely snakes
its way among the flowers;
then, while still a silvery serpent
breaking through, it makes glad music ring,
grateful for its majestic passage,
flowing into the open fields.
Why should I, with greater life
in me, enjoy less liberty?
I rise to such a pitch of anger
that I feel like Etna, volcanic;
I want to rip my chest open
and tear out pieces of my own heart.
By what law, reason, or judgment
is a man deprived of that sweet gift,
that favor so essential,
which God has granted to a stream,
a fish, a brute, a bird?

**Rosaura.** His words move me. I pity him
and am afraid.

**Segismundo.**     Who's been listening
to me? Is that you, Clotaldo?

**Clarín.** [*aside*] Say yes.

**Rosaura.**               Only some lost

unhappy soul among these cold rocks
who heard you in your misery.

**Segismundo.** Then I'll kill you at once
so you won't know that I know
you already know my weaknesses.
You overheard me—that's enough.
For that alone, these two strong arms
of mine must tear you apart.

**Clarín.** I'm deaf, I couldn't hear a word
you said.

**Rosaura.**      I throw myself at your feet.
If you were born human,
my doing so would free me.

**Segismundo.** Your voice moves and softens me,
your living presence stops me,
and your level glance confuses me.
Who are you? I know so little
of the world here in this tower,
my cradle and my tomb.
I was born here (if you can call it
being born), knowing only
this rugged desert, where I exist
in misery, a living corpse,
a moving skeleton.
I've never seen or spoken to
another human being, except
the man who hears my lamentations
and has told me all I know
of earth and heaven; but even
more amazing (and this will make you
say I am a human monster,
living in his fears and fantasies):
though I'm a beast among men,
a man among beasts, and sunk
in misery, I've studied
government, taught by the animals,
and from the birds I've learned to follow
the gentle declinations
of the stars—it is you, and you
alone, who douse the fire of my wrath,
fill my sight with wonder
and my hearing with admiration.
Each time I look at you
the vision overwhelms me
so that I yearn to look again.
My eyes must have the dropsy,
to go on drinking more and more
of what is fatal to their sight.
And yet, seeing that the vision

must be fatal, I'm dying to see more.
So let me look at you and die,
for since I have succumbed and find
that looking at you must be fatal,
I do not know what not looking
at you would mean; it would be worse
than fiercest death, madness,
rage, and overwhelming grief.
It would be life—for, as
I've had so bitterly to learn,
bringing life to one who's desperate
is the same as taking life away
from one who swims in happiness.

**Rosaura.** I look at you astonished,
amazed at what I hear, not knowing
what to say to you nor what to ask.
I can only say that Heaven
must have brought me here
to be consoled, if misery
finds consolation in seeing
someone still more miserable.
They tell the story of a wise man
who one day was so poor
and miserable he had nothing
to sustain him but a few herbs
he picked up. "Can any man,"
he asked himself, "be more wretched
than I am?" Turning his head,
he found the answer where another
sage was picking up the leaves
he had thrown away.
I was living in this world,
complaining of my troubles,
and when I asked myself the question,
"Can there be another person
whose luck is worse than mine?"
pitifully you answered me.
Now, coming to my senses,
I find that you have gathered up
my troubles and turned them into bliss.
So if by chance any
of my troubles can relieve you,
listen carefully and take your pick
among the leftovers. I am. . .

**Clotaldo.** [*within*] Cowards, or are you fast asleep!
Is this the way you guard the tower,
Letting two people break
into the prison . . .

**Rosaura.**                    More confusion!

**Segismundo.** It's Clotaldo, my jailer.
My troubles aren't over yet.
**Clotaldo.** [*within*] Be quick now, go capture them before
they can defend themselves, or else
kill them.
**Voices.** [*within*] Treason!
**Clarín.**                         Oh prison guards
who let us in here, since there's a choice,
capturing us would be simpler now.

> *Enter CLOTALDO with a pistol and the*
> *SOLDIERS, all wearing masks.*

**Clotaldo.** Keep your faces covered, everyone.
It is most important, while we're here,
to let no one recognize us.
**Clarín.** Here's a little masquerade!
**Clotaldo.** You there—you, who out of ignorance,
have trespassed on this forbidden spot
against the order of the King,
who has decreed that no one
dare approach the prodigy
secluded here among these rocks—
put down your arms and lives, or else
this pistol like a metal snake
will tear the air apart with fire,
and spit out two penetrating
shots of venom.
**Segismundo.**           Master tyrant,
before you injure them, I'll give up
my life to these blasted chains,
where, by God, with my hands and teeth
I'd sooner tear myself apart
than let you harm them or regret
the outrage you may have done them!
**Clotaldo.** What's all this bluster, Segismundo?
You know your own misfortunes
are so immense that Heaven
declared you dead before
you were even born. You know
these chains are simply a restraint
to curb your mad, proud rages.
Yes, to rein you in and stop you cold.
—Now throw him back in, and shut
the door to his narrow cell.

> [*He is shut in and speaks from inside.*]

**Segismundo.** Heavens, you were right to take
my freedom from me. Otherwise
I'd be a giant rising up
against you, piling your jasper

mountains up on stone foundations
till I reached the top to smash
the crystal windows of the sun!

**Clotaldo.** Perhaps your being kept from
doing it makes you suffer here.

**Rosaura.** Since I see how much pride offends you
I'd be foolish not to beg you
humbly, at your feet, to spare my life.
Let Pity move you, sir;
it would be bad for me
if you happened to dislike
Humility as much as Pride.

**Clarín.** If neither one can move you (being
the two stock characters we see
traipsing on and off stage
in the same old moralities),
I, who can't say I stand
for Pride or for Humility
but for something in between,
beg only, from where I'm standing,
for your help and your protection.

**Clotaldo.** You there, soldier!

**Soldier.**                          Sir?

**Clotaldo.**                                      Take away
their weapons and blindfold them; they're not
to see how or where they're going.

**Rosaura.** Here is my sword—I can
only yield it up to you, since you are
in command here; it may not be
surrendered to one of lesser rank.

**Clarín.** [*to a SOLDIER*] Here's mine surrendering itself to
the least of all of you—take it, man!

**Rosaura.** And if I must die, I wish you
to have this as a token
for your sympathy, a gift worthy
as its master, who once wore it
at his side. I beg you, guard it well,
for though I do not know
precisely what its secret is,
I know this golden sword
has certain special powers.
Indeed, trusting to nothing else,
I came with it to Poland,
hoping to avenge an insult.

**Clotaldo.** [*aside*] My God, what's this? Old wounds,
reopen, my confusion deepens.
[*aloud*] Who gave this to you?

**Rosaura.**                          A woman.

**Clotaldo.** Her name?
**Rosaura.**                 I swore not to reveal it.
**Clotaldo.** How do you know, how can you assume
  there's some secret about this sword?
**Rosaura.** Because she who gave it to me said,
  "Go to Poland, and use your wits,
  your guile, or some ruse to bring
  this sword to the attention
  of the noblemen and leaders there.
  For I know that one of them
  will favor you and help you."
  Yet since he may have died,
  she did not wish to give his name.
**Clotaldo.** [*aside*] Heaven help me! What's this I hear?
  I still have no idea
  whether all this has really happened
  or is simply an illusion.
  But surely it's the sword
  I left behind with Violante,
  promising that whoever came
  wearing it would find me tender
  and receptive as any father
  to his son. But now, my God, what
  can I do in such a quandary?
  He who brings it to me as a gift
  must lose his life for his doing so,
  and by surrendering to me
  sentences himself to death.
  What a pass to come to now!
  What a sad and fickle thing is fate!
  Here's my son—as every sign
  would indicate, including
  these stirrings in my heart
  which seeing him before me rouses.
  It's as if my heart responded
  like a bird beating its wings
  that can't break out to fly away,
  or like someone shut up in a house
  who hears some outcry in the street
  and can only look out
  through a window. Now, hearing
  that outcry in the street, and not
  knowing what's happening, my heart
  can only use these eyes of mine,
  the windows it looks out of,
  and through them dissolve in tears.
  Heaven help me, what shall I do?
  What is there to do? To take him
  to the King (oh God!) is to lead him

301

to his death. But to hide him
is to break my oath of fealty
to the King. That I cannot do.
Between my selfish interests,
on the one hand, and my loyalty,
on the other, I'm torn apart.
But come, why do I hesitate?
Does not loyalty to the King
come before one's own life and honor?
Let loyalty prevail—let him die!
Just now he said, as I recall,
that he came here in order
to avenge himself, and a man
whose honor hasn't been avenged
is in disgrace. No, he's not
my son! He cannot be my son.
He must not have my noble blood.
But if there's really been
some accident, from which no man
is ever free—honor being
such a fragile thing, shattered by
the merest touch, tarnished by
the slightest breeze, then what choice
had he, what else could he do,
if he's really noble, but risk
everything to come here
to avenge his honor?
Yes, he is my son, he bears my blood.
It must be so, since he's so brave.
Now then, between one doubt
and another, the best recourse
would be to go and tell the King,
"Here's my son, and he must die."
But if, perhaps, the very scruple
which sustains my honor
moves the King to mercy
and merits having my son spared,
then I'll help him to avenge
the insult; but if the King
in strictest justice should execute
my son, then he will die
not knowing I'm his father.
[aloud] Strangers, come with me, and do not fear
you are alone in your misfortunes,
for in such dilemmas,
where life or death hangs by
a thread, I cannot tell
whose lot is worse—yours or mine.

                                                    [Exeunt

### In the capital; a hall in the royal palace.

*ASTOLFO and SOLDIERS enter on one side, and the PRINCESS ESTRELLA
and LADIES-IN-WAITING on the other. Military music and intermittent
salvos are heard offstage.*

**Astolfo.** Drums and trumpets, birds and fountains—
each responds with its own fanfare
to your bright rays that once were comets,
and when joining in the same refrain
of marveling together
at your celestial beauty,
some are feathery clarinets,
others, metallic birds.
Thus, all alike salute you, madame:
to cannonade, you are the queen,
to birds, their own Aurora,
to trumpets, their Minerva,
and to flowers, Flora.
Because your coming pales the daylight
which has banished night away,
yours is the glory of Aurora,
the peace of sweet Flora,
Minerva's martial stance,
who reign as queen of all my heart.
**Estrella.** If what you say is measured
by any human action,
your gallant courtly phrases
are belied by all this menacing
display of arms, which I oppose,
since your lisping flattery
contradicts the sabre-rattling
that I've seen. I'll have you know
such behavior is contemptible
(deceptive, false, corrupt,
and, if you will, just beastly),
which uses honeyed words
to disguise the aim to kill.
**Astolfo.** You've been badly misinformed,
Estrella, if you doubt me
and think my words are insincere.
I beg you now to hear me out,
and judge if they make sense or not.
When Eustorgio the Third,
King of Poland, died, his heirs were
Basilio, who succeeded him,
and two daughters, of whom we are
the offspring. (I do not wish

to bore you with anything
irrelevant.) But there was Her Grace,
Clorilene, your mother—bless her,
gone to a higher kingdom
now veiled among the stars—
and she was the elder sister.
The second daughter was your aunt,
my mother, lovely Recisunda—
God rest her soul a thousand years—
and she was married in Muscovy,
where I was born. But to return now
to the other member
of the family. Basilio,
both childless and a widower,
suffering the usual decline
of age in time, is given more
to study than to women; so you
and I now both lay claim
to the throne. You insist
that being the daughter
of the elder sister gives you
the prior right; and I, that being male,
though born of the younger sister,
gives me precedence over you.
We advised the King our uncle
of our claims, and he has called us here
to judge between us—which is
the reason why we came today.
Having only this in view,
I left my estates in Muscovy
and came here not to fight with,
but to be subdued by, you.
Now may the all-knowing god of love
concur with the subjects of this land
in their prophetic wisdom.
And let such concord lead to your
becoming queen and, as my consort,
reigning over my heart's desire.
And, toward your greater honor,
as our uncle yields the crown,
may it reward you for your courage,
and its empire be my love for you!

**Estrella.** The least my heart can hope for
in response to so much courtesy
is to wish the crown were mine,
if only that I might rejoice
in giving it to you—
even though my love might still suspect
there's reason to mistrust you

in that portrait locket which you wear
dangling over your chest.
**Astolfo.** I can explain it all to you
quite easily . . . but those loud drums

                                              *[Sound of drums.]*

cut me off now, announcing
the King and his council.

               *Enter KING BASILIO with retinue.*

**Estrella.** Wise Thales . . .
**Astolfo.**                    Learnèd Euclid . . .
**Estrella.** You who rule . . .
**Astolfo.**                 . . . you who are immersed . . .
**Estrella.** . . . Among the signs . . .
**Astolfo.**                      . . . among stars and zodiac . . .
**Estrella.** Plotting their course . . .
**Astolfo.**                    . . . tracing their passage . . .
**Estrella.** Charting them . . .
**Astolfo.**                 . . . weighing, judging them,
**Estrella.** Permit me like ivy humbly . . .
**Astolfo.** Permit these arms, wide opened . . .
**Estrella.** To cling around your waist.
**Astolfo.** Lovingly to kiss your feet.
**Basilio.** Come, niece and nephew, embrace me.
Since you so loyally respond
to my affectionate command
and come greeting me so warmly,
you may be sure you shall have nothing
to complain of—you will be treated
equally and fairly, both.
So, while I confess I'm tired
of the heavy weight of all my years,
I beg only for your silence now.
When everything is told,
my story will no doubt amaze you.
Listen to me, then, beloved niece
and nephew, noble court of Poland,
my kinsmen, vassals, friends.
You knew the world in honoring
my years of study has given me
the surname Learnèd. To counteract
oblivion, the paint brush
of Timanthes and the marbles
of Lysippus portray me throughout
the world as Basilio the Great.
As you know, the science
I pursue and love the most
is subtle mathematics,
through which I steal from time and take

from fame their slow-moving powers to
divulge more and more
of what's new to man each day.
For now, perceiving in my tables
all the novelties of centuries
to come, I triumph over time,
forcing it to bring about
the happenings I have foretold.
Those snow circles, those glass canopies
which the sun's rays illuminate
and the revolving moon cuts through,
those diamond orbits, crystal globes,
the stars adorn and the zodiac
wheels into the open—such have been
my main study all these years.
They are the books of diamond paper
bound in sapphire where Heaven writes
in separate characters
on golden lines whatever
is to be in each man's life,
whether adverse or benign.
These I read so swiftly
that only my spirit follows
their rapid traces through the sky.
God! before this skill of mine
became a commentary
in their margins, an index
to their pages, I could wish
my life itself had been the victim
of their rages, so my tragedy
were totally confined to them.
For those destined to melancholy,
their own merit is a knife-thrust,
since he whom knowledge ravages
is most apt to destroy himself!
Though I say this now, my experience
itself tells it more convincingly,
which to give you time to marvel at,
I ask again only for your silence.
By my late wife, I had
an ill-starred son, at whose birth
the heavens drained themselves of signs
and portents. Before emerging
in the lovely light of day
from the living sepulcher
of the womb (birth and death being
so much alike), time and again
between waking and delirium,
she saw a monster in human form

burst savagely out of her womb,
while she, blood-drenched, dying, gave birth
to the human viper of this age.
The prophecies were all fulfilled
(rarely if ever are
the cruelest omens proven false).
His horoscope at birth was such
that the sun, all bathed in blood,
clashed in furious combat
with the moon, the earth serving
as battleground; the two beacons
of the sky fought light to light,
if not hand to hand, for mastery.
It was the hugest, most horrible
eclipse the sun has suffered
since it wept blood at the death of Christ.
The sun sank in living flames, as though
undergoing its last paroxysm.
Skies turned black, buildings shook.
Clouds rained with stones, rivers
ran blood. So the sun in frenzy
or delirium saw the birth
of Segismundo, who giving
indication of his nature
caused his mother's death, as if
to say ferociously,
"I am a man, since I begin by
repaying good with evil."
Hastening to my studies,
I discovered everywhere I looked
that Segismundo would be
the most imprudent of men,
the cruelest prince, the most ungodly
monarch, through whom this kingdom
would be split and self-divided,
a school for treason, academy
of all vices, and he,
swept by fury and outrageous crimes,
would trample on me, and while I lay
prostrate before him (what an effort
for me to say this!), would see
this white beard on my face
become a carpet for his feet.
Who would disbelieve such danger,
especially the danger he witnessed
in his study, where self-love presides?
And so, believing that the fates
correctly prophesied
catastrophe by such dire omens,

I decided to imprison
the newborn monster and see
if human wisdom could dominate
the stars. The news went out
the child had died at birth.
Thus forewarned, I built a tower
in the crags and rocks of those mountains
where the light almost never enters,
protected by such a dense array
of cliffs and obelisks.
Edicts were imposed forbidding anyone
to trespass near the spot,
for reasons I've made clear to you.
There Segismundo lives now, poor
and wretched in captivity,
tended, seen, and spoken to,
only by Clotaldo,
his instructor in humane studies
and religious doctrine, who still is
the only witness of his sufferings.
Now here are three things to consider:
first, that my respect for you is such
that I would spare you from servitude
and the oppression of a despot.
No ruler that's benevolent
would let his subjects and his realm
fall into such jeopardy.
Second, it must be decided
if depriving my own flesh and blood
of rights sanctioned by the laws
of man and God would be in keeping
with Christian charity.
There's no law that says that I,
wishing to restrain another
from tyranny and cruelty,
should practice them myself;
or that, if my son's a tyrant,
to prevent his committing crimes,
I may commit those crimes myself.
Now here's the third and last point—
and that's to see how much in error
I may have been in giving
easy credence to foretold events.
For though temperament impels him
to acts of violence, perhaps
they will not wholly master him;
even if the most unbending fate,
the most vicious temperament, the most
destructive planet, sway the will

in one direction, they cannot force
the will to do their bidding.
And so, having turned the matter
over so much, and weighing one
alternative after another,
I have come to a conclusion
that may shock you. Tomorrow
I will bring him here, who,
without knowing he is my son
and your King, Segismundo
(the name he's always borne),
will be seated on my throne,
under this canopy. In a word,
he will take my place here,
to govern and rule over you,
while you bow and take your oaths
of fealty to him.
In this way I accomplish
three things, each answering
to the three questions I have put.
First, if he is prudent,
wise, benign, and thus wholly
disproves the prophecy about him,
you may all enjoy in him
your native prince as King, who till now
was a courtier in the desert
and the neighbor of wild animals.
The second thing is this:
if he's cruel, proud, outrageous, wild,
running the whole gamut
of his vices, I shall then
have faithfully discharged
my obligation, for in
disposing of him I shall do so
as a king in just authority,
and his going back to prison
will not constitute an act
of cruelty but fair punishment.
And finally, if the Prince
turns out as I say, then I'll give you
(out of the love I bear you all,
my subjects) monarchs more worthy
of the crown and scepter—namely these,
my niece and nephew, who,
conjoining their claims and pledging
holy matrimony together,
will be tendered what they have deserved.
This is my command to you as King,
this is my desire as father,

this is my advice as sage,
and this, my word to you as elder.
And if what Spanish Seneca once said
is true—that a king's a slave
to his own nation—then as slave
I humbly beg this of you.

**Astolfo.** If it behooves me to reply,
who in effect have been
the most interested of parties here,
I would speak for one and all
in saying, Let Segismundo come.
His being your son is enough.

**All.** Give us our Prince, we would
beg him now to be our King.

**Basilio.** My subjects, I thank you all
for your esteem and favor.
And you, my mainstays and supports,
retire to your rooms meanwhile
until we meet the Prince tomorrow.

**All.** Long live King Basilio the Great.

> [*All except BASILIO exeunt with*
> *ESTRELLA and ASTOLFO*

> *Enter CLOTALDO, ROSAURA, and CLARÍN.*

**Clotaldo.** Sire, may I speak with you?
**Basilio.**                                    Ah,
Clotaldo, you are very welcome.

**Clotaldo.** Sire, I have always felt welcome here
before, but now I fear
some sad, contrary fate annuls
my former privilege
under law and the use of custom.

**Basilio.** What's wrong?
**Clotaldo.**                              A misfortune,
Sire, overwhelmed me out of what
appeared to be the greatest joy.

**Basilio.** Tell me more.
**Clotaldo.**                              This handsome youth
recklessly burst into the tower,
Sire, and there saw the Prince,
and he is—

**Basilio.**        Don't disturb yourself,
Clotaldo. If this had happened
any other day I confess
I would have been annoyed.
But now that I have let the secret
out, it does not matter who knows it.
See me later; there are many things

I must consult with you about,
and many things for you to do.
I warn you now, you must be
my instrument in accomplishing
the most amazing thing
the world has ever seen.
And not to have you think I blame you
for any negligence,
I pardon your prisoners.

*[Exit*

**Clotaldo.** Great Sire, long life to you!
  *[aside]* Heaven's improved our luck;
  I'll not tell him he's my son,
  since that's no longer necessary.
  *[aloud]* Strangers, you're free to go.
**Rosaura.** I am in your debt eternally.
**Clarín.** And I, infernally.
  What's a few letters' difference,
  more or less, between two friends?
**Rosaura.** To you I owe my life, sir;
  and since the credit's due to you,
  I am your slave forever.
**Clotaldo.** It is not your life you owe me,
  for a man of honor can't be said
  to be alive if his honor's lost.
  And if as you have told me
  you've come here to avenge an insult,
  I have not spared your life,
  for you brought none to spare;
  a life disgraced is no life at all.
  *[aside]* Now that should spur him on.
**Rosaura.** Then I admit I have none,
  though you have spared it for me.
  Yet when I am avenged
  and my honor's cleansed with all threats
  to it annulled, my life will seem
  a gift worth giving you.
**Clotaldo.** Take back this burnished sword
  you wore; I know it will suffice,
  stained with your enemy's blood,
  to avenge you, for this which was
  my steel . . . I mean that for a while,
  the little while, I've held it . . .
  has the power to avenge you.
**Rosaura.** In your name I put it on again,
  and on it swear to get my vengeance,
  even though my enemy should be
  more powerful.

**Clotaldo.**      Is he—by much?
**Rosaura.** So much so, I may not tell you—
   not that I distrust your confidence
   in such important matters, but that
   at your sympathy and favor, which
   move me so, won't be turned against me.
**Clotaldo.** Telling me would only win me
   further; it also would remove
   the possibility of my
   giving aid to your enemy.
   [*aside*] Oh, if I only knew who he is!
**Rosaura.** Then, not to have you think I value
   your confidence so little,
   know that my adversary is
   no less a personage than
   Astolfo, Duke of Muscovy!
**Clotaldo.** [*aside*] This could hardly be more painful.
   The case is worse than I suspected.
   Let us see what lies behind it.
   [*aloud*] If you were born a Muscovite,
   the man who's ruler of your country
   could not possibly dishonor you.
   Go back to your country and give up
   this burning purpose that inflames you.
**Rosaura.** Though he was my Prince, I know
   he could and did dishonor me.
**Clotaldo.** But he couldn't; even if
   he'd slapped your face, that wouldn't be
   an insult. [*aside*]
         God, what next?
**Rosaura.**                    It was
   much worse than that.
**Clotaldo.**                 Tell me,
   since you cannot tell me more
   than I already have imagined.
**Rosaura.** Yes, I'll tell you—though I cannot say
   why I regard you with such respect,
   or why I venerate you so,
   or why I hang upon your words
   so that I hardly dare to tell you
   these outer garments are deceptive,
   and do not belong to me.
   Consider this enigma
   carefully: if I'm not the person
   I appear to be, and he came here
   with the view of marrying
   Estrella, he could dishonor me.
   There, I have said enough.

[*Exeunt ROSAURA and CLARÍN*

**Clotaldo.** Listen! Wait! Stop! What sort of maze
is this now, where reason finds no clue?
It is my honor that's at stake.
The enemy is powerful.
I'm only a subject, and she—
she's but a woman. Heavens above,
show me the way to go.
There may be none, I know,
since all I see through this abyss
is one portentous sky
covering the whole wide world.

## Act Two

### *A room in the palace.*

**Clotaldo.** It's all done, just as you directed.
**Basilio.** Clotaldo, tell me what happened.
**Clotaldo.** What happened, Sire, was this.
I brought him the pacifying drink,
which you ordered to be made,
a mixture of ingredients
compounding the virtue
of certain herbs whose great strength
and secret power so wholly sap
a man, they steal away
and alienate his reason.
Emptied of aggression, drained of all
his faculties and powers,
he becomes a living corpse.
We need not question, Sire,
if such a thing is possible.
Experience shows it often,
and we know that medicine
is full of nature's secrets.
There's no animal, plant, or stone
without its own determined structure,
and since human malice can
uncover a thousand fatal drugs,
is it any wonder that,
when their virulence is tempered,
such drugs, instead of killing,
are merely sleep-inducing?
We can drop the question, then,
since reason and evidence both
prove the matter creditable.
And so, taking this drug with me

(actually made up of henbane,
opium, and poppies), I went down
to Segismundo's narrow cell
and talked with him a while about
those humane studies taught him
by silent nature under skies
and mountains, that holy school where
he'd learned rhetoric from birds and beasts.
To elevate his spirit further
toward the enterprise you had in mind,
I proposed the subject
of the mighty eagle and its speed,
how, in scorning the lower regions
of the wind, it rises
to the highest realms of fire
where it becomes plumed lightning
or a shooting star; and thus,
glorifying the eagle's flight,
I said, "Of course, as the king of birds,
he should take precedence over them.
That's his right " This was enough
for Segismundo, for on the subject
of royalty his discourse is full
of eager, proud ambition.
Thus moved by something in his blood
inciting him to do great things,
he replied, "So even in
the commonwealth of birds someone
requires they swear obedience.
The example comforts me
in my misery, since if I'm
anybody's subject here, that's
because I'm forced to be. On my own
I'd never bow to any man.'
Seeing how the matter, so close
to his own griefs, roused his anger,
I administered the potion.
It scarcely left the glass
and touched his throat when all
his vital spirits fell asleep.
A cold sweat made its way through every
vein and member of his body,
so that if I hadn't known
it wasn't death but its counterfeit,
I would have doubted he was alive.
Then the people came whom
you'd entrusted to carry out
the experiment; they put him
in a coach and brought him here

to your chamber where all
the majesty and grandeur owing
to his person were awaiting him.
He lies there now in your bed where,
when his torpor ends, he'll be treated,
Sire, as you directed,
just as if he were yourself.
If I have fulfilled your wishes
well enough to warrant some reward,
I beg you only to tell me (pardon
this presumption) what your purpose is
in having Segismundo brought here
to the palace in this way?

**Basilio.** Clotaldo, your scruple
is justified, and I wish only
to satisfy you on it.
You know that the moving star
guiding the destiny of my son
Segismundo threatens
endless tragedy and grief.
I would like to know if the stars,
which can't be wrong and have given us
so many further signs
of his bad character,
may still mitigate or even
slightly soften their influence,
and be allayed by his valor
and discretion, since man himself
can master his own fate.
This I would like to test
by bringing him here, where
he will know he is my son
and where he can show what
his real character is like.
If he's magnanimous he'll rule;
if he's tyrannical and cruel,
back to his chains he goes.
But now you'll ask why, in order
to conduct the experiment, have I
brought him sleeping here this way.
Since I wish to give you
every satisfaction, I'll answer
every question. If he discovers
that he's my son today,
then wakes up tomorrow
to see himself again reduced
to misery in his own cell,
he'll come to know his true condition,
only to despair, for knowing who

he is would be no consolation.
So I wish to mitigate
the possibility
by making him believe
that what he saw was something
that he dreamt. In that way
two things will be tested:
first, his true character,
for when he wakes he'll act out all
he's dreamt and thought; and secondly,
his consolation, for if he has
to see himself obeyed today
and subsequently back in prison,
he'll believe that he was dreaming,
and he'll be right in thinking so,
since everyone alive on earth,
Clotaldo, is only dreaming.

**Clotaldo.** There's proof enough, I think,
to make me doubt you will succeed.
But it's too late—there's no other way.
Besides, there are signs he's wakened
and is on his way here now.

**Basilio.** Then I'll withdraw, as you, his tutor, stay
and guide him through this new perplexity
by telling him the truth.

**Clotaldo.** You mean you give me leave
to tell it to him?

**Basilio.** Yes, for if
he knows the truth perhaps
he'll grasp the danger facing him
and more easily overcome it.

*[Exit*

*Enter CLARÍN.*

**Clarín.** Four whacks I had to take
to get inside here; they were laid on
by a redheaded halberdier
showing off his livery and beard,
but I had to see what's going on.
Now, there's no box seat to be had
that gives a better view of things,
without bothering about tickets,
than the eyes and head a man carries
with him: bright though broke, he can take in
any peepshow, cool as you please.

**Clotaldo.** *[aside]* There's Clarín, that girl's servant—
My God! that girl, such a dealer
in misfortunes, bringing my disgrace
all the way from Poland!

[aloud] Tell me, Clarín, what's new?

**Clarín.** What's new, sir, is that Rosaura,
who believes you sympathetic
to her cause of vengeance, has taken
your advice and put on again
her proper woman's clothing.

**Clotaldo.** That's good—it's right she dresses
properly.

**Clarín.**      Also, she's changed her name
and wisely made it known she is your niece,
whereby her reputation's risen
till now she's maid of honor here to
the incomparable Estrella.

**Clotaldo.** That's fine—at last I now can stand
responsible for her honor.

**Clarín.** Other news: with some such thing in mind,
she now awaits the time and place
when you can act in her behalf.

**Clotaldo.** Yes, that's the safest course.
Only time itself will see such matters
fully settled.

**Clarín.**           Further news:
she's favored so, being your niece,
she's treated like a queen, while I,
who came with her through thick and thin,
I am dying of hunger.
Nobody thinks of me at all.
They forget my name's Clarín,
meaning trumpet—and if I once
sound off, there's a tune will carry all
the news there is to Astolfo,
Estrella, and the King,
because Clarín the trumpet
and Clarín the manservant
are two things which don't keep secrets well.
So it may be, if silence
should ever lose its hold, out of me
will pop some refrain like this:
    *There's nothing sweeter to the ears or eyes*
    *than waking to a trumpet at sunrise.*

**Clotaldo.** There's something in what you say.
I'll see to it you're better treated.
Meanwhile, you are in my service.

**Clarín.** Yes, but here comes Segismundo.

        MUSICIANS *enter singing, and with* SERVANTS *attending*
        SEGISMUNDO, *who appears to be in a state of shock.*

**Segismundo.** Heavenly God, what is this?
What's this I see, God help me!

317

My wonder makes me fear it less
than my belief, which doubts it more.
I, in this sumptuous palace?
I, in silks and in brocades?
I, surrounded by swarms of servants,
all so elegant and attentive?
I, awake from sleep and in a bed
of such magnificence?
I, among so many people
and all eager to dress me?
To say I'm dreaming would be untrue
I know quite well that I'm awake.
I'm Segismundo, am I not?
Heavens, tell me if I'm mistaken,
and tell me what happened to my brain
and my imagination
while I slept that I should
find myself in such a place?
But be that as it may,
why worry over such questions?
Let them all serve me, come what will.

**Servant 1.** [*aside to SERVANT 2*] What a melancholy chap this is!

**Servant 2.** Who wouldn't be, considering
what's happened to him.

**Clarín.**                     I wouldn't.

**Servant 1.** You speak to him, go ahead.

**Servant 2.** [*to SEGISMUNDO*]
Shall they sing again?

**Segismundo.**              No,
I don't want them to sing again.

**Servant 1.** You were so abstracted,
I had hoped it would divert you

**Segismundo.** I don't feel diverted from
troubles with your singing voices.
When the military band
was playing, yes—I liked hearing that.

**Clotaldo.** Your Majesty and Noble Highness:
let me kiss your hand and be
the first to render homage
and my obedience to you.

**Segismundo.** [*aside*] It's Clotaldo—but how can it be
that he who treated me
so miserably in prison
now addresses me respectfully?
What is happening to me?

**Clotaldo.** In the huge bewilderment
brought on by your new situation
you'll find your reason and your
every utterance beset by doubt.

I wish, if possible, to free you
from all doubt, because, Sire, you should know
you are the Crown Prince of Poland.
If you were kept from others
and in seclusion till now,
that was due to fate's bad auguries,
foretelling numberless disasters
for this kingdom once the proud laurel
crowned your august brows. But now,
trusting that your prudence
may yet overcome the stars,
which a strong man's magnanimity
can indeed accomplish,
you were brought here to this palace
from the tower where you lived,
your spirit swathed in sleep.
My Lord the King, your father,
will come to see you, Segismundo,
and from him you'll learn the rest.

**Segismundo.** The rest? You infamous vile traitor!
Now that I know who I am, what more
do I need to learn in order
to express my pride and power from
now on? How do you explain
your treason to this country,
you who hid from me, and so denied,
the rank due me by reason and law?

**Clotaldo.** Alas, unhappy me!

**Segismundo.** You played treason with the law,
a wheedling game with the King,
and a cruel one with me.
And so the law, the King, and I,
after such monstrous misdeeds,
condemn you now to die between
these two bare hands of mine.

**Servant 2.** But, my Lord,

**Segismundo.**                    Don't interfere now—
anybody. It's useless. By God,
if any of you get in front
of me, I'll throw you out the window!

**Servant 2.** Run, Clotaldo.

**Clotaldo.**                    Alas, for you
cannot know that all this
arrogance you turn on me
is only something that you're dreaming.

*[Exit*

**Servant 2.** But you ought to know—

**Segismundo.**                    Get out of here!

**Servant 2.** —that he was obeying the King.

**Segismundo.** If his law's unjust, the King
   is not to be obeyed.
   Besides, I was the Prince.

**Servant 2.** It's not for him to undertake
   to say if any law is good or bad.

**Segismundo.** I suspect something bad's
   about to happen to you,
   since you go on arguing with me.

**Clarín.** The Prince is altogether right,
   and you are in the wrong.

**Servant 2.** And who asked you to talk?

**Clarín.** I just decided to.

**Segismundo.** And you,
   who are you, tell me?

**Clarín.** A meddling
   snoop—I do that job best. In fact,
   I'm the biggest busybody
   the world has ever known.

**Segismundo.** You're the only one who pleases me
   in this brave new world of moribunds.

**Clarín.** Sire, I am the greatest pleaser
   of whole worlds of Segismundos.

*Enter ASTOLFO.*

**Astolfo.** Oh Prince and sun of Poland,
   how fortunate is this day
   when you appear and fill it,
   from one horizon to the other,
   with joyful and blessèd splendor!
   For like the sun you rose to come
   from deep among the mountains.
   Come then, and wear the glittering crown
   of laurel on your brow, and since
   you put it on so late,
   may it never wither there.

**Segismundo.** God save you.

**Astolfo.** Of course you do not
   know me. Only that excuses you
   from honoring me properly.
   I am Astolfo, born Duke
   of Muscovy and your cousin.
   We are of equal rank.

**Segismundo.** If my "God save you" doesn't please you
   and you complain and make so much
   of who you are, next time you see me
   I'll say, "May God not save you!"

**Servant 2.** [*aside to ASTOLFO*] Your Highness should consider
   he is mountain-born and bred,

and treats everyone this way.
[*aside to SEGISMUNDO*]
Sire, Astolfo merits. . .

**Segismundo.** I couldn't stand the way he came in
and talked so pompously. Now the first
thing he does is put his hat back on.

**Servant 1.** He's a grandee.

**Segismundo.**                    And I am grander.

**Servant 2.** However that may be, it would be
better if more respect were shown
between you than among the rest.

**Segismundo.** And who asked for your opinion?

*Enter ESTRELLA.*

**Estrella.** Your Highness, Noble Sire,
you are most welcome to this throne,
which so gratefully receives you,
and wishes to secure you,
notwithstanding all false omens,
and henceforth would have you
live augustly eminent,
not only for years and years
but for centuries.

**Segismundo.** [*to CLARÍN*] Now you tell me,
who is this proud beauty, this human
goddess at whose lovely feet
Heaven strews its radiance?
Who is this splendid woman?

**Clarín.** Sire, your star cousin, Estrella.

**Segismundo.** But more like the sun than a star.
My heart wells up to your well-wishing
my well-being, though seeing you
is the only welcome thing
I can admit today.
So having found in you a sight
more welcome than I merit,
your speech of welcome overcomes me.
Estrella, you can rise
and in your dawning fill
the brightest star with happiness.
What's there for the sun to do
if when you rise the day does too?
Come, let me kiss that hand of yours
from whose snowy cup the early breeze
imbibes its purities.

**Estrella.** Your courtliness is more than gallant.

**Astolfo.** [*aside*] If he touches her hand,
I am lost.

**Servant 2.** [*aside*] I know this puts

Astolfo off. I'll try to stop it.
[*aloud*] Consider, Sire, it is not right
to take such liberties,
especially with Astolfo here . . .
**Segismundo.** Haven't I already told you
I don't care for your opinions?
**Servant 2.** What I say is no more than right.
**Segismundo.** That sort of thing infuriates me.
Nothing's right if it goes against
the things I want.
**Servant 2.**          But I heard you say,
Sire, that one must honor and obey
only what is right and just.
**Segismundo.** You also heard me say
I'd throw anyone off
this balcony who gets me mad.
**Servant 2.** Such a thing as that just can't be done
to someone like myself.
**Segismundo.**          No?
Well, by God, then I'll just try it.

> [*SEGISMUNDO lifts him up bodily and goes out;*
> *the others follow, then return immediately.*]

**Astolfo.** What is this I have just seen?
**Estrella.** Quickly, everyone. Go stop him!

> [*Exit*

**Segismundo.** [*returning*] He fell from the balcony
right into the sea. So, by God,
it could be done after all!
**Astolfo.** Now you should try restraining
your violent temper.
There's as much difference between
men and beasts as between living
in the wilds and in a palace.
**Segismundo.** Now if you get so righteous
every time you say a word,
maybe you'll find yourself
without a head to hang your hat on.

> [*Exit ASTOLFO*

*Enter BASILIO.*

**Basilio.** What has been going on here?
**Segismundo.** Nothing's going on. There was
a man who got me mad,
so I threw him off that balcony.
**Clarín.** Be careful, that's the King.
**Basilio.** So your arrival here
has cost a man his life,
and on the first day too.

**Segismundo.** The man said it just couldn't be done,
   so I did it and won the bet.
**Basilio.** Prince, I am greatly grieved.
   I came to see you, supposing
   that being warned against
   the ascendancy of certain stars,
   you were overcoming adverse fate;
   but I find you in a rage instead,
   and that your first act here
   has been a heinous murder.
   How can I welcome you
   with open arms, knowing that yours,
   so cruelly skilled, have dealt out death?
   Who could view the naked knife
   still dripping from its fatal thrust
   and not be fearful? Who could approach
   the bloody scene where another man
   was killed and not find himself repelled?
   From such a deed the bravest man
   instinctively recoils.
   So I withdraw from your embrace,
   for there I see your arms
   as that death-dealing instrument
   still raised above the fatal scene.
   I who had hoped to meet and clasp you
   warmly in fond welcome
   can only drop my arms,
   afraid of what your own have done.
**Segismundo.** I can do without your fond embrace,
   as I've done without it till now,
   because a father who can treat me
   with such uncanny cruelty,
   being disposed to cast me off
   so scornfully he has me
   brought up like an animal,
   chained up like a freak, and wanting
   to see me dead—what does it matter
   to me if he embraces me or not,
   when he's deprived me of the right
   to be a human being?
**Basilio.** God in Heaven, if only
   I'd never given you a life,
   I'd never have to hear your voice
   or look at your outrageous face.
**Segismundo.** If you'd never given me a life
   I'd have no complaint against you,
   but since you did and then
   deprived me of it, I must complain.
   If giving something freely

is a rare and noble thing,
to take it back again
is as base as one can be.

**Basilio.** Is this the way you thank me
for making you a prince who were
a poor and lowly prisoner?

**Segismundo.** But what's there to thank you for?
What are you really giving me,
tyrant over my free will,
now that you've grown so old and feeble
that you're dying? Are you giving me
anything that isn't mine?
You're my father and my King.
And so all this majesty
is what justice and the law
of nature already grant me.
While this is my true station,
I am not obliged to you at all,
but could call you to account instead
for all the years you've robbed me
of liberty and life and honor.
Indeed, you have me to thank
for making no demands on you,
since it is you who are in my debt.

**Basilio.** Insolent barbarian,
you've confirmed the prophecy
of Heaven, to which I now appeal
to look at you, brash and puffed up
with pride. Though now you know
the truth about yourself
and are completely undeceived,
and though you see yourself preferred
above all others, I am warning you,
be moderate and humble,
for you may find you're only dreaming
though you think yourself awake.

[*Exit*

**Segismundo.** Can it be I'm only dreaming
though I think myself awake?
I am not dreaming, for I know
and feel what I have been
and what I am; now you may be
repentant, but that will do no good.
I know who I am, and however
you bemoan it and regret it,
you cannot rob me of the fact
that I am the born heir to this throne.
And if you once had me bound in chains,
that was because I had

no notion who I was,
but now I know exactly who I am,
and that's knowing I am
partly beast and partly man.

*Enter ROSAURA, dressed as a woman.*

**Rosaura.** [*aside*] Here I come to find Estrella,
but dreading to think that
Astolfo may find me. Clotaldo
wishes him not to know who I am
nor to catch sight of me since,
Clotaldo says, it vitally
affects my honor. And I trust
his interest now, grateful
for his support of me,
my life and honor both.
**Clarín.** [*to SEGISMUNDO*]
What is it here you've liked most among
the things you've seen and wondered at?
**Segismundo.** Nothing has amazed me here
that I had not foreseen.
But if there were anything
in this world that may have struck me,
it's a woman's beauty.
Among the books I used to have
I once read that God put
most of His attention
into creating man,
a little world unto himself.
Instead, I think, it should have been
in His creating woman,
a little heaven unto herself,
encompassing in her a beauty
as superior to a man's
as Heaven is to earth—
and more, if she's the one
I'm gazing at this moment.
**Rosaura.** [*aside*] Oh, it's the Prince—I must go back.
**Segismundo.** Stop, woman—listen to me!
Coming and going so fast, you push
sunrise and sunset together.
With the dawn and the dusk colliding
that way, you cut short my day.
Can I believe my eyes?
**Rosaura.** No more than I do mine, believing
and disbelieving them at once.
**Segismundo.** [*aside*] Her beauty—I've seen it somewhere
before.
**Rosaura.** [*aside*] His magnificence

and splendor I've seen before—
chained up in a narrow cell.

**Segismundo.** [*aside*] At last I've found my life!
[*aloud*] Woman—the most endearing word
a man can utter—who are you?
Though I do not know you,
I adore you, claiming you
on faith alone, and luckily
I have the feeling that
I've seen you once before.
Who are you, lovely woman?

**Rosaura.** [*aside*] I must pretend.
[*aloud*]                           Simply
an unhappy lady
in Estrella's retinue.

**Segismundo.** Say no such thing. Say you are the sun
from whose fire that other star,
Estrella, borrows its flamboyance,
bathing in the splendor of your light.
In the realms of fragrance,
amid whole squadrons of flowers,
I have seen the rose preside
in its divinity,
reigning over all the others
by virtue of its loveliness.
In that fine academy of mines
among the precious stones,
I have seen the admired diamond
ruling over all the rest
by virtue of its brilliance.
In the restless commonwealth of stars
I have seen the morning star
given precedence and chosen
monarch over all the others.
Amid Heaven's perfected spheres
I have seen the sun summoning
to court all its planets and,
as the clearest oracle of day,
in command above the rest.
Now if among the flowers,
precious stones, the planets, stars,
the whole zodiac itself,
only the loveliest prevail,
how is it that you serve
one of lesser beauty, you
who all in one are lovelier
than sun and stars, diamond and rose?

[*CLOTALDO appears at the curtain.*]

**Clotaldo.** [*aside*] I must do something to restrain him;
    I'm responsible, after all,
    I brought him up . . . But what's this now?

**Rosaura.** I esteem your favor,
    but let silence fill the rhetoric
    of my reply. When one finds
    one's reason sluggish, Sire,
    speaking best is speaking least.

**Segismundo.** Stay here, you do not have to leave!
    How can you persist this way
    in evading what it is I mean?

**Rosaura.** I must ask that permission, Sire.

**Segismundo.** Your leaving me abruptly
    is not asking it but taking
    such permission for granted.

**Rosaura.** If you don't give it, I must take it.

**Segismundo.** You'll turn my courtesy
    to impropriety; resistance
    is a poison I can't swallow.

**Rosaura.** But if that poison, full of rage
    and hate and fury, should overcome
    your patience, you still could not,
    you would not dare, dishonor me.

**Segismundo.** I'll try it, just to see if I can—
    once you make me lose the awe
    I feel for your beauty, for when
    a thing's impossible I find
    the challenge to overcome it
    irresistible; only today
    I threw a man off that balcony
    who said I couldn't do it.
    So, just to find out if I can—what
    could be simpler?—I'll let your virtue
    go flying out the window.

**Clotaldo.** [*aside*] From bad to worse—he makes
    an issue of it. Lord,
    What am I to do now that mad lust
    threatens my honor a second time?

**Rosaura.** Then the prophecy was true
    foretelling how your tyranny
    would bring to this poor kingdom
    riots of monstrous crimes and deaths,
    treason and furious contention.
    But what's a man like you to do
    who is human in name only,
    insolent, insensitive,
    cruel, impulsive, savage,
    and tyrannical, someone
    born and bred among beasts?

**Segismundo.** To keep you from insulting me
   I spoke to you gently,
   hoping that way I might win you.
   But if despite my courtesy
   you still accuse me of such things,
   then, by God, I'll give you reason to.
   All of you now, leave us!
   And lock that door behind you.
   let no one enter.

                                 *[Exeunt CLARÍN and SERVANTS*

**Rosaura.** *[aside]*      Now I'm lost.
   *[aloud]* Take care—
**Segismundo.**        I'm a raging brute—
   no use trying to chain me down.
**Clotaldo.** *[aside]* What a situation to be in!
   I must go out and stop him,
   though it may mean my life.
   *[aloud]* Sire, look, be lenient—

                                   *[He approaches.]*

**Segismundo.** You've provoked me once again,
   you crazy, weak old man.
   Do my cruelty and fury
   mean so little to you?
   How did you get in here?
**Clotaldo.** This woman's cries brought me here
   to urge you to be more moderate
   if you wish to rule, and not be cruel
   because you see yourself
   the master of everything about you,
   for all this may only be a dream.
**Segismundo.** Spouting that way about illusions
   makes me fighting mad! Now let's see if
   killing you is real or just a dream.

                 *[As SEGISMUNDO tries to draw his dagger,*
                    *CLOTALDO stops him, falling to his knees.]*

**Clotaldo.** Going down upon my knees,
   I hope to save my life.
**Segismundo.** Take your crazy hand off my dagger!
**Clotaldo.** I won't let go till someone comes
   to check your outrageous fury.
**Rosaura.** Oh God in Heaven!
**Segismundo.**           Hands off me,
   I tell you—enemy, doddering
   old idiot, or you'll see

                                 *[They fight]*

these arms of mine crushing you to death!

**Rosaura.** Help, oh, come and help him!
   Clotaldo is being murdered!

*[Exit*

*[CLOTALDO falls to the ground, ASTOLFO*
*appears and stands between them.]*

**Astolfo.** Well, what's this, magnanimous Prince?
   Is this the way to stain your keen blade,
   in an old man's frozen blood?
   Come, sheathe that shining knife of yours.
**Segismundo.** Not till it runs with your putrid blood.
**Astolfo.** Having put his life in
   my protection should do him
   some further good.
**Segismundo.**              Your own death
   will be that further good.
   Now I can avenge myself
   for your piquing me before,
   by killing you as well.
**Astolfo.** The law justifies my fighting
   royalty in self-defense.

*[ASTOLFO draws his sword and they duel.]*

**Clotaldo.** Do not injure him, my lord.

*Enter BASILIO with ESTRELLA and retinue.*

**Basilio.** What, drawn swords in my presence?
**Estrella.** *[aside]* There's Astolfo! I'm full
   of terrible misgivings.
**Basilio.** Well, what's the reason for this?
**Astolfo.** Nothing, Sire, now that you are here.

*[They sheathe their swords.]*

**Segismundo.** A great deal—even though you're here, Sire.
   I was about to kill that old man.
**Basilio.** And you had no respect
   for those white hairs?
**Clotaldo.**                You see,
   they are merely mine, Sire; nothing
   of importance, you understand.
**Segismundo.** Such futile nonsense— expecting me
   to honor someone's white hairs!
   *[to the KING]* Perhaps some day you'll see your own
   become a carpet for my feet.

*[Exit*

**Basilio.** And before you see that day arrive,
   back to your old sleep you'll go,
   where all that's happened to you here
   will come to seem like all the glories
   of this world, something that you dreamed.

329

[*Exeunt the KING with CLOTALDO
and ATTENDANTS*

**Astolfo.** How rarely fate deceives us
   in foretelling our misfortunes,
   as certain to be right
   in predicting what is evil
   as to be wrong in predicting good.
   He'd be a fine astrologer
   whose forecasts were always negative,
   since no doubt they'd always turn out true.
   In such a light, Estrella,
   consider our experiences—
   Segismundo's and my own,
   each so different in effect.
   For him the auguries foretold
   violence, catastrophes,
   murder, and despair, and so
   his forecast was correct, since all this
   is really happening.
   But consider my case: when, madame,
   I beheld your gaze flashing
   such brilliant rays, it turned the sun
   into a shade and the sky
   into a passing cloud;
   so fate seemed to promise great success,
   quick approval, rewards,
   and gains in property.
   Fate in this was right, but also wrong:
   right, when promising such favors,
   and wrong, when in effect it deals out
   nothing but disdain and scorn.
**Estrella.** I do not doubt your gallantries
   contain a certain weight of truth,
   but they must be intended
   for that other lady
   whose portrait you were wearing
   in a locket on a chain
   that hung around your neck
   when you came to see me.
   And so, Astolfo, she alone
   deserves your compliments.
   Go give them to her quickly
   so she may reward you,
   for in the court of love,
   as in the court of kings,
   gallantries and vows of fealty
   are not the way to valid titles
   when they are addressed to
   other ladies, other kings.

*Enter ROSAURA, standing aside and listening.*

**Rosaura.** [*aside*] Thank God I've reached the end
  of my misfortunes since witnessing
  such sights as this is to fear no more.
**Astolfo.** I'll see to it that portrait
  is replaced with the image
  of your loveliness against my breast.
  When Estrella lights the way
  shadows disappear, just as stars do
  when the sun itself arrives.
  Let me go and get the locket now.
  [*aside*] Forgive me, beautiful Rosaura,
  but when it comes to that,
  both men and women are untrue
  who are absent from each other.

[*Exit*

*ROSAURA comes forward.*

**Rosaura.** [*aside*] I couldn't hear one word they said,
  I was so afraid they'd see me.
**Estrella.** Astrea!
**Rosaura.**          My lady.
**Estrella.** I'm so glad it's you, since you're
  the only one I can confide in.
**Rosaura.** My lady, you honor me
  in serving you.
**Estrella.**          Astrea,
  in the short time I have known you,
  you've won my trust completely.
  And so, knowing what you are,
  I dare confide in you what I have
  often kept even from myself.
**Rosaura.** I am all obedience.
**Estrella.** Then to tell this to you briefly:
  Astolfo, my cousin—
  to call him that should be enough;
  what more he is you can imagine—
  he and I are to be married,
  if one stroke of good fortune
  can do away with much that's bad.
  The first day we met I was troubled
  that he wore the portrait
  of another woman round his neck.
  I told him so politely.
  Since he's so gallant and in love
  with me, he's gone to get the portrait
  and will bring it to me here.
  His giving it to me

will embarrass me no end.
Please stay behind and when he comes,
tell him to give it to you.
I'll say nothing more than that.
Being lovely and discreet yourself,
you know what love is all about.

[Exit

**Rosaura.** Good Lord, if only I didn't!
Who is there so wise and cool
he can advise himself
on such a difficult occasion?
Is there anyone alive
so heavily weighed down
by fate's adversities,
and choked by such bleak sorrows?
What is there for me to do,
confused, perplexed, when reason
cannot guide me nor help me find
a way to any consolation?
After my first misfortune
nothing new has taken place
without additional misfortunes,
as though each one has given birth
to the next, and so on, endlessly,
like the phoenix always rising
out of one form into another,
the living out of the dead,
and always finding in its grave
a bed of warm ashes.
A wise man once said our cares
are cowards—they never come alone.
I say they're more like heroes—
always marching on ahead
and never looking once behind them.
Anyone who's had to bear them
knows he can do anything;
knowing they will never leave him,
he is always fearless.
I can say this since, whatever else
has happened to me all my life,
they've never stopped dogging me,
and they never will grow tired
till they see me, destroyed by fate,
fall into the arms of death.
Good God, what am I to do now?
If I say who I am,
I offend Clotaldo,
whom l must loyally support
since he saved my life; and he tells me

to wait silently until
my honor has been satisfied.
But if I do not tell Astolfo
who I am, and he finds out,
how can I continue this pretense?
For though my voice, my tongue, my eyes
deny it, my heart will tell him
that I lie. What shall I do?
But what's the use of planning to do
this or that when it's obvious
the more I do to prevent it,
the more I plan and mull it over,
when the time comes, my own grief
will blurt the secret out, since no one
can rise above his sorrows.
Since my soul won't dare decide
what I must do, let there be an end
to sorrow. Today my grief is over.
Goodbye to doubts and all pretense.
And meanwhile, Heaven help me.

*Enter ASTOLFO with the portrait.*

**Astolfo.** Here, madame, is the portrait.
But . . . oh God!
**Rosaura.**             What's so astonishing,
Your Grace? What stops you?
**Astolfo.** Hearing you, Rosaura,
and seeing you.
**Rosaura.**             I, Rosaura?
Your Grace must be mistaken, thinking
I'm some other lady. No, I'm
Astrea; in all humility,
I do not merit such extreme
regard as your surprise reveals.
**Astolfo.** Rosaura, stop pretending,
one's heart can never lie;
although I see you as Astrea,
I love you as Rosaura.
**Rosaura.** Since I cannot understand Your Grace
I don't know how to answer you.
I can only tell you
that Estrella, brilliant and beautiful
as Venus, has asked me to wait
for you in her stead; she asked me
to accept the portrait for her
which Your Grace would give me
(a fair enough request), and which I,
in turn, would bring to her.
This is what Estrella wishes,

and even in the slightest matters,
though it result in harm to me,
this is what Estrella wishes.

**Astolfo.** Try as you will, Rosaura,
you are no good at pretending!
Tell your eyes to harmonize
with the music of your voice.
Otherwise they grow discordant
and throw their instrument out of tune,
trying to temper their false notes
with the truth of feeling in it.

**Rosaura.** As I've said, I'm waiting
only for the portrait.

**Astolfo.**                    All right, then,
since you wish to carry this pretense
to its conclusion, I'll go along.
So, Astrea, go tell the Princess,
in answer to her request,
that I respect her too much to send
a mere likeness, and instead,
because I value and esteem her,
I am sending the original.
And you are to carry it with you,
since you already bear it in you,
being yourself the original.

**Rosaura.** A bold man with a fixed purpose,
who bravely undertakes a mission,
then finds a substitute is offered,
even one of greater value,
would feel balked and foolish
returning without the prize
he set out to obtain.
I was asked to get the portrait;
if I bring back the original,
though it be more valuable,
my mission is not accomplished.
And so, Your Grace, give me the portrait.
I cannot return without it.

**Astolfo.** But if I don't give it to you,
how are you to get it?

**Rosaura.** This way! Let go of it,
you scoundrel!

*[She tries to take it from him.]*

**Astolfo.**                    Impossible!

**Rosaura.** So help me, I will not see it fall
into another woman's hands!

**Astolfo.** You're a real terror!

**Rosaura.**                    And you're a fiend!

**Astolfo.** Rosaura, that's enough, my dear.
**Rosaura.** Your what? You lie, you cad!

*[They struggle over the portrait.]*

*ESTRELLA enters.*

**Estrella.** Astolfo, Astrea, what is this?
**Astolfo.** *[aside]* It's Estrella.
**Rosaura.** *[aside]*          Oh Love, grant me
  the wit to get my portrait back!
  *[aloud]* My lady, if you like,
  I'll tell you what it's all about.
**Astolfo.** *[aside to ROSAURA]* What are you up to now?
**Rosaura.** You directed me to wait here
  for Astolfo to request
  a portrait for you. Being alone,
  and finding my thoughts drifting
  from one thing to another,
  and having just heard you speak
  of portraits, it occurred to me
  that I happened to have my own
  here in my sleeve. I intended
  to look at it, like anyone
  alone trying to amuse himself
  with little things of that sort.
  It fell from my hand to the ground.
  Coming in just then to give you
  the portrait of some other woman,
  Astolfo picked mine up, and now
  is not only set against
  surrendering the one
  you asked for but also
  wants to keep the other one.
  I pleaded and protested,
  but he would not give it back.
  In my anger and annoyance
  I tried to snatch it from him.
  The one he's holding in his hand
  is mine; you can tell by looking
  if it isn't a likeness of me.
**Estrella.** Let me have that portrait, Astolfo.

*[She takes it out of his hand.]*

**Astolfo.** Madame . . .
**Estrella.**          Yes, indeed, it's close;
  the drawing doesn't do you any harm.
**Rosaura.** Would you say it's me?
**Estrella.**           Who would doubt it?
**Rosaura.** Now have him give you the other one.
**Estrella.** Take your portrait, and go.
**Rosaura.** *[aside]* I've got it back now; let come what will.

[*Exit*

**Estrella.** Now give me the portrait I asked for.
  Though I'll never look at it
  or talk to you again, I insist
  I won't permit you to keep it,
  having been fool enough to beg you
  for it.
**Astolfo.** [*aside*] How do I wriggle out
  of this embarrassment?
  [*aloud*] Beautiful Estrella,
  though I wish for nothing better
  than to serve you obediently,
  I cannot possibly give up
  the portrait you ask for, because—
**Estrella.** You are a villain and, as a suitor,
  beneath contempt. I don't want it now.
  If I had it, it would only
  remind me how I had to ask you
  for it.

[*Exit*

**Astolfo.**    Wait, listen, look, let me say . . .
  The good Lord bless you, Rosaura!
  How, or why in the world,
  did you come to Poland now?
  Just to ruin me and yourself?

[*Exit*

### The Prince's cell in the tower.

*SEGISMUNDO, in chains and animal skins, as in the beginning, lies stretched*
*out on the ground; CLOTALDO enters with two*
*SERVANTS and CLARÍN.*

**Clotaldo.** You can leave him here now,
  His insolent pride ending
  where it began.
**A Servant.**      I'll attach the chain
  the way it was before.
**Clarín.** Better not wake up, Segismundo,
  and see how lost you are, your luck
  all gone, and your imaginary
  glory passing like life's shadow,
  and like death, all in a flash.
**Clotaldo.** A man who can turn phrases like that
  deserves to have a place apart,
  a room where he can go on prattling.
  [*to the SERVANTS*] Take hold of this man and lock him up
  in that cell.

**Clarín.** But why me?

**Clotaldo.** Because a tight prison cell
   is just the place for trumpeters
   who want to blare their secrets out.

**Clarín.** Did I, by any chance, offer
   to kill my father? No.
   Was I the one who picked up
   little Icarus and threw him
   off the balcony? Is this a dream
   or am I only sleeping?
   What's the point of locking me up?

**Clotaldo.** Clarín, you're a trumpeter.

**Clarín.** Well, then. I'll play the cornet,
   and a muted one at that; as
   an instrument it's miserable!

                *[They take him away, leaving CLOTALDO alone.]*

         *Enter BASILIO, masked.*

**Basilio.** Clotaldo!

**Clotaldo.**          Sire! Is it
   Your Majesty coming here this way?

**Basilio.** Alas, foolish curiosity
   brought me here like this
   to see what's happening
   to Segismundo.

**Clotaldo.**         See him
   lying there in complete abjection.

**Basilio.** Unhappy Prince—oh, the fatal hour
   you were born! You may wake him now,
   his energies and manhood sapped
   by the opium he drank.

**Clotaldo.** Sire, he's restless and talking
   to himself.

**Basilio.**       What will he be dreaming
   now? Let's listen to what he says.

**Segismundo.** *[in his sleep]* A just prince must punish tyrants.
   Clotaldo must be put to death,
   and my father kiss my feet.

**Clotaldo.** He's threatening to kill me.

**Basilio.** To insult and conquer me.

**Clotaldo.** He plans to take my life.

**Basilio.** And to humiliate me.

**Segismundo.** *[in his sleep]* Once my uncontested valor
   finds its way into the vast
   theatre of this world to clinch
   its vengeance, they'll all see
   how Prince Segismundo subjugates
   his father.
   *[waking]*    But, good Lord,

what's this? Where am I now?
**Basilio.** [*to Clotaldo*] He must not see me. You know
    what's to be done. Meanwhile,
    I'll step back here and listen.

                                                   [*He withdraws.*]

**Segismundo.** Is this really me? Can I be he
    who now returns to see himself
    reduced to such a state, bound up
    and clapped in chains? Oh tower,
    have you become my sepulcher?
    Yes, of course. God Almighty,
    what things have I been dreaming!
**Clotaldo.** [*aside*] That's my cue to play illusionist.
**Segismundo.** Is it time for me to waken now?
**Clotaldo.** Yes, it's time for you to waken.
    Or would you spend the whole day sleeping?
    Have you been awake at all
    since I began that disquisition
    on the eagle? Were you left behind
    while I was following its slow flight?
**Segismundo.** Yes, nor have I wakened yet,
    Clotaldo, for if I grasp
    your meaning, I must be still asleep.
    In that I can't be much mistaken,
    for if what I felt and saw so clear
    was something that I dreamt,
    then what I'm looking at this moment
    would be unreal; so since I now
    can see I'm fast asleep, it shouldn't
    be surprising that when
    I am unconscious I dream
    that I'm awake.
**Clotaldo.**           Tell me what you dreamt.
**Segismundo.** If I thought it was a dream
    I'd never tell you what I dreamt.
    But what I saw, Clotaldo—
    yes, I'll tell you that. I woke,
    I saw myself lying in a bed
    —oh, the warmly sinister
    deception of it all!—as in
    some flower bed the spring shoots
    through and through with luscious colors.
    And gathered there around me
    were a thousand noblemen
    bowing and calling me their Prince.
    What they offered me were jewels
    and costumes rich and elegant.
    Then you yourself appeared,

and changed my quiet numbness into
an ecstasy by telling me
(never mind what I look like now)
that I was the Prince of Poland.
**Clotaldo.** Surely you rewarded me
for bringing you such news.
**Segismundo.** Just the opposite. In a rage
I tried to kill you twice
for being such a traitor.
**Clotaldo.** Did I deserve the punishment?
**Segismundo.** I was lord and master there—
of everybody. And I took
revenge on all of them,
except for a woman that I loved . . .
I know that that was true, for
it's the only thing that stays with me.
All the rest has disappeared.

*[Exit BASILIO*

**Clotaldo.** [*aside*] The King was moved by what he heard,
and went away.
[*to SEGISMUNDO*]   So much talk
about eagles put you to sleep
and made you dream of empire. Still
it would be better, Segismundo,
if you could dream, instead,
of honoring the one
who took such pains to bring you up;
for even in a dream, remember,
it's still worth doing what is right.

*[Exit*

**Segismundo.** True enough. And so, put down
the beast in us, its avidity
and mad ambition, since we may
just happen to dream again,
as we surely will, for the world
we live in is so curious
that to live is but to dream.
And all that's happened to me tells me
that while he lives man dreams
what he is until he wakens.
The King dreams he's a king,
and so he lives with this illusion,
making rules, putting things in order,
governing, while all the praise
he's showered with is only lent him,
written on the wind, and by death,
his everlasting sorrow,
transformed to dust and ashes.

Who would ever dare to reign,
knowing he must wake into
the dream of death? The rich man
dreams he's wealthy with all the cares
it brings him. The poor man dreams
he's suffering his misery
and poverty. The fellow
who improves his lot is dreaming,
and the man who toils and only
hopes to, is dreaming too.
And dreaming too, the man
who injures and offends.
And so, in this world, finally,
each man dreams the thing he is,
though no one sees it so.
I dream that I am here
manacled in this cell,
and I dreamed I saw myself
before, much better off.
What is life? A frenzy.
What is life? An illusion,
fiction, passing shadow,
and the greatest good the merest dot,
for all of life's a dream, and dreams
themselves are only part of dreaming.

## Act Three

### *In the tower.*

**Clarín.** I'm kept a prisoner
in an enchanted tower
because of what I know.
What will they do to me
because of what I do not know,
since they're so quick to do away
with me for what I do know? To think
a man like me should have to die
of hunger and stay alive!
Of course, I'm sorry for myself.
They'll all say, "You're right to be,"
and they're surely right to say so,
because this silence doesn't jibe
with the name I've got, Clarín.
I just can't keep still, you see.
Who's here to keep me company?
To tell the truth—spiders and rats . . .
Oh, the dear little twitterers!
and my poor head still stuffed

with those nightmares I had last night—
there were a thousand oboes, trumpets,
and what have you, playing to
long processionals of flagellants
and crosses; some staggering up,
others toppling down, still others
fainting at the sight of blood.
As for me I'm fainting out of
hunger, because I told the truth.
I find I'm in prison where all day
I'm taught the philosophic text
of No-eateries, and all night,
the stuff of No-dineries.
If silence is ever canonized
in a new calendar,
Saint Secrecy should be
my patron saint because
I celebrate his day,
not by feasting but by fasting.
Still, I deserve this punishment
because instead of blabbing, I shut
my mouth, which for a servant
is the greatest sacrilege.

[*The sound of bugles, drums and voices outside.*]

**Soldier 1.** [*offstage*] Here's the tower where they put him.
Knock the door down, everyone,
and let's go in.

**Clarín.**          Good Heavens
its clear they're looking for me,
since they say I'm in here.
What do they want of me?

**Soldier 1.**                    Now go in.

[*Several soldiers enter.*]

**Soldier 2.** Here he is.

**Clarín.**          Here he isn't.

**All Soldiers.**                    Sire . . .

**Clarín.** [*aside*] Are they drunk, or what?

**Soldier 1.**                    You are
our Prince. We want you and won't accept
anyone but a native ruler—
no foreigners! We all kiss your feet.

**All Soldiers.** Long live our mighty Prince!

**Clarín.** [*aside*] Good God, they really mean it! Is it
customary in these parts
to grab someone every day
and make him a prince, then
throw him back into the tower?
Now I see that's just what happens.

Well, so that's the part I'll play.

**Soldiers.** We're at your feet. Let us have them . . .

**Clarín.** Impossible. I need my feet.
Besides, what good's a footless prince?

**Soldiers.** We've told your father, straight out,
we'll recognize only you as Prince,
and not someone from Muscovy.

**Clarín.** You told my father? Oh,
how disrespectful of you!
Then you're nothing but riffraff.

**Soldier 1.** But it was out of loyalty
we said it—straight from the heart.

**Clarín.** Loyalty? If so, you're pardoned.

**Soldier 2.** Come with us and reclaim your kingdom.
Long live Segismundo!

**All.**                               Hurray,
Segismundo!

**Clarín.** [*aside*] So Segismundo's
the one you're after? Oh, well,
then Segismundo must be the name
they give all their fictitious princes.

*Enter SEGISMUNDO.*

**Segismundo.** Who is it here that's calling
Segismundo!

**Clarín.** [*aside*]    Well I'll be a—
pseudo-Segismundo.

**Soldier 1.**                    Now who is
Segismundo?

**Segismundo.**        I am.

**Soldier 2.** [*to CLARÍN*] You pretentious idiot,
how dare you impersonate
Segismundo?

**Clarín.**            Me, Segismundo?
I deny that! Why, you were the ones
who segismundozed me
in the first place. So you're the
pretentious idiots, not me.

**Soldier 1.** Great Prince Segismundo,
the standards we have brought
are yours, though our faith's sufficient
to acclaim you as our sovereign.
The great King Basilio,
your father, fearing Heaven
would fulfill the fate
predicting he'd fall vanquished
at your feet, seeks to deprive you
of your lawful right to succeed him
and to give it to Astolfo,

Duke of Moscovy. To achieve this,
he has convened his council,
but the populace, alerted now
and knowing there's a native
successor to the crown,
has no wish to see a foreigner
come here to rule over them.
And thus, nobly scorning fate's
ominous predictions, they've come
to find you where you've been kept
a prisoner so that, assisted
by their arms, you may leave
this tower and reclaim
the kingly crown and scepter
sequestered by a tyrant.
Now come with us, for in this desert
large bands of rebels and plebeians
acclaim you: freedom is yours!
It is shouting to you—listen!
**Voices.** [*offstage*] Long live Segismundo!
**Segismundo.** Heavenly God, do you wish me
once again to dream of grandeur
which time must rip asunder?
Do you wish me once again
to glimpse half-lit among the shadows
that pomp and majesty
which vanish with the wind?
Do you wish me once again to taste
that disillusionment, the risks
that human power must begin with
and must forever run?
This must not, no, it must not happen!
I cannot bear to see myself
bound down again by a private fate.
Knowing as I do that life's a dream,
I say to you, be gone and leave me,
vague shadows, who now pretend
these dead senses have a voice
and body, when the truth is they are
voiceless and incorporeal.
Because I'm through with blown-up majesty,
I'm through with pompous fantasies
and with all illusions scattered
by the smallest puff of wind,
like the flowering almond tree
surrendering without the slightest
warning to the dawn's first passing breeze,
which dulls and withers the fine
rose-lit beauty of its frilly blooms.

I understand you now, yes,
I understand you and I know now
that this game's the game you play
with anyone who falls asleep.
For me, no more pretenses, no more
deceptions. My eyes are wide open.
I've learned my lesson well.
I know that life's a dream.

**Soldier 2.** If you think we're deceiving you,
just cast your eyes up to
those mighty mountains and see
all the people waiting there
for your commands.

**Segismundo.**          Yes, and this
is just the thing I saw before,
as clearly and distinctly
as I see it now, and it was all
a dream.

**Soldier 2.**   Great events, my lord,
always are foreseen this way.
That is why, perhaps, you saw them
in your dream first.

**Segismundo.**          You're right.
This was all foreseen; and just in case
it turns out to be true,
since life's so short, let's dream,
my soul, let's dream that dream again,
but this time knowing the pleasure's brief
from which we suddenly must waken;
knowing that much, the disillusion's
bound to be that much less.
One can make light of injuries
if one's prepared to meet them halfway.
Thus forewarned, and knowing that
however much it seems assured
all power is only lent
and must be given back to
its donor, let's dare do anything.
My subjects, I appreciate
your loyalty to me.
With my aggressiveness and skill,
I'm the one to lead you
out of servitude to foreigners.
Strike the call to arms; you'll soon have proof
of how great-hearted my valor is.
I intend to wage war against
my father, dragging whatever truth
there is out of the stars of Heaven.
I'll see him grovel at my feet . . .

[aside] But if I wake before that happens,
perhaps I'd better not mention it,
especially if I don't reach that point.
**All.** Long live Segismundo!

*Enter CLOTALDO.*

**Clotaldo.** Good Lord, what's all this uproar?
**Segismundo.** Clotaldo.

           My Lord . . .

**Clotaldo.** [*aside*]              He's sure
to take his fury out on me!
**Clarín.** [*aside*] I'll bet he throws him off the cliff.
**Clotaldo.** I come to lie down at your feet, Sire,
knowing I must die.
**Segismundo.**        Get up,
little father, get up from the ground,
for you're to be my guide,
my true North Star. I entrust you
with my first efforts, aware of
how much I owe to your loyalty
for bringing me up. Come, embrace me.
**Clotaldo.** What's that you say?
**Segismundo.**          That I'm dreaming,
and "Even in a dream, remember,
it's still worth doing what is right."
**Clotaldo.** Indeed, Sire, if doing right
is to be your motto, then surely
it should not offend you if the plea
I make now is in the same cause.
Wage war against your father?
I must tell you that I cannot serve
against my King, thus cannot help you.
I am at your feet. Kill me!
**Segismundo.** [*aside*] Traitor! Villain! Ingrate!
God knows, I should control myself,
I don't even know if I'm awake.
[*aloud*] Clotaldo, your courage
is enviable, thank you.
Go now and serve the King;
we'll meet again in combat.
You, there! Strike the call to arms!
**Clotaldo.** You have my deepest gratitude.

                                *[Exit*

**Segismundo.** Fortune, we go to rule!
Do not wake me, if I sleep,
and if it's real, don't put me
to sleep again; but whether real
or not, to do the right thing

is all that matters. If it's true,
then for truth's sake only;
if not, then to win some friends
against the time when we awaken.

[*Exeunt, to the sound of drums.*

### A hall in the royal palace.

*Enter BASILIO and ASTOLFO.*

**Basilio.** Astolfo, tell me, what prudence
could restrain a wild horse's fury?
And who could check a coursing river
flowing fast and foaming to the sea?
Can valor keep loose rock
from breaking off a mountain top?
Well, any one of these would seem
easier to achieve than putting
down an impudent, rebellious mob.
Once rumor starts up factions,
you can hear the echoes breaking
far across the mountains: from one side,
*Segismundo!* and from the other,
*Astolfo!* while the throne room,
split by duplicity and horror,
becomes again the grisly stage where
urgent fate enacts its tragedies.

**Astolfo.** Then, Sire, we'll defer our happiness
and put aside the tribute
and sweet reward your hand
so generously offered me.
For if Poland, which I hope to rule,
now withholds obedience to me,
it's because I have to win it first.
Give me a horse, and let me show
my fearlessness, hurling lightning, as
I go, behind my shield of thunder.

[*Exit*

**Basilio.** What must be admits no remedy;
what's foreseen magnifies the peril,
impossible to cope with,
while to evade it only brings it on.
This is the circumstance, this the law
grinding on so horribly.
The risk I tried to shun meets me head on;
and I have fallen in the trap
I took such pains to sidestep.
Thus I've destroyed my country and myself.

*Enter ESTRELLA .*

346

**Estrella.** If your Majesty in person
    does not intervene to halt
    this riot swelling with each
    new band fighting in the streets
    and squares, you'll see your kingdom
    swimming in scarlet waves, and caked
    in its own purpling blood.
    Sorrow creeps in everywhere,
    piling tragedy on misfortune
    everywhere. The ear grows numb,
    the eye falters witnessing
    the havoc done your kingdom,
    the bloody, heavy-handed blows
    of sheer calamity.
    The sun pulses in amazement,
    the wind moves up and back perplexed;
    each stone juts out to mark a grave,
    each flower garlanding a tomb.
    Every building has become
    a towering sepulcher, every
    soldier a living skeleton.

                *Enter CLOTALDO.*

**Clotaldo.** Thank God I've reached you here alive!
**Basilio.** Ah, Clotaldo, what news
    have you of Segismundo?
**Clotaldo.** A blind and monstrous mob
    poured into the tower; out of
    its recesses they plucked their Prince,
    who, when he saw himself
    a second time restored to grandeur,
    relentlessly displayed his valor
    and hoarsely swore he'd drag what truth
    there is out of the stars of Heaven.
**Basilio.** Give me my horse. Relentless too,
    I go in person to put down
    an ungrateful son; and, to defend
    my crown, will show that where knowledge failed,
    my cold steel must succeed.

                                        *[Exit*

**Estrella.** And at his royal side, the Sun God,
    I'll be the invincible Bellona;
    hoping to frame my name with his
    in glory, I'll stretch my wings
    and fly like Pallas Athena,
    war goddess and protector.

            *[Exits, as the call to arms is sounded*
        *ROSAURA enters, detaining CLOTALDO.*

**Rosaura.** I know that war is everywhere,
  but though your valor beckons you
  impatiently, listen to me first.
  You well remember how I came
  to Poland, poor, unhappy,
  and humiliated, and how,
  shielded by your valor,
  I took refuge in your sympathy.
  Then, alas, you ordered me
  to live at court incognito
  and, while I masked my jealousy,
  endeavor to avoid Astolfo.
  Finally, he saw me,
  but though he recognized me,
  still persists in trampling
  on my honor by going nightly
  to the garden to meet Estrella.
  I've taken the garden key
  and can now make it possible
  for you to enter there
  and wipe my cares away.
  So, with daring, courage, strength,
  you will restore my honor,
  determined as you are
  to avenge me by killing him.

**Clotaldo.** It's true, Rosaura, that from
  the moment I met you
  I was inclined—as your tears
  could testify—to do all
  I possibly could for you.
  My first thought was to have you change
  the costume you were wearing, so that
  if Astolfo happened to see you,
  at least he'd see you as you are,
  and not think that your outraged honor
  had filled you with such mad despair,
  it had made you wholly licentious.
  Meanwhile I tried to think of some way
  to restore your honor, even though
  (and this shows how much your honor
  meant to me), it should involve
  murdering Astolfo. But oh,
  it must have been the madness
  of senility in me!
  I do not mean the prospect fazed me.
  After all, who is he? Surely
  not my King. So here I was,
  about to kill him when . . . when
  Segismundo tried to murder me.

348

And there was Astolfo, on the spot,
to save me— despite the danger,
all heart, all will, and boundless
courage! Now think of me,
touched to the soul with gratitude—
how could I kill the man who saved
my life? So here I am,
split between duty and devotion:
what I owe you, since I gave you life,
and what I owe him, who gave me life.
I don't know whom to help
nor which one of you to support:
you, to preserve what I have given,
or him, for what I have received.
In the present circumstance, my love
has no recourse at all, since I am
both the one to do the deed
and the one to suffer for it too.

**Rosaura.** I'm sure I needn't tell a man
of honor that when it's nobler
to give, it's sheer abjection
to receive. Assuming that much, then,
you owe him nothing, for if
he's the one who gave you life,
as you once gave me mine, it's clear
he's forcing you, in good conscience,
to do a thing that's mean and base, and
I, a thing that's fine and generous.
By that token, he insults you,
and by it you remain obliged to me
for having given me
what you received from him.
Therefore, as giving is worthier
than taking, you must apply yourself
to the mending of my honor,
a cause far worthier than his.

**Clotaldo.** While nobility lives on giving,
gratitude depends on taking
what's given. And having learned by now
how to be the giver,
I have the honor to be known
as generous; let me now be known
as well for being grateful.
That I can achieve, as I achieved
nobility, by way of being
generous again, and thereby show
I love both giving and receiving.

**Rosaura.** When you granted me my life,
you told me then yourself

that to live disgraced
was not to live at all.
Therefore, I received nothing from you,
since the life your helping hand held forth
to me was not a life at all.
And if it's generosity
you admire above gratitude
(as I've heard you say), then I'm still
waiting for that gift of life
you've neglected giving me.
For the gift grows greater
when before you practice gratitude
you indulge your generosity.

**Clotaldo.** You've won; first I'll be generous.
Rosaura, you will have my estate,
but live in a convent.
I've thought the matter through:
this way you'll commit yourself
to safety rather than to crime.
Surely at times like these,
with the kingdom so divided,
I could not, as a born nobleman,
add to my country's misfortunes.
In following my proposal,
I continue loyal to the crown,
generous to you, and grateful
to Astolfo. Now choose this way
which best suits you between extremes.
If I were your father, God knows
I couldn't do more for you.

**Rosaura.** If you were my father,
I'd endure this insult silently.
But since you're not, I won't.

**Clotaldo.** Then what do you intend to do?

**Rosaura.** Kill the Duke.

**Clotaldo.**                    A woman
who has never known her father,
and so courageous?

**Rosaura.**                    Yes.

**Clotaldo.** What inspires you?

**Rosaura.**                    My good name.

**Clotaldo.** Think of Astolfo as . . .

**Rosaura.** The man who utterly disgraced me.

**Clotaldo.** . . . your King and Estrella's husband.

**Rosaura.** That, by God, he'll never be!

**Clotaldo.** This is madness!

**Rosaura.**                    I know it is.

**Clotaldo.** Well, control it.

**Rosaura.** I can't.
**Clotaldo.** Then you'll lose . . .
**Rosaura.** Yes, I know.
**Clotaldo.** . . . your life and honor.
**Rosaura.** Yes, of course.
**Clotaldo.** Why? What do you want?
**Rosaura.** To die.
**Clotaldo.** That's sheer spite.
**Rosaura.** No, it's honor.
**Clotaldo.** It's hysteria.
**Rosaura.** It's self-respect.
**Clotaldo.** You're in a frenzy.
**Rosaura.** Angry, outraged!
**Clotaldo.** So there's no way to curb
   your blind passion?
**Rosaura.** No, there's not
**Clotaldo.** Who's to help you?
**Rosaura.** Myself.
**Clotaldo.** And no other way?
**Rosaura.** No other way.
**Clotaldo.** Consider now, if there's another . . .
**Rosaura.** Another way to ruin myself, of course.

[*Exit*

**Clotaldo.** Daughter, wait for me—I'll go
   with you, and we'll be lost together.

[*Exit*

### *An open field.*

*SEGISMUNDO in animal skins; SOLDIERS
marching, drum beats; CLARÍN enters.*

**Segismundo.** If Old Rome, in its triumphant
   Golden Age, could see me now,
   how she'd rejoice at the strange sight
   of a wild animal leading
   mighty armies, for whom,
   in his high purposes,
   the conquest of the firmament
   is but a paltry thing. And yet,
   my soul, let us not fly too high,
   or the little fame we have
   will vanish, and when I wake
   I'll plague myself for having gained
   so much only to lose it all;
   so, the less I feel attached to now,
   the easier to lose it later.

[*A bugle is sounded.*]

351

**Clarín.** Mounted on a fire-eating steed
    (excuse me if I touch things up
    a bit in telling you this story),
    on whose hide a map is finely drawn,
    for of course his body is the earth,
    and his heart the fire locked up
    in his breast, his froth the sea,
    his breath the wind, and in
    this sweltering chaos I stand
    agape, since heart, froth, body, breath,
    are monsterized by fire, earth, sea, wind—
    mounted on this dappled steed,
    which feels the rider's spur
    bidding it to gallop (say to fly
    instead of gallop), I mean, look here,
    there's a very lively woman
    riding up to meet you.
**Segismundo.** Her light blinds me.
**Clarín.**                     God, it's Rosaura.

                                      *[He withdraws.]*

**Segismundo.** Heaven has restored her to me.

      *ROSAURA enters in the loose blouse and wide skirts of a
           peasant woman, and wearing a sword and a dagger.*

**Rosaura.** Magnanimous Segismundo,
    your heroic majesty rises
    with the daylight of your deed
    out of your shadowy long night.
    Like the sun regaining lustre
    as it rises from Aurora's arms
    to shine on plants and roses,
    seas and mountains, gazing
    golden-crowned abroad and shedding rays
    that twinkle in the foam
    and flash upon the summits,
    so too you come now, a bright new sun
    of Poland rising in the world.
    Oh aid this poor unhappy woman
    who lies prostrate at your feet,
    and help her both because she is
    a woman and is unprotected,
    two reasons to obligate
    any man who prides himself
    on being valiant—either one
    should do or be more than enough.
    Three times now I've surprised you and
    three times you've failed to recognize me,
    because each time you saw me I was
    someone else and dressed differently.

The first time you took me for a man.
That's when you were heavily confined
in prison, where your life was so
wretched that it made my own sorrows
seem trivial. The next time
you admired me as a woman,
when all the pomp of majesty
was to you a dream, a fantasy,
a fleeting shadow. The third time is
today, when I appear before you
as a monstrous hybrid:
armed for combat as a man,
but in woman's clothing.
Now to rouse your sympathy,
the better to dispose you
to my cause, hear my tragic story.
My mother was a noblewoman
in Muscovy, who, since she was
unfortunate, must have been
most beautiful. Her betrayer
saw her there, whose name I cannot tell
because I did not know him, yet know
there was something valiant in him
because the same stuff stirs in me.
Sometimes when I think he fathered me,
a perverse idea seizes me:
I'm sorry I wasn't born a pagan
so I could tell myself
he was like one of those gods
who changed himself into a shower
of gold, a swan, a bull,
on Danae, Leda, and Europa.
That's odd: I thought I'd just been
rambling on, telling old tales
of treachery, but I find
I've told you in a nutshell
how my mother was deceived
by tender love's expression,
being herself more beautiful
than any woman, but like us all,
unhappy. His promises
to marry her she took
so guilelessly that to this day
the thought of them starts her weeping.
As Aeneas did on fleeing Troy,
this scoundrel fled, leaving her his sword.
It's the same one sheathed here at my side,
which I'll bare before my story ends.
This was the loosely tied knot—

neither binding enough
for a marriage nor open
enough to punish as a crime—
out of which I myself was born,
my mother's image, not in beauty
but in bad luck and its aftermath.
I needn't stop to tell you how,
having inherited such luck,
my fate has been as grim as hers.
All I can tell you is that the man
who destroyed my honor and good name
is . . . Astolfo. Simply naming him
floods and chokes my heart with rage,
as if I'd named my worst enemy.
Astolfo was the faithless wretch
who, forgetting love's delights
(for when one's love is past, even
its memory fades away),
came here to Poland, fresh for new
conquest, to marry Estrella,
her torch lit against my setting sun.
Who'd have thought after one happy star
had brought two lovers together
that another star (Estrella)
should then rise to pull them apart?
Hurt, insulted, my sadness turned
to madness, and I froze up inside—
I mean that all of Hell's confusions
went sweeping through my head
like voices howling out
of my own Tower of Babel,
I decided to be silent,
and speak my troubles wordlessly,
because there are anxieties
too painful for words and
only feelings may express.
Alone with her one day,
my mother Violante
tore wide open in my breast
the prison where these were hidden.
They came swarming out like troops tripping
over one another.
I was not ashamed to speak of them.
For, knowing that the person to whom
one confesses one's weaknesses
has herself been prone in the same way
makes the telling easier
and the burden lighter.
Sometimes there's purpose in

a bad example. And so,
as she listened to my troubles,
she was sympathetic
and tried to console me
by telling me of her own.
How easily can the judge who sinned
excuse that sin in another!
Sad experience had taught her
not to entrust the cause of honor
to lapsing time or to occasion.
She applied this lesson
to me in my unhappiness,
advising me to follow him
and, with relentless courtesy,
persuade him to restore my honor.
Also, to minimize the risks,
fate designed that I should go
disguised as a gentleman.
Mother took down this ancient sword
I wear (and the time approaches,
as I promised, to unsheathe it)
and, trusting in its power, told me,
"Go to Poland, and make sure that
those at court see you wearing this blade.
For surely someone among them
will be sympathetic to you
and defend you in your plight."
Since it's known and not worth retelling,
I'll only mention the wild horse
that threw me and left me at your cave,
where you saw me and were astonished.
We may also pass over how
Clotaldo first became my close
supporter, interceded for me,
and got the King to spare my life;
then, when Clotaldo found out
who I was, convinced me I must
change back into my own dress
and join Estrella's retinue,
where I managed rather skillfully
to block Astolfo's courtship
and his plans to marry her.
Again we can pass over details:
how you saw me there once more,
dressed as a woman, and how
confused you were by all those changes.
Let's pass on to Clotaldo.
Convinced that now the fair Estrella
and Astolfo must marry and rule,

he urged me to drop my prior claim
against the interest of my honor.
And when, oh valiant Segismundo,
I now see you, ripe for vengeance,
since Heaven permits you to break out
of your crude prison cell
where your body lay, an animal
to feeling, a rock to suffering,
and since you take up arms
against your father and your country,
I have come to help you fight.
You see me wearing both the precious
robes of Diana and the armor
of Minerva, for I'm equally
adorned in cloth and steel. And so,
brave captain, let us go together
to prevent the projected marriage,
a matter which concerns us both:
me, to keep the man who's vowed
to be my husband from marrying
another, and you, to keep them
from joining forces, whose greater strength
would make our victory doubtful.
As a woman I come hoping to win you
over to my honor's cause;
but also as a man would, I come
to swell your heart, battling for your crown.
The woman yearning for your sympathy
kneels down here at your feet;
the man who comes offering his service
lends you both his person and his sword.
But should you turn to take
the woman in me as all woman,
the man in me would kill you,
in strict defense of my good name;
for, to triumph in the war of love,
I must be both the humbled woman
who appeals to you and the man
who's out for honor and for glory.

**Segismundo.** [*aside*] If it's true that I'm still dreaming,
oh God, suspend my memory,
for it's impossible to crowd
so many things in one dream.
God, let me escape from all this,
or else give up thinking of it!
Who ever found himself confronting
such terrible ambiguities?
If I only dreamed the grandeur
in which I saw myself before,

how can this woman bring up details
known patently to me alone?
Then it was true and not a dream;
but if true—which would only make things
more, not less, confusing—
how can my life be called a dream?
Are all glories like dreams—
the true ones taken to be false,
and the false ones, to be true?
There's so little difference
between one and the other
that we cannot be sure if what
we're seeing and enjoying
is simple fact or an illusion!
Can it be the copy is so like
the original that no one knows
which is which? If this is so,
and one must be prepared to find
all pomp and majesty,
all the power and the glory,
vanishing among the shadows, then
let us learn to take advantage
of the little while that's granted us,
because all we can enjoy now
is what's to be enjoyed between dreams.
Rosaura's in my power;
my soul adores her beauty . . .
Let's take advantage of the moment.
Let love break all laws of gallantry
and the trust that lets her lie there
at my feet. It's all a dream,
and being such, let it be glad;
it'll turn sour soon enough.
My own reasoning convinces me
again, but let's see now.
If it's all a dream, all vainglory,
who'd want to substitute vanity
that's human for glory that's divine?
Is not all our former bliss a dream?
Does not a man who's known great joy
tell himself, when the thought of it
returns, "Surely it was all a dream"?
If this proves I'm disillusioned,
knowing that pleasure is a lovely flame
soon turned to ashes by the wind,
let me aim at what is lasting,
that longer-living glory
where joys are not a dream
nor greatness swallowed in a sleep.

Rosaura has lost her honor.
The duty of a prince is not
to take it but to give it back.
By God, then, I shall restore
her reputation before I claim
.ny crown. Meanwhile I turn my back
on her; the temptation
is more than I can bear.
[*to a* SOLDIER]          Sound the call to arms! This day
must see me fighting before darkness
buries its gold rays in dark green waves.
**Rosaura.** But, Sire, is this the way you'd leave me?
Without a single word?
Doesn't my plight affect you?
Doesn't my anguish move you?
Sire, how is this possible—
you neither listen nor glance at me.
Won't you even turn and look at me?
**Segismundo.** Because your honor hangs by a thread,
Rosaura, I must be cruel now
in order to be kind.
Words fail me in reply
so my honor will not fail.
I do not dare to talk to you,
because my deeds must do the talking.
I do not even look at you because,
as someone sworn to look after
your honor, I have all I can do
to keep from looking at your beauty.

*[Exits with the SOLDIERS*

**Rosaura.** God, why all these riddles now?
After all my troubles,
to be left with piecing out
a meaning from such puzzling replies!

*Enter CLARÍN.*

**Clarín.** Madame, is it all right for me
to see you?
**Rosaura.**          Clarín! Where have you been?
**Clarín.** Cooped up in a tower, and reading
my fortune—life or death—in a deck
of cards. The first card frowned at me,
thumbs down: my life is forfeit. Poof!
that's when I came close to bursting.
**Rosaura.** But why?
**Clarín.**                    Because I know the secret
of who you are and, in fact,
Clotaldo . . . But what's that noise?

*[The sound of drums.]*

**Rosaura.** What can it be?
**Clarín.** An armed squad's left the besieged palace
    to fight and overcome
    Segismundo's wild armies.
**Rosaura.** Then how can I be such a coward
    and not be at his side
    to scandalize the world that basks in
    so much cruelty and anarchy?

*[Exit*

**Voices.** Long live our invincible King!
**Other Voices.** Long live our liberty!
**Clarín.** Long live both—liberty and King!
    Let them live together;
    I don't care what they're called
    so long as I'm not called.
    I'll just take French leave now
    from all this ruckus and, like Nero,
    not give a damn who gets it or how,
    unless it's for myself.
    This spot here between the rocks
    looks mighty well protected
    and out of the way enough for me
    to watch all the fireworks.
    Death won't find me here—to hell with it!
           *[He hides; drum beats, the call to arms; BASILIO,*
                *CLOTALDO and ASTOLFO enter, fleeing.]*

**Basilio.** No king was ever more regretful,
    no father more beset, ill-used.
**Clotaldo.** Your army is beaten,
    and retreating everywhere pell-mell.
**Astolfo.** The traitors are victorious.
**Basilio.** In such wars the victors
    are always considered loyal,
    the vanquished, always traitors.
    Clotaldo, let us escape the wrath
    and ruthlessness of a tyrant son.

           *[Shots are fired offstage; CLARÍN falls,*
              *wounded, out of his hiding place.]*

**Clarín.** Heaven help me!
**Astolfo.**               Who is
    this unhappy soldier, fallen
    so bloodily at your feet?
**Clarín.** A man whose luck ran out.
    Trying to hide from death,
    I ran straight into it.
    I discovered it by fleeing it;
    for death, no place is secret.
    From this you clearly may conclude,

the man who most avoids its sting
is stung the quickest. Turn back, therefore—
go back to that bloody battlefield;
there's more safety in the midst
of clashing arms and fire
than in the highest mountain passes.
And there's no safe highway leading past
the force of destiny
or fate's inclemency.
So if by fleeing you now attempt
to free yourselves from death, remember,
you die when it's God's will you die.

*[He stumbles out and falls offstage.]*

**Basilio.** "Remember, you die when
it's God's will you die." Good Lord,
how convincingly this corpse
reflects upon our error,
showing our ignorance the way
to greater understanding,
and all this spoken from the mouth
of a wound trickling out its gore,
a bloody tongue lengthening
with eloquence, to teach us how vain
are men's deliberations when set
against a higher will and cause.
So in endeavoring to free
my country of murder
and sedition, I succeeded
only in giving it away
to murderers and traitors.
**Clotaldo.** Although it's true, Sire, that fate
knows all the ways and byways,
and can pick its man out of a crack
between two heavy boulders,
still it isn't Christian to believe
there's nothing to pit against fate's wrath,
Because there is—a manly prudence
will conquer fate's adversities.
But since you're not yourself exempt
from such contingencies, do something
now, in order to protect yourself.
**Astolfo.** Clotaldo speaks to you, Sire,
as a man of prudence and ripe years,
and I, simply as a valiant youth.
Hidden in some nearby thickets,
there's a horse that runs like lightning.
Take it and escape, and I'll
keep you covered from behind.
**Basilio.** If God intends that I should die here,

or death awaits me somewhere nearby,
I should like to meet it face to face.

    *A call to arms; SEGISMUNDO and the whole company enter.*

**Soldier.** Somewhere among these twisting paths
    and heavy branches, the King
    is hiding.
**Segismundo.**    Go after him.
    Comb every plant and tree,
    trunk by trunk and twig by twig,
    until you find him.
**Clotaldo.**             Sire, escape now.
**Basilio.** Why?
**Clotaldo.**       What will you do?
**Basilio.**                    Step aside,
    Astolfo.
**Clotaldo.**    What have you in mind?
**Basilio.** To do something, Clotaldo,
    that has long needed doing.
    [*to SEGISMUNDO*] If you've come to find me, Prince,
    here I am now, at your feet.
    [*He kneels.*] Here's a snowy carpet for you,
    made out of my white hair.
    Here's my neck—stamp on it!
    Here's my crown—trample on it!
    Smash my honor, disgrace me,
    drag down my self-respect.
    Make sure you take revenge on me.
    Chain and use me as your slave!
    After all I've done to ward it off,
    let fate receive its due, and the word
    of Heaven be fulfilled at last.
**Segismundo.** Distinguished court of Poland,
    witnesses of these astonishing
    events, listen to me:
    your Prince addresses you.
    What's written in the stars,
    on that blue tablet which
    God's hand inscribes with swirling figures
    and his ciphers, like so much gold
    lettering on blue fields of paper—
    such markings never are mistaken,
    and they never lie. Those who lie
    and are mistaken are such men
    who'd use them to bad purpose trying
    to penetrate the mystery
    so as to possess it totally.
    My father, at my feet here,
    using as his excuse

the auguries of my foul nature,
made of me a brute, a half-
human creature, so that
even if I'd been born gentle
and sweet-tempered, despite my noble
blood and inbred magnanimity,
such bizarre treatment, such upbringing,
would have been enough to turn me
into a wild animal.
Strange, because this was what
he wanted to avoid!
If any man were told,
"One day you'll be murdered
by some inhuman monster,"
would he deliberately go
and rouse the sleeping beast?
If he were told, "That sword
you're wearing at your side
is the one that will kill you,"
wouldn't it be foolish if,
to keep this from happening,
he unsheathed his sword so as
to turn it toward his chest?
Suppose that he were told,
"Deep waters, under silvery foam,
will one day be your grave"—
it would be a pity if he
put out to sea when the waves
were curling whitecaps like
foaming silver mountains.
But this all happened to the man
who, feeling threatened by a brute,
went and woke it up; and to the man
who, fearing the sword, unsheathed it;
and to the one who, fearing waves,
churned up a storm to jump into.
And, though my rage (listen to me)
were like a sleeping beast,
my latent fury like a sword still
sheathed, my hidden violence a sea
becalmed—no vengeance nor injustice
would alter the course of fate,
but, if anything, would incite it.
And so, the man who wishes
to control his fate must use
judgment and be temperate.
He cannot keep an injury
from happening, even though
he sees it coming; though, of course,

he can mitigate the shock
by resignation, this cannot
be done till after the worst
has happened, since there's no way
to ward it off. Let this strangest
of spectacles, this most amazing
moment, this awesome, prodigious scene
serve as an example. Because
nothing better shows how,
after so much had been done
to prevent its happening,
a father and a king lies subject
at his own son's feet. For such was
Heaven's verdict and, do what he might,
he could not change it. How then can I,
with fewer white hairs, less courage,
and less knowledge, conquer fate
when he could not?
[*to the KING*]            Rise, Sire,
and give me your hand. Now
that Heaven's disabused you
of the illusion that you knew the way
to overcome it, I offer myself up to you. Take
your vengeance. I kneel before you.

**Basilio.** My son—because your noble deed
has re-engendered you in me—
you are a prince indeed!
The laurel and the palm belong to you.
You've won the day. Your exploits crown you!

**All.** Long, long live Segismundo!

**Segismundo.** If my valor is destined
for great victories, the greatest
must be the one I now achieve
by conquering myself.
Astolfo, take Rosaura's hand.
You know the debt of honor due her.
I mean to see it paid her now.

**Astolfo.** Though it's true I've obligations
to her, let me point out that she
does not know who she is.
It would be base and infamous
for me to marry a woman who . . .

**Clotaldo.** Enough, don't say another word now.
Rosaura is your equal
in nobility, Astolfo,
and I'll defend her with this sword
on the field of honor.
She's my daughter—and that's enough.

**Astolfo.** What's that you say?

**Clotaldo.** Simply that until
I saw her married, nobly
and honorably, I would not
reveal the fact. It's a long story,
but it ends with this: she's my daughter.
**Astolfo.** Well, if that's the case, of course
I'll keep my word.
**Segismundo.** And now,
not to leave Estrella downcast,
since she has lost this brave
and famous prince, I offer her
my own hand in marriage,
with the virtues and fortune
that go with it, and though
they do not exceed, at least
they equal, his. Give me your hand.
**Estrella.** I gain by meriting this good fortune.
**Segismundo.** For Clotaldo, who served
my father loyally,
my gratitude waits to grant
whatever wish he has.
**Soldier.** If you're about to honor someone
who treated you dishonorably,
what about me, who incited
this kingdom's overthrow,
and took you out of that tower
you were in? What'll you give me?
**Segismundo.** The tower. And—so that you'll never
leave it till you die—a constant guard.
Once the cause of treason's past,
there's no need to keep the traitor.
**Basilio.** Your judgment astonishes us all.
**Astolfo.** What a changed disposition!
**Rosaura.** What prudence, what discretion!
**Segismundo.** Why are you surprised? What's there
to wonder at, if my master in this
was a dream, and I still tremble
at the thought that I may waken
and find myself again locked in a cell?
Even if this should not happen,
it would be enough to dream it,
since that's the way I've come to know
that all of human happiness
must like a dream come to an end.
And now, to take advantage
of the moments that remain, I'd like
to ask your pardon for our mistakes;
for such noble hearts as yours,
it would be fitting to forgive them.

# THE CROWN OF ABSALOM

# (LOS CABELLOS DE ABSALÓN)

## The Crown of Absalom

The initial action of the play concerns the rape of Tamar by her half-brother Amnon, Israel's crown prince. Subsequently the vengeful pursuit of her honor is climaxed when Absalom, her blood-brother, murders Amnon at a banquet table to which the whole family has been invited. For all the melodramatic brio and high romantic sentence surcharging the action, the play is more intricately concerned with King David, once the legendary hero, now the aged and love-begging father enmeshed in the struggle for the crown he must soon relinquish to one son or another.

The play's narrative follows the main events in Samuel II of the Old Testament up to the death of Absalom; David's story re-enacts the proverb about the sins of the father being visited upon the children. But, in effect, the question of honor lost is engulfed by the greater question of man's destiny as a labyrinthine journey, largely unaided by his ability to control it. As an exemplum of the theme, the heroic stature of the king is overcome in old age by resources he can no longer implement. And the love he seeks to share with his sons and daughter is turned into an unending series of punishments and humiliations which questions the value of his existence. Suffering then becomes an almost reflex action which can neither be shared nor predicted, as his heroic deeds once were, but now must be simply endured, and even welcomed, as a just punishment by the victim. The implications of these developments give strong dramatic substance to Calderón's treatment of the old story and probe for a new depth to the honor question.

From the start to the end of the play, there is a dominant sense of slippage and eroding focus in David's character. The source is his guilt and a degraded feeling for himself, emerging from his past actions, and now reflected in the behavior of his sons and daughter. His children all appear to be hypocritical failures except for Solomon, whose life of true ruling power is reserved for developments still to come, beyond the events of the play. It is Amnon and Absalom who abortively re-enact their father's life of victories and crimes. In their search for power, they mirror aspects of David's earlier lust and powerful ambition, hollowed out now by his inadequacies as a father, and giving way to self-punishment as he witnesses the death of two sons and the disgrace of his only daughter. We see Absalom's and Amnon's desperately extravagant deeds turn into moral defeats, and, by the same token, how they reflect upon the crown—through which the youthful heroic legend of David was incarnated—now reduced by his weakened character and subsequent misjudgments laying waste to his children's lives. Amnon calls Tamar, after he rapes her, "poison in a golden cup." Absalom, grossly proud of his golden hair, believes it outdoes the glory of the royal crown itself, before being ensnared by the former and and fatally deprived of the latter. David can only assume these events are due punishment from God for his sins.

On the other hand, the two women, Tamar and Teuca, reveal in different ways the fatal missteps of male authoritarian power. Although once her honor is satisfied and Tamar turns into a warrior, she has been mainly instrumental, with Teuca, in exposing the hypocrisy of Amnon and the disorder of David's misrule. Characters who serve for personal profit and political power, like Achitophel, Joab, and Ensay (though no one in the play is exempt from crime and offense, including rape and murder), are shaped by the dramatist to demonstrate the roles of councilors around David and Absalom. And so in this play, as in **The Mayor of Zalamea,** where suddenly sharp characterizations similarly give way to closer delineations based on social disposition and personal temperament, the diction has greater snap and luster. Here it is present in the highly theatrical exchanges between the princes and the bitter rivalry of the councilors contending for Absalom's favor. But the play's soft ending leaves no doubt of Calderón's intentions. Consummate technician and dramaturge that he is, he brings the involved action to a close with his main character devastated, but intact enough to receive punishment in a way that even King Lear, another fond and foolish old man, is spared by dying.

There is also a deeper level in which the weaknesses of character and the aftereffects of honor lost and then resolved are made to interact, thereby suggesting something of life's meaning beyond the disasters of tragic consequences.

In the plays represented here, starting with **Secret Vengeance for Secret Insult,** Calderón's treatment of honor is engaged with psychological and social involvements, through which an inflexible code, imposed on an individual, by some accident suddenly traps and inexorably victimizes him. The tyranny of the code enforces an act of violence and a blood-shedding to eliminate the source of insult, the offending antagonist. Besieged by jealousy, or a spontaneous reaction to insult, the typical victim feels robbed of identity, which only vengeful murder may restore. But such a resolution may not wholly reinstate the injured person; more often it degrades his sensibility and causes further injury, social ostracism, self-imposed exile. This is the case in these plays, except for the comedic/ironic treatment of honor in **The Phantom Lady.**

The erotic compulsion sparking the honor quandary is based in each instance on either some suspected or an actual antecedent event, in which sexual identity is closely linked to personal identity, with all its murky uncertainties attached. Gradually the evolving situation reveals the problem in greater depth as the characters confess or speculate on their dread and their gnawing desires. What ultimately incites a crucial action is the obsessive attachment to a beloved or the alarm and emptiness brought on by a lost or unreciprocated affection.

In **The Crown of Absalom,** David's increasing sense of emptiness grows out of the feeling that everything is slowly fading from him after his attempts to yield his royal crown or grapple over it with his sons. Now, as an old man, he feels at the core of his existence an all-pervading nothingness. The repeated disaffection of his sons makes him almost greedy to accept punishment with the same alacrity with which he once sought their love.

In **Devotion to the Cross,** Eusebio's empty erotic passion for what turns out to be his own sister, Julia, parallels Amnon's self-frustrating passion for his half-sister Tamar. Confounded by its startling appearance in Eusebio, Julia observes, "Are you the phantom of desire or the shadow of a dream?" But, as she turns criminal herself and follows him in immensely destructive acts, she finds something better than Tamar's recourse of burying herself in a nunnery: Julia can follow her redeemable brother in his thaumaturgic rise to Heaven on the giant Cross. In effect then, striving for love—familial, filial, erotic or a combination of them all—appears to end in some refuge of self-drained desire; and ultimately regicide, fratricide, incestuous rape become vain attempts to find love or self-fulfillment that end in death or powerlessness.

Similarly in **Life Is a Dream**, the men in authority (Clotaldo, Astolfo, Basilio) have all been well-meaning but guilty of brutalizing a son or a daughter; these children then proceed to challenge the repressive law which subsists on the lies of a false honor code. At the end, Segismundo's triumph and consolation are not self-serving but self-proving: he discovers that to be fully conscious, one must strike through the mask and be reborn in oneself. While others may say that life is a dream, Segismundo must find out whether this is true or not by living his own life, through one delusion after another, for no other reason than that it is his own and only life. He must fight for the power he has been denied and then wear it lightly, pardoning his enemies and renouncing his love.

As in more than a few of Calderón's plays dealing variously with oppressive parents and subsequent actions of lost honor and incest, **The Crown of Absalom** employs the popular subject as skillfully as ever, but with a notable difference. King David, as a defeated hero in a story and an environment crumbling into widespread havoc and failure, is an unusual figuration to sustain according to the well-known story and morality. The play seems to lack conclusiveness as a result—unless one sees that the meaning lies in David's survival: David the lyricist, musician and poet, author of the Psalms, must, in fact, survive for his art as well as for his towering exploits. But the meaning of his life in terms of the play cannot simply reside in his ability to withstand punishment. It is what the body, the aged body itself in its longevity, subsumes by surviving. Thus the meaning must reach out further than the code, and it must do so through the reason of the body.

Curiously enough, there is a message to this effect in another dramatic work of Calderón's which directly applies to this necessity. It occurs early in the allegorical *auto*, **El pleito matrimonial del cuerpo y el alma (The Matrimonial Dispute of the Body and the Soul.)** The Body's speech is translated by A. A. Parker, the noted Calderón scholar, in his book, **The Mind and Art of Calderón** (p. 356).

> Without hearing, speaking, or seeing,
> I lie in perpetual night. If I am nothing
> before I have life, what shall I be when
> I have it? But, confused nature of mine,
> I do not want to know the answer, nor do
> I want to be; for this would be to anticipate
> the sadness of my life if I could see that

> I, who am beginning by being nothing,
> should be nothing when I end. Nonetheless,
> I want to live; for it is a mistake not to love
> life if having it depends on me, since it is
> better to have life on the lowest level than
> not have life at all; and already
> I feel such love for my life that I hope to have,
> that I must strive to exist, judging it
> to be a greater misery to be deprived of
> existence now, than not to live now
> in order not to die.

The sense of the Body's speech here is related to the least hope needed in order to live life: "it is/ better to have life on the lowest level than/ not to have life at all." In the play the illusion of love filial and erotic is destroyed; and David's need for love, when it is denied, puts him "on the lowest level." One might add that he has already experienced the deprivation of Donne's "else a great Prince in prison lies," the equivalence of the body's lying senseless: "Without hearing, speaking, or seeing,/ I lie in perpetual night." For behind the illusion of David's love is his uncorrupted dream of childhood: the love to be given and had effortlessly without question, without apparent struggle, between parent and child, that goes begging, and with that to contend with, the weight of love sought becomes a way of thickening the substance of illusion.

Hence David's love for his children is not reciprocated but *pro forma*, meaning that basically it is neither generated nor returned. And, as between the children themselves, as the example of rape exemplifies, there is no possibility of love being effortlessly consummated. Again, the sharp differences Calderón creates between the societies of Court and country vividly stress the distinction between a life of intrigue, murder, and war, where there is no love, and the values of natural life: peace, beauty, affectionate discourse, productivity. The energy that should go into love and natural desire is diverted into the intrigue and jockeying for the crown. As for Absalom, the anti-hero, one might say an intense narcissism that generates self-intoxication leads to a choking off of love in the labyrinthine and entangling woods, where he is ultimately hung by his hair from a bough. And the culminating insult that precedes this event occurs when, at Achitophel's advice, Absalom's troops are sent in to ravish the concubines in David's palace, and then parade through the streets of Jerusalem with the doors of the harem aloft as a triumphant gesture to humiliate David.

Implicit in these examples is Calderón's fabling on the Old Testament story to show how rape, as the gross sexual affront to honor, signifying the detestation of woman ("poison in a golden cup"), spreads to all forms of abuse in love and politics against the humane values of civilized society. The bitter lesson Amnon and Absalom exact, accommodated by their father, is that sexual possessiveness and the unstinted lust for power are two lethal ingredients brewed in the selfsame cup.

# THE CROWN OF ABSALOM

# LOS CABELLOS DE ABSALÓN

## DRAMATIS PERSONAE

| | |
|---|---|
| DAVID | Old King of Israel |
| ABSALOM | Golden-haired son of David |
| ADONAI | Envious son of David |
| JONADAB | Amnon's servant, *gracioso* |
| TEUCA | Ethiopian sorceress |
| ELIAZAR | Servant |
| JOAB | David's general |
| SOLOMON | Son of David |
| AMNON | Eldest son of David; Crown Prince |
| TAMAR | David's daughter; Absalom's sister |
| ACHITOPHEL | Conspirator |
| SEMEY | David's emissary |
| ENSAY | David's counselor |
| Shepherds | |
| Musicians | |

*The scene is laid in Jerusalem, Baalhazor, and Hebron*

## ACT ONE

### *Jerusalem. The Royal Palace.*

*Sound of drums; DAVID enters through one door, ABSALOM, SOLOMON,
ADONAI, TAMAR, and ACHITOPHEL through the other.*

**Solomon.** Israel's champion, slayer
   of the sacrilegious Moabite,
   o happily return, with your
   noble forehead laurel-crowned.
**Adonai.** Defender of God and his holy law,
   terror of the Gentile idolator,
   o let your snow-white head
   be crowned with circlet
   of the immortal olive branch.
**Absalom.** Through diamond voice and metal lip,
   let Fame chant hymns to
   Jehovah's royal chief and all
   the tragic blades of Philistines.
**Tamar.** Garlanded with stars and flowers,
   let the lovely daughters of
   Jerusalem intone his glory—
   as great as David's triumph was
   once upon Goliath.

> *[DAVID embraces SOLOMON first, then ABSALOM,
> ADONAI and TAMAR]*

**David.** Come, my precious loved ones:
   renew my ancient days
   with these glad and loving bonds
   of your embrace! Come now,
   valiant Adonai, come to me again.
   And you, my prudent Solomon,
   once more you touch a heart
   dissolved in loving tears.
   You too, my handsome Absalom,
   renew the pleasure you bring me
   on this happiest of days.
   And you as well, Tamar—
   do not withdraw, my dear—
   for my heart would not leave off
   embracing you, at such
   a glorious moment, to hurry
   for someone next in line . . .
   I left proud Rabbat, the walled
   and well-armed city of the Ammonites,
   defeated, its wondrous walls

demolished, its high towers
prostrate and in ruins,
its streets bathed in blood—
thanks mainly to the Great Lord
of Israel, then to Joab,
my valiant general,
to whose bravery I owe my success.

**Joab.** Sire, in your exploits lies my honor.

**Achitophel.** [*aside*] Unhappy me who serves without reward;
as his loyal soldier, not so much
as a single word is granted me.

**David.** So singular a victory
would not be complete
without returning here to see you.
Although so many tidings blend
your joy, considering
that this happy day when
triumphant, entering
the sumptuous house of Zion
as all of you come forth
so eagerly to greet me
at your threshold upon
this signal occasion,
only Amnon is missing among you—
Amnon my eldest son and heir,
whom I esteem and love as such.
What's the reason, Adonai,
he does not augment my happiness?

**Adonai.** Sire, there's none I know of.

**David.** Solomon, a pain imagined
is greater than a pain experienced.
Tell me, on your life,
what has happened to Amnon?

**Solomon.** Absalom will tell you. I'm not
aware of anything that has.

**Absalom.**                     Nor I.

**David.** Your uncertainty prolongs my pain.
Tamar, what ails your brother?

**Tamar.** Sire, you ask me this in vain.
Sequestered in my rooms, I'm ignored
even by chance events.

**David.** Will no one tell me about Amnon?

**Achitophel.** As your servant, Sire, love obliges
me to keep nothing from you
Although common sense might urge me
not to inform you of a painful matter,
for which reason all refrain, my soul
fills with another thought: that is,
to release you from that suspense

because hiding what is ill allows
no means to act, while knowing it may
permit a remedy. Amnon,
your son, spends long days suffering
a heavy siege of melancholy.
In his overwhelming sadness
he cannot drive away, he receives
the sun's light so impatiently
he's come to live among the shadows,
even loath to open a window
to greet the sovereign daylight.
Amnon hates himself so much
he lacks the appetite
for normal sustenance.
Refusing all medical attention
he is, in a word, dying
of a grave unhappiness, a burden
implicit in the laws of Nature.

**David.** Although the news you bring
bespeaks your loyalty,
I might have pardoned your
omitting it, Achitophel.
For displeasure is so discomforting
that the very wish to know it
means coping with such heaviness
that I prefer not knowing
what now I am aware of.
The plight of one afflicted
is so hard to live with
that knowing it or not causes
the same anxiety.
What's known and what's unknown
are equally disquieting.
Oh God, I cringe from finding rest
in my own chambers now. Let's first
go to Amnon's. Come join me, everyone.
Lord, I am ungrateful. I say
ungrateful for your favor to me;
for the satisfaction I feel
in finding my four children well
now gratifies me less on finding
one of them afflicted and unwell.
Oh the ingratitude
of human discontent—
moving always to extremes . . .

**Absalom.** This is Amnon's room, to which
your feelings and not your feet guide you.

**David.** Open this door.

*The curtain is opened and AMNON is found in a chair,*
*close to a buffet table, and opposite JONADAB.*

**Joab.**                    Here, Sire,
  the door is now open
  and through the slim light the great star
  sends us the prince seated in a chair.
**Tamar.** Who would not wonder, seeing him
  so absorbed by his sorrow, that
  he still has no sense of our presence?
**David.** Amnon!
**Amnon.**              Who calls me?
**David.**                         I do.
**Amnon.** Sire! Why . . . are you here?
**David.** Does my happiness give you
  so little pleasure, my love
  so little joy, that you
  forego embracing me?
  Though being so harshly met,
  I am still compelled, my son,
  to come to you myself.
  Now, with such stirring of
  my love for you, how is it there's
  no glimmer of response from you?
  What is this, Amnon?   What is wrong?
  Hearing of your sorrow,
  I thought my coming here to you
  might temper your vexation.
  No welcome do you give me
  on my victorious return to
  Jerusalem? My victories
  have not overcome
  your present irritations ?
  For a prince who is heir
  to Israel, whose heroic
  valor should resist,
  with spirit and daring,
  fortune's frown and fate's opprobrium,
  to give in to such temperament,
  such sorrow—and be so absorbed
  in it that he'll not permit his eyes
  the light of day? Amnon,
  what is this? If your trouble
  has a cause, I am confident of
  my power to overcome it.
  All my empire, from one end
  to the other, is at your disposal,
  and open to your will.
  And should your grief have

no other cause than what
our human dust is naturally
disposed to, take heart. Man holds sway
over himself, and when
his human capacities
are enlisted, call one
and all will come together.
Do not surrender or
enslave yourself so basely
to your quandary. Take heed:
the monstrous pain that preys
on human lives battens
on idleness. Quit this room, or since
all your kin have come with me,
speak with them. Come now, all of you,
since my affection for Amnon
can do so little.

**Adonai.**             Prince . . .
**Absalom.**                    Brother . . .
**Solomon.**                         Sir . . .
**Tamar.** Amnon . . .
**Amnon.** [*aside*] To that voice I respond.
**Tamar.** What ails you?
**Solomon.**                 What is it you feel?
**Absalom.** What is it torments you?
**Adonai.** What is it frightens you?
**David.** What is it you crave?
**All.** What is it you want?
**Amnon.** Only that you let me be.
**David.** Since your stern desires consist
     of this alone, let us leave this place.
     [*aside*] I promise to return
     and speak with him alone,
     since he may not speak
     his mind before the others.
     [*aloud*] Come, now you are alone.
     Ah, unhappy soul: the happiness,
     the joys, the pleasures which
     a single pain turns to bitterness!

                                                        [*Exit*

**Joab.** What a strange melancholia!
**Achitophel.** Such an unseemly silence!

                                                        [*Exit*

**Adonai.** Such a cruel compulsion!

                                                        [*Exit*

**Solomon.** Such overpowering emotion!

                                                        [*Exit*

**Tamar.** Heaven only knows, Amnon,
  how much your sorrows weigh on me!
**Absalom.** Not on me!
**Tamar.**                What's that you say?
**Absalom.** Yes, indeed, for he is David's
  proud heir, and if he dies,
  I come closer to the throne; for
  one aspiring to the kingship,
  each brother is an obstacle.
**Tamar.** Although his death would sadden me,
  I'd be glad to see you on the throne,
  for the truth is we are children
  of the same father and mother.

                      *[Exeunt Tamar and Absalom*

*AMNON and JONADAB*

**Amnon.** Have they left now, Jonadab?
**Jonadab.** Yes, sir, one after the other,
  like the coins of someone
  spending his money bit by bit,
  thinking now one coin, now
  another, won't make a difference
  and when he least expects it
  he finds the fattest money bag
  dissappears and is actually a
  skeleton in a shroud.
**Amnon.** Well, now you can disappear
  and be done with it once and for all.
**Jonadab.** Are you forgetting I'm your favorite?
**Amnon.** I'm not forgetting it,
  since you alone have leave
  to wait on me when I
  am in perplexity;
  but now I want to be left alone.
**Jonadab.** I comply gladly. It's not
  so pleasant having a master
  when he is saturnine
  and hypochondriacal.
  Yet before I leave, I'm bound to ask,
  how is it you respond
  to your father and your siblings
  in such a manner? Can
  it be there's no one merits
  being told the reason for
  your distemper?
**Amnon.**             No. If I were able
  to deny it to myself, I would
  do so since I see that I myself
  must feel ashamed of naming it.

The truth is I live in fear
of my own silence, as I've been told
that eyes are known to speak in silence.
The reason for my pain I keep
so deeply buried in my heart
that sometimes I hide it from
the heart, lest startled by the shock
of recognizing it, my very heart
would then beat on the louder.
I've imprisoned it so deeply
in my life that even the breath
that brings vital sustenance
knows nothing of it lest
the curious air should tell
by the distemper of a sigh
that I bring forth: "This breath
knows of it since it expires burning."
In sum, my sorrow is so lashed down
in my soul's depths that the soul itself—
the warden of my prison—
knows not what prisoner it holds,
being its own jailer.

**Jonadab.** You are a sodomite, no doubt;
otherwise I find no reason that
obliges you to be so silent.

**Amnon.** What is that obliges you
always to be so stupid?

**Jonadab.** Because it's not given me to be wise.

*[Footsteps offstage]*

**Amnon.** Whose footsteps do I hear?

**Jonadab.** Tamar, your sister's—she has left
David's sumptuous chambers and
now returns down this corridor
to her own.

*[Music]*

**Amnon.** *[aside]*  O silent passion,
how should I control myself?
But oh, my desire, it must be
that even only to glimpse her face,
I must not leave this door.
But, alas, how vainly I oppose
the influence of my star,
for scarcely do I say decisively
I shan't go out to see her,
when I begin to lie in wait.
Heavens, what is all this? Don't I
myself recognize the harm?
Then how do I give in to it?
Does something other than myself

dwell inside me? No. Then how does something
other make such imperious
demands that it carries me
where I have no wish to go?

**Jonadab.** Either I'm stupid or someone's approaching . . .

**Amnon.** What are you looking at?

**Jonadab.** I've got something to look at a moment.

**Amnon.** Haven't I told you to leave?

**Jonadab.** Yes, you have, but for that reason
  I've not done so yet.

**Amnon.**                    Get in there somewhere!

**Jonadab.** Yes, I'll install myself in the entryway.
  [*aside*] Which is why they say
  we servants are like suitors,
  since the crassest servant
  never stops prying.

                                        [*Hides himself*]

**Amnon.**                    I'll have
  a glimpse of Tamar from back here,
  for I need not be afraid,
  considering that in effect
  she'll be coming this way after all . . .
  And also, so that my pains may see
  how I'd struggle and stand up
  to them, I shall see and even
  speak with her, since no heart
  is valiant or heroic
  that calls itself victorious
  before it faces danger.

                    *TAMAR enters.*

Ah, most beauteous Tamar!

**Tamar.** [*to her retinue*] No need to come in with me;
  wait inside this doorway.
  —Amnon, how much I appreciate
  your having called me
  as I go back to my room
  while the whole court waits
  upon my father. Though
  with loving heart I feel for
  your unhappiness, I would not
  intrude, knowing that the least
  company disturbs one's
  melancholy. But since I owe you
  this occasion, having heard my name
  upon your lips, Amnon, I
  would do ill not to respond.
  I beg you, let me be the one worthy
  of hearing why such harsh pain

afflicts you, for the illness is
in no small measure alleviated
when reported to another,
assured that he will share it, and as
I am ready to exchange
your complaints with my tears
my sincerity is worth trusting.
Let your lips perform their part,
and my eyes will do theirs:
let me hear your grief and
see how my tears respond.

**Amnon.** Divine Tamar: if I could word my pain,
if I could voice the burden
of it all; if it were
in my power to explain,
it would be told to you alone,
and so it would be spoken.
This being so, if I keep it
from you, please believe me,
I'll tell it to no one else.
However great and rare the pain,
however intense it may grow,
I'd tell it only to you,
and from you alone withhold it.
Just imagine the perversity
of my suffering, when here you are,
the only one ignorant of it,
and I'd tell it to anyone else
but never at all to you.

**Tamar.** If you find the same reason for
withholding as for telling of
your troubles, then in keeping them
from me you do now offend me.
Curiosity does battle
on the side of finding out
what they are. Bear in mind I am
a woman, and as such will insist
on knowing and hearing it, just
because I'm kept from knowing it.

**Amnon.** Leaving me no way out,
your insistence obliges me,
on my part, to remain silent,
and on yours to speak out.
So as not to let silence and
confession be at odds within me,
I'm compelled to obey you.
Hear me . . . but be aware
that I shall tell it to you,
and you'll not take it in.

I am in love, Tamar,
and my affliction is
unquestionably a love
impossible —which shows how great
it is: with both loves out of the question.

**Tamar.** Now my confusion mounts. Tell me who!
For though your words inform me,
they do not make any sense.

**Amnon.** Oh my dear Tamar! I said I'd tell
you why I'm dying, but not for whom.

**Tamar.** Amazed, I question how there can be
someone, beloved by you,
not grateful to be so beloved.

**Amnon.** Oh no. She is not to blame,
for though I am dying for her,
she does not know I love her,
nor shall she ever know it.

**Tamar.** Why not?

**Amnon.** Because I value what
I love more than what I hope for.
Not to mention I'm so fearful of her
that I'd gamble on being loved
in order not to find myself hated.
So I prefer to keep silent,
knowing I will offend her.
O Tamar, let my star be my death
but hers not to suffer.
For I would rather die
than see her thus offended.

**Tamar.** But why should she be offended
at finding she is loved by you
when the most retiring of women
is still a woman after all?
She may well rebuff you, putting on
a show of honor, but to suffer,
no; don't be backward in the least,
for the most tyrannic scorn is shown
him who is quick to complain of,
but late to declare, his love.
And so, declare it!

**Amnon.** I cannot.

**Tamar.** Why?

**Amnon.** Because
I fear and doubt.

**Tamar.** Speak your pain.

**Amnon.** I am mute.

**Tamar.** Let her know your illness.

**Amnon.** I am afraid to.

**Tamar.** Speak.
**Amnon.** Words fail me.
**Tamar.** Write to her.
**Amnon.** It would offend her.
**Tamar.** Give her some sign.
**Amnon.** I fear to look at her.
**Tamar.** Is she anything but a woman?
**Amnon.** Yes.
**Tamar.** Then the fault is all yourself.
**Amnon.** Not myself, but my star's
whose influence is so oppressive,
Tamar, that it obliges me to die
rather than tell my lady: oh,
you are the mistress that I love,
you, the glory for whom I die,
you, the cause of my lament,
you, the one I've no way of telling,
you, the goddess that I yearn for,
yours the beauty I idolize,
and yours the loveliness I adore.
Take pity on me, with all
your beauty out of reach
who see me so taken by you,
that you see me dying because of it.
**Tamar.** Enough, no more—for if now
I gave you such advice,
it was only to encourage you
to tell her about it, not me.
**Amnon.** Then have I, perhaps, told you more
than I should have said?
Your counsel was so good,
I should tell you it encouraged me
so much my early fear deserts me:
thanks to my self-examination,
so far, I may now begin,
bit by bit, to lose my fear
of speaking out; so as such tricks may
allay the fancies of a mad man,
let us go on, Tamar, with
this rehearsing of my ailment,
so I may better understand it
when I tell it to my beloved.
**Tamar.** Your ailment so much concerns me
that if I may thus mitigate
your pain, I'll play along with you
for whatever comfort it may bring.
**Amnon.** Then pretend you are the beauty
for whom I die, to see if

I'll know how finally
to penetrate her disdain.
**Tamar.** I'll play my part but don't know
if I can do it very well.
**Amnon.** Impossible beauty to whom,
since I spied you in a garden,
I yielded up my life and soul,
which now I offer you again,
although, being what I abhor,
it can be no gift to you.
For such effrontery I am not
to blame, since only my free will
was born enslaved. I know not
what impious planet
predominated on that day,
for though I beheld your beauty
other times, that was the first time
I loved you, Tamar, my sweetest beauty.
But what have I been saying?
**Tamar.**                                    Stop, wait!
Remember, though I take that lady's role,
I am not Tamar.
**Amnon.**              Yes, of course,
but somehow lips and eyes, in fiercely
apprehending my distemper,
so confused the prize that being
so equivocally wise,
the lips absconded with
what the eyes beheld.
**Tamar.** That being so, I absolve
lips and eyes from such error
and return to my former make-believe.
Amnon, my prince and lord,
though I continue disguised
as your beloved, the person that I am
forbids you take so high a risk,
because if you speak that way again
I shall not, on my life,
come back to listen to you, ever.
**Amnon.** Is that your answer to me?
**Tamar.** Yes. But why torment yourself
if all this is make-believe?
**Amnon.** Then if it's make-believe,
tell me, why reply that way to me?
What can it matter to you, Tamar,
to offer some hope through
such a true rendition?
Should the pleasure of the make-believe
be dearer than the suffering?

**Tamar.** No, but the way your lips and eyes
    confused your troubles persuading you
    that I was your lady-love
    involves as well my own confusion
    of the senses which, in listening
    to you, were more wisely mistaken
    when my lips responded
    to what my ears had heard.
    And so, since little good
    is served by such make-believe
    (for in it danger grows
    the more it is suppressed),
    let it remain the way it is,
    for neither pain nor pleasure,
    dear Amnon, is easy to disguise.
    Let her who loves you love your heart,
    for Tamar need not play the lady
    who does not speak like Tamar.

*[Exit*

**Amnon.** Who has seen greater unhappiness?
    For even the compassion of a make-believe
    is converted into injury greater
    than the true one I experienced.
    Who will advise me now?

           *Enter JONADAB.*

**Jonadab.**                 I will,
    whose blind curiosity
    has brought home to me today
    what your illness is and through whom
    it comes, for in the end
    the same fortune is revealed to him
    who witnesses as to him who plays.
**Amnon.** Then you've now understood
    what underlies my passion?
**Jonadab.** Indeed, sir, for there's no sponger
    who wasn't first a gambler.
**Amnon.** I am asking for your advice.
**Jonadab.** Though it's a strange opinion
    that deception requires greater craft
    than strength, the same is not true
    of love, where strength is needed
    more than craft.
**Amnon.**             Tamar's my half-sister.
**Jonadab.** I'll tell you what I'd do
    if she were my full sister
    and she aroused my anger.
**Amnon.** What can I do to reassure her
    since it's clear now Tamar won't come back?

**Jonadab.** An unusual stratagem
   is called for to compel your love
   to return, and in bringing her here . . .
**Amnon.** Take heed, for my father
   is entering this chamber.
**Jonadab.** Well, let's not talk about it.
**Amnon.** It doesn't matter, for now
   I am totally resolved
   since my unhappiness requires
   exceptional remedy
   for exceptional hurt.

         *Enter DAVID.*

**David.** I could not return before this,
   Amnon, since I was kept from doing so
   by the people who came to offer
   me their prolix congratulations.
**Amnon.** Sire, I thank you for your deep regard.
**David.** Well, then, return the compliment
   with another, since it is not without
   asking for your counsel that I come
   to see you.
**Amnon.**       I am ever
   bound to you and subject
   to the obedience I owe you.
**David.** Then let the cause be known
   of your desperate affliction.
**Jonadab.** Sire, I shall tell you that.
**Amnon.** [*to JONADAB*] Silence, fool.
   —Physicians distinguish
   melancholy from sadness:
   where sadness rises from
   some unhappy circumstance,
   melancholy is caused
   by innate feeling; and so,
   I cannot tell you which it is.
**David.** What gives rise to your suffering,
   if it is that? For what illness
   is there not some remedy?
**Amnon.** For me, the best that's applicable.
**David.** And what is that?
**Amnon.**             To feel what I feel.
**David.** That's no remedy but rather
   giving illness greater power.
**Amnon.** Then what is it I can do?
**David.** Seek happy diversions.
**Jonadab.** [*aside*] One diversion I've spoken of
   already—scarcely happy.

**Amnon.** Good enough, but all grow wearisome,
    none uplifting, for since I lack
    the appetite, all resolve into
    greater pain, since the dominant
    humor is certain to
    convert the sustenance.
**David.** You speak of it as metaphor
    but I'd have you speak literally
    of food. Isn't it a sort of
    desperation when a prudent man
    denies himself even such
    a human offering?
**Jonadab.** Yes, of course. I've just been telling him
    to eat, almost anything,
    but he won't take any heed.
**Amnon.** I have found nothing to my taste,
    and therefore—or because it would
    preserve my life—I hate it.
**David.** Then there is one thing you
    will have to do for me.
**Amnon.** I offer then to do it.
**David.** What offering, Amnon, would
    most please you? For I'll surely
    see to it for you, and bind you
    to what you desire.
**Amnon.**               I doubt
    I'll profit from any such choice
    since I've no appetite for anything
    but if there is something to eat
    of the kind of preparation
    and décor Tamar's servants devote
    to her, then, Sire, I believe eating
    such viands may pleasantly relieve
    tedium; and all the more so
    if she herself would bring the meal;
    for a sick man is better pleased
    by fond attention, Sire,
    than by the food itself.
**Jonadab.** That's the truth, because a lady,
    with the pincers of her fingers
    forking in the mouthfuls
    can start a dead man chewing.
**David.** Amnon, I shall speak to Tamar;
    then she'll come here herself
    bearing your meal, and at the same time
    I'll have musicians serenade you
    and see if that does not divert you.

                              *[Exit*

**Amnon.** May Heaven augment your life as I
    in this abode await that favor.
    Come now, Jonadab.
**Jonadab.**              So far so good.
**Amnon.** No—say, rather, ill, because
    I intend treacherously,
    in desperation, to add
    sin to sin, fire to fire,
    pain to pain, error to error,
    injury to injury, peril to peril.

                                              *[Exit*

          *Enter DAVID to a fanfare of trumpets.*

**David.** What new salvo is this,
    with martial accents turning
    to shouts upon the air,
    whose echoes weakly answer?
            *Enter SOLOMON and ABSALOM.*

**Solomon.** Reward us for our good news, Sire.
**David.** Why, if the pleasure is unlooked for?
**Absalom.** For the news that the ships
    have arrived safely from Ofir.
          *Enter JOAB and ACHITOPHEL.*

**Joab.** You have already heard the reason
    for this military clamor?
**David.** Yes, Joab.
**Achitophel.**        Now once again
    repeated on the wind.
      *Sounds of fanfare as SEMEY and TEUCA enter,*
        *accompanied by Ethiopians and soldiers.*

**Semey.** [*kneeling*] Allow me, Sire, to kiss your royal hand.
**David.** Rise from the ground. You are
    most welcome, Semey.
**Semey.**               Necessity
    impels my coming here to see
    myself at your feet. King Hiram
    of Tyre has sent me with
    an armada of war vessels,
    monsters of two elements:
    among varied riches of gold
    and silver are the cedars,
    that incorruptible
    material, for building
    the Temple, which you have reserved
    to house the Ark of the Covenant.
    But of all the booty I bring you
    I especially extol

this divine Ethiopian maid,
in whose foreign accent
there's a spirit foretelling
events, whether good or ill.

**David.** Semey, you have given me equal
portions of pleasure and of pain:
the pleasure, your company,
with a solicitude that pleases
me; the pain, your ignorance,
since you think that in the grandeur
of my palace I harbor fortune-
tellers. God speaks through hearts
tyrannically oppressed.
Therefore, remove at once this dull
sorceress from my court,
and after that let
the materials brought me
be guarded. The time is not yet ripe
to begin building the Temple,
since I am not worthy to labor
on the house of the Lord. Whoever
succeeds me will build it. And so,
my sons, take heed and learn to be
devout, for Almighty God
disallows my building his Temple
because my hands are stained
with the blood of an idolater.

*[Exit*

**Teuca.** Although I wished to answer the King,
by Heaven, I could not do it,
for there's a spirit in his breast
nobler than my own, and
on seeing him, my own went dumb;
avenging itself on me,
it broke my heart in pieces.
Woe is me, I live wracked in madness!
Woe is me, I die wracked in madness!

**Absalom.** What insensate frenzy infuses
this Ethiopian woman?

**Solomon.** What's the matter with her?

**Achitophel.** She is tearing out her hair,
and ripping her clothes to shreds.

**Semey.** Teuca . . .

**Teuca.**                    Perfidious sacrilege
desist! I see you and tremble.

**Joab.** Take heed . . .

**Teuca.**                    Despicable assassin,
out of my way. I must escape

from you—you hurling
lances recklessly, you
gathering rocks to throw,
and spreading terror till
you become the very heir
of your own death—your death a
codicil to your last testament.
**Achitophel.** Your words are strangely mad.
Now listen here . . .
**Teuca.**                I won't listen to
your advice, Achitophel. That's enough!
Your advice will lead to a heavy
desperation, denying you
a decent grave.
**Solomon.**            Control yourself.
**Teuca.** Solomon: Your fortune I will
foretell, but my lips are sealed
since the world won't have to know
if your fate is good or bad.
**Absalom.** How she rambles on! Look here,
my Ethiopian sorceress . . .
**Teuca.** Your ambition, I foresee, will lead
to being lifted to
the heights by your own crown!
Woe is me, I live consumed by madness!
Woe is me, I die consumed by madness!
**Solomon.** Look after her, lest her fury
drive her to extremes.
**Semey.** I shall follow her footsteps doubting
predictions I do not understand.

                                                *[Exit*

**Solomon.** Such strange delirious words!
**Absalom.** Although I take them to be such,
I do not find myself displeased
by what they have to tell me.
**Solomon.** What have they to tell you?
**Absalom.** That I shall see myself—
if I recall the words—lifted to
the heights by my own crown.
**Solomon.** And how do you interpret that?
**Absalom.** Beauty, a letter of favor
sent by Heaven, is addressed
to men, as well as to
everything in general affection.
Such beauty is in me—all agree,
so I needn't leave it to
my mirror—so abundantly that
clippings from its domain every

single year (and from throw-aways alone)
should be worth a fortune.
Ladies from Jerusalem buy them
from me, since for their grooming
I leave for their sustenance
a thing most adorable.
Being as I am thus loved by all,
I may well infer that such
general adoration
means that all the people
must acclaim me as their king when
the kingdom comes to be divided
among the sons of David.
I therefore justly infer
that since my hair is one
of my beauty's prime endowments,
it will see me set upon the heights:
and so, lifted up on high,
I'll be by my own hair crowned.

**Solomon.** How you twist the application
to fit the concept! However,
do you imagine that effeminate
beauty in everyone's heart
will engender more love than hate?

**Absalom.** Why not, when such beauty
hinges on the valor I possess?

**Solomon.** Because among the sons of David
are merits totally above your own.

**Absalom.** Are you not yourself, to say the least,
the reliquary of a double crime:
homicide and adultery—say
of Beersheva and Uriah,
one unchaste, the other murdered?

**Solomon.** Absalom, you have besmirched
your father, and though I can
castigate such presumptuous
misdeeds with my two hands, Heaven
has tied them, perhaps because God
would do so himself; paternal
offenses are always
in the hands of Heaven.

*[Exit*

**Joab.** His words are most prudent.

**Achitophel.** Fear is always very prudent.

**Joab.** Time was when prudence was
always very valiant.

**Absalom.**                 What is all this?

**Achitophel.** Joab.
　He takes Solomon's side.
**Absalom.** You've been opposing me all my life!
**Joab.** I've always defended reason, sir.
**Absalom.** My father's favoring you at court
　has made you very arrogant, Joab.
　You'll have cause to remember me
　when I am elevated to that position
　my worthiness prepares me for.
**Joab.** I'll go on doing the same thing then,
　and maybe then I'll have even
　more occasion to do so.

　　　　　　　　　　　　　　　　　　　　　　　　　　　*[Exit*

**Absalom.** Me—he is threatening me!
**Achitophel.** Hold on, sir, and take heed—it's not yet
　time to say aloud what we've hatched
　together; it's important to find allies first.
**Absalom.** Achitophel, I shall follow
　your advice in everything.
**Achitophel.** It will bring you where your thoughts aspire.

　　　　　　　　　　　　　　　　　　*[Instruments strike up]*

**Absalom.** I put my trust there and in myself.
　Then with both . . . But what's that sound?
**Achitophel.** It's Tamar, moving from her chamber,
　and well accompanied, towards
　Amnon's rooms.
**Absalom.** 　　　　　　She wishes to
　entertain his senses
　with some music. Let us depart,
　Achitophel, for I do not wish
　to speak of any thing
　other than our mutual designs.

　　　　　　　　　　　　　　　　　　　　　　　　　　*[Exeunt*

　　　　　　*Enter all the Musicians and the Ladies with plates
　　　　　　　　　　and towels, and TAMAR.*

**Musicians.** *Of the sorrows of Amnon,
　love's the cause, it's clear.
　For only love would dare
　assault a noble heart like his.
　But oh, it's vain to think
　that love has slain him, for
　who lays claim to silence
　cannot lay claim to love.*

　　　　　　　　*Enter AMNON and JONADAB.*

**Jonadab.** Tamar is entering your chamber.
**Amnon.** How daring are my thoughts

　　　　　　　　　　　　　　　　390

when I do not see her; how cowardly
when I do! I'm trembling all over.

**Tamar.** Do not thank me, Amnon,
for this visit; I come today
to serve you because my father
has ordered me to do so.

**Amnon.** Yes, I do thank you,
because your obedience
brings me happiness.
[*aside*] I am nearly dead.

**Tamar.** I bring you music and savories
to while away the time delighting
your two senses.

**Amnon.**               Much injury
has been done to the most
sensitive of them all.

**Tamar.**               Which is?

**Amnon.** Sight. Because bringing music
for the ear and viands for
the tastebuds, you forget . . .
[*aside*] Oh, I am dying! . . .
—you bring beauty to the eyes.
I don't infer you think you do not,
unless you think me blind.

**Tamar.** If from that former self-delusion
any flirtation lingers on,
you cast it now in vain before me,
for I intend today to lighten
actual pains, not your
imaginary ones.

**Amnon.**               I'll eat, then.
And let them sing—but not here.
Their dulcet tones are sweeter elsewhere;
they do not sound so well nearby.
So have them sing some other place.

**Jonadab.** Indeed, since art and music from
afar are less discordant.

**Tamar.** You may sing outside.

*[Exeunt MUSICIANS*

**Amnon.** [*aside*] Jonadab, over there!

**Jonadab.** [*aside*] I understand: close the door
and have them all sing behind it.
Just as you told me, am I right?

*[Exit*

**Amnon.** Yes.

**Musicians.** [*offstage*] *Who lays claim to silence*
*cannot lay claim to love.*

**Amnon.** And so, divine Tamar,

do not wonder at my daring,
if I break the laws of
decorum and respect.
Let this lovely white hand,
instead of playing lily to an asp,
be the antidote to my poison.

**Tamar.** Let go my hand, Amnon,
for your complaining now
is but sheer illusion.

**Amnon.** If that were so, you put it well,
but the time has come for passion
to burst its prison bars
and break its chains, because . . .

> [*Spoken and sung together with the MUSICIANS.*]

*Who lays claim to silence*
*cannot lay claim to love.*
I am dying for you, Tamar,
No greater end can I attain
than to die for you:
My hope in this is killing me.

**Tamar.** [*aside*] But who could have expected this?
—Now look, Amnon . . .

**Amnon.**                    I see nothing now.

**Tamar.** I am your sister.

**Amnon.**                    True enough,
but as the saying goes:
"Blood boils without fire."
Now what will blood do *with* fire?

**Tamar.** Our law permits kin to marry kin.
Go ask my father for my hand.

**Amnon.** It's too late for me to ask.

**Tamar.** Listen to me, out there!

> Enter MUSICIAN.

**Amnon.** Tamar bids you go on singing.

**Tamar.** I?

**Musician.** Yes, as you command.

> [*Exit*

> [*Offstage, MUSICIANS go on singing*
> *what they wish while the actors speak*]

**Amnon.** I cannot resist enjoying you.
—Jonadab, shut the door at once.

**Jonadab.** The door is already shut.

**Tamar.** The risk!

**Amnon.**           I am not afraid!

**Tamar.** O father! O Sire! Absalom!

**Amnon.** How can your cries avail
against such dulcet harmonies?

392

[*MUSICIANS continue singing.*]

**Tamar.** Then I'll shout to Heaven.

**Amnon.** Heaven's answer is late in coming.

**Tamar.** [*drawing her sword*] Then this sword will answer fatally
  if you continue coming at me.
  I have strength and I have valor!

**Amnon.** Your drawing it already wounds me.
  But even if it augurs ill,
  I no longer fear a thing
  since I intend to have you.
  Now I must persevere, for once
  my love has been declared it's certain
                     [*Both AMNON and MUSICIANS speak/sing.*]

*Who lays claim to silence*
*cannot lay claim to love.*

                              [*Exeunt omnes*

## ACT TWO

### The Royal Palace.

#### Enter AMNON and TAMAR.

**Amnon.** Out, get out of here! Away with you,
  poison in a golden cup,
  angelic harpy, sepulchral
  beauty outwardly, yet
  nothing but a loathsome beast,
  casting glances, like the basilisk,
  full of venom—don't look at me.
  Evil-eyed monster, your looks
  are killing, sapping my youth,
  crippling me forever. How
  could I ever have loved
  or felt any desire for you?
  Putrid fruit of Sodom, skin smooth
  but coal-black at the core.
  Horror that you are, punishing
  my life, get out of here! Get out!
  The loathing you fill me with
  is greater than any love
  I ever felt for you.
  Come and throw her out of here!

**Tamar.** Now the offense and injury
  you heap upon me are greater
  than your amorous fury was.
  Go and honor some servant girl
  with the spoils you've torn from me,
  and pile your anger over me.

**Amnon.** If only I'd been born deaf and blind
    so I'd never heard nor seen you!
    Woman, won't you get out of here!
**Tamar.** And where would I go, ingrate,
    now my honor's lost? Who would ever
    take me in, a disgraced woman,
    like a merchant whose goods are gone?
    Pay some heed to your sister, you
    who've paid none to yourself.
    Do not add insult to injury
    lest you perish in the linked chain
    of sin you thus augment.
    In your gamble for my honor
    you have stolen under false pretense
    the jewels I begged in vain to keep.
    Now take my life, I've lost all the rest.
    No, don't get up so quickly.
    My loss is too immense.
    However tiresome the loser is,
    a noble gambler does not rise
    while there's something on the table.
    The stake left over is my life,
    a life without honor, scoundrel,
    and that deal I mean to lose.
    Traitor, finish up the game;
    my death will be your winner's tip.
**Amnon.** Hellion you still are, but without fire,
    who torment me with frost.
    Get out, monster, get out, you snake!
**Tamar.** To stay in the game, a loser
    suffers any insult;
    and so proceed, you tyrant,
    and let me play until you take
    what little there is left of me.
    Now raise your hand and strike me dead,
    then, villain, sweep up the final hand.
**Amnon.** Such torment is unheard of!
    Hello! Is there no one out there?
    Such madness is unparalleled!

        *Enter ELIAZAR and JONADAB.*

**Eliazar.** Sire . . .
**Amnon.**            Now, throw this viper,
    this pestilence, out of here!
**Eliazar.** Pestilence, viper? What has she done?
**Amnon.** Drag this woman out of here,
    and lock the door behind her!
**Jonadab.** She was a letter he ripped open,
    which he read and wants to throw away.

**Amnon.** Throw her in the street!
**Tamar.**                              That would
   suit you fine and serve me right, for
   the crime committed here in private
   I'm now cast out like a street crier to
   proclaim dishonor brought down on me!
**Amnon.** I take my leave, not to vex you more.

                                       *[Exit*

**Jonadab.** What a strange business, Eliazar:
   so much hate after so much love!
**Tamar.** Soon, soon, you wretch, you'll live
   to see the vengeance of Tamar.

                 *[Exit as AMNON and JONADAB enter*

**Absalom.** Barbaric schemer! If you were not
   my brother or in this palace now,
   you'd lose your impudent ambition
   and your life, on this very spot!
**Adonai.** If the blood in your veins were not
   that which my father honored
   so unworthily, I would
   see to it that it went dry, standing
   with my feet here planted in your gore.
**Absalom.** So, you wretched madman, you want
   to reign, do you? When Amnon dies
   of the illness consuming him,
   you aspire to mount the royal throne
   encompassing a dozen tribes?
   Are you aware I am your elder
   brother? How do you dare presume
   to rival Absalom, at whose feet
   Fortune heaped such valor, beauty, wealth?
**Adonai.** If the throne of Israel
   should pass to the most flaccid, self-
   preening, most delicate of men (though
   I'm not myself a freak of nature),
   the kingdom would bend its neck under
   your yoke, each tribe magically bewitched
   and threaded through your charming gold locks,
   converting martial exploits into
   divertissements, sending you tithes
   of ribbons and cosmetics:
   your royal council become
   a bevy of ladies, your crown
   a head of tresses, your poor father's
   court a ladies' salon, and your arms
   reduced to Holland linens
   and brocades, while your shield became
   a looking glass fastening

your own self-loving image.
For the sword, which is my preference,
you'd no doubt accost me with a fan.
For nature gave you the endowment
to spellbind the eyes of Israel.
Heaven heaped a fortune on your head
to sell your locks of hair to ladies,
making a harvest of its beauty.
Pretending you are only
lightening the weight,
you distribute the treasure
through the ladies' shops, receiving
two hundred shekels for a lock.
You should be the King of May, and leave
to me the crown of Israel
lest it bruise your dainty head.

**Absalom.** Scoundrel, shut your impudent mouth!
Gainsaying your envy, a wise man
once said that beauty resides in
governance; the sign of nobility
is the soul that lives within.
So handsome is as handsome does.
When my father wars against
the enemy, I do not tarry here
at court, engaging idleness in
debaucheries, nor by any
reckoning showing that valor
is absent from my deeds; my blade gleams
with uncircumcised blood. Wars, from which
the priesthood is exempted,
prove in my case how well matched
beauty is with valor. Why,
with anything so certain, should I
bolster argument with reason?
Let this sword do my boasting
against anyone like you who claims
I'm a coward because I'm handsome.

**Adonai.** You wear that sword as pure adornment.
God forbid, and self-love save you,
don't draw it; the sight might make you faint.

**Absalom.** If the King were not approaching . . .

**Adonai.** . . . not approaching—then what?

*Enter DAVID with SOLOMON.*

**David.** Your mother, Beersheva, petitions
for you, dear Solomon:
grow into your proper manhood
and if God indeed loves you,
as your name confirms, I trust

that when you ascend the royal throne,
He will see to it your celebrity
astonishes centuries to come.
**Solomon.** Such celebrity, if it come,
great Sire, will, in image
and in likeness, reflect you.
**David.** Royal princes . . .
**Absalom.**                           Great Sire!
**David.**                                       What's your news?
**Adonai.** With peace, time engrosses novelties.
Youth on fineries expends its pleasures,
the truths of age in disillusionment.
**Absalom.** The hunt defends us from idleness,
then invites to needed solitude.
Such are my plans, and a banquet
afterward—Good heavens,
what was that outcry?

> *Enter TAMAR, weeping.*

**Tamar.** O Israel's great monarch,
descendant of the Lion
old Jacob gave Judea
to redress its injuries—
if tears, if sighs, my quavering voice,
my mourning clothes, my outcast state
should stir your pity, and that not be
enough, I, as your daughter
should incite you, as one who stained
your blood, through these eyes I pour
out my soul. In mourning
for my lost honor, these sighs
are dredged up from the ice
of my avenging innocence.
My head is decked with ashes,
for love that's only fiery lust
leaves as consequence the ashes
that the wind must sweep away.
Such ashes do not obliterate
the stains of honor,
for which only purple blood will do.
The infectious illness of
the scoundrel prince Amnon
has poisoned my honor and struck me
down. You ordered me to cook something
savory to rouse his jaded appetite.
Poison would have done better.
I made him a tasty dish,
but what good is such a dish
if the palate is corrupted?

In his soul was lustful hunger which
to my misfortune incited
his shamelessness to disgrace me.
He seized the opportunity
and brushed aside my pleas as
to being your royal daughter
and his sister, and disregarding
rank, the law, and God,
threw the attendants out
and behind locked doors, he forced his way
into the temple of my self-
esteem and holy honor. Having
raped me, he abhorred me.
That does not surprise me, for
after all, desire and possession
are sworn enemies. Finding pleasure
and revilement, my assaulter
threw me, damaged and abused,
straight out of this palace.
Imagine the conceit
of such a creature! In my grief,
I crept dishonored through the streets
of your city. The sun, roused
to compassion, behind clouds withdrew
its rays so as not to see
an event so vicious and atrocious.
All this demands justice, Sire,
unconquerable Justice!
You'll say Amnon has your blood
but his crime has corrupted it;
blood must be let if you wish
to keep your valor uncorrupted.
Your sons, your heirs, like you,
are virtuous and courageous.
Let no one who succeeds you
to the throne defame his sister
and scorn your reputation.
Let him offend his servants
rather. Behold, you of Abraham's
generous blood, who stalwartly
raised a knife against
an innocent son: he had one son,
you have many; his was guiltless,
Amnon is not. As Abraham served
the Lord, you'll have served the Good Lord too.
O King, conquer yourself,
let passion be separated
from justice, in which there is
more glory than in tearing

a lion to pieces. Brothers,
join me in my plea for justice.
Handsome Absalom, one father
sired us both, one mother
bore us. As half-brothers,
the rest of you are not bound
to rectify my honor
and disgrace—not entirely
but rather half of it.
You who are my blood brother
must take full satisfaction,
or live in perpetual infamy
and disgrace from this day on.
Father, brothers, Israelites,
streets and doors, moon and sun,
beasts, fishes, birds, wild creatures,
of whatever element you are,
I beg justice from all of you
upon this traitor who has raped
his sister and the law.
**David.** Rise from the ground, my poor Tamar.
Have Prince Amnon brought here.
Good Lord, is this what having
children means? Painful sorrow
leaves me speechless. These tears
will be the words to tell you
what is in my heart. As your King,
it is justice calls me.
As your father, it is love.
Obliged by one, impelled by the other,
which one will overcome the other?
**Absalom.** My sister . . . O that you never were!
In reason find refuge that's never
found in vengeance, and dry your tears.
Amnon is your brother and, since
the same blood binds you both,
disgracing you, he's disgraced himself.
Let the insult and your dishonor
remain here behind locked doors.
There's an estate of mine in Ephraim,
with granges in Baalhazor
that have served for recreation,
which now will serve you in your sorrow.
There you will abide with me;
the court is no place for a woman
who has lost her honor.
Let us go there and see if time,
the wise healer, whose balm is
to forget, can divert your sorrows.

**Tamar.** [*aside*] You are right, since whoever
   is banished by society
   lives among the beasts. Among
   the beasts honor, I know,
   would not be lost.

                                                  *[Exit*

**Absalom.** [*aside*]     And so,
   incestuous tyrant prince,
   Absalom will soon repay you—
   rid you of life and crown,
   and see your debt to honor paid.

                                                  *[Exit*

**Adonai.** [*aside*] There are no words for such
   portentous happenings, no reason
   in their counsel and consolation.
   In sorrow and confusion I depart.

                                                  *[Exit*

**Solomon.** [*aside*] The Crown Princess is my sister
   and I the Prince, her brother.
   I feel the insult she is suffering
   and fear the danger for Amnon's life.
   His deed incites horror,
   the King is wise and prudent,
   but in the end it's best
   to let time work its wonders.

                                                  *[Exit*

        *Enter AMNON; DAVID is weeping.*

**Amnon.** [*aside*] My Sire, the King, has summoned me.
   How shall I appear before him?
   Do I dare to look him in the face
   without fear or shame? I tremble
   before the snowy whiteness of
   his locks, for they are dead ashes
   of sins love's fire had ignited.
   How zealously the sinner moves
   to act; then, once done, how cowardly.
**David.** Prince . . .
**Amnon.** [*from a distance*] I am at your feet.
**David.** [*aside*] Justice here is no more powerful
   than affection. I'm a father,
   but also I am the King.
   He's my son, and the offender.
   His eyes implore me for mercy;
   and the Princess, for satisfaction.
   I'll imprison him for his crime.
   But no, from his pale visage
   he appears just wakened fearfully

from bed; this his pale cheeks tell me.
But what's happened to my courage?
What will they say in Israel
to my foolish backsliding?
Let justice prevail and let
the offending prince die.
[aloud] Amnon . . .

**Amnon.**                    Beloved father . . .
**David.** [aside] He's called me "beloved father,"
and he has pierced my heart.

                        [ABSALOM appears at the curtain.]

He begs for mercy. But let him die!
[aloud] How is it with you?
**Amnon.** Merciful father, better, better.
**David.** [aside] Looking at him, I turn to wax
melted by the sun. The homicide
and adultery I committed
on becoming king, the Great Judge
on high forgave me when I said
it was a sin of the heart.
God's mercy triumphed over justice,
and I am God's image. The left hand's
his punishment, the right, his pardon.
But being left means sinister.
[aloud] Look to yourself, Prince,
and mind your royal privilege.
[aside] O dearest son of all my heart!

                                                    [Exit

**Amnon.** O the powerful deeds of love,
wrought by the only God,
which today have conquered
David the conqueror himself!
Lovingly he warned me,
"Look to yourself": the prudent
chastisement in the unvoiced rebuke.
Anxious not to leave me burdened,
he assumed I understood him.
I shall repay his great love by
never crossing him from this day on.

                                                    [Exit

**Absalom.** Not a single reason did he give
to denote displeasure!
Not one look of disapproval!
Tamar is his daughter as much as
Amnon is his son; but let that pass—
I've chosen the proper reprisal.
Compassionate love blinds my father
so he cannot see the issue.

With Amnon's death I'll satisfy
royal justice and my ambitions.
Any man who can't govern his appetite
should not be let to rule a kingdom.
My claim to rule I base entirely
on his crime and my own good fortune.
Although second in line to the throne,
now Amnon's crime makes me first.
I'll speak to my father, urging him
to waken from the dream
with which love, always the beguiler,
so often has enchanted him.
Here's his chamber. But now what's this?

*[A crown lies on a buffet table.]*

This crown on a tray has encircled
my father's royal forehead
with such composed solemnity.
On this table this royal plate
was put before me containing
all that I so much desire:
indeed, it seems an invitation.
If to rule is as appetizing
as the ambitious claim, one should not
forego a taste of it.
O circlet now enclosing all my
pleasure, Amnon must not
enjoy you, for you are made of gold,
and he who raped my sister
deserves only to be put in irons.

*[He picks up the crown.]*

I want my head distinguished
by your lovely circlet,
but that honor you may refuse
although it would extol you,
because my golden locks
would put you in the shade.

*[He puts on the crown.]*

There, that's fine! You'll take to me
as though I were born for you. And that's
not far wrong, since I was born
of royal blood, and you were born for me.
Will I be worthy of you? Yes,
of course. And guard you well? That too.
Is there anyone in
Jerusalem to prevent it?
Amnon? I shall kill him.

*[DAVID appears backstage.]*

Then my father will avenge him?
Then kill my father . . .

**David.** Kill who?

**Absalom.** [*kneeling*] Good Lord! Why, whoever does not
    swear allegiance to Your Highness.

**David.** [*entering*] It's unseemly to be kneeling
    at my feet with that crown on your head.

**Absalom.** I was thinking of succeeding you
    later, since the Crown Prince
    is so indisposed now.

**David.** You assume it all too hastily:
    you won't be anyone's successor,
    for I'd say that if this crown required
    someone of a certain talent, it
    would be one greater than yours.
    Now then, do you want to kill me?

**Absalom.** I?

**David.** Isn't that what you just said?

**Absalom.** If you'd heard me accurately,
    you'd reward me for my love.
    I said, if it were my turn to rule,
    with you living in Jerusalem,
    I'd search out someone well known
    for his treachery, and because he is
    a tyrant, wants to kill my father.

**David.** Well, then, who would fit that description?

**Absalom.** I believe he who'd rape his sister
    would also kill his father.

**David.** Since yours and Tamar's mother are the same,
    you're full of wrath against Amnon.
    But take heed that anyone
    who is an enemy of his
    has no chance of being my friend.

**Absalom.** You've no reason to grow angry with me.
    I only find you cruel toward me.

**David.** How much so, if you are
    so cruel toward him?

**Absalom.** Nobody
    in Israel loves him more than I.
    But first, let me say, great Sire,
    I should like to invite him
    and the other princes to honor
    your presence in Baalhazor
    for the sheep-shearing just begun there,
    and I hope that you will attend.
    Far from the foolish talk of anger
    and revenge, I now hasten there
    to prepare the festive banquets
    for my worthy guests. Your presence,
    dear Sire, will honor our fleece

and divert you from the sorrows
of past events. There you will learn
how much my wish is now
solely to regain your love.

**David.** You'd be that love's phoenix
if you'd forgive the prince. Forgetting
those past events, you'd be
Abel, and not vile Cain.

**Absalom.** Since you bring it up now
I swear to God, if any land
beneath the sun makes war against me,
and if I rebelled against you,
may I be hanged by my hair
somewhere between earth and sky,
and there be left to die.

**David.** If you are in earnest, dear Absalom,
I pardon your youthful pranks;
now let my encircling arms
be your coronation: they
are better than any crown.

**Absalom.** If you press your feet to my lips
and add to that another favor,
namely that you'll gladly extend
to us the honor of your presence
at the sheep-shearing, then peace
will make room to lighten your thoughts.

**David.** No, my son; we'd be a burden to you.
Enjoy your landed heritage.
I should let the state
take care of me in my old age.

**Absalom.** Then since I cannot bind you
to grant this favor, do give me
leave to invite instead
Adonai and Solomon, so that they
may come to know, along with Amnon,
the love that I bear them.

**David.** Amnon? I'm afraid not, my son.

**Absalom.** If he is melancholy, then
his sorrows will be dispelled
by the farm, the countryside,
and the river.

**David.**              What I fear
is that some new outburst will
heap more sorrow on my own.

**Absalom.** I am surprised you harbor
so little faith in my love.

**David.** I followed my experience in this:
when disruption of the peace
is wearing some disguise,

it comes on as the worst enemy.
**Absalom.** Rather the pleasures and regalements
  I've prepared for him should credit me:
  in that I have taken great pains.
**David.** A certain caution can do no harm.
**Absalom.** Heaven be the bailiff to see me
  hanging from a tall tree
  if I so much as harm the prince;
  I shan't rise from your feet, father,
  until you grant me Amnon.
**David.** He is dearest to my heart,
  but in token of my trust in you,
  I hereby give you my consent.
**Absalom.** Now I am confident of your love.
**David.** [*aside*] Why then this doubting
  chill of fear?
**Absalom.**       I'm on my way to tell him.
**David.** Dear son, put past grievances aside.
**Absalom.** Have no fear.
**David.**            Oh Absalom,
  how deeply you test my love!
**Absalom.** Farewell.
**David.**         Now see, you bear
  half my heart away with you.

                            *[Exeunt*

      *Enter TAMAR, disguised, with shepherds singing.*

**Lead Shepherd.** *To the shearing, all you shepherds:*
  *the lambs and sheep are bleating.*
  *Now is the time for shearing:*
  *the master shearer calls the shepherds.*
**First Shepherd.** Henceforth, from this day on,
  the cattle will be happy
  drinking from the Jordan's
  crystal waters and the salt
  they lick from off the thyme.
  [*addressing TAMAR*] To welcome your beauty's prospect,
  the meadow grass bursts open,
  and though the sun would parch it,
  your light foot keeps it green.
  Beauteous Tamar, why
  are you crestfallen—you
  whose lovely glances gladden
  all these hills? If, as they say,
  the Court is anywhere the King is,
  you now, as Queen of Beauty,
  hold court here, as anywhere.
  Do take heart, dear Princess,

and gaze upon these waters
whose crystals are your mirror.
**Tamar.** I'm too afraid to look at myself.
**Second Shepherd.** Yes, you're well advised: otherwise
you'd fall in love with yourself.
An angel brought you here.
Still, come, look anyhow,
and see how your likeness
is enhanced on the river's
gentle surface, while blossoms
blue and gold serve to frame
your portrait from the shore.
Come, honor it with your glance.
**Tamar.** You call me beautiful,
but a shameful stain besmirches me.
If I looked, I'd start to weep.
**Lead Shepherd.** A shameful stain, you say?
Well, for that very reason,
mirrors here are such that
whatever stains appear
are instantly erased,
and thus display their friendliness.
Back at Court, a mirror's good
just to show one's blemishes;
since it's only made of glass,
all it does is cast them
back into your face. Here
a mirror's made of water
and those who come to gaze
find, the instant they stoop to wash,
all stains are erased.
**Tamar.** If water could erase this stain
my own tears would suffice;
only a traitor's blood would do
to expunge it totally.
**Lead Shepherd.** I've not heard of such cosmetics,
though virgin honey's used here,
since even faces nowadays
traffic in some artifice
of virginity . Are they
your freckles?
**Tamar.** [*aside*]     My freckled sins.
**Lead Shepherd.** Quicksilver is a good covering.
**Tamar.** It's not for lack of covering,
shepherd: my whole being
is filled with poison.
**Lead Shepherd.**      Some mole
or birthmark, then? Something
your toque might hide?

**Tamar.** [*aside*]                    It won't
change like the moon. Dishonor is
no mole to be hidden.
**Lead Shepherd.** Then be that as it may,
by God, for now we must sing
and dissipate the gloom,
else all is madness.
But now here comes Teuca,
and I think I shall cut
some flowers in the garden.

*Enter TEUCA, veiled, with some flowers.*

**Tamar.** All is heaviness and grief.
**Lead Shepherd.** Dear Teuca, although you won't
take off that veil, you can rest assured
the sun won't try to burn you;
it knows you well from years back.
**Teuca.** All these lovely flowers
I have stolen from the spring,
and since love has brought them here,
you yourself may rival them.
My little basket freshly
overflows with lovely herbs,
with jasmines and with roses,
with carnations and with thyme.
Here is your manutisa, star
of the sea with turquoise petal,
and here's the purple violet which,
with love that's gone, is stepped upon.
Take them up, the spoils of the meadows,
and clasp them to your lips, your breath
and hair, your eyes and brows.

[*Gives TAMAR a bouquet.*]

**Tamar.** Everything that April tinctures, friend,
has through me been drained of color,
since the flower I most prize
I have been deprived of.
**Teuca.** Then take your vengeance quickly!
**Tamar.** That's my only consolation;
if not, let the earth swallow me.
**Teuca.** You will surely be consoled.
Take heart. How will you manage it?
**Tamar.** It seems all the princes have arrived
who mean to honor us today.
**Lead Shepherd.** Then what are we waiting for?
**Other Shepherd.** Since they are here, let us hasten
to the gentle grove, and
with flowers, wild grass, and branches
let us decorate the house.

**Lead Shepherd.** Ardenio is right: shepherds,
  make haste now; but who will
  bother with flowers and branches
  when there's Absalom to look at?

  *[Exeunt SHEPHERDS*

**Tamar.** Teuca, let us leave this place.
**Teuca.** But why? You are well enough disguised.
**Tamar.** Yes, and totally despised.
  This I cannot abide.

  *Enter from hunting: ABSALOM, ADONAI, SOLOMON
  and AMNON, with ACHITOPHEL and JONADAB.*

**Amnon.** How beautiful the country is today!
**Absalom.** It is the gallant month of May,
  with blossoms everywhere.
**Jonadab.** Down to the least peasant
  in a smock trimmed with braid.
**Amnon.** Look, there are mountain girls here too.
**Jonadab.** Lively, and not bad-looking either.
**Absalom.** They are all from my estate,
  and I assure you, they'd make
  anyone at Court envy their
  freshness and composure.
**Amnon.** Beauty sits best on her who owes it
  all to Nature, not cosmetics.
**Absalom.** There's that curious woman
  who tells fortunes, and whom
  the rustics think a sorceress.
**Solomon.** And is that of some importance?
**Amnon.** To make much of such folk
  is sheer vanity. Perhaps for
  every truth they utter, twenty lies
  will follow. But why are they veiled?
**Absalom.** That one's a pretty shepherdess
  bemoaning some injury of hers;
  the other's her maid who follows her.
**Jonadab.** She is quite phlegmatic.
**Amnon.** Can we take a look at her?
**Absalom.** She prefers not to show herself
  since she's a case of honor lost.
**Jonadab.** A delicate subject.
**Amnon.** Ah, that's fine now. You seem
  to read my mind. Come here,
  my little mountain girl.
**Teuca.** Your Highness would be a suitor,
  then he'll run away like the wind.
**Amnon.** You appear to read the future.
  You come laden with flowers.

Why would you not share them
if courtesy inclines you?
**Teuca.** These meadows are like the theater
where Amalthea displays
her horn of plenty—so that
you won't complain, I shall
give you each a different flower.
**Amnon.** Now this one, is she a mute?
Why won't she speak?
**Teuca.**                                   Mute, a case
of honor lost, a molting bird.
**Amnon.** Is there honor among peasants?
**Teuca.** I should say! And much stricter,
since there are no princes here,
and no glib noblewomen.
But let the matter rest
and let's return to flowers.

*[She takes out the flowers.]*

**Amnon.** Which one then would suit me?
**Teuca.**                                   *[Giving him a lily with a reed.]*
This, the gentle lily.
**Amnon.** That will test my chastity.
**Teuca.** I know the scent will please you.
But do not tear the petals,
for the stalk you see has the shape
of a sword, and those specks of gold, though
you find the sight amusing,
will stain if you maul them
since their value depends on
being left intact; so beware,
Amnon, of mishandling the lily
stalk of love. If you do, watch out!
**Amnon.** I value your advice.
*[aside]* This woman is the very devil.
**Solomon.** What then did she tell you?
**Amnon.** Nothing to worry about;
I just assume she's mad.
**Adonai.** What flower then would suit me?
**Teuca.** Strange. It is the larkspur.
**Adonai.** I love the name—gentleman's spur.
**Teuca.** The spur may hurt at times.
**Adonai.** I am prudent.
**Teuca.**                                   Yes, sufficiently;
but, if you fancy some married lady,
don't get lost by overreaching.
**Adonai.** I do not understand you.
**Absalom.** *[to SOLOMON]* I'm last in line; go ahead, brother.
**Solomon.** *[aside to TEUCA]* Both of them left in confusion.

I'll make it worth your while if
in my case you're more enlightening.
**Teuca.** This trefoiled cup of majesty,
flower of vision, smell, and law:
enjoy all its properties,
for though as king you'll be a model,
the best of all the better ones,
I fear you'll be a lusty old man,
trapped in the garden of love.
**Amnon.** A good flower then?
**Solomon.**                    With a little sting.
**Absalom.** Which of them will suit me?
**Teuca.** This narcissus.
**Absalom.**                    The one
who fell in love with himself.
**Teuca.** Absalom, beware of it, and don't
love yourself overmuch, for to value
self-aggrandizement, and loving
yourself excessively
will leave Israel wondering.
You infatuate your nation
with your beauty: you are
Narcissus, Absalom,
and that may be your undoing.
Trim those graceful locks,
for if you let them grow,
they'll soon have you displayed
uplifted by a crown of hair.
**Absalom.** [*aside to TEUCA*] Take note, Teuca—your seeing me
uplifted by my hair
will receive its due reward,
and Israel receive a rude assault.

*[Exit TEUCA*

**Amnon.** We are all left wondering now.
**Absalom.** Princes, enough! Let us dine.
[*aside*] I see myself on the throne,
crowned king by my father.
With my supper guest Amnon
put away, Tamar is avenged,
and the path cleared for Absalom
to inherit the crown.

*[Exit*

*Enter PEASANT.*

**Peasant.** The supper is growing cold
and calling for your Highnesses.
**Amnon.** I'd really like to see what
that mountain girl looks like.

410

She has left me wondering.
**Adonai.** Do not keep us waiting.

[Exit

**Amnon.** Oh mountain girl, I am taken by
those bewitching eyes of yours.
They must be gamblers, since
they have won my heart. Do you need them
to goad me on?
**Tamar.** You will quickly tire
of this game. On winning the first hand
you'll want to raise the ante.
**Amnon.** Such good hands!
**Tamar.** For a shepherdess.
**Amnon.** I'll have one.
**Tamar.** It's useless to give
a hand to someone who plays offhand:
now in love, now hating.
**Amnon.** I'll just come and take it,
since I'm forced to by your beauty.
**Tamar.** Take it? How?
**Amnon.** By force.
**Tamar.** How
inclined you are to forcing!
**Amnon.** That's enough. Everyone today
seems inclined to mystify.
**Tamar.** We here are inclined to learn how
to deceive you, since you
do that so well yourself.
**Amnon.** Flowery words you bring off so well?
**Tamar.** Each of us, well-off or humble,
hopes on what he's lost he'll stumble.
**Amnon.** O mountain girl, I love you well:
give me your flower.
**Tamar.** You do end up well
and flourishing. Believe me, sir,
ever since a flower was lost to me,
I've no taste for the evil I see.
**Amnon.** I mean to take (to mar), a flower.
**Tamar.** Tamar's flower is the one you mean.
**Amnon.** Give it willingly, or I'll force
you to, and take it.
**Tamar.** You are much
inclined to forcing.
**Amnon.** Uncover yourself!
**Tamar.** That will never happen.
**Amnon.** I tell you I must look at you!
**Tamar.** Stand back.

**Amnon.** In that case
I must do it to you. Come on, woman.

[*He unveils her.*]

Good Lord! Monster! Is it you?
You who suck the eyes out of
the first man to look at you,
a disgrace to all womanhood!
I'll leave, but as it seems,
without my life; the sight
of you has killed me. Heavens
above, I never did expect
such hors d'oeuvres to my supper.

[*Exit*

**Tamar.** An even worse dessert awaits you—
cruel, ungrateful savage that you are,
because your last plate will be
the vengeance of Tamar. Amnon,
the day to face your death has come,
for having wronged a woman.
**Solomon.** [*offstage*] This is hideous treachery!
**Absalom.** [*offstage*] Your supper should repay you,
villain, by serving you your death.
**Amnon.** [*offstage*] Brother, why have you killed me?
**Absalom.** To fulfill the vengeance of Tamar.

*A table is revealed with a service of silver plate and the tablecloth thrown back,*
*AMNON pitched over it, bloodied, with a napkin tied onto him.*

**Absalom.** This banquet was intended, sister,
for your sake; although the main dish was
disagreeable, it has avenged our insult
and worked well to your benefit.
Drink his blood, Tamar, and let it
purge your reputation, sullied
until this moment. It is still warm—
and now revenged, you can draw the blood
easily. I am off to Gesur, fleeing
to the king my grandfather,
father of our injured mother.
**Tamar.** My thanks I give to Heaven
since no more will I lament
my insult, o valiant Absalom.
My honor now restored,
I can face the world again.
The traitor's blood is the blazonry
of innocence. Rest there,
ungrateful savage,
you who put my honor up for sale;
a sepulchre of concupiscence

is this table, cup and plate.
**Absalom.** Now to the throne I aim to inherit.
**Tamar.** May fair Heaven be your guide.
**Absalom.** I have good friends, and through them,
as Teuca promised, all Israel
will rise to see me lifted to the heights.

*[Exeunt ABSALOM, masked*

*Enter DAVID.*

**David.** O Prince Amnon, my dear son—
is that you? I asked hopefully
for the good news whose minutes
I count by centuries eternal.
Dear Amnon, where are you?
Let the sun of your handsome face
undo this frozen fearfulness, and
renew your countenance for this old man.
Will Absalom really have been avenged?
If so, has Absalom been ungrateful
to me? No, for his vow must be kept.
I trusted him, and Amnon is
his brother, to say the least.
Oh, what is it I am debating?
Blood boils without fire. But oh,
it is hereditary blood, and
Amnon is guilty in effect.
Absalom, did you not swear to me
not to injure him? What am I
afraid of? Yet love and insult
never do abide by sworn vows. Hope
and fear in this confused debate
reduce to pro and contra.
O Heaven, judge favorably.
—I hear their horses. Are they
my beloved sons? My soul,
find windows through these eyes;
eyes, open up to take them in.
Now unshackle fear from these feet
when the wish casts itself from
the windows. O my sons! . . .

*Enter ADONAI and SOLOMON.*

**Adonai.** Sire!
**David.**       Is your news good?
How is it with your brothers,
Amnon and Absalom? What is this?
Why do you not answer me?
You are silent! Silence
always was the speechless envoy of
misfortune. Do you weep? Sufficient

413

messengers, confirming my
suspicions. So my mistrust was not
in vain. Did Absalom kill his brother?
**Adonai.** Yes, Sire!
**David.**          Then let consolation lose
all hope of returning to the soul,
for I have lost Amnon! Eternal
grief—because it is eternal—
takes possession of these unhappy
eyes, unless I blind them and let my
grief-stricken ears hear nothing but
lamentation. Oh, my son Amnon,
my crown prince! Now go in haste,
go find Absalom, and go
send armies out to find him,
**Adonai.** Sire, look here . . .
**David.**          In this I need
no one's counsel. Dear
heart of mine, Amnon! You
and Absalom have slain me.

## ACT THREE

*Enter JOAB, SEMEY, and JONADAB, speaking clandestinely.*

**Joab.** Now where is that woman?
**Semey.** Jonadab, who went to fetch her
in Baalhazor, will tell you where.
**Jonadab.** She is awaiting you here outside,
cloaked and masked now in Israelite
attire—if you'd just excuse
the rest, since nature, lacking fair skin,
shrouded her in black.
**Joab.**          In a word,
Semey, are you satisfied she knows
how to speak with the King?
**Semey.** No woman on earth has more learning,
more subtle ingenuity.
**Joab.** Where does she hail from and what's her name?
**Semey.** Teuca's her country and her name.
**Joab.** Is she a sorceress?
**Semey.**          Yes,
and I've had her veiled to see
just what effect her prophesying
might have on both of us.
**Joab.** It seems a final testament
ending with our deaths, as she's told us
both: with me hurling lances,

and with you throwing stones.
At the moment that's not important,
nor do I fear what may occur.
But tell me, if you can, what deeds
my loyalty to Absalom
would now make desirable.

**Semey.**                              Yes,
but first, before entering the Court,
I beg you, tell me what
proposal you intend to make.

**Joab.** Since that unhappy day turned into
a tragedy with Absalom
staining his table with the royal
blood of Amnon, and Absalom
fleeing the royal court for Gesur,
where his grandfather, Ptolomy, reigns,
I do not know if Tamar went
with him, for no one in Israel
speaks of her since she complained
to David of her rape, and she
was sent to Baalhazor to be
protected there by Absalom.
But anything I'd say, from this point
on, would be conjecture, and not
a certainty. So seeing that
my loyalty to David might grow
suspect, to cover up the trick,
I'd throw them off the track
by saying Absalom had arrived,
and thereby not sacrifice my prime
status at Court; and the King's
clemency, being such, I'd find
a way of being pardoned even
while all doors to his affections
are now locked and replaced throughout
the kingdom with lamentations.
And so, seeing finally that there's
no middle way between one
difficulty and another,
and that any petition is now
unfeasible, I took precautions
to seek out the lady fortune-teller.
Since you had spoken of her, and
she already knew the matter
I have at heart, let her request
an audience with the King.
There's no risk in his seeing her:
widows customarily are veiled
when speaking with the King. And since

I want to be present
in pleading the cause
of Absalom through her, my pretext
might thus dissuade his verdict.
**Semey.** The King is now approaching.
**Joab.** Do not let him see us talking.
**Semey.** Sir, in all things I obey you.
   —Now, Jonadab, consider this:
After speaking with the King,
this woman must return with you
to Ephraim. And you should know
she harbors a spirit in her breast.
So if it happens you find her in
a fury, have no fear,
for she is tormented by a demon.
**Jonadab.** Yes, one must be cautious, very
   cautious, and for that very reason.
**Semey.** Quiet now. Here comes the King.

> *Enter the KING, holding several petitions, followed*
> *by several soldiers and ACHITOPHEL.*

**Achitophel.** This is my petition.
**David.** I have already granted you
   a place on my war council.
**Achitophel.**                    Sire,
   that is not what my heart desires.
**David.** That is the reason I placed you there.
   That way you will learn what duty is
   for those who give counsel.
   —Does Joab seek an audience here?
**Joab.** Yes, Sire: I am the first petitioner.
**David.** You? What is your petition?
**Joab.** That you end your hostility
   with Absalom. It's been two years since . . .
**David.** Wait, stop! Don't speak to me
   of Absalom.
**Joab.**          Be advised . . .
**David.** I want no advice.—See if
   someone else wants to speak with me.
**Semey.** Sire, there's a woman here in black
   who begs an audience with you.
**David.** Bring her in, then.
**Joab.** [*aside*]               Heaven grant
   this enterprise success!

> *Enter TEUCA in mourning, in a black cloak.*

**Jonadab.** [*aside*] Wasn't it enough this sorceress
   *is* black, but wearing black as well?
**Teuca.** I am Tekoah's poor widow, Sire,

kneeling at your feet to seek redress
for a great violence done me by
your judges. Though based on justice and
on reason, there are times, perhaps,
when prudence should modify justice;
otherwise there is no doubt that law
will extend into tyranny.

**Jonadab.** [*aside*] Watch her now break into a fit!

**David.** Arise and tell me more.

**Teuca.** Sire, I had two sons who, when my
husband died, were the consolation
of my grief. One day in the fields
a quarrel rose between them—
a bitter heritage from
our earliest brotherhood!
Since no one was there to intervene,
in a fit of rage, one killed the other.
Once roused, such blind fits of anger
blot out blood's kinship!
Returning home, the fratricide
begged me for the means to go into
hiding to evade Justice.
With one son dead, and plunged in grief,
one half of me weeping,
the other half seeking to rise
against it, I attempted
to hide the living son so that
both should not have perished.
But the judges of Israel, taking
great pains to search for him, have passed
this sentence against me: either
I surrender my son, or for sheltering
him, I must die. Sire, decide if
it is just that I surrender
an only son in whom
his father's ashes are preserved.
Although I am the one involved in
the offense, my concern is to save
his life, since losing one
and surrendering the other would
double the forces of my sorrow.
I beg your mercy, great Sire.

**David.** Weep not, fear not, woman,
you do not deserve to die
for defending your son. First:
mercy to you is justified.
The greater error would have been
that with one son dead, you'd let
the other one be condemned.

For one thing is most certain:
it is greater to pardon
out of grief than to seek vengeance.
**Teuca.** You say that?
**David.**                That is what I say,
and what my tongue will say a thousandfold:
the greater mercy is safeguarding him.
**Teuca.** Then according to such reasoning
you agree . . .
**David.**           To what?
**Teuca.**                  To what's concerned
in the anger you still feel toward
Absalom, since against
your better judgment, with one son
dead and the other fled,
you'd want them both defunct. Restore
Absalom to your favor or let
Israel see your error in
not doing so, since your deeds
do not accord with your beliefs.
**David.** Wait now, woman, be careful—and not
because I'd punish you
for deception, but to find out if
it was Joab who was behind
your testing my judgment.
Tell me now, and do not lie.
**Teuca.** Sire, it was.
**David.**              Then go in peace
and I shall do what's fitting.
**Semey.** [*aside to ACHITOPHEL*]
This time Joab is done for,
and all his privileges.
**Achitophel.** [*aside*] God willing!
**Semey.** Go with her.
**Jonadab.**                If she is going to
the devil why should I go with her?

                      [*Exeunt TEUCA with JONADAB*

**David.** Joab!
**Joab.**        Me?
**David.**               Don't worry; just see that
Absalom returns to my court, for
it's not fair if I pronounce in
favor of one thing, and then do
otherwise. I've already said as much,
and now I recognize that, having
one son dead and the other living,
I must warn the one and protect
the other, so that with one lost,

anger is to no avail,
and the right thing is to help
the other, so both may not be lost.
**Joab.** A thousand times your humble slave!
**Achitophel.** And now, with such permission,
Absalom will come and see you.
**David.** Where is he?
**Achitophel.**          Trusting, I believe,
in your great clemency, he is
alive and well in Hebron.
**David.** [*aside*] It is not so bad that he should be
there as that you should know it.
[*aloud*] Go and fetch him, leave at once.

> [*Exit ACHITOPHEL*

**Voices.** [*offstage*] Long live our great King of Judea!
**David.** What's the noise and shouting for?
**Joab.** It's the whole city, bursting with
the news, and rejoicing at
the pardon and release of Absalom.
**David.** Oh you masses, so patently
evident in your shifting opinions,
you are a many-headed monster:
inveighing yesterday against
Absalom, and now approving him.

> *Enter ENSAY, an old man.*

**Ensay.** I'm but a poor old soldier, Sire,
so much a son of battle that
I was born in one and hope to die
serving you in another. I now
aspire to be on your war council.
My long experience in war and
years of service encourage
me in my petition to you.
There is a place now vacant . . .
**David.** I've already given it
to Achitophel in deference
to the wish that I reward him. . .
[*aside*] or for the fear he sparks in me
[*aloud*] but I'll reward your white hairs
on some other occasion.
**Ensay.** Given it to Achitophel?
God forbid, but while he's rewarded
and I who serve you do complain,
it's he who will betray you!

> [*Exit ENSAY*

> *Enter ADONAI and SOLOMON.*

**Adonai.** Your favor to Absalom today

419

is good, and strengthens our friendship.
**Solomon.** Through him our love grows stronger.
**David.** Time's passing file of hours begins to
    wear down our feelings and silently
    has exhausted all my wrath.
    If my heart speaks truly now,
    Absalom is slow in coming here.

                              *[The sound of bagpipes]*

**Joab.** Not by much; it appears
    he was awaiting your summons.
**Solomon.** And is now entering the palace,
    and very well accompanied.

        *Enter ABSALOM and ACHITOPHEL with others.*

**Absalom.** Multiply a thousand times this day
    of gladness when, after many routs
    and tempests, fortune brings me to
    this blessed harbor, Sire,
    of your royal presence.
**David.** Absalom, rise from the ground and come,
    dear Absalom, to my arms; then let
    their love encircle Solomon
    and Adonai as well.
**Solomon.** You are dearly welcome, Absalom.
**Adonai.** May Heaven augment your days.
**Absalom.** And safeguard your own, dear brothers.
**David.** To stir no rancor on
    this occasion, I'll ask you
    nothing about Tamar.
    But having witnessed my welcome
    of him back, you may all
    withdraw within. For though
    between son and father
    a public reconciliation
    is in order, not so
    the deliberations of pardon
    between father and son. Leave us now.

                  *[Exeunt SOLOMON, ADONAI,*
                          *and ACHITOPHEL*

Absalom, you surely must be
thinking to yourself that, as my
reason to be alone with you here,
I intend scolding you
for your disobedience.
I trust you don't believe it!
Because the pardoner pardons
poorly who leaves nothing to be
said of fear nor anything to be

done about disgrace. And to show you
how much to the contrary my love
intends, it is to offer you
apologies and not complaints,
Absalom, for my delay
in pardoning you. The first of which
is that I desire it for you
more certainly than in truth you do.
How often I cursed my own obstinacy!
It was imperative, dear Absalom,
not without any lack of courage
in me to pardon greater
disobedience, but rather that
I fear the possibility of
your further actions more than your deeds
heretofore, according to what
everyone tells me of your temperament.
I do not wish to list the malicious
tales, suspicions, scruples, doubts
about you that reach my ears, and do
not feel obliged to spell them out.
I wish you to be aware only
that I live and rule and that
the holy diadem is fixed
upon my brows, although
more oppressive than its real weight,
so that I will know . . . But today
is not the time to speak of
these things. I do not fear and have
no doubts of your love and obedience.
Absalom: Let us be friends.
Contending as I have with love's
rebuffs, I beseech you now with tears;
if it were no impropriety
to this royal purple, these silver
hairs, you'd see me on my knees
before you, and begging prostrate
at your feet that since I love you
as a father, you may obey me
as a son. So now that you see
how little I doubt your fine spirit,
I'll not wait for your reply
for I desire you not to think
or to believe that I could doubt
what your reply would be.

[Exit

**Absalom.** What an old dotard my father is—
when I know that he intends to give
the throne to Solomon, he wants

421

to see me dissolving in his tears.
But before that . . .

*Enter ACHITOPHEL.*

**Achitophel.** I was
waiting for the King to leave.
What was it like with him?

**Absalom.** Endless irrelevancies.
Is there anything remarkable
in telling me to be grateful
for pardoning me? Did he not
pardon Amnon? Is it not
a greater crime to commit rape
than it is to avenge it?

**Achitophel.** Yes, of course, but if you think it
over, you are to blame.

**Absalom.** For what?

**Achitophel.** For letting him think he leaves you
to act as if you're obliged to him.
Wouldn't it have been much better
for you to come back under arms,
turning your plea into
military action? Aren't there
many provinces now gathered
together waiting only to decide
to act when your army blows
its trumpets in Hebron?
Then what's all this ceremony for?
Wouldn't action be wiser, more prudent:
instead of pardoning you,
obliging him to fear you?

**Absalom.** It's true I'm in touch with divers
other armies that when I give
the signal to follow, I'll see them
set forth into the field of battle.
But for all that, I have wanted
this reconciliation
with its pretense of friendship
because it makes a war much easier
having a single domestic
enemy than many foreign ones.
Besides, I do not yet have
sufficient troops to follow me,
while being present here
I can try to win them over.

**Achitophel.** In what way?

**Absalom.** In this way:
You are aware that royal hearings
were always held at the city gates.

I'll go into the countryside
and there, finding a disappointed
petitioner, complaining of
a bad settlement, or of some
contrary judgment, I'll summon
and tell him if he follows me,
I'll see to it he gets justice.
That way the malcontents must surely
follow and acclaim me.
**Achitophel.** Well said, for when you talk of justice,
it happens when the verdict proving
one is right clearly shows the other wrong.
So you'll always find at least one
complainer for your army.
**Absalom.**                          Meanwhile
as I go about this business,
you'll now leave and tell everyone
to come in single file and meet
in Hebron. Tamar goes disguised
among the populace in Gesur;
I'll write for her to come and join us
nearby, and you'll see to the standards
raised aloft in Jerusalem, where
with blood and fire I make war
against my father and my brothers,
crowning my head with their laurels.
**Achitophel.** That you'll surely do, if you get
the malcontents behind you, though
of all who think they are deserving
very few merit recompense,
and most of them complain.

                                                      *[Exeunt*

### Enter *JONADAB and TEUCA.*

**Jonadab.** [*aside*] I may well congratulate myself
on being, just a bit,
incredibly afraid,
but as for the present,
accompanying this antipode
of flesh-colored dawn, neither
have I been possessed nor have I
ever been taken in.
**Teuca.**                          What is it
distracts you so much, Jonadab?
**Jonadab.** I distracted? It is nothing . . .
[*aside*] Well, it's because I'm traveling with
the devil for a companion.
**Teuca.** [*aside*] I wish I did not have a reason
to proceed in a wild fury,

depressed, confused, and driven mad
by a doubt that rocks my heart.

**Jonadab.** [*aside*] There she goes, talking to herself.
So what's the devil up to,
bedeviling herself?

**Teuca.** [*aside*] If the great spirit that dwells in me
is a spirit of hate and wrath,
of rancor and of discord
how does it now turn round to making peace
between Absalom and David?

**Jonadab.** [*aside*] She is talking to herself: the devil,
it seems, is a self-diabolist.

**Teuca.** [*aside*] Am I an instrument for
creating amity and uniting
two contrary wills? But surely
it will all turn into
some ferocious warring wrath.

*Enter TAMAR with soldiers.*

**Tamar.** Who is making such a fearful row?
But isn't that you, Jonadab?

**Jonadab.** That was me, once; however,
I'm no longer who I was.

**Tamar.** Were you not the go-between
in that disgraceful insult I once
avenged upon my enemy
as now I mean to do
upon all of Israel
in sight of great Jerusalem
witnessing my exploits?

**Jonadab.** Once I was a servant with a good
bag full of tricks; now I am a saint.

**Tamar.** From where and how did you get through?
And what are all those outcries?
Tell me, what is wrong with you?

**Jonadab.** On this dark day, I and this,
my dark companion, traveled through
this dark mountain. What dark roads
we took she'll tell you all about.

**Tamar.** [*aside*] Now that's the servant, and
come into my power at last . . .

**Jonadab.** [*aside*] Ah, woe is me!

**Tamar.** [*aside*] . . . and I will seize him!
[*aloud*] Teuca?

**Teuca.**                Oh, divine Tamar!

**Tamar.** How did you find your way here?

**Teuca.** I came here after speaking with David
in his council chamber, and left him
making peace with Absalom.

**Tamar.** Your telling me that my brother
  has made peace with the King
  is very welcome news to me,
  because I'm sure that false peace
  could serve his designs better
  than it could my own.
  And they must be a strategy
  aligning with our hopes to fulfill
  his glorious ambition
  together with my vengeance.
  In Hebron I await his orders,
  girded by my blade of steel,
  and commanding the army of Gesur
  with the tribes they've gone to join;
  although fame will say one day that
  my past insults spurred me on.
  [*To her company*] And now, since that servant here
  has come to know my plans,
  and to prevent him from divulging
  them, let him be hurled off the mountain
  top; tie his hands behind him.
**Jonadab.** Heavy fate!

                                       [*Offstage voices*]

**Voices.** To the valley.
**Other Voices.**          To the mountain.
**Soldiers.** Through the backwoods yonder.
**Tamar.** Now listen, wait. What harsh accent
  does the wind break in four parts?
**Jonadab.** I'll go out and see what it's about.
**Teuca.** A confused soldiery
  now crowns the mountaintop,
  another squadron garrisons
  that forest, while over there the trees
  seem to bear another army, while
  still another squadron, down
  below, cuts off the road.
**Tamar.** If all that soldiery were now
  in combat, they wouldn't be
  proceeding quietly.
  But in this way I find they come,
  forewarned to where I am,
  to capture me. But before
  I haggle for my life,
  I'll haggle with my sword thrusts.
  Of such soldiery I'm not much afraid.

             *ACHITOPHEL enters with a letter.*

**Achitophel.** You ennoble everyone
  around you. I bow to you.

**Tamar.** Achitophel, my friend!
**Achitophel.** Human sunflower in whose rays
   I follow the sunlight of your
   beauty. This letter is from Absalom.
**Tamar.** I'll see what he wishes.
**Achitophel.** [*aside*] Isn't that the sorceress there?
   I'll have a bit of fun and learn
   what fate she has in store for me.
**Tamar.** Listen to what Absalom writes me.

   *I am putting together*
   *a huge army from those now following me.*
   *They'll be arriving with*
   *Achitophel in Hebron today,*
   *without stopping a moment till*
   *they reach you, lovely Tamar.*
   *Let each trumpet go mute, and*
   *no drumbeat bound for combat be heard*
   *but come on so silently one*
   *would think that Fear was their General.*
   *I'll be waiting for them*
   *in the field outside of Hebron,*
   *and there, when I find them,*
   *greeting them with salvos,*
   *and picking up the cry Long Live*
   *Absalom!, they'll attack, coming on*
   *as suddenly as lightning without*
   *any warning thunder.*

   This is what my brother writes me,
   through whose swelling honors
   I thrive; so he may see
   how much I venerate his commands,
   my reply to him is silence.
**Teuca.** I would love to come with you.
**Tamar.** That servant there . . .
**Jonadab.** [*aside*] I thought they'd forgotten me!
**Tamar.** . . . he should be the first to die.
**Teuca.** May I beseech you on his behalf,
   since he brought me here . . .
**Jonadab.** [*aside*] Your coloring was ever so
   ingratiating.
**Teuca.**       . . . that he may not
   be put to death.
**Tamar.**          All right, then.
   Keep him as a prisoner
   so he won't inform about the event.
   Now let the army, still dispersed,

march on in smaller units,
for once I reach the walls with them,
Jerusalem, sunk in blood and fire,
will see its battlements overthrown,
its towers toppled, its palace
lying there in dustless ruins.
As the decrepit sun goes down
let another youthful sun arise
to spread its rays in beauty
with the curling splendor of its hair.

*[Exit*

**Jonadab.** Well, then whose prisoner am I?
**Achitophel.** Release him. I want him as my prisoner.
**Jonadab.** Well then, sir, let them release me
    from these bonds. They're chafing me to death.
**Achitophel.** Yes, do it—and wait for me here.
**Jonadab.** Let the devil wait, and not go off,
    as long as I'm unbound.
**Achitophel.** [*to TEUCA*] Listen.
**Teuca.** Tell me, what is your request?
**Achitophel.** I should like to know what it was
    you wished to tell me. O gnawing pain!
    Did the voice you heard with horrid
    accent say the air would be my stone?
**Teuca.** I do not know, for now the spirit
    that dwells within me dictates nothing;
    but seeing that rope dangling
    from your hands as though between
    two dark shadows in a dream,
    I'd say the rope seeks its owner.
**Achitophel.** Well, if it seeks an owner, it has
    already found him. There's nothing
    surprising or confusing, for when
    Absalom is King, I fully expect
    to be chief justice of the realm. Let
    wickedness beware, for I shall be
    owner of the role of justice:
    let each and everyone fear punishment,
    for mine shall be a harsh ministry.

*[Exit*

*Enter ABSALOM and ENSAY.*

**Absalom.** I've brought you to this chamber
    to speak more privately where
    friendship wishes to reward you
    for the good service you've rendered me.
    I know you're angry with my father,
    and I, seeing that you're elderly,

and anxious no vassal should complain,
will try to satisfy one and all.
So I'll see to it that your cause
is left in my hands for just repair,
and that way I'll reward you.

**Ensay.** You are a true prince, and savior
of this poor humble old man.

**Absalom.** Since he did not satisfy you
by putting you on his council,
I will have you put on mine.

**Ensay.** I do not understand you—
what tribunal do you have, and of
what would you make me minister?

**Absalom.** We two are the only ones,
and I want to speak of it more clearly.
In good time things will improve,
and though I have no others now,
I hope to have them very soon.

**Ensay.** As long as the King is alive, no
law permits me to assume that post.

**Absalom.** If being still alive is in the way, the
King will soon not be alive.

**Ensay.** His advanced age, I admit,
puts him at death's door, but
who names you his successor?

**Absalom.** That's the reason I name myself, since
I am a descendant of kings;
and so in naming you with me,
take note that I have cast the dice.
I must have your vow to aid me
and my cause—or I'll kill you.

**Ensay.** [*aside*] What greater straits can I be in?
What am I to do, dear God—I am
a traitor if I say yes, a corpse
if I say no. But why do I doubt
since the pain of infamy
is greater than the pain of death?
But now, dear God, if I am dead, how
would David learn of what he is not
privy to? Therefore I must concede
and go along with Absalom.

**Absalom.** What is it your conscience
is still doubting?

**Ensay.**                Matters
of such import always try
the conscience with vacillation.
Not that I doubt, sir,
what my reply must be.

**Absalom.** Then say what it must be.
**Ensay.**                              It is this:
  that my life, my honor,
  my estate I'll always render you,
  and I needn't add, there's reason
  to seek vengeance on the King
  who ill rewards my service to him.
  Yours I've been, and yours I am, and
  my life is yours from this day on.
**Absalom.** All these are signs of your valor;
  and so, go to your house, arm yourself
  and your servants, then the instant
  you hear the cry, *Long Live Absalom!*
  arising here, you will leave,
  for that's our signal and the role
  you'll follow in acclaiming me.

*Enter SOLOMON.*

**Ensay.** That's Solomon approaching.
**Absalom.** Let him hear nothing of this
  And let us both withdraw.
**Ensay.** [*aside*] By God, I shall tell the King.
**Absalom.** Go to your house, while I leave
  to alert the forces I
  momentarily expect from
  Hebron, and whom I hope to govern.
  Onward, to reign or die!

[Exeunt

**Solomon.** The entente my father has arranged
  with Absalom, though not vexing to me,
  has stirred up some anxiety, for
  I fear it will disturb my own
  smooth succession. And though their entente
  may not undo that day, it may
  defer it. I shall therefore speak
  to my father on behalf of
  Beersheva concerning my succession,
  for I detect in such delay
  some danger. But since he's sleeping,
  it 's not proper to awaken him now.

[He draws the curtain, revealing DAVID asleep;<br>on the buffet table lies a gold crown.]

**David.** My son, do not put me to death.
**Solomon.** His deep restlessness indicates
  an exhausting dream. Best to wake him
  and lift his senses from so profound
  a lethargy. Sire!
**David.**                    What strange
  severity! Dear son, are you

429

aiming to destroy me? Strike me?
Kill me?

*[He wakes.]*

**Solomon.** I woke you, Sire; observing
your disquietude, I seek
to restore your equanimity—
and not, as you imagine, because
I'd kill or strike against you.
**David.** Ah, my own dearly beloved son!
What a sad, macabre dream
cast me in mortal constraint
these moments I was asleep!
But now with your embrace,
that shock has all vanished.
Asleep, somebody was killing me;
awake, someone else embraces me.
And so, I would give thanks to God
for having mercifully permitted
heavy sorrow to be imaginary
and happiness become reality.
**Solomon.** What was it you were dreaming?
**David.** I don't know: fantasies, deliriums,
phantoms risen from long ago.
**Solomon.** Tell them to me.
**David.**                          Gladly.
May I find pleasure in the telling,
for otherwise there was none.
I dreamed an army was entering
Jerusalem, and repeating . . .

*[An army beyond the gates]*

**Outside.**                    *Long Live Absalom!*
**David.** Good God! What's that uproar I hear?
**Solomon.** A scandalous wild horror!
**David.** Now sadness is reality
and happiness imaginary.

*Enter ENSAY with drawn sword.*

**Ensay.** David, o unhappy king of Israel,
though I arrive to give voice now
to the dangers besetting you,
you must know that Absalom,
together with large numbers
of soldiery, has entered the city,
spreading the news and making
such a din that all who . . .
**Outside.** *Long Live Absalom!*
**Ensay.** Achitophel is coming with him.
Now see whom you favored there

and whom you scorned here,
since he incites men to kill you
while I safeguard your life.
I could not counsel you before;
but so that you'll always have
warning of his designs
concerning plots to succeed you,
I shall be your loyal traitor.
Those with his group who saw me
may know that though I'm on his side,
my loyalty is with yours.

*[Exit*

*Enter ADONAI and SEMEY.*

**Adonai.** Sire, don't wait another moment,
the city is a volcano,
exhuding smoke, pouring flame.
**Semey.** The whole high wall is one Red Sea
in flood, stanchioned in blood, it seems
a gulf incarnadined.
**David.** Then what am I waiting for?
I'll be the first to go and . . .

*Enter JOAB.*

**Joab.**                              No, Sire:
stand back, do not go out; know now
the monstrous rabble is loose;
restraints cannot stop them
while their own fury spurs them
to discharge itself. At first,
moment by moment, novelty
feeds and heightens it, permitting
them to be carried away by it.
Then, following the first blow,
it shatters of itself, whereupon
subdued, they fall to bickering
and quarreling. Avert your glance, Sire;
Take note, the city, unprepared
for so sudden a happening,
has been shaken. In the rout,
traitors and loyalists cannot
be told apart; neutral and
indifferent, most are waiting
watchfully—for among
the populace, the traitor
always is defeated,
and the loyalist wins out.
**David.** What risk would there be of dying,
in waiting to resist?
**Joab.** We shall defend each and every gate;

go through that one, leading to the hills.
**Solomon.** We shall all of us defend you
    to the death.
**David.**        Oh, my son,
    how misconceived your valor is
    if I alone escape and leave you
    all behind, abandoned.
    Either all of us escape
    together, or we die.
**Joab.** If that is your resolve,
    escape is a lesser evil
    than risking your life alone.
    This is not being cowardly,
    for while you're still alive
    your very courage and vitality
    will make possible
    a reversal in your fortune.
**David.** Then come along, all of you, with me.
    Who would believe that David
    would be running off this way,
    fleeing his eminent royal fortune?
    O Absalom, how poorly
    you repay me for what you owe me!

                    *[Exit omnes, taking their arms*

          *Enter JONADAB.*

**Offstage Voices.** *Long Live David!*
**Jonadab.** *Long Live David!*
**Other Voices Offstage.** *Long Live Absalom!*
**Jonadab.**               Live and reign,
    for I don't think I shall kill myself
    because this one or the other reigns.
    I've got to be a soldier
    without an army, as I've been
    before, for this capon sword—
    a sword in name only  is none
    to force an entry in the lists,
    since there is nobody
    it can open or close for.
          *Enter ABSALOM.*

**Absalom.** Enter now or forfeit your lives—
    those of you who do not raise the cry,
    *Long Live Absalom!*
**Jonadab.**         *Long Live Absalom!*
    Don't stop for me.
          *Enter omnes.*

**Achitophel.** The city has surrendered, sir—
    they are yours, and the countryside

as well as where Tamar
and her followers are.
**Absalom.** Then garrison all the walls with my
troops, while I level the palace.
**Achitophel.** This is the King's chamber.
**Absalom.** Prisoner or corpse, let him not escape.
**Ensay.** That triumph you prepare too late,
for he has fled into the hills.
**Absalom.** How careless of them—not
to have taken the doors!
**Offstage Voices.** *Long Live David!*
**Absalom.**                                             What is that?
**Achitophel.** The rabble, the King's followers,
trying to reach him in the hills.
**Ensay.** The city is empty:
children, elders, women—
all have taken to the hills.
**Absalom.** How can we put a stop to it?
Kings without subjects can
not call themselves kings.
**Achitophel.** Sire: since scandalous outbursts
between father and son always end
in reconciliation, so that hatred
in the end turns to love, many
subjects now do not declare themselves
for you because they fear
you will yet be pardoned
and they will be found traitors.
And so to reassure them
it might be well to demonstrate
to them that no possibility
of amity again exists
between the two of you.
Then you'll soon find them
acclaiming you by name.
**Absalom.** What sort of action should that be?
**Ensay.** [*aside to ABSALOM*]
Take heed and do not follow his
advice; it will spell your downfall.
**Achitophel.** Friendships often fall out
because of grievances and insults,
indignities and murders,
trickery and treachery.
There's only one thing over which
ties of friendship can be broken:
friendships can be broken
over jealous passion only.
For no man who is noble,

433

honorable, reasonable, or
valiant renews his friendship with
one who rouses his jealousy;
and moreover, jealousy in honor
is a pain that sears the soul.
That being so, all the women
in that chamber are merely
your father's concubines . . .

**Absalom.** Hold on, stop: don't say another word.
I understand you clearly: that
is enough. There are things that
do not seem as badly done
as said: like some pleasures,
which are none the worse for
being indulged. Let my troops
go in there, let them all
be gratified. Let the world
forever echo to their jollity.
Get in there, comrades, all of you!

        *[Exit*

**Jonadab.** A dog to bitches, cock to ladies-
in-waiting!

        *[Exit*

**Ensay.** What man, what rough beast,
what monster, however irrational
his behavior, would give such filthy
advice?

**Achitophel.** Don't you recognize how rarely
the stern demands of statecraft
accord with religious teachings?
The present instance is but a case
of temporary expedience.

**Ensay.** The point here is rather one
of your treacherous intentions.

**Achitophel.** My intentions are loyal,
for they endeavor to assure
that the Crown act in
strictest justice always.

**Ensay.** Yes, but with such foul advice . . .

**Achitophel.** Suspicions grow, Ensay, that you
are not partisan to Absalom.

**Ensay.** You draw the wrong conclusion.
Wanting him perfect,
means I *want* him King.

**Achitophel.** Would all this not end in tyranny?

**Ensay.** Yes, I admit it's tyranny, but
at least it's benevolent,
and not duplicitous.

> [*A loud uproar offstage, and the
> voice of ABSALOM is heard.*]

**Absalom.** Now the doors are battered down,
  let in the soldiers to parade them
  through the streets and squares
  and thus shame them publicly.
**Ensay.** Oh, all your counseling be damned!
**Achitophel.** Thank God for his return,
  so I can make you understand
  at what risk you've offended me.

*Enter ABSALOM.*

**Absalom.** What's all this? What's the outcry for?
**Achitophel.** It's Ensay here, taking exception
  to your actions, sir.
**Ensay.**　　　　　　The fact is
  that since you made me your counselor
  such matters are left up to me.
**Absalom.** Then what were you saying?
**Ensay.** Sire, as you are about to enter
  your reign, may you begin by
  excelling in the virtues
  of mercy and of clemency,
  since a monarchy that is founded
  on severity cannot endure;
  for whoever founds a house
  wishes to see it strengthened.
**Absalom.** Well said, but it grows late now,
  and because time is short,
  tell me, the two of you, putting
  your rivalry aside, what you think
  I should do now. Jerusalem
  has submitted to my armed forces;
  my father, fled, has penetrated
  and passed through the depths
  of the mountains: would I do well
  to remain here and secure
  the city or had I better
  try to pursue and overtake him?
**Achitophel.** My loyalty bids me counsel
  that he be overtaken,
  seized, and put to death; and
  so that everything's attended to
  equally and at once, you yourself
  remain here in the city
  while I and a company of men
  pursue and hunt him down.
**Ensay.** [*aside*] Oh, if I could just help him take flight!
  [*aloud*] Sire, your good fortune

should not be trifled with.
To preserve your gains involves
greater battle now.
You have already subjugated
great Jerusalem. If you withdraw
your troops you'll be handicapped
twice over: first, on noticing
there are fewer men to guard it,
nonpartisans may be tempted
to join the uprising.
Secondly, if by chance those
now pursuing David
should lose a single soldier
in the labyrinthine passes,
the slightest loss would cause
the rest to lose heart, even with
the "lost" soldier but one step behind.
Take heed, it won't all happen in a day—
let one victory today suffice;
you may hunt him down tomorrow.

**Absalom.** You counsel wisely; not only
are you my counselor
but Israel's chief magistrate.

**Achitophel.** Did you not offer me that office?

**Absalom.** Oh, how quick you are, Achitophel,
to score me with all you've done for me!
What a punctual creditor you are!

**Achitophel.** I know creditors who by making
and unmaking kings will be able...

**Absalom.** To make another one tomorrow.
Is that what you were about to say?
Ensay, come with me;
and you, Achitophel, beware:
there's no point in using
a traitor more than once.

*[Exeunt*

**Achitophel.** That I should hear this from one of whom
I expected so many favors.
Insults are my compensation?
How sharp, how strong the viper
of envy that bites my heart!
My life's over—no spirit left in me:
the sun in me eclipsed, the earth
departing under me, the wind
itself affronts me. My heart
yearns to quit my breast
bit by bit, my life's abhorrent,
in love with bitter death.

This asp coiled up in my heart
[*he takes out the rope*] (woe is me!), now grips me.
Not for nothing did Teuca tell me a rope
like this one was hastening
to find its master in me.
I am the minister of my death,
and now that there is nothing
to hope for from Absalom,
who hates me, nor from David, whom I
abhor, it's best I give up hope.
Let air be my monument
since earth denies it to me;
for one who wishes to hang his life
upon a man, will find his justice
in a rope that leaves him
hanging in the air.

                  *[Exit ACHITOPHEL*

      *Enter ADONAI, JOAB, SOLOMON and DAVID.*

**Solomon.** Sire, this is the most secluded part
  of the forest.
**Adonai.**        The most
remote, the most concealed.
**Joab.** Wait here—if not safe from
  threats of death, at least safeguarded.
**David.** Who would believe that David, in his
  misfortune, should make his way on foot,
  weary and pursued by Absalom?
  Flow gently, tears, flow unstintingly.
**Adonai.** A thousand souls have fled the city
  and now follow you, my lord.
**Solomon.** Their number is dispersed
  in troops throughout the mountain.
**Joab.** Halt here and prepare to rest
  while we swiftly take account
  along the horizon
  of the troops we can muster.
**David.** Flow gently, tears, flow unstintingly.
  Go then, muster and regroup them,
  not because I seek such security,
  but because they'll find more security
  in unity, and the rigors
  less offensive.
**Joab.**         I'll go to muster
and regroup them.
**Adonai.**        We'll all go now.
**Solomon.** Each take a different path,
  searching through the forest.

                       *[Exeunt*

**David.** Flow gently, tears, flow unstintingly.
 Oh, Absalom, dear son of mine, how
 ill-advised is your behavior!
 My tears do not grieve for
 your impious error; they grieve
 lest God punish you; to Him
 I send these tears in your name
 to pardon you the ambition
 that induced your actions.

*Enter SEMEY.*

**Semey.** [*aside*] Ill luck strike him who has brought us
 such grief. But woe is me that
 he should sit here all alone.
 Now what if by chance he's heard my voice?

**David.** Yes, I did, Semey, but do not
 let that worry you. The grief
 you suffer excuses you.
 You are right, but curse fate,
 not me. I'm not to blame; fate is.

**Semey.** You have put us both in a hole, but
 it's against you I'll cast these stones.

**David.** Throw them, and give me my just deserts,
 for my vassals stoning me is just.

**Semey.** I shall not be satisfied until
 these hands avenge me with your life.

*Enter ENSAY.*

**Ensay.** Sacrilegious murderer, what are
 you doing, throwing stones against
 your King? Now I must punish you
 since I arrived . . .

**David.**                    Don't try—
 for since I pardon him,
 he's not committed an offense.

                                                    [*Exit SEMEY*

 Ah, Semey, don't quit my sight—
 for I give you my word: never in
 my life to punish you or your anger.
 You are God's messenger sent to
 punish me, for it's his judgment
 I must never in my life complain
 of you. Now tell me, friend,
 what has been happening?

**Ensay.** Absalom in Jerusalem is crowned king.

**David.** If only Jerusalem
 were the world's great capital,
 so that my Absalom's high forehead
 could be crowned lord of all this world!

**Ensay.** He's delayed too long to be your friend,
    but he's dared to go against
    the most revered worship
    of your honor, in violating . . .
**David.** Don't go on, and if it's what I think,
    don't say it: I do not want to know
    because—oh God, I do not wish uttering
    the sad truth to force from me
    some malediction, since I still hope
    Heaven will pardon and not punish him.
**Ensay.** I submit Achitophel was
    the villain, but being desperate . . .
**David.** Oh God, let Your Judgment
    mitigate his punishment.
**Ensay.** Your barbaric enemy
    has committed suicide.
    And combat with Absalom today
    is averted, since yesterday
    through me it was postponed.
    Through the forest, great Sire,
    pressing now against you,
    come his troops armed in fury.
    My duty is to remain here
    with you, my life dedicated
    to defend you.

    *Enter JOAB, ADONAI, and SOLOMON to the sound of drums.*

**Joab.**                Now the army
    is deployed in three regiments.
**David.** Very well done, Joab,
    in seeing to that. As Absalom
    comes to engage us first, I shall be
    the first to die in combat.
**Joab.** No, Sire. If your person is discovered here
    all will be lost in losing you.
**Solomon.** It's not safe, Sire, to hazard it:
    the two of us suffice to defend you.
**David.** Seeing you in danger starts up
    a new war in my consciousness;
    for if I consider that all my sons
    are everywhere in combat,
    it's a clear sign I cannot expect
    a good outcome for myself,
    for the arm that thrusts forward
    and the arm that redresses are
    one and the same. And so,
    with the self-same sword, I shall come
    to die in such strange confusion
    that whatever blow is struck

against me is both the person's
inflicting it and the victim's suffering it.
**Joab.** You put that well, let Solomon
and Adonai withdraw with you now.
**Solomon.** That way hastens our defeat . . .
**David.** Do as I say.
**Adonai.** You impugn
our valor and our judgment.
**David.** Good friend Joab, since you divide
the field in three parts, thereby
intending to animate our hope,
your command will be Abisay, and yours,
Ensay, the other two.

*[Sound of trumpets]*

**Joab.** That's our trumpet sounding.
**David.** Then let us withdraw. You go out
and receive them. Come, my sons.
**Solomon.** That way you'll have us surrounded.
**David.** Our commanders engage in battle now.
**Adonai.** What a misguided precaution, Joab,
you have to look forward to!

*[Sounds of trumpets and drumbeats]*

With the battle sounds approaching
you can see their banners.
**David.** Joab!
**Joab.** Why are you turning back?
**David.** Since I entrust you with my honor,
remember that Absalom is my son.
Don't let him be killed in
the battle's furor; he is all
the heart I have left in this breast,
the most precious gift in my sight.
You look at me when you see him.
I shall die if anyone attacks him.
**Joab.** See how the tide of battle rises.
**David.** See to it. Absalom is my son.

*[Exit DAVID, SOLOMON, and ADONAI on one side, JOAB and ENSAY on
the other; and as drumbeats sound within, battle cries resound,
and ABSALOM is revealed on his horse.]*

**Absalom.** Fleeing Israelites, who in the wild
wastes of these mountains seek
shelter for a life that I abhor,
turn out into the plains,
turn there where I invite you to fight,
vassals that you are twice over: of
my ancestral blood and of my power.
Go tell my father David

(for he must never stop being so,
even as I now pursue him,
thereby heightening my daring),
tell him that if he remembers
when he was young and in his breast
some reliques remain of
his former daring, let them
not be hidden from me,
for I await him in the field
to put to shame, with his death,
his crown and his empire.
Tell him to bring along his sons,
for in dying in my hands,
one blow exterminates them all.
Fellow soldiers, take up your arms,
and as our forces clash
let the oppressed earth wail,
the weary wind begin to roar.

> *Trumpet sounds, drumbeats, and the battle begins*
> *as some enter and others retreat, fighting.*

**Voices.** [*offstage*] Onward to battle!
**Other Voices.** [*offstage*]　　　　　　Long live Absalom!
**Others.** [*offstage*] Long live our true King David!
**Absalom.** What is this I see? Some rearguard regiment
　hidden in the mountains cuts across
　and does us grievous harm.
　Go out and assist our troops.
　Oh you brutal swift forces
　of the earth and wind, run and fly,
　for your kin are perishing,
　go and save them. But oh my God!
　Here am I, without restraint,
　spewed forth and thrown through the thickets
　of these oaks, and in their midst
　set down, oh my God! Oh what is this,
　Heavens above, what is it? I am
　suddenly ensnared by
　my own hair in these thickets!

> [*His horse keeps whirling around; a call to arms, and*
> *ENSAY, JOAB, and soldiers enter with lances.*]

**Voices.** [*offstage*] Onward to battle! Long live Absalom!
**Other Voices.** Long live our true King David!
**Ensay.** Do not follow the advance, Joab,
　without first reflecting on
　the portent I saw in these hills.
**Joab.** What did you see?
**Ensay.**　　　　　　　　Absalom hanging,
　caught by his hair, seized by the wind

441

instead of by his fatherland.

**Joab.** Well then, if you saw him,
why did you not run him through
with your lance? I would have
showered you with gifts.

**Ensay.** I would not touch one hair
on his head for all the gold
in the world, for he's the son
of my king, who has forbidden
any of us to do so.

**Joab.** The single life of one man,
even if it be the Crown Prince,
means less than the common welfare
of the rest of the kingdom.
The just law of the land
is not reducible to the precepts
of love: I shall have to kill him.
Vain youth, die, even though the King
bade me not to touch you.

*[JOAB throws the lance at him.]*

**Absalom.** *[offstage]* Heaven save me!

**Joab.** He's still alive. Give me another.
Israel's beautiful Narcissus,
die in the air.

*[He hurls another lance.]*

**Absalom.** *[offstage]* Heavens above!

**Joab.** Even a pair do not satisfy.
Three's the number Heaven bids me
hurl against you: the first
for fratricide; the second
for lewdness; the last for being
a disobedient son.

*[ABSALOM is shown hanging by his
hair, and pierced by three lances.]*

**Absalom.** Fixed by the will of God, I die;
hung by my crown of hair on high,
touching neither earth nor sky,
between sky and earth I die.

**Joab.** Israelites, cease your loud
long outcries and hasten here,
all of you: come and witness
this rarest of all portents.

*Enter omnes.*

**Ensay.** Oh, this sad spectacle!

**Teuca.** Heaven's promise is fulfilled!

**Semey.** I come flying here from the King
and this stops me in my tracks.

**Jonadab.** Acorns from this oak I shall not eat,

even if I were a swine.
I shall inform the King of this event,
providing he's alive and well.
What does it matter if I go slowly
with news I got so quickly?

[*Exit*

*Enter TAMAR.*

**Tamar.** Cruel sons of Israel,
what are you gawking at?
Although the punishment
for his misdeeds is merited,
who would not be moved to pity,
gazing now at Absalom?
Cover him with leaves and branches,
and seek no pleasure in
so sorrowful a tragedy,
so ill-fated a punishment;
for I, who never again shall see
even the least flurry of a wind,
will go and bury myself alive
in the darkest corner where
my life goes on unheeded
and my death as well.

[*Exit*

**Teuca.** From this day hence, I too
shall follow in her dispensation.
For great is God who sees to
meting out reward and punishment.

[*Exit*

*Enter DAVID, SOLOMON, and ADONAI.*

**David.** Oh, my dear son Absalom,
that I did not die before you!
**Joab.** David comes here weeping.
I tremble to look at him.
**Semey.** And I as well, for I committed
a great sacrilege against him
**Joab.** Sire . . .
**David.**          Joab, say no further word,
I know that I am left the victor . . .
I'd give my entire victory
to pay the price of a single life.
Semey, were you here too?
**Semey.** [*kneeling*] O Sire, I . . .
**David.**                    Arise and
have no fear. To your daring,
Joab, I owe many victories.
I cannot be ungrateful; my life

443

I owe you too. And you [*to SEMEY*],
driven mad by wrath against me,
hurled stones and maledictions.
My word I give you both, though
you have offended me—you
by throwing stones, you
with lances—it is certain
that never in my life will I
seek vengeance, and I pardon
you. I seek no vengeance.
Solomon, whatever is in store
for you to do, my testament
will advise you . . . And now,
no joyous salvos but rather
hoarse outcries, yes, let sad voices
accompany this victory;
as I take my way back
to Jerusalem, more conquered
than conqueror, let Absalom's
crown of hair be our present monument,
and pardon our many faults.

# Appendices

# About the translator

Edwin Honig has taught at several colleges and universities, including Harvard and Brown, where he is Emeritus Professor of English. He was poetry editor of *The New Mexico Quarterly* and the founder of Copper Beech Press. He is known for his translations of works by Cervantes, Lope de Vega, García Lorca, Miguel Hernández and Fernando Pessoa. He was decorated with the Cross of St. James by the President of Portugal for his service to Portuguese letters. Among other citations are those granted by the New England Poetry Club, the Poetry Society of America, PEN Club, and the National Institute of Arts and Letters.

Among Professor Honig's works are books of poetry including **The Moral Circus, The Gazabos, Survivals, Spring Journal, Four Springs, Interrupted Praise, Gifts of Light,** and **The Imminence of Love.** Representing books of fiction, non-fiction and plays are **The Foibles and Fables of an Abstract Man, García Lorca, Calderón and the Seizures of Honor, The Poet's Other Voice,** and the **Mentor Book of Major American Poets** (with Oscar Williams).

## Texts of the Six Plays

Calderón de la Barca, Pedro. **Obras completas, I, Dramas,** ed. Luis Astrana Marin. Madrid, 1951. (**La vida es sueño,** pp. 221-255; **A secreto aqravio, secreta venganza,** pp. 295-323; **El alcalde de Zalamea,** pp. 523553; **Los cabellos de Absalón,** pp. 939-974; **La devoción de la cruz,** pp. 975-1004.) (Aguilar)

——————. **Obras completas, II, Comedias,** ed. Angel Valbuena Briones. Madrid, 1956. (**La dama duende,** pp. 233-270.) (Aguilar)

——————. **A secreto aqravio, secreta venganza,** ed. Angel Valbuena Briones. Madrid, 1956, pp. 1-96. (Clásicos Castellanos)

——————. **La devoción de la cruz,** ed. Angel Valbuena. Madrid, 1953, pp. 1-117. (Clásicos Castellanos)

——————. **La vida es sueño,** ed. Augusto Cortina. Madrid, 1968, pp.1-110. (Clásicos Castellanos)

——————. **Los cabellos de Absalón,** ed. Gwynne Edwards. Oxford, 1973, pp. 1-140. (Pergamon Press)

——————. **El alcalde de Zalamea,** ed. Augusto Cortina. Madrid, 1955, pp. 111-209. (Clásicos Castellanos)

——————. **La dama duende,** ed. Angel Valbuena Briones. Madrid, 1954, pp. 1-110. (Clásicos Castellanos)

——————. **Los cabellos de Absalón,** ed. Evangelina Rodriguez Cuadros. Madrid, 1989, pp. 132-182. (Clásicos Castellanos)

## Translations by Edwin Honig

**Calderón: Four Plays**, Hill & Wang (New York), 1961
**Cervantes: Interludes**, New American Library (New York), 1964
**Calderón: Life Is a Dream**, Hill & Wang (New York), 1970
**Fernando Pessoa: Selected Poems**, Swallow Press (Chicago), 1971
**Lope de Vega: La Dorotea** (with A. S. Trueblood), Harvard University
   Press (Cambridge), 1985
**Fernando Pessoa: Poems** (with S. M. Brown), Ecco Press (New York), 1986
**Fernando Pessoa: The Keeper of Sheep** (with S. M. Brown), Sheep
   Meadow Press (New York), 1986
**Federico García Lorca: Divan & Other Writings**, Copper Beech Press
   (Providence), 1977
**Fernando Pessoa: Always Astonished — Selected Prose**, City Lights
   Books (San Francisco), 1988
**Miguel Hernández: The Unending Lightning — Selected Poems**, Sheep
   Meadow Press (New York), 1990
**Federico García Lorca: Four Puppet Plays; Divan and Other Poems;
   Prose Poems and Dramatic Pieces, Play Without a Title**, Sheep
   Meadow Press (New York), 1990


## Selected Books by Edwin Honig

**García Lorca**, New Directions (New York), 1944, 1963: Octagon Books
   (New York), 1981
**Dark Conceit: The Making of Allegory**, Northwestern University Press
   (Evanston), 1959; Faber & Faber (London), 1960; Oxford University
   Press (New York & London), 1966; Brown University Press
   (Providence), 1972; New England University Press (Hanover), 1982
**Calderón and the Seizures of Honor**, Harvard University Press
   (Cambridge), 1972
**The Foibles and Fables of an Abstract Man**, Copper Beech Press
   (Providence), 1980
**The Poet's Other Voice: Conversations on Translation** (University of
   Massachusetts Press), 1986
**Mentor Book of Major American Poets** (with O. Wllliams), New
   American Library (New York), 1962
**Major Metaphysical Poets** (with O. Willlams), Washington Square Press
   (New York), 1968
**Spenser**, Dell Editions (New York), 1968

## MATERIALS AVAILABLE FROM IASTA

### FILMS—VIDEOCASSETTES—BOOKS
All films are available on VHS or Beta videocassette.

### SPANISH-RELATED FILMS AND BOOKS
THE SPANISH GOLDEN AGE OF THEATRE, PT. I, 38 minutes. Scenes from Lope de Vega's **The Knight from Olmedo**
THE SPANISH GOLDEN AGE OF THEATRE, PT. II, 26 minutes. Scenes from Calderón de la Barca's **The Phantom Lady**
THE SPANISH GOLDEN AGE OF THEATRE, 13 minutes, Spanish soundtrack
STAGING A SPANISH CLASSIC: **THE HOUSE OF FOOLS** (paperback, 312 pages)

### FILMS
ASPECTS OF THE CLASSIC GREEK THEATRE, 13 minutes
EURIPIDES' LIFE AND TIMES: **THE TROJAN WOMEN**, 38 minutes
ROMAN COMEDY, PT. I, 22 minutes. Scenes from Plautus' **Amphitryon** and Shakespeare's **A Comedy of Errors**
ROMAN COMEDY, PT. II, 24 minutes. Scenes from Terence's **Phormio** and Molière's **Scapin**
ITALY: ORIGINS OF THE THEATRE TO PIRANDELLO, 20 minutes
MEDIEVAL THEATRE, 16 minutes
ASPECTS OF THE COMMEDIA DELL'ARTE, 14 minutes
**THE GREEN BIRD**, 35 minutes. Carlo Gozzi's *commedia dell'arte* classic
SHAKESPEARE'S THEATRE AND **MACBETH**, 16 minutes
SHAKESPEARE'S **KING LEAR** AND THE MIDDLE AGES, 31 minutes
SHAKESPEARE AND WEBSTER: JACOBEAN ENGLAND,33 minutes
SHAKESPEARE'S **HENRY VIII**, 40 minutes
MARLOWE'S **EDWARD II**,45 minutes
MARLOWE'S **TAMBURLAINE**, 30 minutes
MARLOWE'S **DR. FAUSTUS**, 30 minutes
MOLIÈRE AND THE COMÉDIE FRANÇAISE, 17 minutes
ASPECTS OF THE NEOCLASSIC THEATRE, 13 minutes. Scenes from Jean Racine's **Phèdre**
SHERIDAN'S 18TH CENTURY ENGLAND, PT. I, 33 minutes. Scenes from **The Rivals**
SHERIDAN'S 18TH CENTURY ENGLAND, PT. II, 36 minutes. Scenes from **The School for Scandal**
ASPECTS OF THE 18TH CENTURY COMEDY, 12 minutes. Congreve and Marivaux
PARIS AND THE 19TH CENTURY NOVELISTS, 26 minutes. Balzac, Flaubert, Dumas, Stendhal, Hugo, George Sand, Zola